Criminal Justice in Crisis

Law in its Social Setting

Criminal Justice in Crisis

Edited by
Mike McConville
*Professor of Law and Director of The Legal Research Institute,
University of Warwick*

and

Lee Bridges
Principal Research Fellow, School of Law, University of Warwick

Edward Elgar

Published by
Edward Elgar Publishing Limited
Gower House
Croft Road
Aldershot
Hants GU11 3HR
England

Edward Elgar Publishing Company
Old Post Road
Brookfield
Vermont 05036
USA

British Library Cataloguing in Publication Data

Criminal Justice in Crisis. – (Law in Its
Social Setting Series)
  I. McConville, Michael II. Bridges, Lee
  III. Series
  344.105

Library of Congress Cataloguing in Publication Data

Criminal Justice in Crisis / edited by Mike McConville and Lee
  Bridges.
    p. cm. – (Law in Its Social Setting)
    "This book arose out of a conference held at the University of
Warwick on Saturday, 18 September 1993 at which most of the papers
were presented" – Acknowledgement.
  Includes bibliographical references and index.
    1. Criminal justice, Administration of–Great Britain–Congresses.
  I. McConville, Michael. II Bridges, Lee. III. Series.
KD7876.A75C738 1994
364.941 – dc20
                                       94–5165
                                        CIP

ISBN 1 85898 003 8

Printed and bound in Great Britain by
Hartnolls Limited, Bodmin, Cornwall

Contents

General Editor's Preface

The publication of *Criminal Justice in Crisis* marks the launch of a new series of books under the auspices of the School of Law's Legal Research Institute at the University of Warwick.

Law in its Social Setting aims to foster the established commitment of Warwick to the contextual study of law. The series will bring together authors from other research centres in Britain and abroad to enrich debates on issues of contemporary importance in the area of socio-legal studies.

The first in the series, *Criminal Justice in Crisis*, is a timely contribution to the debate started by the report of the Royal Commission on Criminal Justice published in July 1993 and fuelled by the Home Secretary's proposed changes to the criminal justice system which were announced at the Conservative Party Conference later in October of that year. The papers included in this volume are highly relevant to current political debate and will also have enduring importance for theoretical discussions of the nature and direction of criminal justice.

Mike McConville
University of Warwick
November 1993

Acknowledgements

This book arose out of a Conference held at the University of Warwick on Saturday, 18 September 1993, at which most of the papers were presented and discussed. Planning for the Conference was undertaken by Mrs Bernadette Royall, Conference Organiser of the Legal Research Institute, to whom our greatest debt is owed. As well as making all conference arrangements and taking care of speakers' needs, Bernadette translated all papers onto disk, created camera ready copy, and was responsible for the final layout of the book.

Bernadette was helped in the Conference organisation by Pauline Earp, who photocopied papers and created files of contributions for all conference participants, a set of tasks she carried out uncomplainingly and with good humour. On the day of the Conference, Bernadette and Pauline were assisted by Ian Bryan who is tireless in his efforts to help the Legal Research Institute. Aileen Stockham, the Institute's Research Secretary, helped with typing and liaison with speakers.

Our final thanks must go to the speakers themselves who delivered their papers on time and at very short notice following publication of the Royal Commission's Report.

List of Contributors

Chris Boothman is a solicitor; Legal Director – Commission for Racial Equality; Member of the Law Society's Criminal Law Committee; Member of the Law Society's Race Relations Committee; and former Chairman, Society of Black Lawyers.

Lee Bridges is Principal Research Fellow at the School of Law, University of Warwick and was Research and Policy Officer of the Public Law Project until the end of 1993. He is a joint author of *Standing Accused: The Organisational Practices of Criminal Defence Lawyers in Britain.* He has also worked as a consultant to the Law Society and the Legal Aid Board on duty solicitor schemes

Mike Brogden is E. Rex Makin Professor of Criminal Justice at Liverpool John Moores University. He has written several texts on policing, including most recently *Policing for a New South Africa* (with C.D. Shearing). He is currently acting as adviser to the transitional Government in South Africa, and the reform of the South African Police, and is primarily concerned with the legitimation of non-state policing.

Ed Cape is an experienced criminal solicitor and Principal Lecturer in Law at the University of the West of England. He is a consultant to a firm of legal aid solicitors and is an approved police station duty solicitor. In addition to regularly presenting courses for practitioners in the area of criminal litigation, he is the author of a recent book *Defending Suspects at Police Stations.*

Madeleine Colvin is a barrister who left practice after 10 years to help set up the Children's Legal Centre in 1980. Subsequently she has worked as Legal Officer at Liberty (1987–91) and presently at JUSTICE, the all-party human rights organisation.

Jane Creaton has studied at the Universities of Warwick and Edinburgh, and is now researching the impact of DNA profiling on the criminal justice system at the University of Birmingham.

Richard V. Ericson is Principal of Green College, Professor of Law and Professor of Sociology at the University of British Columbia. He was formerly Professor and Director, Centre of Criminology, University of Toronto. He holds Ph.D. and Litt.D. degrees from the University of Cambridge, and is a Fellow of the Royal Society of Canada. His research interests include: policing; mass communications; organisational communications; law reform; knowledge society theory and risk society theory. His books include: *Making Crime, Reproducing Order, The Ordering of Justice* (with P. Baranek); *Visualising Deviance* (with P. Baranek and J. Chan); *Negotiating Control* (with P. Baranek and J. Chan); *Representing Order* (with P. Baranek and J. Chan) and *The Culture and Power of Knowledge* (with N. Stehr).

Andrew Hall, formerly a solicitor, now practises as a criminal defence barrister at Doughty Street Chambers in London. He has broadcast, lectured and written extensively on many aspects of the criminal justice system, and has been closely associated with attempts to re-open a number of miscarriage of justice cases. In particular, he acted for Winston Silcott in his trial for the murder of PC Blakelock during the Broadwater Farm disturbances and the subsequent successful appeal.

Paddy Hillyard is a Senior Lecturer in Social Policy at the University of Bristol and a member of the editorial board of *Social and Legal Studies: An International Journal*. He is also a former Chair of Liberty (the National Council for Civil Liberties) and a long-standing member of its Executive Committee. He has written widely in the fields of the sociology of law and civil liberties.

Jacqueline Hodgson is a Lecturer in Law at the University of Warwick. As well as conducting research into the provision of custodial legal advice and the right to silence for the RCCJ, she has carried out and co-authored an extensive study of the organisation and practices of criminal defence lawyers. She is currently engaged in a research project in France, as Chercheuse invitée at the Université de Bordeaux I, comparing the process of criminal justice in England and France.

John Jackson is a Reader in Law at Sheffield University and was formerly a Lecturer in Law at Queen's University Belfast. His research interests lie in the fields of evidence, criminal justice and human rights. He has recently completed a study with Sean Doran of Manchester University, funded by the Leverhulme Trust of Northern Ireland's non-jury 'Diplock' trials which is to be published by Oxford University Press.

Nicola Lacey is Fellow in Law at New College Oxford. She works in the areas of legal, political and social theory and criminal justice. Her publications include: *State Punishment: Political Principles and Community Values; Reconstructing Criminal Law* (with Celia Wells and Dirk Meure); and *The Politics of Community* (with Elizabeth Frazer).

Roger Leng is Senior Lecturer in Law at the University of Birmingham. He has acted as consultant for the Law Reform Commission of Canada and for the RCCJ for whom he conducted research on the right to silence. He is also co-author of *The Case for the Prosecution* and *A Guide to the Criminal Justice Act 1991.*

Gerry Maher has taught at the Universities of Edinburgh and Glasgow and currently holds a Chair of Law at Strathclyde University. He is a member of the Scottish bar where he recently practised. Professor Maher has written on many areas of criminal justice and is currently engaged in research on theoretical aspects of the criminal process.

Mike McConville is Director of the Legal Research Institute, University of Warwick and is Chair of the School of Law. He has written extensively in the field of the administration of criminal justice. His books include: *Negotiated Justice* (with John Baldwin); *The Case for the Prosecution* (with Andrew Sanders and Roger Leng) and *Watching Police, Watching Communities* (with Dan Shepherd).

Chester Mirsky is Professor of Clinical Law, New York University of Law. He is co-author of *Criminal Defense of the Poor in New York City* (with Mike McConville) and *Federal Criminal Practice: Prosecution and Defense* (with Harry Subin). His current interests include the RCCJ, research on criminal courts and the guilty plea system, and on the evolution of the criminal justice system in the nineteenth century.

Richard Nobles is a Lecturer in Law at the London School of Economics. Together with David Schiff, he submitted evidence to the Royal Commission on the role of the Court of Criminal Appeal, with particular reference to the re-assessment of expert evidence.

Edward Phillips is currently Principal Lecturer in Law and Course Director of the LLB programme at the University of Greenwich. He teaches Criminal Law and Evidence and is primarily interested in comparative law and, in particular, comparative criminal justice.

Mike Redmayne is a Lecturer in Law at the University of Manchester.

Andrew Sanders is Deputy Director of the Centre for Criminological Research at the University of Oxford, and a Fellow of Pembroke College, Oxford. He previously lectured in the Faculty of Law, Birmingham University. He is author of *The Case for the Prosecution* (with Mike McConville and Roger Leng) and was a member of the Parole Board from 1990 to 1993.

David Schiff is a Lecturer in Law at the London School of Economics, specialising in the law relating to emergencies and terrorism. With Richard Nobles, he submitted evidence to the Royal Commission which involved a detailed case study of the Birmingham 6 and Maguire 7 appeals.

Philip Scraton is a Professor of Criminology and Director of the Centre for Studies in Crime and Social Justice at Edge Hill University College. His current research interests include: custody deaths and human rights; advocacy and justice in the aftermath of disasters; the politics of imprisonment; the regulation of sexuality. Publications include: *The State of the Police*; *In the Arms of the Law*; *Law, Order and the Authoritarian State*; *Prisons Under Protest*. He is also a member of the *Statewatch* collective.

Satnam Singh studied law at the University of Warwick and Oxford and is presently qualifying as a barrister.

Roger Smith is Director of the Legal Action Group and an honorary Lecturer in Law at the University of Kent. He qualified as a solicitor in 1973. He has worked in law centres and for national pressure groups such as the Child Poverty Action Group.

Russell Stockdale is a partner in the independent forensic science consultancy, Forensic Access. A practising forensic scientist for over 23 years, he was formerly a principal scientist in the Home Office Forensic Science Service.

John Wadham is a solicitor and is the Legal Director of Liberty. He has been working for Liberty since 1990. He is the author of a number of articles on civil liberties and human rights, the civil liberties section of the *Penguin Guide to the Law* and the *Liberty Guide to Civil Liberties* (forthcoming).

Celia Wells teaches at Cardiff Law School and is co-author of *Reconstructing Criminal Law.* Her most recent book is *Corporations and Criminal Responsibility.*

Jane Winter is the Chairperson of British Irish RIGHTS WATCH, a non-governmental organisation concerned with the human rights aspects of the conflict in Northern Ireland.

Foreword

The Royal Commission on Criminal Justice (the Runciman Commission) was the only body of this type appointed during the whole period since the Tory Party returned to power in 1979. Its immediate predecessor, the Royal Commission on Criminal Procedure (the Philips Commission), had been appointed under a Labour Government as far back as 1977 and reported in 1981. It is indeed a mark of the depth of the crisis into which British criminal justice was plunged by the release of the Guildford 4 and then the Birmingham 6 (followed by many more victims of miscarriages of justice) not only that Mrs Thatcher's successor had to quickly abandon the distrust of 'government by committee' but also that criminal justice should have been subject to two such major investigations within just over a decade.

In the event, the Conservative Government need not have concerned themselves, since the Runciman Commission has produced a report which, although gaining support in establishment circles and among some legal professional insiders, has been universally condemned by all those victimised by the miscarriages of justice and others who campaigned and fought for so long, in the face of dogged resistance from the same legal establishment, to free them. Indeed, the Commission's Report has endorsed several key changes to the criminal justice system – extending police questioning beyond charge, abolition of a defendant's right to elect jury trial, introduction of open plea-bargaining, advance defence disclosure to the prosecution – that have long been on the agenda of the 'law and order' lobby but which even successive Conservative Governments, with overwhelming parliamentary majorities, never dared to push forward. The Runciman Commission has therefore helped to effect a dramatic reversal in the political climate over criminal justice, from a situation of crisis engendered by miscarriages of justice to one of triumphal 'law-and-orderism'.

All the papers in this volume, for the most part first presented at a Conference on Criminal Justice in Crisis held at the University of Warwick in September 1993, just over two months after publication of the Royal Commission Report, reflect a common sense of disappointment, even betrayal. We have divided the papers into three broad sections.

Part I provides a variety of critical responses to the Runciman Commission, starting with our own general analysis of the Report's approach and key recommendations first published in the *Modern Law Review*, January 1994, and reproduced here with kind permission. We also include an edited text (reproduced with kind permission of the Legal Action Group), of an earlier talk delivered by Professor McConville to a conference on the Royal Commission's Report held at the London School of Economics in July 1993. Three further papers – by Lacey, Nobles and Schiff, and Wells – critically examine the Commission's claim that they were not informed by theory but instead 'guided throughout by practical considerations' (*RCCJ*, p. 3), each showing how the Commission's work was in fact implicitly grounded in particular theoretical assumptions about the 'balance' and 'rationality' of criminal justice.

The Commission itself carried out visits to Scotland in order to examine aspects of its more 'inquisitorial' system, and Maher shows in his paper how few lessons were in fact drawn from the Scottish experience. Perhaps a more telling influence on the Commission's work, although it was explicitly left out of their terms of reference, was the experience of policing Northern Ireland. Where it suited the Runciman Commission to do so, as in the recommendation to give the police new powers forcibly to take mouth swabs from suspects, the Northern Ireland experience is cited favourably to justify changes giving the police and prosecution extended powers. But the Commission completely ignored the Northern Ireland experience regarding the intimidation of suspects and the dangers inherent in any watering down of suspects' rights, including the 'right to silence'. The lesson has not been lost on the Government, however, which intends to base its planned abolition of the 'right to silence' precisely on the Northern Ireland model. Hillyard and Winter in their papers both examine the work of the Runciman Commission from this perspective, while Boothman exposes the Commission's failure to tackle in any serious way the issue of racial discrimination within the criminal justice system.

The final paper in this section, by Scraton, provides a timely reminder of the political functions of Royal Commissions as vehicles for 'official discourse' and social and political control. These are functions which the Runciman Commission appears to have amply fulfilled.

The papers in Part II begin the much more difficult task that we now face, in the aftermath of the Runciman Commission's failure of political will, to once again challenge the 'official discourse' on criminal justice and to present more critical accounts of its working and impact on ordinary people. The Warwick Conference was honoured to have as its keynote address the paper which opens this section, by Professor Richard Ericson, in which he presents an alternative theory of criminal justice, as based not on traditional concepts of 'crime control and suspect's rights' but on 'surveillance and system rights'. He shows in the process how the Runciman Commission's various recommendations help to shift our system in this latter direction. Sanders in turn identifies the repressive functions of the police and criminal justice as a missing dimension in the Commission's analysis.

The remaining papers in this section trace these alternative models through the various stages of criminal justice, beginning in the papers by Brogden and Singh with that meted out on the street, in the exercise of police powers of stop and 'moving on' and their targeting operations against particular 'problem' populations. These were aspects of policing arbitrarily ignored by the Runciman Commission, although as Leng points out in his paper they deliberately chose to leave police powers in relation to informal questioning of suspects and the subsequent admissibility of confession evidence virtually untouched by reform. Cape and Hodgson extend the analysis into the police station, exposing the inadequacies of the Runciman Commission's analysis of the interrogation process and the role of legal advisers in this context. Similarly, Creaton (in relation to DNA profiling), Redmayne (on forensic science services), and Phillips (on scientific evidence in general) look critically at the Commission's examination of various issues of criminal evidence.

Wadham, writing from the perspective of one of the bodies that has campaigned tirelessly to expose miscarriages of justice, provides a broad survey of the Runciman Commission's approach to pre-trial and trial issues, while Jackson looks at one of the Commission's most controversial proposals, to abolish the right to elect jury trial, and its failure to consider alternative modes of trial. McConville and Mirsky address another of the Commission's key recommendations, to introduce an open form of plea-bargaining through formalised sentence discounts and a system of 'sentence canvassing'. Bridges analyses the failure of the Commission to fulfil one of its specific terms of reference, to examine 'the arrangements for the defence of accused persons', while Colvin, writing from the standpoint of JUSTICE and its long experience of working on miscarriages of justice, looks critically at the Commission's recommendations on appeals and the proposal to establish a new Criminal Case Review Authority.

We end the volume with three papers, in Part III, which attempt to look forward towards future action. Roger Smith of the Legal Action Group reminds us that, whatever the evident failings of the Runciman Commission, the issue is to fight the draconian 'law and order' measures that the Government has announced in its wake. Stockdale sets out a plan for improving access to forensic science services. Finally, Hall takes us back to the miscarriages of justice, to which the Runciman Commission owed their existence, and reminds us of the key issues – coercive police investigative powers, the primacy of confession evidence in the criminal justice system, the undermining of the presumption of innocence and the burden of proof – which these cases so cruelly exposed.   The Royal Commission, far from tackling these problems, has actually served to re-inforce and institutionalise them even more deeply into the structures of criminal injustice in Britain.

PART I

1. Keeping Faith with their own Convictions: The Royal Commission on Criminal Justice

Lee Bridges and Mike McConville

Our criminal justice system deals perfectly well with the overwhelming majority of cases .... The cases that are now a cause of our concern represent only a tiny proportion of the work that is carried out to a very high standard. I would wish that to be clearly understood, so that we don't get carried away with the quite erroneous belief that everything in our current arrangements is flawed.[1] Kenneth Baker, Home Secretary, announcing establishment of Royal Commission on Criminal Justice, 14 March 1991.

The great majority of criminal trials are conducted in a manner which all the participants regard as fair, and we see no reason to believe that the great majority of verdicts, whether guilty or not guilty, are not correct .... But the damage done by the minority of cases in which the system is seen to have failed is out of all proportion to their number.[2] Royal Commission on Criminal Justice, *Report*, July 1993, Cmnd 2263.

Like all such bodies, the work of the Royal Commission on Criminal Justice (the Runciman Commission) must be assessed within a political context, and the political context in which this Royal Commission has reported is very different from that in which it was established just over two years ago. It was set up when Margaret Thatcher was still Prime Minister (the only Royal Commission appointed during her over twelve years in office) and Kenneth Baker the Home Secretary, as an immediate, damage limitation exercise following the release of the Guildford 4 and the Birmingham 6 from long terms of imprisonment after their convictions for terrorist bombings in the 1970s had finally been overturned by the Court of Appeal. At the time it was known that the line of miscarriages of justice would continue even while the Runciman Commission was sitting, and indeed this proved to be case. There followed, among others, the cases of the Maguires, Judith Ward, Stefan Kiszko, the Tottenham 3, the Darvell Brothers, the Cardiff 3, the Taylor Sisters, Ivan Fergus, and various

---

[1] HC Debates, *Hansard*, 14 March 1991, Col. 1109.
[2] Royal Commission on Criminal Justice, *Report*, Cmnd 2263 London: HMSO, 1993 (hereinafter RCCJ).

individuals falsely convicted as a result of misconduct over a number of years by the now-disbanded West Midlands Serious Crime Squad and by Metropolitan Police officers based at Stoke Newington police station in North London. The original convictions in some of these cases post-dated the Police and Criminal Evidence Act 1984 (PACE), which itself had emerged out of the Royal Commission on Criminal Procedure (the Philips Commission)[3] just over a decade earlier.

The miscarriages of justice therefore cast significant doubt on the reforms of police practice and procedures represented by PACE and on other measures, such as the setting up of the Crown Prosecution Service and a national duty solicitor scheme for providing legal advice to suspects in police stations, that had resulted from the Philips Commission. But their political impact potentially extended much further, threatening the political consensus over crime, policing and criminal justice that had begun to develop between the political parties from the mid-1980s onward. Underneath the competing rhetoric of each party claiming to be the true upholders of 'law and order', there was a striking agreement not only between politicians but also the judiciary, senior police officers, the Home Office and reform groups, on the need to modernise the police, to divert many more minor offenders outside the criminal justice system altogether, and to reduce the use of imprisonment as a punishment for a range of non-violent offences. Much of this consensus was reflected in the Criminal Justice Act 1991 which was completing its passage through Parliament even as the Runciman Commission was settling down to its work. The miscarriages of justice (and the long-running legal and political campaigns that had led to their official acknowledgement) stood as an indictment of many of the past and current practices of various participants in the criminal justice system and as such opened up a much more radical reform agenda.

The political context in which the Runciman Commission has reported is very different. Margaret Thatcher has been replaced as Prime Minister and the Conservative Party has (perhaps unexpectedly) won a further General Election, although with a significantly reduced parliamentary majority. Kenneth Baker has also departed office, replaced as Home Secretary first by Kenneth Clarke and subsequently, just a few months before the Runciman Commission reported, by Michael Howard (both former practising barristers). By this time, the underlying consensus over criminal justice reform had broken down, not as a result of the fallout from the miscarriages of justice but in an outbreak of populist anti-reformism, particularly following the October 1992 implementation of the Criminal Justice Act

---

3   Royal Commission on Criminal Procedure, *Report*, Cmnd 8092 London: HMSO, 1981.

1991. Even prior to this, public anxiety was growing, especially over juvenile crime, yet this group of offenders was seen as one of the main beneficiaries of the reformed sentencing regime introduced under the Act. Added to this was a widespread revolt by magistrates over the new 'unit fine' system that was seen as unfairly discriminating against middle-class offenders. The resulting pressures forced the Government into a rapid legislative reversal of these key sentencing reforms. In the meantime, publication in the Sheehy Report[4] of proposals for radical police management and pay reforms had the effect of re-politicising the police of all ranks, while the unpopularity of the Government raised the political stakes over 'law and order', not least as a means of reconciling (or at least diverting attention from) divisions within the Conservative Party over other issues.

In this context, the question we might pose about the Runciman Commission Report is not whether it provides a continuing impetus for reform of criminal justice, but rather how far it can be used to stem the growing tide of reaction on 'law and order' issues. For either purpose we would look to the Report to provide a clear statement of the basic values which the criminal justice system should seek to uphold and a consistent, comprehensive account of the workings of that system. Our evaluation of the Runciman Commission is that it fails on both of these counts, fudging and compromising on issues of principle and providing a strangely piecemeal, incoherent and seemingly contradictory analysis of the system and set of proposals for change. These weaknesses of the Report stem as much from the approach and method which the Runciman Commission adopted towards its inquiry as they do from the limitations that were imposed on it by the Government or the wider political environment in which the Commission was operating.

I SCOPE OF INQUIRY

The terms of reference[5] set for the Runciman Commission have been subjected to wide criticism, both when they were first announced and more so following publication of the Report. These directed the Commission 'to examine the effectiveness of the criminal justice system in England and Wales in securing the conviction of those guilty of criminal offences and the acquittal of those who are innocent, having regard to the efficient use of

---

4 Inquiry into Police Responsibilities and Rewards, *Report*, Cmnd 2280 London: HMSO, 1993.
5 RCCJ, p. iii.

resources'. The terms went on to specify a number of particular aspects of the system to be investigated, including the conduct and supervision of police investigations; the role of prosecutors and arrangements for prosecution disclosure to the defence; the role of experts and of forensic science services; criminal defence arrangements and access to expert evidence; the powers of courts in directing criminal proceedings and their possible investigative role; the courts' duty to consider evidence, especially uncorroborated confessions; the role of the Court of Appeal in considering new evidence; and arrangements for considering alleged miscarriages of justice once appeal rights have been exhausted.

> There was one further item specified in this list, namely the opportunities available for an accused person to state his position in matters charged and the extent to which the courts might draw proper inferences from primary facts, the conduct of the accused, and any failure on his part to take advantage of an opportunity to state his position.[6]

This was a somewhat disingenuous way of asking the Commission to consider whether accused persons should continue to have a 'right of silence' in the face of police questioning or charges against them and, if so, whether their exercise of this right at any stage should leave them open to adverse comment or inferences at trial. It was also taken by the Commission to cover consideration of whether accused persons should be required to take the 'opportunity' to disclose details of their defence prior to trial.

The inclusion of a reconsideration of the 'right of silence' within the remit of a body set up in direct response to the miscarriages of justice, a number of which had involved allegations of the police fabricating or forcing confessions out of suspects, caused a sense of unease over the likely direction of its work. The same was true of the equation drawn in the terms of reference between the objectives of 'securing the conviction of those guilty of criminal offences and the acquittal of those who are innocent'. This was seen as calling into question the principle of the 'presumption of innocence' and its corollary of the 'burden of proof', which together implied a need to weight the criminal justice system towards the protection of accused persons, even at the cost of some guilty persons being acquitted.

As we shall see, the Commission adopted a similar linkage between 'conviction of the innocent' and 'acquittal of the guilty' in its own formulation of what constitutes a miscarriage of justice. Arguably, however, it was less constrained by its terms of reference than by the two-year time limit set by the Government to complete its review. This time-

---

6   Ibid.

table certainly restricted the Commission in the research it was able to set up. Altogether, twenty-two special research studies were undertaken for the Commission,[7] twelve of which related to the conduct and supervision of police investigations and interrogations or to the provision of legal advice to suspects at police stations. Two further research studies were concerned with the role of expert or scientific evidence, one with the availability of evidence to corroborate confessions, one with ordered and directed acquittals in the Crown Court, one with legal advice to convicted persons on appeals, one with a general literature survey on ethnic minorities in the criminal justice system, and one with criminal justice in France and Germany. These studies were carried out over a relatively short six- to nine-month period and a number of them relied on evidence already collected for other purposes which was then re-analysed to meet the Commission's requirements.

Special reference should be made here to the Crown Court study,[8] conducted on the Commission's behalf by one of its members, Professor Michael Zander, which is singled out in the Report as providing 'through questionnaires issued to the main participants, virtually comprehensive information' on all Crown Court cases dealt with over a two-week period in February 1992.[9] In fact, the full text of this study did not appear until just a week before publication of the Commission's Report, and the study itself suffered from poor questionnaire design, an under-representation of guilty pleas, and a low response rate from both defence lawyers and defendants,[10] all of which undermined its usefulness. Nonetheless, it is the one piece of research most frequently cited in the Commission's Report .

Two further features of the Commission's working method should be mentioned. First, in addition to the normal processes of receiving written and oral evidence, the Commission held a series of seven seminars with unidentified 'practitioners and other experts' to discuss the main issues of

---

[7] For a list of these studies, see RCCJ, pp. 254–5.
[8] Michael Zander and Paul Henderson, *The Crown Court Study*, London: HMSO, 1993.
[9] RCCJ, p. 236.
[10] See our critique in 'Pleading guilty whilst maintaining innocence', *New Law Journal*, 5 February 1993, p. 160 and 'Guilty pleas and the politics of research', *Legal Action*, April 1993, pp. 9–10. When the Report of the study was finally published in July 1993, it became clear that it over–estimated the response rates for various categories of respondent (see Appendix 1), as these were calculated against the number of cases for which at least one participant (other than a jury member) returned a questionnaire, thereby ignoring the estimated 14 per cent of cases (mostly guilty pleas) for which no replies whatsoever were received. The true response rate for defence barristers was 56 per cent, for defence solicitors 37 per cent, and for defendants just 16 per cent (8 per cent for defendants in guilty plea cases).

its review.[11]   Indeed, the Commission appears to have spent as much time on these seminars as on hearing oral evidence.[12]

The second particular feature of the Commission's methodology was its circulation, along with the initial invitation to submit written evidence, of a detailed list of eighty questions to be addressed. This provided an early, and in some respects a misleading indication of the scope of the Commission's work. For example, it contained no reference at all to the possibility of extending police investigative powers, although in the final Report several such recommendations are put forward, often explicitly on the basis of police evidence. The questionnaire also provided the first indication of the Commission's ambiguous approach on some basic issues of principle:

> Subject to the fundamental presumption that the accused is innocent till proved guilty, should the function of the criminal justice system be altered in the direction of establishing the validity or invalidity of the case against the defendant and away from deciding whether the prosecution overcome that presumption?[13]

II THE COMMISSION'S APPROACH

How, then, did the Runciman Commission eventually come to perceive its task? As noted, it followed its terms of reference to the extent of asserting that 'law-abiding citizens have a common interest in a system of criminal justice in which the risks of the innocent being convicted and of the guilty being acquitted are as low as human fallibility allows.'[14] In other respects, however, it adopted a flexible, even arbitrary, approach to its terms of reference. Lord Runciman has subsequently pointed out, for example, that the Commission's consideration of police discipline was technically beyond its strict remit.[15] It is also worth noting that, although its general remit to review 'the effectiveness of the criminal justice system' was a fairly broad one, none of the detailed matters listed in the Commission's terms of reference could be said to encompass the issues of 'mode of trial' and 'plea negotiation' which figured so prominently in its eventual Report. Similarly, although the Commission regarded 'police powers of both arrest and stop

---

[11] RCCJ, p. 236.
[12] The Commission sat over seven days to hear oral evidence from a total of 17 organisations and four individuals, one of whom was the then Home Secretary, Kenneth Clarke.
[13] Royal Commission on Criminal Justice, *Terms of Reference*, Annex 1 on 'Some of the questions on which the Commission would be glad to have views', 1991, Question 40.
[14] RCCJ, p. 9. It assumed without argument that only law-abiding citizens had such an interest.
[15] In his talk to *The Times*/LSE Mannheim Centre Forum, 'Criminal Justice After the Royal Commission', 27 July 1993.

and search' as falling outside its terms of reference,[16] it was content to give consideration to and to recommend several extensions in police powers to take samples from suspects once arrested and to question them both before and after arrest and, most significantly, after charge as well. Arguably, its remit to examine 'the conduct of police investigations' related to the manner in which the police exercise their existing powers, not to proposals to extend them. On the other hand, if the terms of reference did cover the latter, then there is no logical reason why the 'conduct of police investigations' should not also have encompassed police powers of arrest and stop-and-search.[17]

Indeed, it is instructive to see how the Commission fashioned a remit for itself in this area. Although no indication was contained in the Commission's initial questionnaire that specific police powers in relation to questioning and sample taking might be increased, there was a question that asked, 'How could the criminal justice system be made less reliant on confessions for evidential purposes?'[18] In view of the role of doubtful and coerced confessions in many of the miscarriages of justice, this would have appeared to most consultees as a reasonable question designed to elicit views, for example, on the possibility of imposing new restrictions of the use to be made of confessions in criminal trials. Yet, in the chapter of the Commission's Report dealing with police investigations, an entirely different twist is put on this matter. After noting the view of a majority of the Commission that 'confession evidence should not be subject to a new supporting evidence requirement', it goes on to state that:

> we expect as a result of our recommendations that it should be rare for a prosecution to proceed in the absence of some other evidence against the accused. We accordingly consider below the process of obtaining additional forms of evidence.[19]

There then follows the recommendations for extending police investigative powers over suspects, apparently put forward to 'balance' the non-recommendation that use of confession evidence should be legally restricted.

---

[16] RCCJ, p. 1.
[17] By contrast, the Commission was requested in several submissions to consider the relationship between the police and the press during the course of investigations and the courts' powers to prevent media bias before and during the course of trials. The Commission declined to do so, despite the significance of media bias in such miscarriages of justice as the Tottenham 3 and the Taylor Sisters. It is ironic that, following the Commission's Report, media bias connected with the Birmingham 6 case was given official recognition but only to abort the trials of three police officers on charges arising out of their conduct during the original investigation (see, *The Guardian*, Friday, 8 October 1993).
[18] *Terms of Reference*, Annex 1, Question 1.
[19] RCCJ, p. 10.

III MINIMALISING MISCARRIAGES OF JUSTICE

Beyond this, the Commission's Report is notable as much for what it leaves out of its examination of the criminal justice system as for what is included. Despite its immediate background as a response to the miscarriages of justice and the then Home Secretary's statement that its 'aim ... will be to minimise so far as possible the likelihood of such events happening again',[20] the Commission undertook no specific analysis of these cases or the lessons to be drawn from them.[21] (Admittedly, it might have had difficulty in keeping pace with them.)   On the other hand, it cites the miscarriages of justice and the fact that 'they concerned serious criminal cases' as grounds for addressing its review 'much more to the procedures at Crown Court than to the magistrates' courts', even while accepting that:

> 93 per cent of criminal cases are dealt with by magistrates. Indeed, this proportion may rise further if our recommendations are accepted. But most of our recommendations are directed at offences sufficiently serious to be tried before a jury.[22]

Similarly, although charged with examining 'the arrangements for the defence of accused persons' generally, the Commission focused its attention primarily on the work of defence solicitors and their representatives in advising suspects at police stations and, at the other end of the system, on defence preparation and representation in Crown Court trials and subsequently in advising convicted persons on their rights of appeal. The vast bulk of the work of criminal defence solicitors (and of criminal legal aid expenditure) in preparing and presenting cases before magistrates' courts was simply ignored in the Report.

The Commission's prospects of providing a coherent analysis of the criminal justice system in fact foundered at the very outset of its inquiry when it misread its own terms of reference.   These, it will be recalled, enjoined the Commission:

> to examine the effectiveness of the criminal justice system in England and Wales in securing the conviction of those guilty of criminal offences and the acquittal of those who are innocent, having regard to the efficient use of resources ....

---

[20] HC Debates, *Hansard*, 14 March 1991 Col. 1109.

[21] Michael Zander has subsequently revealed that a disproportionate amount of time and effort would have been required to 'tell the story of each case accurately and to analyse the lessons' and, had the Commission nonetheless done this, it would 'have provoked much further unprofitable controversy' (*New Law Journal*, 24 September 1993, 1338 at p. 1339).

[22] RCCJ, p. 2.

Whilst these terms are inartfully drafted in several respects,[23] they acknowledge the system's twin objectives of convicting those legally guilty of offences and acquitting any who might be innocent. Nonetheless, the Commission made the fundamental error of elevating the background resource context to co-equal status with these traditional concerns. The instruction to conduct their investigation 'having regard to the efficient use of resources' became, for them, not only an organising principle but a systemic *objective* of criminal justice which could, willy-nilly, take precedence over and frustrate the other conventionally-accepted objectives. As Michael Zander subsequently put it:

> Our conception ... was to look at each part of the criminal justice process and to consider how it contributed to the three overall objectives we were asked to consider: securing the conviction of the guilty, the avoidance of convicting the innocent and efficiency in the use of resources.[24]

The direct consequence of the Commission's framework of analysis was an idiosyncratic approach in applying what it took as the three main elements of its terms of reference. Despite claiming in the Report that it saw these as 'closely inter-linked', so that changes to 'rules and procedures governing one part of the criminal justice system will have a consequential effect on the others',[25] Professor Zander has since explained that:

> when considering each separate topic we had to give due – which does not mean equal – weight to such of the three parts of our remit as were relevant to that topic ....[26]

It now emerges, for example, that whilst most weight was given to protecting the innocent when recommending retaining the right to silence (i.e. preserving the status quo) and to conviction of the guilty when recommending the re-classification of saliva as a non-intimate sample (i.e. a change favouring the prosecution), efficiency of resources became the dominant concern in considering guilty pleas and in proposing direct judicial involvement in those pleas through the 'sentence canvass' (i.e. an innovation where resource considerations were explicitly placed above the need to protect the innocent). Through this approach, the Commission disregarded the burden of proof inherent in the adversarial system and the

---

[23] As, for example, by failing to recognise that the objective of the system is to acquit those who *may be* innocent rather than simply those who *are* innocent, and by ignoring the burden of proof and the distinction between legal and factual guilt.

[24] Michael Zander, 'Where the critics got it wrong' *New Law Journal*, 24 September 1993, p. 1364.

[25] Ibid., p. 3.

[26] Michael Zander, 'Where the critics got it wrong', *New Law Journal*, 24 September 1993, p. 1338.

reason why it is placed on the State, and thus lost sight of the underlying purpose of the criminal justice process. It is rather like learning from your dentist that, in future, the completion of appointments in the fastest and cheapest way possible will from time to time and on an entirely arbitrary basis, take precedence even where it contradicts the normal concerns to preserve healthy teeth and treat or discard those which are decayed.

Unfortunately, the disclosures of Michael Zander, whilst troubling, do not provide an explanation of how the Commission decided which of the three elements of its remit were relevant – or irrelevant – to any given topic. The Commission itself says that it was 'guided throughout by practical considerations' (p. 3), but this does not get us much closer to the underlying rationale of its work.

A key to such understanding may be provided by a statement in the Report, immediately following the disclaimer of interest in magistrates' courts quoted above, to the effect that:

> convictions of the innocent and acquittals of the guilty in serious cases are always jury decisions.[27]

This is a remarkable statement since it implies that the Commission, in so far as it was concerned with miscarriages of justice, directed its attention exclusively to that small minority of criminal cases that result in jury trial. Otherwise the Commission, as a matter of definition rather than inquiry, assumed that the outcome reached in the vast majority of cases dealt with through other court processes are correct or, at the very least, unproblematic in that, if mistakes do occur, they are not to be regarded as 'serious'. The statistics on criminal cases show just how narrow an application of the Commission's terms of reference this was. Even if we consider only the half million cases annually involving defendants charged with 'indictable/either-way' offences, who currently would be eligible for jury trial, only 7 per cent of these cases ever reach the stage of Crown Court trial and less than 5 per cent are subject to an actual jury decision (as distinct from an ordered or directed acquittal). Of the remaining 93 per cent of defendants on these 'serious' charges, around a quarter have the cases against them dropped or dismissed at an early stage before trial or committal in the magistrates' court and two-thirds are convicted as a result of a guilty plea.

Of course, the Commission did give consideration to certain aspects of the criminal court process between the police station and the pinnacle of Crown Court trial. Two of its most controversial recommendations were that the

---

[27] RCCJ, p. 2.

right of defendants in 'either-way' cases to elect jury trial should be abolished[28] and that the system of sentence discounts for early guilty pleas at Crown Court should be regularised and reinforced through direct judicial involvement under the 'sentence canvass'.[29]   The Commission also proposed that committal proceedings in magistrates' courts should be ended.[30]   But the minimalist basis of the Commission's concern with miscarriages of justice, as applicable only to jury trials, meant that it was able to address most of these intermediate issues primarily in terms of efficiency criteria and cost savings, with little or no evident regard for the 'consequential effects' its proposals might have in increasing the risks of innocent persons being convicted (or of the guilty being acquitted). And, given that the majority of non-jury cases actually result in convictions, for the most part on guilty pleas, this emphasis on efficiency would be bound to reinforce the bias of the criminal justice system in that direction, for example, by restricting more 'either-way' cases to magistrates' courts where conviction rates are higher, or by inducing more defendants into guilty pleas through the sentence discount and canvass.

Underlying the Commission's pragmatic approach, therefore, is an unstated policy to minimise even further the number of criminal cases reaching the uncertain, fully adversarial stage of jury trial, where serious miscarriages of justice are deemed – and are seen – to occur. There is also an implicit assumption on the part of the Commission that the vast majority of non-jury outcomes in criminal cases, especially convictions, are correct. Of course, the Commission does reaffirm the principle of an accused *individual's* presumed innocence in the face of criminal charges, even if its formulation of the related 'burden of proof', as 'the obligation on the prosecution to establish the defendant's guilt on the basis of evidence which the defence is entitled to contest',[31] may be regarded as so anodyne as to lose all moral force. But, overlaying this is a more general, system-based presumption of guilt, which is reflected in a number of otherwise unsubstantiated statements that the Commission uncritically adopts as 'facts':

> Nor do we recommend an absolute rule that a confession should be inadmissible unless tape-recorded. To do so would mean that some reliable confessions might be lost. Many witnesses suggested to us that spontaneous remarks uttered on arrest are often the most truthful. We agree.[32]

---

28 Ibid., pp. 85–9.
29 Ibid., pp. 110–4.
30 Ibid., pp. 89–91.
31 Ibid., p. 4.
32 Ibid., pp. 60–1.

A significant number of people plead guilty after a confession who might [under a corroboration rule] be strongly advised by their lawyers not to do so if the confession were the only evidence against them. There is no reason to believe that most of them are not guilty.[33]

As the Seabrook Committee [Working Part of the Bar Council] argued, the most common reason for defendants delaying a plea of guilty until the last minute is a reluctance to face the facts until they are at the doorway of the court.[34]

IV SAFEGUARDING CONVICTIONS

As the above quotations indicate, another concern running through the Runciman Commission's Report is to ensure, whatever demands for improved safeguards for suspects and accused persons the miscarriages of justice might have thrown up, that convictions are not 'lost'. This theme underlies the Commission's recommendations spanning increased police investigative powers, the rejection of any specific restrictions on the use of confession evidence, right through to the Court of Appeal and the majority proposal that material irregularities in pre-trial or trial procedure, such as serious breaches of PACE or fabricated confessions, should not lead to the quashing of convictions which are or might be supported by other evidence. It is worth quoting the dissent on this latter point by Professor Zander (on behalf of himself and one other Commissioner), as it is one of the few places in the whole Report where matters of principle come to the fore:

Where the integrity of the process is fatally flawed, the conviction should be quashed as an expression of the system's repugnance at the methods used by those acting for the prosecution .... At the heart of the criminal justice system there is a fundamental principle that the process must have integrity .... If the behaviour of the prosecution agencies has deprived a guilty verdict of its moral legitimacy the Court of Appeal must have a residual power to quash the verdict no matter how strong the evidence of guilt. The integrity of the criminal justice system is a higher objective than the conviction of any individual.[35]

This principled dissent can be contrasted with the manner in which a majority of the Commission have sought to uphold the accused person's 'right of silence' in the police station. Here it is argued that:

---

[33] Ibid., p. 65.
[34] Ibid., p. 112.
[35] Ibid., pp. 234–5.

the possibility of an increase in convictions of the guilty is outweighed by the risks that the extra pressure on suspects to talk in the police station and the adverse inferences invited if they do not may result in more convictions of the innocent.[36]

The Report then goes on to cite the earlier Philips Commission that allowing adverse inferences to be drawn from silence would 'put strong (and additional) psychological pressure upon some suspects to answer questions without knowing precisely what were the substance of and evidence for the accusations against them.'[37] In fact, this was one of two arguments used by the Philips Commission to uphold the 'right of silence', the other being that:

> any attempt ... to use a suspect's silence as evidence against him seems to run counter to a central element in the accusatorial system of trial. There is an inconsistency of principle in requiring the onus of proof at trial to be upon the prosecution and to be discharged without any assistance from the accused and yet in enabling the prosecution to use the accused's silence in the face of police questioning under caution as any part of their case against him at trial.[38]

The problem for the majority of the Runciman Commission was that any similar statement of principle would have contradicted their separate recommendation that accused persons should disclose their defence in advance of trial or risk adverse comment for not doing so or subsequently changing the nature of their defence.[39] It was again left to Professor Zander (this time as a sole dissenter) to point out that this proposal also raised the:

> fundamental issue ... that the burden of proof lies throughout on the prosecution. Defence disclosure is designed to be helpful to the prosecution and, more generally, to the system. But it is not the job of the defendant to be helpful either to the prosecution or to the system. His task, if he chooses to put the prosecution to the proof, is simply to defend himself.[40]

As a result of its dilemma, the Runciman Commission's final recommendation on silence in the police station ended up being phrased in such a qualified, almost negative way as to be unrecognisable as a 'defence' of this right or to carry much moral or political (let alone intellectual) weight:

---

[36] Ibid., p. 54.
[37] Royal Commission on Criminal Procedure, *Report*, p. 86.
[38] Ibid.
[39] RCCJ, pp. 97–100.
[40] Ibid., p. 221. Professor Zander also observes that, if the limited form of defence disclosure proposed by the Commission proves ineffective, 'the next thing will be a call for much more defence disclosure' (p. 222). As we write, the Government appears to have moved more quickly and further in this direction than even he anticipated, announcing its proposals to abolish the 'right of silence'.

it is when but only when the prosecution case has been fully disclosed that defendants should be required to offer an answer to the charges made against them at the risk of adverse comment at trial on any new defence they then disclose or on any departure from the defence which was previously disclosed.[41]

The Runciman Commission's concern over 'the extra pressure that might be put on suspects to talk in police stations' if adverse comment were allowed on silence also rings somewhat hollow in the light of its recommendations to increase police powers over suspects in other respects. Thus, it is proposed that all requests by the police for samples, whether of an intimate or non-intimate nature, should be backed by the sanction of the courts being able to draw inferences from a suspect's refusal to provide them and to treat such refusal as corroboration of other evidence.[42] Given the Commission's view that allowing such inferences to be drawn in relation to the 'right of silence' could result in undue psychological pressures on suspects, this recommendation virtually negates at a stroke any notion of voluntariness in police sample-taking from suspects. For good measure, however, it is also proposed that the category of 'serious arrestable offences' be expanded in order to allow non-intimate samples to be taken without consent in a wider range of offences, that saliva be re-classified as such a non-intimate sample, and that the police be empowered to conduct forcible searches of suspects' mouths.[43] The Commission's further recommendation that DNA samples can be taken without consent from all suspects arrested on 'serious criminal offences, whether or not DNA evidence is relevant to that offence', and retained on conviction, has already been endorsed by the Government and extended to the much wider category of 'recordable offences'.[44] All of these proposals appear to have been in direct response to demands by the police, and in relation to the re-classification of saliva the Report cites specific police evidence 'that mouth swabs may be taken without consent in Northern Ireland and that the provision has worked satisfactorily there.'[45] As the Commission's terms of reference did not extend to Northern Ireland, and it failed in any event to apprise consultees that it was considering new powers of sample-taking, it is not surprising that the Commission appears not to have received any contrary views on this point.

Another recommendation for which there was virtually no prior consultation is that the police power to question suspects in custody should

---

[41] Ibid., p. 54.
[42] Ibid., p. 15.
[43] Ibid., pp. 14–5.
[44] Ibid., p. 16 and report of speech of Home Secretary, Michael Howard, to Conservative Party Conference, *The Times*, 7 October 1993, p. 4.
[45] RCCJ, pp. 14–5.

be extended until after they are charged.[46] This is a radical proposal since, as the Commission itself notes:

> Traditionally, questioning even before charge has been regarded as of doubtful legality. It was only shortly before the enactment of PACE that the House of Lords finally gave clear approval to detention for questioning before charge.[47]

Yet, the Commission puts forward this recommendation in an almost casual, matter-of-fact manner, claiming that few people 'would nowadays regard the role of the police as being confined to arrest and questioning leading to charge.'[48]   More significantly, it notes that its proposal would serve to legitimate a common police illegality, by removing ('at least to some extent') the temptation 'to prolong questioning beyond the point at which there is sufficient evidence to charge.'[49] Of course, the new power would be subject to 'the usual caution' (soon to be out-dated with the removal of the right to silence) being repeated and to the person charged having the right to consult a legal adviser. But nothing in the Report indicates that the Commission gave any consideration to the capacity of the legal profession to meet this new demand, although there was considerable evidence available to it on the present inadequacies of solicitors and their staff in providing legal advice even just for pre-charge interrogations. Nor was this the only 'consequential effect' of the extension of questioning to after charge that appears to have been ignored. For example, there is no mention of the implications for custody time limits under PACE (under the proposal a suspect might be held and questioned for several days over a weekend) or, more crucially, for the increased risk of false confessions which research and the miscarriages of justice have clearly shown would result from such prolonged questioning in custody.

A further proposal which the Commission put forward as a 'safeguard for suspects' is to regularise the currently dubious police practice of conducting interviews with suspects outside police stations (leading to 'scenic route' confessions). This would be done by extending the PACE codes of practice and possibly tape-recording to cover them.[50] In fact, the Commission was urged by a number of those giving evidence to adopt a different tack, of making statements taken outside the police station and in the absence of such normal safeguards as tape-recording and access to legal advice inadmissible as evidence in court. However, as we have seen, the

---

[46] Ibid., pp. 16–7.
[47] Ibid., p. 17, in which the RCCJ refer to *Mohammed–Holgate* v. *Duke* [1984] A.C.437.
[48] Ibid.
[49] Ibid.
[50] Ibid., pp. 26–8.

Commission specifically rejected this suggestion on the grounds that 'spontaneous remarks uttered on arrest are often the most truthful' and for fear of 'losing' confessions. It also refused to adopt other legal restrictions on the admissibility of confession evidence, in particular any form of corroboration requirement, choosing instead to rely on the most minimal protection of a judicial warning to juries on the dangers of convicting on confession evidence alone.[51] Moreover, in a separate section of the Report, the Commission recommends that the prosecution should no longer be required to disclose to the defence information about a police officer involved in the case who has previously been disbelieved by a jury or of disciplinary proceedings against such an officer that are not considered 'relevant'.[52] It is a mark of just how timid the Commission were in respect to this whole area that, as Roger Leng has pointed out,[53] it would still be possible under these various proposals for a criminal conviction to be based on the allegation of a single police officer that the defendant made an informal and unrecorded confession, where the defendant denies this and there is no other evidence to support it, and where neither the defence nor the jury are made aware that the police officer has been disbelieved in similar circumstances before.

V ERODING RIGHTS

One important consequence of the Commission's various proposals to extend police powers, especially in relation to interviewing outside police stations, and generally to assist them in 'obtaining additional evidence', will be to marginalise the effect of the existing protections for suspects' rights inside police stations. As we have seen, the Commission rejects the notion of altering rules on the inadmissibility of evidence so as to provide a disincentive to police malpractice, choosing instead to rely on better internal police supervision and more effective police disciplinary arrangements to stop abuse.[54] Nor does the Commission recommend any major changes to

---

[51] Ibid., pp. 59–68. The Commission failed to consider, despite its proposal that a defendant's right to elect jury trial in an 'either-way' case be abolished, how such a warning could be made effective in magistrates' courts.

[52] RCCJ, p. 97.

[53] Roger Leng, 'A Recipe for Miscarriage: The Royal Commission and Informal Interviews', paper delivered to University of Warwick Legal Research Institute Conference on Criminal Justice in Crisis 18 September 1993.

[54] It is interesting to observe that there was no apparent dissent within the Commission on this approach, despite the view expressed by Professor Zander, in relation to the Court of Appeal's powers to quash convictions (see p. 14 supra), that disciplinary proceedings against police or prosecution 'wrongdoers' are an ineffective safeguard and also 'irrelevant to the point of

the PACE custody codes, for example, to limit the overall time for which a suspect can be held and questioned (let alone revising them to take account of the proposed extension of questioning beyond charge).

Potentially the most significant 'safeguard' for suspects is the right of access to free legal advice while in police custody. As noted, the Commission had available to it a very substantial body of evidence showing that, as well as difficulties in the police obstructing such access through the use of various 'ploys',[55] there are very substantial problems in terms of the quality of police station advice provided by the solicitors' profession. In particular, the work is frequently delegated to unqualified and often inexperienced and poorly-trained staff within solicitors' firms, and all types of defence adviser, including solicitors, tend to adopt a passive, non-interventionist role in police interviews.[56] More generally, the evidence indicated that police station advice work places a considerable strain on the organisational resources of many private solicitors' firms, not least because of what is widely regarded in the profession as inadequate rates of payment under legal aid for all forms of defence work.[57] Yet, the Commission's approach to these problems was primarily to bring them 'to the attention of the Law Society and of the Legal Aid Board' and to look to these bodies 'to take the necessary action.'[58] More specifically, it recommended that Law Society guidelines on 'good practice' in advising suspects at police stations, in existence since 1985, should be made better known; that 'own' solicitors and their representatives should be subject to the same (fairly minimal) standards of selection and accreditation as 'duty' solicitors in order to continue to receive legal aid payments for police station advice work; and that 'in the longer term, the training, education, supervision, and monitoring of all legal advisers who operate at police stations be thoroughly reviewed.'[59]

---

principle' of upholding the integrity of the process by which the police and prosecution operate.

[55] See in particular A. Sanders, et. al., *Advice and Assistance at Police Stations and the 24-Hour Duty Solicitor Scheme*, London: Lord Chancellor's Department 1989.

[56] This subject was covered by two of the Commission's research studies: John Baldwin, *The Role of Legal Representatives at the Police Station*, London: HMSO, 1993 and Michael McConville and Jacqueline Hodgson, *Custodial Legal Advice and the Right to Silence*, London: HMSO, 1993. The Commission also had referred to it by the Court of Appeal (see *Report*, p. 62) the transcript of police interviews in the case of the Cardiff 3, where the Court criticised the solicitor for 'being gravely at fault for sitting passively through this travesty of [a police] interview' during which his client denied involvement in a murder over 300 times before confessing after lengthy and oppressive police questioning (see *R. v. Miller, Paris and Abdullahi*, Court of Appeal, official transcript).

[57] See RCCJ, pp. 38–9.

[58] Ibid., p. 38.

[59] Ibid. Also, on problems with quality of 'duty' solicitors and their selection, see Sanders et. al., op. cit.

The adequacy of these recommendations in protecting the rights of suspects in police stations can perhaps be judged by reference to two other parts of its Report . First, in its consideration of a possible requirement that confessions only be admissible as evidence if made in the presence of a solicitor, the Commission states that:

> regrettably, the quality of work done by solicitors and their representatives in police stations is far from satisfactory. There is therefore no basis for believing that the presence of a legal adviser would necessarily ensure that the interview was conducted fairly or that the suspect would be relieved of his or her anxiety.[60]

Even more telling is the criticism made by Professor Zander, in a further dissenting note, of the Commission's majority proposal to introduce Pre-Trial Reviews (PTRs) and what he regards as the improbability that the legal profession would comply with fairly basic requirements of completing forms and adhering to time limits. He goes on to note that:

> My fellow Commissioners ... believe that the problem can be solved by a mixture of 'sticks', in the form of wasted costs orders and the like, and 'carrots' in the form of attractive remuneration. I regard this belief as unrealistic.[61]

Among the reasons he states for this scepticism are that 'it is not credible that severe sanctions would be imposed on sufficient numbers of practitioners to make the threat of such sanctions an effective deterrent'; that 'professional bodies would be unlikely to ... impose significant penalties for minor procedural failings'; and that one could not 'realistically have faith in the Lord Chancellor's Department (LCD) paying so well for this work that the "carrot" of sufficient remuneration would ensure compliance.'[62] If such doubts could be expressed about the feasibility of using professional sanctions and obtaining better remuneration under legal aid in order just to improve the profession's form-filling and adherence to procedural time limits, how much more 'unrealistic' was it for the Commission (including Professor Zander) to rely on these same mechanisms to resolve the more intractable problem of poor quality legal advice in police stations?

In the same note of dissent, Professor Zander acknowledges research evidence that:

> One of the most serious defects in the existing system is inadequate preparation of routine cases by defence lawyers. Among the many reasons for this is that the work in most

---

[60] RCCJ, p. 62.
[61] Ibid., p. 226.
[62] Ibid., pp. 226–7.

solicitors' firms is done by clerks, with insufficient guidance from solicitors in their own firms and, too often, no guidance from a barrister.[63]

However, the problem of poor quality defence work, other than in respect of direct preparation for and representation at Crown Court trials, is largely overlooked in the rest of the Report, despite the fact that the Commission intends many more cases to be 'made routine' by being restricted to magistrates' courts or otherwise disposed of through guilty pleas. Indeed, the majority of the Commission come close to endorsing the types of defence practices described by Professor Zander in explaining how they anticipate that a new requirement for defence disclosure would work in practice:

> In most cases disclosure by the defence should be a matter capable of being handled by the defendant's solicitor .... Standard forms could be drawn up to cover the most common offences, with the solicitor having to tick one or more of a list of possibilities, such as 'accident', 'self-defence', 'consent', 'no dishonest intent', 'no appropriation', 'abandoned goods', 'claim of right', 'mistaken identification', and so on.[64]

It is only 'complex cases' that 'may require the assistance of counsel in formulating the defence'.[65] Otherwise, the disclosure of the defence, which will in turn restrict both the further material to be made available by the prosecution and the scope of the defence case at trial, is portrayed by the Commission as just one more bureaucratic step in the processing of cases. Moreover, it is one which, given what was known to the Commission about the extent of delegation within defence solicitors' firms, could have been anticipated would be routinely carried out by unadmitted staff.

Of course, the Commission's recommendations on the abolition of defendants' right to elect jury trial in 'either-way' cases and on the introduction of more open sentence discounting/canvassing would directly compromise accused persons' rights and interests. In the latter respect, the Commission openly accepts that 'to face defendants with a choice between what they might get on an immediate plea of guilty and what they might get if found guilty by jury does amount to unacceptable pressure'[66] and also runs the risk of inducing more innocent persons to plead guilty.[67] It then immediately proposes that just such a system be established, with a standardised set of graduated discounts on sentence depending on the stage

---

[63] The research cited is our book with Jacqueline Hodgson and Anita Pavlovic, *Standing Accused: The Organisation and Practices of Criminal Defence Lawyers in Britain*, Oxford: Clarendon Press, forthcoming.

[64] RCCJ, p. 99.

[65] Ibid.

[66] Ibid., p. 113.

[67] Ibid., p. 110.

when a guilty plea is entered and an opportunity for the defence lawyer to approach the judge at any stage to obtain an answer to the question, 'what would be the maximum sentence if my client were to plead guilty at this stage?'[68] That the Commission should fall into such an open contradiction with itself in the space of two paragraphs in the Report is a reflection of the extent to which it surrendered itself to expediency, failing to relate this proposal in any coherent way to established principles of sentencing or, so far as the innocents who might be induced to plead guilty are concerned, to considerations of justice.

The recommendation to abolish election for jury trial has been so widely condemned since publication of the Report (it appears to have been endorsed only by the Director of Public Prosecutions, Barbara Mills QC, who was primarily responsible for putting it to the Commission in the first place) as to call into question the adequacy of the Commission's consultations among 'practitioners and other experts', let alone more generally.   The weaknesses in the Commission's reasoning and its misinterpretation of empirical research in advancing this proposal have already been discussed at length elsewhere.[69]

VI DEPOLITICISING INJUSTICE

The one major recommendation by the Commission that has met with virtually universal approval is to establish a Criminal Case Review Authority, to take over from the Home Office the function of investigating and reviewing potential miscarriages of justice and referring them back to the Court of Appeal.[70]   This is not to say that the proposal is entirely unproblematic, as the Commission has left unanswered many key questions about how well the new authority would be funded and staffed and its criteria for selecting cases for review.   More generally, there is a danger that such a body will lead to a 'depoliticisation' of miscarriages of justice, removing them from the ambit of family and community campaigning and dedicated legal and investigative work on the part of lawyers, the press and pressure groups which has been so vital to exposing cases of injustice in the past.

But our overall assessment of the Runciman Commission Report is that it will lead, in any event, to a 'normalisation' of miscarriages of justice,

---

[68] Ibid.
[69] See Michael McConville, 'An error of judgment', *Legal Action*, September 1993, p. 6 and subsequent exchanges with Michael Zander in *Legal Action*, November 1993.
[70] RCCJ, pp. 182–7.

transferring them out of the open arena of the jury trial and re-integrating them into the criminal justice system's routine processing of suspects and defendants toward conviction at magistrates' courts and otherwise in guilty pleas.   Under the Commission's proposals, the system's overall presumption of guilt will be reinforced in various ways – by greater powers for the police to obtain evidence from suspects, formally and informally and in and outside police stations; by accused persons continuing to suffer from poor quality legal defence work, not just in police stations but throughout the criminal court process; by the greater inducement and 'unacceptable pressure' that a system of open sentence discounting and canvassing will entail; by new requirements for routine defence disclosure (and related restrictions on prosecution disclosure); and by new limitations on the Court of Appeal. The Report's lack of principle and of consistency and coherency in analysis deprives it of the moral and political authority to be useful in resisting a renewed 'law and order' backlash. And, in many other respects, the Commission's rag-bag of recommendations provide a useful 'law and order' agenda of its own, which the Government has already begun to plunder.

2. An Error of Judgment

Mike McConville

My overall assessment of the Royal Commission on Criminal Justice's Report is that it is not empirically grounded, deploys defective reasoning in support of its recommendations, is based upon a flawed understanding of the organising principles of criminal justice, and often amounts, to coin a phrase, to little more than opinion and assertion. As a result, the Report does not have the intellectual weight and moral authority needed to support the significant changes to the existing system which it advances.

I shall illustrate my position by looking at the two recommendations I regard as the most important and then draw out some general lessons.

I MODE OF TRIAL

To effect a shift of cases into the lower courts, the Commission wants to abolish the right of defendants in either-way offences to elect trial by jury; instead, where prosecutors refuse to agree jury trial, magistrates would decide the venue.

The stated objective is to achieve 'a more rational distribution of cases between the higher and lower courts' and benefit overall efficiency (p. 89, para. 19).[1] The evidence relied upon, however, contradicts the claim to rationality.

According to the Home Office research relied upon by the Commission, chief prosecutors, magistrates and justices' clerks all felt that 'in most instances, the mode of trial decision was clear cut'.[2] In 1990, 64 per cent of either-way offences were sent to the Crown Court by magistrates. These decisions could be rational only if magistrates were right in their view that their sentencing powers were insufficient or that the cases were otherwise too serious for summary trials. Actually, in over six out of every 10 cases

---

[1] All page references in the text are to Royal Commission on Criminal Justice, *Report,* Cmnd 2263, HMSO, 1993.

[2] C. Hedderman and D. Moxon, *Magistrates' Court or Crown Court? Mode of Trial Decisions and Sentencing,* HMSO, 1992, p. 15.

(62 per cent), the sentence imposed in the Crown Court did not exceed the maximum available to magistrates (p. 85, para. 5).

So much for rationality.

There is another rationality which the Commission sidesteps, namely, the decision-making of defendants. By comparison, this appears eminently rational. First, the Commission fails to point out that in 70 per cent of cases, the defendant's decision was made on the basis of legal advice. Second in either-way offences, election to Crown Court results in an acquittal rate of 57 per cent in contested cases, which is significantly higher than the 30 per cent of magistrates' courts.

These decisions are not just rational in a statistical sense. There is the question of perception. Home Office research found that a clear majority of defendants (62 per cent) and an even bigger majority of defence solicitors (70 per cent) believe that 'magistrates are on the side of the police'.[3] This finding parallels that of Janet Gregory for the James Committee (on the distribution of criminal business between the Crown Court and magistrates' courts) that over two-thirds of defendants saw magistrates' courts as 'police courts'.[4]

This perception would also appear to have a material foundation. Research undertaken a decade ago by the Home Office casts serious doubt upon the quality of summary justice. The research found a substantial bias in favour of police evidence which tended to be accepted where there was no confession and where the defendant's credibility was not impugned at trial. Reviewing the available research evidence, Professor Andrew Ashworth concluded that the information 'hardly demonstrates faith in magistrates as triers of fact and appliers of law'.[5] The Commission's failure to deal with this is all the more surprising, given that the key Home Office study was carried out by its own research director, Julie Vennard.[6]

One other result of the Commission's proposal would be a further push to indirect discrimination, given the greater tendency of black people to elect trial in the Crown Court.

Against this background, it is rich to be told by the Commission that 'Magistrates' courts conduct over 93 per cent of all criminal cases and should be trusted to try cases fairly' (p. 88, para. 18). Yet such is the Commission's own confidence in magistrates that, after the abolition of committal proceedings, lay magistrates will not be permitted to rule on a

---

[3] Ibid., Table 3.1, p. 20.

[4] Janet Gregory, *Crown Court or Magistrates' Court?*, HMSO, 1976.

[5] Andrew Ashworth, *The English Criminal Process: A Review of Empirical Research*, 1984, p. 62.

[6] J. Vennard, *Contested Trials in Magistrates' Courts*, Home Office Research Study 71, HMSO, 1982.

submission of no case to answer, the decision being transferred to stipendiaries (p. 90, para. 28).

II PLEA BARGAINING

Let me briefly track the Commission's reasoning:

1. A sentence discount of 25–30 per cent induces considerable numbers of defendants to plead guilty (p. 100, para. 41).
2. This is not based on any recognised sentencing principle relating to deterrence, retribution, punishment or reform. Instead, it nakedly rests upon cost savings (p. 110, para. 41).
3. This system induces the innocent to plead guilty ('it would be naive to suppose that innocent persons never plead guilty because of the prospect of the sentence discount' (p. 110, para. 42)), but any concerns in this regard are to be set against (i.e., subordinated to) the benefits to the system which cost-savings will bring (p. 111, para. 45). Note that here the Commission turns its own terms of reference on their head. It was asked to examine the effectiveness of the system in convicting the guilty and acquitting the innocent having regard to the efficient use of resources; not to achieve cost savings at the expense of the innocent.
4. Were a defendant to be confronted with a choice between one sentence on a plea and another greater sentence if found guilty at trial, this, we are assured, would 'amount to unacceptable pressure' (p. 113, para. 50). The Commission claims to avoid this result by stipulating that defendants are to be told only what would be the maximum sentence were they to plead guilty at that stage (p. 113, para. 51). But, given the discount system and knowledge of the maximum they will receive on a plea, all defendants will face unacceptable pressure because the sentence on conviction after trial can be calculated using elementary mathematical principles.
5. Relying upon Roger Hood's study,[7] the Commission recognises that, because of their greater tendency to go to trial, the sentence discount 'puts black and other ethnic minority defendants at a greater risk of being sentenced to custody and serving longer sentences' (p. 114, para. 58).

In response, the Commission supports Hood's recommendation that 'the Crown Court ... monitor the ethnic origin of everyone who appears there' (p. 114, para. 58).

---

[7] *Race and Sentencing: A Study in the Crown Court*, Oxford, 1992.

Actually, Hood pointed out that, despite cost-saving advantages, the discount policy itself should be reconsidered because of the grave dangers of injustice in its practical operation and that, so far as any graduated discount of the kind proposed by the Commission was being contemplated: 'It would be important to monitor any ethnic differences *before* putting such a proposal into effect' (emphasis added).[8]

The result of the Commission's proposals on plea-bargaining will be to make true of this country Lenny Bruce's description of the American legal system, that 'In the Halls of Justice the only justice is in the halls'.

III RESEARCH

The Commission does violence to research in a variety of ways. First, it undertook no research on crucial issues. Thus:

- More cases are to be tried by magistrates, but there is no research on the quality of summary justice.
- More guilty pleas are to be extracted by pressure, but there is no research on the reliability of guilty pleas.
- There is no research on the quality of defence services, although the Commission's recommendations are premised on the availability of good legal advice.
- There is no research on what was seen as the Commission's central mission, namely, miscarriages of justice.

Second, the Commission has also failed to use misstated or misapplied research that is in the public domain, including that which it itself funded. For example, it feels able to impose disclosure obligations upon the defence even though its own commissioned research by Roger Leng demonstrates unequivocally that moral panics over defence ambushes do not withstand empirical scrutiny. In its discussion of disclosure, no reference is made to Roger Leng's important research.

Finally, it persistently advances contentious, dubious or wrong headed propositions, unsupported by empirical evidence, as if they were founded in research. For example:

- 'the most common reason for defendants delaying a plea of guilty until the last minute is a reluctance to face the facts until they are at the door of the court' (p. 112, para. 48);

---

[8] Ibid., p. 182.

• 'spontaneous remarks uttered on arrest are often the most truthful' (p. 61, para. 50).

IV ILLOGICALITIES, INCONSISTENCIES AND CONTRADICTIONS

The Report is littered with these. For example:

• On the one hand, plea-bargaining results in the conviction of the innocent; on the other, plea-bargaining is solely for the benefit of defendants (p. 113, para. 51).
• On the one hand, prosecutors should not be required to oversee police investigations because they could not maintain the necessary independence from arresting and investigative officers (p. 31, para. 25); on the other hand, the Commission gives this task to the police who, its own research shows, lack this independence, pass on bad habits to new recruits and fail to supervise at all in most cases.
• The obligation on the defence to disclose its case is legitimated on the basis that it might well lead to the prosecution being dropped (p. 97, para. 59).

V THE UNDERLYING PHILOSOPHY

According to the Commission, its Report is pragmatic rather than value-laden, based upon practical and not theoretical considerations (p. 3, para. 12). This is not true. There is a clear ideological agenda which infects the whole Report. Four elements can be stated briefly.

1. By explicitly imperilling 'the innocent' and others through such means as plea-bargaining, the drawing of adverse inferences and defence disclosure obligations, it runs counter to the foundational principles of the burden of proof and the purposes of our trial system.
2. This misunderstanding and misapplication of the burden of proof can be traced directly to the terms of reference, which enjoin the Commission to examine the effectiveness of the system in convicting the guilty and acquitting 'those who are innocent', rather than its correct formulation, namely, acquitting 'those who may be innocent'.
3. Having adopted this fallacy, the Commission constructs two categories of persons, the guilty and the innocent, and, on this basis, rest

recommendations which move the system closer to creating an equivalence of obligations on prosecutor and defence alike.

4. As a result, it is no surprise to find that the Commission not only rejects the inquisitorial system, but also rejects the adversarial model itself. In its place, through such things as mutual disclosure obligations, the removal of rights from defendants and the incorporation of defence representatives into a coercive plea system, it begins the creation of a new system. This seeks to harmonise the functions of the prosecution, the defence and the courts, all of whom would be expected to combine in the cost-efficient disposition of presumptively guilty defendants.

Set up to deal with a system which had miserably let down defendants, failed society as a whole and sullied the face of justice, the Commission's bizarre solution is to strengthen the prosecution and weaken the defence by converting the administration of criminal justice into an administrative criminal process. The end result of its efforts is a miscarriage of judgment.

3. Missing the Wood ... Pragmatism versus Theory in the Royal Commission

Nicola Lacey[1]

The Report of the Royal Commission on Criminal Justice (RCCJ 1993) has been received with widespread disappointment. Quite apart from disagreement over specific recommendations, this disappointment relates to a sense that a rare and crucially important opportunity to look critically at the criminal justice 'wood' as well as its constituent 'trees' has been missed. By the 'wood' I mean the underlying, structural factors which give rise to many of the particular problems in the administration of criminal justice addressed by the Commission, and the basic assumptions, values and goals which ought to inform criminal justice practices. Certainly, the Commission's focus on myriad aspects of detailed practice as opposed to controversial questions of value and theory has meant that most commentators can find things to agree with in the Report. Yet this very reaction to the Report as a 'curate's egg' is itself illustrative of some of the problems inherent in its lack of any underlying theoretical vision. For, on the face of it, such a general vision might have held its recommendations together and helped to persuade people unconvinced by certain aspects of the Report that, taken as a whole, its vision of criminal justice could be regarded as a sound and humane basis on which to undertake reform.

In this paper, I want to reflect on the apparent theoretical vacuum which lies at the heart of the Royal Commission's Report. I shall argue that this aspect of the Commission's approach is related to broader features of contemporary governmental culture in this country – features which are reflected both in the terms of reference with which the Commission was set up and in its mode of operation. By looking carefully at the terms of reference and the Commission's interpretation of them, I hope to throw light on the way in which governmental concerns with efficient resource

[1] I should like to express my very warm thanks to David Soskice, with whom I discussed this paper and who helped me in particular to clarify the argument about the Royal Commission's mode of operation. Remaining errors and infelicities, needless to say, are all my own work.

management and with a particular construction of the 'law and order problem' fed into the Royal Commission's proceedings.[2] This analysis will help to illuminate the processes through which the Commission was 'co-opted' by governmental managerial concerns, as opposed to the civil libertarian concerns about wrongful convictions which constituted the impetus for the Commission's creation. I shall suggest that this claim can be defended and explained quite straightforwardly, in terms of the logic of the Commission's terms of reference and of its status as a reform-oriented body operating within a particular political context. Ultimately, I shall therefore suggest that the Commission's Report *is* informed by an *implicit* theoretical framework – and by one which looks unpalatable when exposed to critical scrutiny. Furthermore, the rejection of 'theory' professed by the Commission can be shown to be counter-productive in terms of several of its own articulated concerns.

I THE COMMISSION'S TERMS OF REFERENCE

Following the Courts' tardy recognition of miscarriages of justice in the Guildford, Maguire and Birmingham cases, there was a widespread sense of relief that the injustices done in these cases had finally been acknowledged. But the relief was accompanied, for many people (though apparently not for the Courts themselves), by a sense of collective shame about and responsibility for the failings of a system in which we were involved – as practitioners, as academic commentators, as politicians, as citizens. The setting up of the Royal Commission seemed to represent the only appropriately general institutional response to the underlying problems which had led to the miscarriages of justice. In this context, even relatively sceptical commentators (this one included) were perhaps somewhat slow to read the writing on the wall which, with hindsight, the Commission's terms of reference represent. The Commission was asked to 'examine the *effectiveness* of the criminal justice system in England and Wales in *securing the conviction of those guilty of criminal offences* and the acquittal of those who are innocent, *having regard to the efficient use of resources* ...' (emphasis added). The centre of gravity of these terms was, therefore, clearly distanced from that which would have been indicated by the circumstances which led to the Commission's appointment. Whether a more vociferous public debate about the

---

[2] I shall continue to put the expression 'law and order problem' in inverted commas, to draw attention to the fact that I am referring to an ideological construct rather than an empirically defined set of issues.

assumptions underlying these terms of reference would have had any effect in encouraging the Commission to take a more critical approach to them is questionable. What is not in doubt is that the terms themselves reflect a clear view of the priorities of the criminal process, and one which is at odds with values which have long been taken, in establishment as much as oppositional ideology, to be at its heart.

On the face of it, the terms of reference construct the acquittal of the innocent, the conviction of the guilty and the efficient use of resources as joint and *equally important* instrumental concerns of the criminal process. In effect, they express a crude version of utilitarianism, with no recognition that special weighting should be given to individual justice – an idea which has long informed liberal critique of utilitarian theories of criminal justice (Hart 1968, Chapter 1). This implicit 'theory' calls into question the tenet that all are presumed to be innocent until proven guilty beyond reasonable doubt – perhaps the central institutional realisation of the critical liberal concern. As we are all aware, this 'golden thread' of criminal justice is all too often broken in practice – in the conduct of interviews in police stations (McConville, Sanders and Leng 1991), in the practice of plea-bargaining (Baldwin and McConville 1977), in the construction of certain doctrinal features of criminal law (Lacey, Wells and Meure 1990, Chapter 3; Smart 1976, Chapter 4), in the style of judicial summing up to the jury and general conduct of trials (McBarnet 1981; Pattenden 1982), to mention just a few examples. Nonetheless, one would have expected a Royal Commission to concern itself with strengthening the institutionalisation of this principle rather than the reverse. Yet, arguably, several of its key recommendations – notably in relation to plea-bargaining and the removal of the defendant's right to opt for jury trial – constitute just such an institutional erosion of the presumption of innocence. Furthermore, these recommendations are a direct result of the Commission's uncritical acceptance of the theory of criminal justice implicit in a literal reading of its terms of reference – terms which place efficiency on all fours with justice, and which construct the conviction of the innocent as no more important than the acquittal of the guilty.

This acceptance is expressed very directly in the Report's introductory chapter. One particularly relevant passage is worth quoting at length, because it gives important clues about further ways in which the Commission's interpretation of its brief was informed by a very particular approach to the criminal process as an administrative system devoted to the management of the 'problem of law and order':

All law-abiding citizens have a common interest in a system of criminal justice in which the risks of the innocent being convicted and of the guilty being acquitted are as low as human fallibility allows. For a person to be deprived of his or her liberty, perhaps for many years, on account of a crime which was in fact committed by someone else is both an individual tragedy and an affront to the standards of a civilised society. If innocent people are convicted, the real criminals, who may be very dangerous people, remain undetected. Conversely, justice is made a mockery in the particular case and the credibility of the system in general is undermined whenever a guilty person walks free because, for example, technical loopholes have been exploited, prosecution witnesses wrongly discredited, jurors improperly influenced, or victims intimidated. We recognise that there is no way of finding out, or even plausibly estimating, the frequency with which miscarriages of justice in either sense occur. It is widely assumed – and we are in no position to contradict it – that the guilty are more often acquitted than the innocent convicted. To some extent, an inevitable and appropriate consequence of the prosecution being required to prove its case beyond reasonable doubt must be that not every guilty person is convicted. (p. 2–3, para. 9)

Several features of this key paragraph call for comment. First, note that it is only 'law-abiding citizens' who have an interest in the adequate working of the criminal justice system. Those who have (?ever) committed an offence are excluded from the category of citizens with legitimate interests in the fair administration of criminal justice. The implications of this exclusion are as remarkable as they are alarming. The second sentence is a direct and reasonable gesture to the miscarriage of justice cases. But it is immediately followed by a statement of the instrumental implications of the conviction of the innocent: that the guilty – the 'dangerous' – have gone free. (This interpretation is echoed later in the chapter at the other main point at which the recent miscarriages of justice are mentioned and where they are discussed under the heading of 'public confidence' – and hence constructed primarily as a question of managerial efficacy rather than of individual injustice.) In a discursive sleight of hand, the focus is quickly shifted away from civil libertarian concerns, and the conviction of the innocent reconstructed as the flip-side of non-conviction of the guilty.

We then proceed to an analysis in which acquittals of the guilty are constructed as first and foremost a problem of system management – justice is made a 'mockery' and the system in general 'undermined'. Note here the positivistic assumptions about the nature of crime: throughout, 'guilt' and 'innocence' are constructed as unproblematic, factual questions rather than as the outcomes of a complex series of interpretative decisions on the part of a number of official and unofficial groups. This assumption, of course, flies in the face of the insights generated by the vast majority of intelligent research undertaken on the criminal justice system in the last twenty years (see for example McBarnet 1981; Box 1983, 1987; Carlen and Worrall (eds) 1987; McConville, Sanders and Leng 1991). It is particularly clearly shown up by the reference to the 'exploitation' of 'technical loopholes': does this, one wonders, include the burden of proof beyond reasonable doubt?

Next, we have the construction of miscarriages of justice as a term applying equally to the acquittal of the guilty and the conviction of the innocent. This construction both contradicts normal usage and expresses a symmetry which is contradicted, as we have already observed, by the presumption of innocence and the burden of proof. We end with the (somewhat grudging) acknowledgement that the (presumed) greater frequency of acquittals of the guilty is '*to some extent*' an 'appropriate' consequence of that presumption and burden. One wonders to what extent the Commission thinks it is *not* such a consequence, and what they would like to see done about it. One also wonders how much the Commission actually values the presumption of innocence, and how far they have implicitly reconstructed it, consistently with their terms of reference, as an institutional impediment to the efficient management of criminal justice seen as a system geared symmetrically to 'the conviction of the guilty and the acquittal of the innocent'.

II THE COMMISSION'S MODE OF ANALYSIS

I have already noted that the Commission eschews any explicit discussion of what might be called a general 'theory' of criminal justice. Indeed, this rejection of theory is explicit: in their initial reference to the debate about adversarial and inquisitorial processes, they assert that 'we have not arrived at our proposals through a theoretical assessment of the relative merits of the two legal traditions. On the contrary, we have been guided throughout by practical considerations in proposing changes which will, in our view, make our existing system more capable of serving the interests of both justice and efficiency.' (p. 3, para. 12). In this section, I want to consider how this anti-theoretical stance, which explicitly sets up theory in opposition to practice – 'on the contrary' – informed the Commission's mode of operation, and what the implications of this aspect of its stance are for the quality of its analysis and the prospects for the success of its proposals judged on its own terms.[3]

---

[3] In a recent article ('Where the critics got it wrong Part II', (1993) *New Law Journal* 1364), Professor Michael Zander, a member of the Royal Commission, has defended its lack of 'expressed theoretical structure'. Zander concedes the relevance of theories and principles of criminal justice to the questions the Commission had to address. However, he argues that their explicit incorporation within the Commission's deliberations or its Report would have made no practical difference to the nature of its proceedings or to the shape of its ultimate recommendations. My objective in this section is precisely to identify the respects in which the failure explicitly to advert to issues of principle allowed an *implicit* and ethically

One of the most striking features of the Report is the level of detail at which it operates. Much of its analysis, and most of its 352 recommendations, engage with particular practices at specific stages of the criminal process. This focus on specifics was evident right from the start of the Commission's proceedings: for example, it was reflected in the consultation paper circulated to interested groups, which set out and solicited views on dozens of questions about detailed institutional reforms. Whilst its grasp of detail is certainly impressive, and was inevitably an important part of the Commission's enterprise, questions can be raised about whether its near-exclusive focus on practicalities debarred it from picking up on the underlying *causes* of the problems it sought to address, as opposed to the *symptoms* represented by the problems themselves.

For example, many of the Commission's initial consultative questions, like many of its recommendations, focused on questions such as how far video-recording, tape-recording and other procedural reforms relating to the interviewing of suspects inside and outside police stations were feasible and might be expected to reduce the chances of inaccuracy and abuse in the construction of suspects' statements. Whilst these are undoubtedly important questions, there are equally important, broader questions which fall into the cracks between the detailed questions. These questions have to do with why abuses occur in the first place, and they can only be addressed through reflection on issues such as the way in which policing is socially constructed within a society preoccupied by 'law and order' as a major social problem; how adequate and humane policing is defined and rewarded; the institutional culture of the police and police work.

The nearest we get to a recognition of these broader questions in Chapter 1 is in the recognition that 'police malpractice, where it occurs, may often be motivated by an over-zealous determination to secure the conviction of suspects believed to be guilty in the face of rules and procedures which seem to those charged with the investigation to be weighted in favour of the defence' (p. 7, para. 24). There is no analysis of the context in which this 'over-zealousness' occurs, nor any hint of recognition that it might be related to a system in which 'clear-up rates' have been a prime measure of police efficiency. We do get a glimpse of the Commission's awareness of the relevance of such issues later on, when it expresses its approval of the fact that Home Office Circular 104/1991 provides for the assessment of police officers' performance 'on the basis of their skills, abilities and attitudes rather than chiefly on numbers of arrests, searches and stops in

---

questionable set of theoretical assumptions to dominate the Commission's deliberations, with clear and direct implications for its analysis.

the street' (p. 21, para. 62; see also Recommendation 31). But this insight is not developed in terms of any substantive discussion of what the relevant indicators of good performance should be (an omission which also characterises other recent reports on the police: *Police Reform* (1993), HMSO; *Inquiry into Police Responsibilities and Rewards* (1993) HMSO). Nor is there any reflection on the way in which governmentally-encouraged public preoccupation with 'law and order' helps to construct a particular and very pressing set of imperatives for policework, and feeds into the aspects of policing culture which are most problematic from a civil libertarian point of view (Reiner 1985). One highly relevant factor here is the idea that policing is, as the recent White Paper on police reform (*Police Reform* (1993), HMSO) confirms, first and foremost about 'the fight against crime'. This arguably fosters both an instrumentalist and a conflictual 'them-and-us' mentality which, in helping to construct (particularly certain groups of) suspects as presumptively guilty, is directly hospitable to the kind of rule-bending which the Commission decries (Hillyard 1993b).

Perhaps most damagingly of all, the Commission fails to recognise the link between this instrumentalist, divisive 'law and order' mentality and its own undermining of the presumption of innocence *via* the construction of miscarriages of justice as symmetrical. In the context of the passage already quoted, this means that the Commission does not see fit to point out that the 'rules and procedures' are indeed *meant to be* 'weighted in favour of the defence'. Arguably, their systematic failure to achieve their purpose in upholding the presumption of innocence – a failure which was closely related to the miscarriages of justice which led to the Commission's creation – had to do with the utilitarian reconstruction of these rules as unreasonable and inefficient obstructions to police investigations. This is, of course, precisely the reconstruction to which the Commission's uncritical acceptance of its utilitarian terms of reference implicitly lends weight.

The predominant focus of the Commission's analysis on the level of practical detail therefore obscures some of the most important general issues which one might have expected it to address. The stance brings with it what might be called a technocratic approach to reform. The mode of analysis is to identify a specific 'problem' – abuses of power in police interviewing, wastage of resources as a result of 'cracked' trials, incompetence on the part of defence and prosecution lawyers – and to suggest a specific, 'practical' solution. The assumption underlying this way of proceeding is a deeply instrumentalist and yet practically dubious one in which all functional problems are presumed to have regulatory solutions. Furthermore, a very significant proportion of the solutions proposed either take the form of *coercive* regulations backed by detailed sanctions or consist in rather general prescriptions for procedural reform which evade central substantive questions which would be likely to be politically controversial.

For example, the proposed solution to lawyers' incompetence and inefficiency is to set out detailed procedural rules backed up by disciplinary sanctions such as loss of fees; the solution to police malpractice is in terms of an extraordinarily comprehensive system of human and electronic surveillance (see Recommendation 50) and adjustments to the disciplinary structure. Failures within a system of coercive regulation are therefore dealt with by means of the elaboration of more and more coercive regulations – a mode of reform familiar to all acquainted with the criminal process and exemplified by the Police and Criminal Evidence Act 1984. It is all too obvious that such over-regulation is likely to be counter-productive. This is because perceptions among relevant practitioners that their activities have become regulated and bureaucratised to an unrealistic degree will breed precisely the kind of instrumentalist rule-avoidance which the Commission itself recognises is already a feature of the system; because those charged with the sanctioning process may see the regulations as neither feasible nor fair; and because, most of all, the regulations respond to the problems but fail to address their causes. In this last respect, one particularly relevant factor is the extensiveness of the criminal justice system, whose growth over the last ten years has been very marked. This, arguably, is a direct result of an over-ready governmental resort to criminalisation as a quick 'fix' for a variety of perceived social problems. And this resort has been necessitated in part by the effects of the Government's own economic and social policies in damaging the networks and institutional infrastructure which supported more informal, consensual and local means of resolving conflict, and hence in reducing the array of repertoires available for the reproduction of social order.

Arguably, then, the resort to coercive regulation is one of the few tools available in a system which has become impoverished in terms of fora for substantive debate about the values underlying criminal justice practice and in which such values are deeply contested. The same is true of the other main kind of reform proposal – the instantiation of at first sight more proactive solutions such as better and more extensive training. For systems of police, judicial and legal practitioner training to have any hope of improving standards of criminal justice, there will have to be some consensus about what the values which inform the system are. Yet the nearest we get to any such substantive discussion lies in the ethically unsatisfactory consideration of the presumption of innocence and the undeveloped expression of approval for broader performance indicators for the police mentioned above. Beyond this, the Commission provides us with little above the level of platitudes, apart from the Report's thorough-going commitment to 'value for money' and the efficient use of resources. The key question of how effective resource management can be made compatible with the operationalisation of the presumption of innocence in a society with an over-extensive, under-resourced, criminal justice system and a commitment to a divisive 'law and order' politics is outside the scope of the Commission's analysis.

Perhaps the Royal Commission simply thought that the values underlying the presumption of innocence were so obvious and uncontested as not to merit specific discussion. If so, the assumption is unfortunate, because it is contradicted by the inroads on that presumption which are implicit in its own approach. It is also unfortunate because the presumption of innocence may be based on a number of different evaluative concerns. Notably, it may be supported on the basis of a concern to ensure a relative equality of power between an individual defendant and a powerful prosecuting state. Additionally or alternatively, it may be based on the idea that the conviction of the innocent is an especially grave form of injustice and inhumanity. Which of these and other relevant concerns is foremost has implications for the extent to which and the thoroughness with which the presumption of innocence will be institutionalised. The inevitable implication of the Commission's evasion of such contested questions of substance – as it might say, of 'theory' – will be that, in so far as its recommendations are implemented, they will be likely to be ineffective or even counterproductive in terms of efficiency or justice. An important opportunity to articulate and defend the basic values *underlying* institutional rules such as the 'right to silence' has been missed. This evasion has arguably contributed to the ease with which the Government has already been able summarily to announce its intention to abolish the right, notwithstanding the Commission's qualified defence of it.

III REFORMING THE CRIMINAL PROCESS IN A 'LAW AND ORDER' SOCIETY

Finally, I want to consider whether it would have been realistic to expect the Royal Commission to produce anything other than a Report characterised by the features I have mentioned. Given the context in which it was set up, many commentators have been taken aback by its focus on concerns of managerial efficiency and by the relatively small place occupied by an analysis of how miscarriages of justice as usually understood come about in a system which professes to be weighted in the defendant's favour. There has been talk of 'co-optation' by governmental concerns. Certainly, the Royal Commission could have adopted a more critical and independent-minded stance on certain key issues. Yet it can be argued that the style of its Report is eminently understandable as having been dictated not only by its terms of reference but also by the broader logic characterising the enterprise of a reform-oriented public body of its type.

The Royal Commission was created by a Government which, in its successive manifestations since 1979, had made its status as the upholder of 'law and order' a central plank of both its ideology and its political programme. By the time the miscarriage of justice cases were acknowledged, this 'law and order' approach had begun to constitute something of a self-created noose around the Government's neck. For, as it poured resources into the police and the prison system and resorted liberally to criminalisation as a response to a wide range of 'social problems', the most apparent result of its policies was an increase in the level of crime. This presented a major political problem, for once 'law and order' is set up as an index of governmental competence, it is hard to dismantle. The Government had consistently held up the image of the 'law-abiding' citizen as distinct from the 'criminal' – the ultimately undeserving and threatening 'other', excluded from political society by reason of his or her own individual wickedness (Lacey, Wells and Meure 1990, Chapter 2). In doing so it had shifted political attention away from the social causes of crime and, in particular, the relevance of its own libertarian social policies to the increasing poverty, relative deprivation and urban infrastructural decay which are associated with many forms of crime in most 'developed' countries. But it had also constructed a Frankenstein's monster whose exigencies in terms of political capital and economic resources were huge – a monster which by this time was being fed by an Opposition which was keen to demonstrate its macho credentials in an area in which it was generally regarded as electorally vulnerable (Hall 1980).

In this context, the miscarriage of justice cases presented the Government with a very tricky problem. As a result of its own policies, the (in itself proper) social concern with the threat of and harms done by crime to its actual and potential victims had become extraordinarily intense. So much so, in fact, that almost any substantial political concern with injustice to actual or suspected offenders at a *systematic* level (rather than in the context of particular sensational cases) was in danger of being seen as the Government 'going soft' on crime and undermining its own 'law and order' credentials.   Its solution, expressed clearly in the Royal Commission's terms of reference, was to reconstruct those cases as instances of a more general problem of the *efficient management* of the criminal process, and in particular of the process's failure in securing the conviction of the guilty. At a stroke, a spectacular instance of individual injustice and the abuse of power was converted into an instance of systemic inefficiency and wastage of resources.

Since this analysis was so very clear in the Commission's terms of reference, it is hardly surprising that it informed the Commission's own analysis. For the very logic of such a body is that it hopes to be judged a success – and success, most obviously, is judged in terms of the acceptance and implementation of its reform proposals. Thus such bodies always have a clear incentive to 'second-guess' what will find favour with the Government of the day.[4] There is, of course, a certain paradox to this mode of operation. For the proposals of such bodies are almost always diluted in any event: even the compromises made in the process of second-guessing rarely reach the statute book unamended. This has the inevitable result that principled commitments tend to suffer a double attrition in the very reform process which one might expect to strengthen them. It seems reasonable to suggest, therefore, that a rational reform body, forseeing the limited prospects of successful implementation of even its most modest proposals, might well take a long-term view of its role. And if it did so, it might well see sense in throwing down the gauntlet to both Government and Opposition by laying emphasis on the enunciation of values and principles which it genuinely believed ought to inform public debate and policy.

The Royal Commission's horizons, however, were fixed firmly on the short- and medium-term law reform process. Given the Labour Party's own pragmatic stand on 'law and order', there was no reason, notwithstanding the forthcoming election, for the Royal Commission to envisage any fundamental change in governmental analysis pending its Report. It therefore picked up the baton the Government handed to it, and produced a large number of detailed recommendations which are predominantly utilitarian and managerial in orientation. As we have seen, most of these have no bearing whatsoever on the cultural and structural features of the system which led to the miscarriages of justice, and some of

---

[4] Cf. Richard Ericson's argument, in this volume, that the 'reform discourse' of the Royal Commission simply confirms a *'fait accompli'* rather than proposing anything new.

those which do are likely to exacerbate those underlying causes rather than the reverse.

Given the political and institutional context in which it operated, it was therefore always highly unlikely that the Royal Commission would engage in the kind of thoroughgoing critical analysis which many citizens and many commentators on and practitioners within the criminal justice system would have welcomed. For the really basic questions – questions about the social and economic conditions which foster crime; about the patterns of social division which mark out the social groups against whom criminal justice is enforced and, equally importantly, those against whom it is *not* enforced; about the long-term implications of a socially divisive 'law and order' politics, supported, in effect, by both major political parties; about the proper functions of the criminal justice system in a society such as ours; about the nature and role of policing and police culture; about the values underlying the presumption of innocence – are simply not on the political agenda in this country.

We might, on the other hand, have expected the Royal Commission at least to push these fundamental issues a little closer to that agenda. At root, these are questions about the nature of criminal justice in a socially divided society which aspires to become more civilised than it currently is. Royal Commission or no Royal Commission, what we have to recognise is that these fundamental questions must find their way on to the political agenda, and our democratic institutions must develop in a way which will facilitate a wide-ranging debate about the crisis within and beyond criminal justice which has been occasioned by our construction of ourselves as a 'law and order society' (Hall 1980). Until this happens, the hope that law reform can effect significant and lasting improvements in the quality of criminal 'justice', broadly and properly understood, will be an illusion.

4. Optimism Writ Large: A Critique of the Runciman Commission on Criminal Justice

Richard Nobles and David Schiff

> Integrity without knowledge is weak and useless, and knowledge without integrity is dangerous and dreadful (Samuel Johnson, *Rasselas* 1759, Ch. 41)

This Royal Commission was set up in response to cases in which large (or at least important) sections of the public had come to the conclusion that, in a number of cases, the wrong persons had been convicted of serious offences. Thus, whatever its specific terms of reference, its role was to respond to public awareness that the English system of criminal justice had produced miscarriages of justice. But beneath a consensus that miscarriages of justice had occurred, there are radically different notions of what constitute miscarriages of justice, and how one should respond to them.

Miscarriage of justice, as interpreted by the Royal Commission, is essentially about getting the verdict wrong – it is a rational conception linked to the outcome of trials. The Royal Commission's terms of reference required them to consider the effectiveness of the criminal justice system in securing the conviction of the guilty, as well as the acquittal of the innocent. These terms of reference immediately moved the focus away from another view of miscarriage of justice, one which could equally well be said to have concerned the public at the time the Commission was set up: the view that convictions had been secured in flagrant breach of the rules of criminal procedure – through, for examples, non-disclosure (Stefan Kiszko, Darvell brothers, Judith Ward) and police malpractice (Guildford 4, Birmingham 6).

In the Commission's terms of reference, effectiveness is also a rational concept linked to the outcome of trials, associated in some way with probability. It is unacceptable to fail to convict too many of the guilty, or to convict too many innocents. 'Too many' is not quantified, but it is accepted that there will inevitably be some mistakes. As a Report in the rationalist tradition,[1] it is perhaps not surprising to find that it is a-historical. Although the Commissioners must be presumed to be aware of the long history of debate over the appropriate processes for separating the innocent from the guilty,[2] their Report repeatedly reads as if the issue can be solved by a process of balancing, applied now, taking account of new evidence, or the effects of recent reforms. There is no sense of fundamental conflicts over ways of interpreting the criminal justice system. Perhaps this is deliberate. A brief statement of the history of the reform of criminal justice might have forced them to confront the fact that balances and trade offs are not matters of common sense or logic, but politics. In the absence of a consensus as to the appropriate aims and procedures for criminal justice there can be no simple balance. This may be the major reason why criminal justice has spawned so many commissions of enquiry, with such regularity.[3]

The Commission's commitment to the Enlightenment project (the rational pursuit of truth)[4] is well captured in the final paragraph of their introductory chapter:

> It may be argued that however practical our recommendations, and however cogent the reasoning behind them, there is a potential conflict between the interests of justice on the one hand and the requirement of fair and reasonable treatment for everyone involved, suspects and defendants included, on the other. We do not seek to maintain that the two are, or will ever be, reconcilable throughout the system in the eyes of all the parties involved in it. But we do believe that the fairer the treatment which all the parties receive at the hands of the system the more likely it is that the jury's verdict, or where appropriate the subsequent decision of the Court of Appeal, will be correct. As will become apparent from our recommendations, there are issues on which a balance has to be struck. But we are satisfied that when taken as a whole our recommendations serve the interests of justice without diminishing the individual's right to fair and reasonable treatment, and that if they are implemented they will do much to restore that public confidence in the system on which its successful operation so much depends. (para. 27)

The Commissioners' most important concern is the pursuit of truth in terms of the justice of 'correct' decisions. Fairness is welcomed to the extent that it contributes to the pursuit of truth, but must occasionally be balanced where the two conflict. The pivot for that balance is concern

---

[1] See 'The Rationalist Tradition of evidence scholarship', Twining 1985: Ch. 1. The ghost of Bentham hangs over this Report, and Bentham's close association of reason and truth in his theory of utility. The Report attempts, as did Bentham and his Enlightenment predecessors, to present sound, uncomplicated reasons rather than be bound by superstition and fiction (see Harrison 1983: Ch. 1).

[2] See for example, the exchange between Paley 1809 and Romilly 1810.

[3] See the Bibliography of Parliamentary Papers: Reports of Commissions and Committees, in Radzinowicz and Hood 1986: 830–45.

[4] See footnote 1.

with public confidence. Without this, measures which might at first glance seem to increase the efficiency of criminal justice (e.g. increased police investigatory powers, the admissibility of all available evidence) can actually reduce efficiency (through a decline in the public's willingness to report crimes, be witnesses at trials, and, as jurors, to convict defendants).

But while the Royal Commission pursues truth at the point of trial court decisions, it fails to explore the 'truth' of public confidence in the system. Although it commissioned twenty-two separate pieces of research, none of them examined the basis of public confidence in, or public disquiet with, criminal justice. The Commissioners proceeded from the somewhat naive assumption that public confidence in criminal justice is based solely upon the statistical likelihood of mistakes. Therefore, measures which increase the accuracy of outcomes would also restore public confidence. The consequences of failing to consider other possible bases for public confidence (whether or not they can be measured empirically) is best illustrated by the fate of their recommendation for the abolition of the right to opt for jury trial (immediately questioned by the Home Secretary).[5] Despite stating in their introductory chapter that the jury is 'widely and firmly believed to be one of the cornerstones of our system of justice' (para. 8), they recommended taking away the defendant's right to choose trial by jury. In making that recommendation, they only discussed the reasons why defendants might wish to take advantage of such a right and, believing that most defendants chose jury trial in order to maximise their chance of an acquittal, felt this was an illegitimate basis for the right. But the appropriate question is not simply why, or who, takes advantage of the right to jury trial (or many other rights) but why the availability of such a right creates public confidence in the legitimacy of the system. By making the crude assumption that legitimacy is mainly a function of accuracy, the Commission was led to make the crass mistake of recommending the abolition of such an important legitimating right.[6]

The strength of the Commission's commitment to accuracy over rights led the majority of them, in their discussion of the powers of the Court of Appeal, to recommend that convictions obtained through procedurally defective trials should nevertheless be upheld, provided that the Court of Appeal were satisfied that the conviction was 'safe'. As for the minority (which includes Zander, Newbold and one other) Zander points out in his dissent that allowing defendants to serve prison sentences 'on the basis of

---

5 'Howard wary on proposal to limit right to trial by jury', *The Guardian*, 7 July 1993.
6 Lord Runciman admitted that he was 'very surprised' by the degree of critical reaction to the proposals for restricting jury trial. See 'Critics of jury plan surprise Runciman', *Financial Times*, 8 July 1993.

trials that are seriously flawed' (para. 64) is to subordinate 'the integrity' of the criminal justice system to the conviction of particular individuals.

In light of the strength of the Commission's commitment to accurate results at trial, one cannot but question the motives for recommending the maintaining or strengthening of suspects' rights whilst in detention. Consider its treatment of the defendant's rights to remain silent, and to receive legal advice before answering police questions. Retaining the first of these rights has little to do with accuracy, unless one believes that those suspects who remain silent are also the ones who, if the right of silence were abolished, would be most likely to make false confessions. The majority felt unable to recommend the termination of this right, feeling a) that the right to comment on silence at trial would make little or no difference to the jury's decision (the prosecution is already allowed to bring the fact of silence to their attention) and b) that abolishing the right to silence would result in the police informing suspects that their silence might lead to adverse comment at their trial, which could lead to an increased number of innocent persons incriminating themselves. This attempt to present its conclusion in rationalist terms is singularly unconvincing. One feels in the end that the right to silence is simply something that is not worth taking away – it has no appreciable effect on the outcome, it is not exercised by the majority of defendants, and it is therefore an extremely cheap (both in terms of expense and likely number of wrongful acquittals) concession to those bodies who are concerned to uphold the rights of suspects in detention.

At first glance, the Commissioners treat the right to legal advice more seriously. They commissioned extensive research into the number of people who ask for solicitors to be present during its interrogations, were pleased with the increase in numbers following PACE, and made suggestions to further increase those numbers. But if the basis of concern is that uninformed answers to police questions may lead to unreliable evidence, why rely on the suspect's *right* to ask for a solicitor. Their concern with numbers leads one to believe that higher numbers are better than lower ones, and a 100 per cent take up would be ideal. But if one wants 100 per cent of suspects' interrogations to take place with the benefit of legal advice there are more effective means to ensure this than granting a right to legal advice. One simply requires all interviews in detention to take place in the presence of a solicitor which, like the Commission's recommendation of the 'safeguard' of video cameras in interview suites, cannot be waived by the suspect. This could be achieved through the provision of duty solicitors at every police interrogation centre. In comparison with this, the granting of a right to legal advice is a cheap alternative, and one which will always be hard to defend. Since the right will never be taken up by 100 per cent of suspects, and common sense indicates that it will be the most vulnerable who will waive it, the right to legal advice will always favour the confident against the unconfident, the literate against the illiterate, the adequate against the inadequate. This example leads one to question the Commission's approach to rights, as set out in its introductory chapter (quoted above). For truth has not been sacrificed to rights, but to expense and police convenience. Granting and upholding rights has simply disguised this trade-off. That the basis for rejecting more radical protections than rights is cost is demonstrated by its reaction to suggested reforms which might increase the use of solicitors by the more vulnerable groups – the reading out of notices setting out the right to free legal advice, which would put the illiterate and literate on an equal footing. This reform is rejected on the basis of consequent inconvenience to the police.

Although the Commissioners define justice in terms of accurate results, their understanding of rights is inchoate. Where rights are not seen as procedures for assisting the search for truth, they appear to have two other bases. First, rights based on ideas of liberty – the freedom to be left alone by the state unless the state can show cause why you are to be processed through the criminal justice system. This idea of rights supplements the adversarial system, which otherwise depends on the (often unconvincing) assertion that leaving the full burden of proof on the State assists the search for truth.

A second basis for rights appears to be traditions or history. Ideas that the 'fair' treatment of suspects depends upon them continuing to enjoy rights which they have had in the past. Again, this supplements the adversarial system. The continued enjoyment of past rights can be supported on the basis that some balance of power between the State and the individual is 'fair' or that it contributes to the process of discovering truth. The second assertion is unconvincing. The first suffers from the self-evident inequality of power between the individual and the State, such that any assertion of balance appears simply arbitrary.[7] It also fails to take account of the interests that are served by the State, in particular the interests of those who suffer from the perpetration of crimes: victims. Those who seek to balance the rights of the suspect and the State can be

---

7   Bentham contemptuously referred to the desire to redress this balance of power as 'The fox-hunter's reason': 'Every villain let loose one term, that he may bring custom the next, is a sort of bag-fox, nursed by the common hunt at Westminster. The policy so dear to sportsmen, so dear to rat-catchers, cannot be supposed entirely unknown to lawyers. To different persons, both a fox and a criminal have their use: the use of a fox is to be hunted; the use of a criminal is to be tried.' Bentham 1827: 238–9.

accused of neglecting the 'rights' of victims.

Running through the whole of this Report is an attitude which threatens to undermine its original project. Brought into being in response to a perceived collapse of confidence in criminal justice, one might have expected the members of the Commission to exhibit a degree of scepticism towards the present system.[8] Whilst they were unlikely to adopt the scepticism of radical criminologists,[9] who see criminal justice as a process of social control, class oppression, or labelling, they might have accepted that the commitment to truth of many actors within the system is open to question. As Mr. Justice Bridge had said, at the trial of the Birmingham 6, if the defendants were telling the truth then 'consider the scale of the conspiracy in terms of those involved. It ranges, does it not, from detective constables and police constables right up through the police hierarchy to .... Assistant Chief Constable .... If the evidence of the defendants is true, it shows the police not only to be masters of the vile techniques of cruelty and brutality to suspects. It shows them to have a very lively and inventive imagination.'[10] In these circumstances what is most surprising about its Report is its optimism about the ability of legal fora to identify truth.[11] This optimism makes them reluctant to rule out any type of evidence.[12] Police malpractice is better dealt with through improved police discipline and training. Interviews which occur outside the police station may still contain true incriminations. Rules of corroboration are technical and likely to exclude reliable proof. And even convictions obtained in the face of serious breaches of the rules may be upheld where they are still considered 'safe'.

This faith in the ability of adjudicators to identify reliable evidence without reference to procedures or rules has echoes of the tension between act and rule utilitarians.[13] Just as pursuit of utility may undermine the institutions and rules which make utility possible, so acceptance of one's ability to identify the reliability of evidence obtained in contravention of rules or processes intended to ensure its reliability may lead to a lowering of the amount of truth in the system or, and equally important in the context of this Commission, a loss of public confidence in the ability of the

---

[8] Especially given that one of the Commissioners was Sir John May, whose earlier report (May 1990) had been so critical of the police, prosecution, judiciary and Forensic Science Service.

[9] See for example, Inciardi 1980.

[10] Quoted in Mullin 1990: 201.

[11] Although this optimism forms part of the rationalist evidence tradition and, in particular, Bentham's concept of free proof. See Twining 1985: 3.

[12] In Bentham's words: 'Evidence is the basis of justice: exclude evidence, you exclude justice.' (Bentham 1827: 1).

[13] See Smart 1973: 9–12.

system to deliver truth.

This same optimism also serves to undermine the Commission's commitment to rights. A more sceptical approach to truth might have led the Commission to place more emphasis on rights. If we cannot with confidence state that every person selected for punishment was in fact guilty of the crime of which they were accused, we must be able to say that the processes which led to its conviction were 'fair'. And though concern with truth remains, paradoxically, part of the process of justification (for if one is indifferent to truth conviction can best be justified by lottery), it cannot be the whole basis for a just conviction.

The Commission's commitment (rhetorical if not actual) to the pursuit of truth, leaves it open to the criticism that the aims of the criminal justice system cannot be reduced to a single value. The feature which most obviously belies such a claim is the enormous reliance placed in the Report upon the guilty plea. This represents a one-word confession, obtained through inducements and the fear of increased punishment, unproved by the full process of trial and cross-examination. Belief in the reliability of such pleas in these circumstances is either hopeless optimism, or the use of such optimism to disguise a fatalistic acceptance that the cost of processing persons through criminal justice without this device is simply prohibitive.

This Royal Commission should prompt those interested in reforming the criminal justice system to engage in a debate about the enterprise of reform itself. The evolution of the reform of criminal justice procedure has been guided by the move from superstition to truth; the elimination of those characteristics of the system which cannot be supported by direct proof as correlated to the 'correctness' of trial decisions.[14] The information put before this Commission both from its funded research reports and the vast list of individual witnesses and organisations, included much evidence not predicated upon justice as a rational search for truth. With that narrow focus the Commission has been able to ignore most of this evidence because, in the application of its criteria for reform, and within its narrowly defined analytic framework, most of it is at best tangential to its concerns. Far from not having a clear starting point from which to examine the criminal justice system, this Commission has one definite standard consistent with the rationalist tradition and constructed out of its

---

[14] This project clearly has its origins with Bentham's extensive writings. As he states in the Conclusion to the final volume of *Rationale of Judicial Evidence*: ' ... in principle there is but one mode of searching out the truth: and (bating the corruptions introduced by superstition, or fraud, or folly, under the mask of science,) this mode, in so far as truth has been searched out and brought to light, is, and ever has been, and ever will be, the same ... see every thing that is to be seen; hear every body who is likely to know any thing about the matter ... ' (Bentham 1827: 743)

interpretation of miscarriage of justice.

Whatever the fate of the Commission's recommendations, its general approach has implications for the future of reform. If reform continues to be discussed in terms of the pursuit of truth, then many aspects of the present system, and many of the demands of those who seek radical reforms, will be hard to justify. The pursuit of what Bentham called free proof,[15] is best undertaken without reference to rules or rights. All one needs is an impartial, totally rational adjudicator, of superior intelligence. There is little reason to believe that the further research recommended by this Commission will reveal that the jury fits this ideal.[16] And here again, the parallels with utilitarianism are instructive. When truth is treated as an objective and rational value, rights which conflict with truth appear irrational and often subjective. But truth cannot be found in legal fora without confidence in the veracity of the institutions and actors of the criminal justice system. And such confidence is reliant upon irrational ideas of fairness and adherence to procedures and rules as well as commitment to truth. It may also require measures which lead to a decrease in the number of convictions. But one cannot restore a loss of confidence in the institutions and personnel who make up the criminal justice system, and who are responsible for presenting the evidence upon which verdicts are to be based, if one starts from the premise that no opportunity to obtain evidence should be lost, and no person genuinely believed to be guilty should be acquitted.

The Commission's Report raises difficult questions about the appropriate praxis for reform. Does one continue to concentrate on miscarriages of justice as the central expression of the weakness of the system? By stressing the need to acquit the innocent (even apart from convicting the guilty), one is in danger of undermining concepts of rights. Rights which do not self-evidently contribute to the accuracy of result, or at least reduce the likelihood of wrongful convictions, are difficult to defend. Those who are at most risk from wrongful conviction ('the vulnerable'[17]) are likely to be the least able to exercise rights. The desire to protect the innocent is likely to lead to arguments not for rights but safeguards – measures designed to protect vulnerable individuals from themselves as well as from

---

[15] Arguments about this conception are discussed by Cohen 1983.

[16] Ch. 1, para. 8

[17] The use of inverted commas is intended to indicate our view that the vulnerability of suspects to make false self-incriminations cannot be simply read off from a list of categories of persons who are generally thought to be vulnerable in other contexts.

others.[18]   And whether one argues for rights or safeguards, if the
organising principle is the desire to avoid the wrongful conviction of the
innocent, one is always vulnerable to optimism whether this takes the form
of faith that malpractice will be low, or in the ability of legal fora to
identify whether particular abuses have led to unreliable evidence. And
one must, after the experience of this Commission, doubt the ability of
empirical research, or concrete examples of wrongful conviction, ever to
destroy such optimism on the part of those whom the establishment
entrusts with the process of reform.

---

[18] One can talk of inalienable rights, but the moving from rights to 'safeguards' is intended to
refer not only to things which the suspect may not choose to waive, but to abandon any
concept of correlative individual duties. It is the system which must ultimately afford the
necessary protection.

5. The Royal Commission on Criminal Justice: A Room Without a View

Celia Wells[1]

The announcement in 1991 that the crisis of criminal justice was to be addressed by a Royal Commission naturally provoked a mixture of responses (Royal Commission on Criminal Justice 1991). For some there was already an air of world-weary cynicism including a prescient warning that the very function of Royal Commissions was to bury rather than to deliver. For others its establishment represented an overdue recognition that there was something seriously wrong with the 'best system of criminal justice in the world'. It was a case of scepticism and a claimed realism on the one hand and faith and trust on the other. By the time the Commission reported two years on, the chorus was more in unison; even the optimistic were, it seems, disappointed by the decision to play safe.

My task is broad and reflective adopting a position once-removed from the arguments deployed or recommendations made. In resonance and tone the Report misjudges wildly the complexities of the relations with which people engage in the criminal justice system. I describe below the two senses in which it seems to me that the Commission has chosen a partial and limited perspective on criminal justice, and then consider more closely some of the conceptual questions which the Report raises. First, though, some initial observations through which I try to capture what might be called the disappearing vapour, the essence which is missing from the Report's deliberations.

We cannot make sense of the Runciman Report nor work out how to incorporate it in our thinking unless we comprehend the importance of the initial loss of faith and disenchantment with the system which prompted and preceded it. Royal Commissions cannot be neutral observers; they are part of the process by which criminal justice is played out in particular societies at particular times. The historical, social and political contingency

---

[1] Without research assistance by Tess Newton, funded by Cardiff Law School, this paper would not have been written. I happily take responsibility for any errors and shortcomings.

of criminal justice should not be understated. More than anything, it is the Report's failure ever to locate itself and the system it addresses which bespeaks its limitations.

Although set up as a clear result of the public exposure of miscarriages of justice arising from the Birmingham and Guildford bombs, the Report fails to acknowledge the reverberating shock which those cases caused especially amongst hitherto trusting observers of the system. Given the symbolic position which Royal Commissions command, it is extraordinary that no attempt is made to orchestrate through it some kind of wake or memorial to those whose lives have been blighted by the driving force of 'criminal justice'. Irrespective of the detail of the Report's recommendations, or their overall thrust or even of any theoretical underpinnings on which they might rest, this is a significant omission.

I AN INCOMPLETE VISION

One obvious point about the Commission's picture of criminal justice is that it is fragmentary and incomplete. With a few exceptions, it is a conception which starts when a suspect arrives at a police station and ends at the court; there is no attempt to address the whole of what might reasonably be thought to come under the term 'criminal justice'. The piecemeal tinkering which results can be traced to two causes. The terms of reference themselves excluded significant parts of the system and thus deprived the Commission of the opportunity to examine it from enforcement policy through to investigative practice, and from prosecution through to punishment (Editorial (1991) *New Law Journal* 141, p. 373). The effect of this is not only to leave some crucial parts of the system untouched, it also reinforces the primacy of the police as enforcers of criminal law; other enforcement agencies are forgotten or regarded as insignificant.

Additionally, the picture which emerges seems unfinished because of the way the Commission conceived some of the matters which clearly were within its terms. Although the relationship between enforcement and prosecution was included, we learn a lot more about delivery of the former by the police, than about the latter, by the Crown Prosecution Service.[2] There appears to have been no attempt to conduct research into the CPS, an omission all the stranger given the criticism it has attracted during its short life. Two of the terms of reference (numbers ii and vi) refer specifically to

---

[2] Eleven of the Commission's research studies focus on aspects of police investigation, and only one touches on prosecution (apart from the study on serious fraud).

questions of prosecution yet the nearest the Report comes to considering the key issue of the relationship between investigation and prosecution is the unimpressive Chapter 5. A sample of the levels of sophistication displayed can be taken from the discussion of the research paper on the French and German systems: '[I]t should not be supposed that to put the prosecution in the position of being able to direct and supervise police inquiries would remove all scope for argument between the two services. Leigh and Zedner were told that the police sometimes resent having to carry out the prosecutor's directives.' (para. 5.16). But it would be an extremely odd system of supervision which did not involve tension and resentment some of the time.

The second broad sense in which it can be said that the Commission achieves only an inhibited vision arises from an inability to see the wood of criminal justice as a social institution for the trees of the process by which that institution is translated into practice. I argue in the remainder of this section that the failure to look at criminal justice in a broader context is a significant detraction from the usefulness of the Commission's work.

It is unarguable that the criminal justice system is a taken for granted part of the apparatus of state, however defined (Lacey 1994); that it is itself a social institution from which spring other social institutions such as those of punishment; and that it interacts with numerous other institutions such as those associated with school, work, family and so on (Garland 1990). And this is not just a reworking of the idea that punishment through criminal law is merely one amongst a number of sources of social control, although that of course is worth recalling. More than that, it is a reminder that criminal justice does not come plucked from the pages of a Report or an Act of Parliament. It is a series of practices which interlock with many others, not least of which are those aspects of the organisation of contemporary Western society which perpetuate class and wealth differentials. While the establishment of the Commission ensured that the investigation of the details of the Birmingham 6 and other miscarriage cases would not be examined, there was nothing to stop the Commission trying to identify some common factors, the most obvious being that the suspects in all these cases were either Irish, working class or in some other way regarded as outside the broad spectrum of respectable English. Little evidence emerged that the Commission recognised the unspoken assumption identified by Roger Smith that 'the major protection of the innocent is that they are simply not arrested. This accords with the personal experience of most judges, lawyers or even the vast majority of the population.' (Smith 1991).

Critics have voiced their concerns that the Commission has not proposed any radical overhaul of those parts of the system it surveyed. But it is useful to remember that even a radical overhaul of the system is unlikely to accomplish anything unless it relates to or emerges from the asking of much broader questions about the everyday experiences of those who come into contact with crime, or with the police, as Scarman did post Brixton (Scarman Report 1981). This would have helped to underline the point that the criminal justice system relates to a wide variety of client groups from victims of crime, to suspects, offenders and officials, as well as being subject to government manipulation in support of its claim to authority. Our relationship with it is intricate, contradictory, at times personal, at others political, often social and frequently experienced through forms of entertainment. The criminal justice system both responds to and exploits deep-seated fears about personal safety and protection of property. It is easy to forget that most people subjected to its coercion threaten neither of those interests and that criminal justice can be used as a vehicle for state intervention over an extremely broad range of activities (Uglow 1988). The harm of wrongful imprisonment is not only greater than that inflicted by 'rightful' imprisonment, it is often far greater than the harm of the offence alleged to have been committed.

Blame generally, and criminal blame in particular, is used as a way of people making sense of the world.[3] People select certain risks for attention to defend their preferred life-styles and as a forensic resource to place blame on other groups (Douglas 1992). The pressure for vengeance greets us every day. It manifests itself in a number of ways, including greater use of civil litigation to claim compensation as well as in calls for criminal justice to answer problems ranging from terrorism through to joyriding. An increased tendency towards greater legalisation has accompanied a decline in confidence in major institutions, business and government (Galanter 1992). In terms of criminal justice, while the last twenty years have seen a constant (perceived) threat to order from terrorism, in other respects there have been important changes in the vocabulary of public affairs.

I began by referring to a range of responses to the Commission. The patterning can be fitted to a typology which cultural theorists have developed which seeks to classify people's responses to different threats (see Douglas 1992, n. 11, p. 104). Two key variables in this approach to cultural diversity are the continuums of social relationships and of social interactions. On the first, social identity runs from strong individualism to strong collectivism and the second has extremes of restriction and

---

[3] A number of writers point to the effect of the increasing secularisation of society on perceptions of crime and risk. Taylor, I. (1983), *Crime, Capitalism and Community*, Toronto: Butterworths, p. 107; Lee, T.R. (1981), 'The Public's Perception of Risk and the Question of Irrationality', in Warner F. (ed.), *The Assessment and Perception of Risk*, London: Royal Society, p. 5.

independence (explained by Milton 1991). Four institutionalised ways of responding emerge from the intersection of these two continuums: the entrepreneur, the egalitarian, the hierarchist and the fatalist. The entrepreneur quadrant, where high levels of individualism and independence meet, is characterised in the prevailing political ideology of pursuit of personal profit; this squeezes out egalitarians who combine strong group membership with a high degree of independence. Criminal justice appears most strongly to relate to the needs of the hierarchist who represents high levels of collectivism and prescription, with strong emphasis on central control. Fatalists, combining high degrees of individualism and prescription, experience a sense of being manipulated by a system over which they have no control. These ideal types are useful for considering how we relate to criminal justice and how it relates to us.

Culture renders the construction of categories into a seemingly natural, unconscious, process. It affects the way we look at ourselves and the rest of the universe. But at the same time in a highly interdependent society culture is fragmented. Its reflection and refraction through the maze of social institutions will be diverse and enigmatic. Two connected trends in recent writing about crime help underline this theme. First, there has been a revival of interest in Durkheim's theory of the relationship between legal sanctions, social structure and public sentiment (Calavita et al., 1991). The second is the renewed concern with ideas of vengeance and shame and their role in modern society (Braithwaite 1991). In Durkheimian analysis, punishment is a social institution which reinforces matters of morality. Punishment is neither rational nor instrumental, it is irrational and emotional. But it is also ultimately functional, in giving vent to outbursts of common sentiment it strengthens the social bond.

This connects with Braithwaite's argument for a reintegrative theory of shame, on the grounds that it is crucial to crime control. What is interesting here is the essential functionalism ascribed to shame and to vengeance. Durkheim saw law as either repressive or restitutive. Repressive laws inflict suffering and punishment, and penal laws are therefore characteristic of them. Restitutive laws seek to return things as they were, and their sanctions are characteristic of civil laws.

Braithwaite uses the notion of shaming as specifically non-repressive. Shame can be used in a reintegrative rather than stigmatising way. Forgiveness, apology and repentance need to be elevated to cultural importance. Restitutive sanctions can have a place in criminal law. It is a mistake, argues Braithwaite, to see shame as connotative of pre-industrial, folk society with clear networks of relationships. Modern communications may mean more interdependencies rather than less.

In this section I have tried to bring to the surface some of the issues which lie behind the familiar terrain of crime and criminal process. The Runciman Commission provided an opportunity for contemplation about the conflicting expectations people have in relation to criminal justice, to provide a theoretical framework for understanding some of the paradoxes which it inevitably engenders. Perhaps to expect the Commission to do more than acknowledge some of the tangled tensions inherent in the criminal justice system would have been unrealistic or even naive. But there is a real danger in becoming victims of our own scepticism, of making the easy transition from recognising the political and social realities in which we are operating to forgetting the underlying truths to which they should alert us. It would not have been difficult to begin to look at or even beyond the foundational premises of the terms of reference. After all, as Chris Price commented when the Commission was set up, unless issues such as the composition of the judiciary are addressed, any recommendations are as likely to be rendered ineffective as changes in the appeal system since 1907. 'If there had been any propensity over the past decade to accept criticism and act on it, there would be no need for a Royal Commission' ((1991) 'After Birmingham' *New Statesman and Society*, 4, p. 18, at 19).

II CONCEPTUAL REFLECTIONS

A radical analysis would have been an essential precursor to any radical overhaul. This truth seems somehow missing from many of the comments both before and after publication of the Report. And more important, it would have led the way to challenging the uncritical use of terms such as 'the interests of justice' or 'the acquittal of the guilty' (para. 1.27).

From the start the pitch was wrong with the terms of reference placing the need to secure the conviction of the guilty in a position of apparent preeminence over the objective of ensuring acquittal of the innocent.[4] This is not just perpetuated but intensified and amplified when translated into the crude deployment of a binary opposition between the two; between the need to avoid the acquittal of the guilty and the conviction of the innocent. For these are not harms of equal or even equivalent gravity.

Apart from the obvious objection that the Commission was clearly set up to address the former, the juxtaposition of wrongful convictions with 'wrongful' acquittals[5] obscures the very real differences between them. Conviction of a person, whether they are 'innocent' or 'guilty', is a

---

[4] Rightly criticised, by Lee, S. (1993), *The Times*, 27 July.
[5] The use of inverted commas on the latter and not the former is of course deliberate.

judgment with consequences, placing them in a new legal and social category, one from which they will find it difficult to escape, and one which in most cases renders them subject to a number of state-enforced limitations. Adoption of a wider notion of criminal justice in the first place might have helped to ensure that this would not have gone unspoken and unnoticed in the invariable pairing of 'wrongful' acquittals with wrongful convictions. Even if the system were 99 per cent perfect there would still be 600 wrong convictions each year (Editorial (1993) *The Guardian*, 7 July). That should be of far more concern than achieving some mythical balance between the harm involved in those cases and that where the 'guilty' go free.

This leads to another point, reflecting on the use of the phrase 'acquittal of the guilty' and of the word 'guilty'. If acquittal means 'not guilty', is not the notion of the 'acquittal' of 'the guilty' something of an oxymoron? This is more than a semantic point; it raises the extremely important question of who decides on 'guilt'. 'It is widely assumed,' says the Report, 'and we are in no position to contradict it that the guilty are more often acquitted than the innocent convicted.' (para. 1.9). Unless there is some basis to the proposition being advanced, it is somewhat disingenuous first to elevate it by stating it and then to throw in the qualification that there is no evidence in possession to contradict it. No reference is made to the lack of any evidence in support of it. The point can be demonstrated by substituting the following assertion: 'It is widely believed that academics have nothing useful to say, and we are in no position to contradict it.'

But when does a person become 'guilty'? This is a central issue in miscarriage cases. An assumption that guilt can be identified leads to the 'noble cause corruption' which afflicts police officers and probably many others.[6] The problem, as Chris Mullin has pointed out, is not that a small number of officers are dishonest in fabricating confessions, but that expectations placed on police and the culture in which they operate makes this kind of thing almost inevitable. ((1993) 'A New Travesty is Waiting to Happen' *The Independent*, 7 July). This is especially so in the terrorism cases, but it would be an example of mass delusion if we were to believe that the pressures to confess occur only in high profile, serious offences.

And lastly, the problem of balance. '[A]s will become apparent from our recommendations there are issues on which a balance has to be struck.' (para. 1.27). These include, the Report continues, a potential conflict between 'the interests of justice' on the one hand and the requirement of 'fair and reasonable treatment for everyone involved, suspects and

---

[6] The phrase was used by Paul Condon, Commissioner of Metropolitan Police, to the Home Affairs Select Committee of House of Commons, 24 March 1993.

defendants included'.[7] By the 'interests of justice' is meant, it would seem, arrival at a correct verdict by the jury. But this begs all the questions of what a 'correct' result is:

> But we do believe that the fairer the treatment which all the parties receive at the hands of the system the more likely it is that the jury's verdict ... will be correct .... But we are satisfied that when taken as a whole our recommendations serve the interests of justice without diminishing the individual's right to fair and reasonable treatment, and that if they are implemented they will do much to restore the public confidence in the system on which its successful operation so much depends (para. 1.27).

This encapsulates one of the persistent problems in analyses of criminal justice. It should not be reduced to a system of neatly balanced scales, the victim and the offender, the police and the suspect, the prosecution and the defence, the Home Office and the Court of Appeal, as symbolised in the iconography of justice so frequently portrayed. As long as at each weighing the two sides 'balance', it would appear that no complaint can be made. It is as though there could be no other objective.

It would be absurd to argue that no system can be improved. Equally it would be foolish to believe that a Royal Commission, or any other body set up to consider criminal justice, could fully detach itself from the wider institutional structure from which it was begotten. But between those two extremes is a position in which a spirit of inquiry, openness and self-awareness can fuel a step towards a different way of understanding things. That the Commissioners might stand firm against the tide of public, media and government pressure to resolve complex issues through a simplistic reliance on a vengeance-led criminal justice system was a legitimate, if optimistic, expectation. That they would fail to acknowledge the seriousness of the crisis was unexpected and self-defeating. Her Majesty's right, trusty and well-beloved friends have treated and greeted us but have neither illuminated nor reassured us.

---

[7] Ibid. Simon Lee complained of a lack of philosophy, above n. 4.

6. Reforming the Criminal Process: A Scottish Perspective

Gerry Maher

I INTRODUCTION

The Royal Commission on Criminal Justice, when discussing its terms of reference, described them as far-reaching (Royal Commission Report, para. 1.5). In one sense this is so as the Commission was asked to consider a very wide range of topics, covering virtually every stage of the criminal process. However in another, and crucial, sense the terms of reference of the Commission were very narrow. The Commission was asked to examine

> the effectiveness of the criminal justice system in England and Wales in securing the conviction of those guilty of criminal offences and the acquittal of those who are innocent, having regard to the efficient use of resources.

The first comment which can be made about these terms of reference is how restricted they are in respect of the normative principles which the Commission had before it. In particular no place seems to be provided by the terms of reference for concepts such as individual rights of suspects and other persons in the criminal process; or ideas such as process or intrinsic values. One general point of weakness in the Commission's approach, therefore, is the narrowness of the range of justificatory principles which it sought to appeal to and to apply in its discussions.

Another restriction which follows from the Commission's terms of reference is that the scope of its inquiry was limited to the criminal justice system in England and Wales. Nonetheless the Commission itself reported that it looked at the Scottish system of criminal justice in some depth (para. 1.13) and the Report contains various examples where a justifying strand in one of its recommendations is that a similar sort of procedure is to be found in the Scottish criminal process, as well as several examples where the Commission noted the position in Scotland but did not feel inclined to recommend that England and Wales should adopt or adapt that position. In this paper I will examine critically the use made by the Commission of Scots law as a model, suitable or otherwise, for the English criminal process. My conclusion will be that the Commission's approach to Scots law never really goes beyond a superficial level and that if fuller consideration had been given to the rules and practices of Scots law some of the Commission's recommendations might well have been different. I will also note that on one or two occasions some of the critics of the Commission might have reached a different view if they had looked to the position north of the border.

II SCOTS LAW AS A MODEL FOR THE ENGLISH CRIMINAL PROCESS TO ADOPT

In relation to several issues the Royal Commission considered the position of Scots law as support for a recommendation that England and Wales should adopt a similar position. There are several examples of this approach, for example in relation to diversion away from the full panoply of the criminal justice system. (See para. 5.62 where the Commission discusses the system of fiscal fines introduced into Scotland by section 56 of the Criminal Justice (Scotland) Act 1987.)

Three further examples call for more detailed comment:

1. Trial procedures

One area where Scots law is clearly the model for the Royal Commission's recommendations is in respect of trial procedures at the Crown Court. One of the striking features for a Scots criminal lawyer observing a Crown Court trial is the amount of time which is spent by various parties talking to the jury about evidence rather than leading it. In Scotland there are no opening addresses to the jury by the Crown or by defence counsel, closing addresses are relatively short, and the judge's address to the jury at the end of the trial concentrates mainly on the law (including the burden and standard of proof, and the different verdicts) but the judge does not 'sum up' by rehearsing the evidence led (*King v. HM Advocate* [1985] SCCR 322).

A further difference is that in Scotland the indictment served on the accused is fully narrative and sets out the facts at some length. The indictment is read out to the jury at the beginning of the trial by the clerk of court and copies of the indictment are handed to members of the jury. The lack of a fully specified indictment in English practice is surprising to Scots lawyers. Indeed Scottish court practice in both civil and criminal cases requires written pleadings to be legally relevant and factually detailed. (Rules are set out in the Criminal Procedure (Scotland) Act 1975 about how indictments are to be framed.) An indictment which is lacking full specification of the facts to be proved against the accused would be subject to challenge as irrelevant.

It therefore comes as no great shock to a Scots lawyer to read the recommendation of the Royal Commission supporting the introduction of full narrative indictments (para. 8.6). However there is some surprise that the Royal Commission still accepts that opening speeches may be allowed in some cases and backs away from recommending change to the practice of the judge's address to the jury (a factor which was said to have contributed to the jury's verdict in the trial of the Birmingham 6 (Jackson (1993), 146)). There is further puzzle about some of the reactions in England to these modest proposals by the Royal Commission. One critic has described the proposals as not only 'half-witted' but as leading to possible breaches of article 6 of the European Convention on Human Rights (Mackenzie (1993), 1035). These are certainly interesting perspectives if they are intended to apply to the Scottish criminal process but I doubt whether this is an area where any Scots lawyer would want to abandon practice and adopt instead current English procedures.

2. Grounds of appeal

The Royal Commission (paras 10.27 et seq.) refers to various problems arising from the present law (in section 2 of the Criminal Appeal Act 1968) on the grounds which the Court of Appeal are to consider when dealing with an appeal. The majority view is that there should be one broad ground of appeal and a suggested formulation is that the verdict 'is or may be unsafe'. By contrast a minority of the Commission take the view that the term 'unsafe' is too broad as a ground of appeal and that the Court of Appeal should be given more detailed guidance. This would be done by setting out two separate categories of appeal, namely a verdict based on an erroneous view of the evidence, and material irregularities or error of law or procedure (para. 10.34).

It is interesting that the majority counter the argument of the minority by pointing to the position in Scotland where there is a single broad ground of appeal (para. 10.32). The majority argue that this approach would give the Court of Appeal sufficient flexibility to deal with all categories of appeal. However a closer look at the Scottish experience tends to give support to the minority reasoning on this point. Prior to the Criminal Justice

(Scotland) Act 1980, the High Court of Justiciary sitting as a Court of Appeal had three grounds on which to decide an appeal, subject to the standard type of proviso. After that Act, those grounds were replaced by an apparently straightforward provision that the Court may adopt various modes of disposing of appeals where there has been 'a miscarriage of justice', and the proviso was abolished.

It was thought that this new general statement of a ground of appeal would provide the Court with a clean sheet and enable it to disregard the previous case-law (which indicated a restrictive approach by the Court to allowing appeals) (Gordon (1981), 101). However this has not happened. The old case-law, and the former grounds of appeal which it explained, remain as 'guides' to the new provision, and some of the former grounds which were interpreted narrowly (including the ground that the jury's verdict was unreasonable or unsupported by evidence) continue to be interpreted under the new law in the same restrictive manner. According to some commentators the situation has been made worse. By a very questionable process of statutory interpretation, the Court of Appeal has re-invented the proviso, and has held that it is possible for the Court to find that there has been a miscarriage of justice in a particular appeal but nonetheless to refuse the appeal because the miscarriage was not serious or material enough (*McCuaig* v. *HM Advocate* [1982] SCCR 125; Gordon (1982), 128–9; McCluskey (1992) 171–4). The lesson to be taken from this experience is that simply changing the wording of the grounds of appeal will not in itself make a Court of Appeal more inclined to interfere with jury verdicts and to allow appeals; and that if that goal is to be achieved it would be safer (and more satisfactory) to do so by explicit and detailed statutory language.

3. The defendant's right to elect trial by jury

Clearly the most controversial proposal made by the Royal Commission is that in respect of offences triable either-way. The Commission recommend that a defendant should no longer have an automatic right to elect trial by jury in respect of such offences. Instead where the prosecution wish to try a case summarily but the defence favour jury trial the defence will have its way only if it can persuade magistrates that trial by jury is appropriate. In arriving at this unanimous recommendation the Royal Commission (para. 6.11) noted the position in Scotland where the decision on the forum and mode of trial of a case is made by the prosecution (apart from certain types of crime and offence where mode of trial is determined by fixed rules).

The Commission noted an objection against using Scotland as a precedent that the Scottish system works against a different history and context.

Unfortunately the Commission did not provide any detail of these differences in history and context and this particular objection was simply ignored by the Commission.

What is the clearest element in the differences between Scottish and English practice in this area is the relatively high role played by *professional* judges in criminal trials in Scotland. Table 1 shows the distribution of criminal cases in the Scottish court in 1991:

Table 1   Source: – Scottish Office, Review of Criminal Evidence and Criminal Procedure
1993, Annex B

High Court of Justiciary	746
Sheriff and jury	2,643
Sheriff without jury	76,500
District court	89,230

The powers of lay magistrates (the district court) in Scotland is nothing like as extensive as those possessed by magistrates' courts in England and Wales, and in practice district courts handle only very minor cases. Many of the cases which in England and Wales are either-way are tried in Scotland by a sheriff (a professional lawyer) sitting without a jury.

As the Royal Commission itself noted (para. 6.11) the Scottish system whereby mode of trial is largely determined by exercise of prosecutor's discretion is uncontroversial in Scotland. There is an old case where the High Court of Justiciary stated that if an offence were more suited for trial by indictment but the prosecution decided that it should be heard under summary procedure, the proceedings would be quashed (*Clark and Bendall* v. *Stuart* [1886] 1 White 191, at 208–9). However I have been unable to discover any subsequent case where this remedy was invoked by an accused who wanted trial by jury but was confronted instead with trial before a sheriff or lay magistrate.

Accordingly there *are* differences in the context in which the jury operates in the two legal systems, the major one being the role of professional judges in Scotland who deal with the most serious cases which are tried without a jury. However this and other differences in context were not explained by the Royal Commission. The Royal Commission's proposal was motivated rather by consideration of costs and efficiency in the use of resources. In this section of its Report there are various references by the Commission to such considerations as:

a more rational division of either-way cases; (para. 6.13)

savings may be made available which would enable more resources to be devoted to ensuring that the more serious cases going to the Crown Court are not only better prepared but more quickly heard. A trial in a magistrates' court is many times cheaper than a trial in the Crown Court; (para. 6.15)

a more rational distribution of cases between the higher and lower courts; (para. 6.19)

benefits for the overall efficiency of the criminal justice system. (para. 6.19)

Given the lack of any basis for its recommendation other than cost cutting, it might be thought that critics of this particular proposal would easily be able to point to the weaknesses of the Royal Commission's approach. But the nature of the reaction, or at least the initial reaction, to this proposal has surprised commentators in Scotland. Included among comments on the Royal Commission recommendation are the following:

> The *concept* of jury trial is worth *nothing* unless it is supported by an *inalienable* right to be tried by a jury. (Enright (1993) 1024 (emphases added))

> Once you start tinkering with that, you are tinkering with a fundamental freedom. (Richard Ferguson QC *The Times*, 7 July 1993)

> The choice to opt for a jury trial is an essential safeguard against miscarriages of justice. (John Rowe QC *The Times*, 7 July 1993)

> in cases where the CPS does not agree to trial by jury, the magistrates would have the power to decide. This would be madness. (Lord Williams of Mostyn QC *The Times*, 7 July 1993)

> There are delays and inefficiencies at present, but the way to deal with them is to improve the mechanics, not to erode a fundamental civil liberty. (Lord Williams of Mostyn QC *The Times*, 7 July 1993)

It is difficult to gauge whether these statements are intended to be taken as serious argument rather than rhetoric. Two points might be made. The first is that all of the *causes célèbres* which led to the setting up of the Royal Commission involved jury trials and it is difficult to see how the right to elect for jury trial (or even jury trial itself) is a protection against miscarriage of justice. Jury trial does not seem a sufficient condition for achieving the goal of preventing or minimising miscarriages of justice. If not a sufficient condition, is jury trial a necessary condition? My second point is that assessed by the critics' comments quoted above the Scottish criminal process is one which has done away with fundamental freedoms and fundamental civil liberties, and has a system of jury trial which is completely worthless. I am quite sure that those critics did not mean to imply these types of conclusion about Scotland, and it may be that what is being discussed are not concepts or principles of jury trial but the application of general principles or concepts of jury trial to the specific conditions of the English criminal process. But those specific conditions have not been identified by the Royal Commission's critics and both sides of this debate look destined to continue with a form of shadow boxing where the real issues are never made clear.

III SCOTS LAW REJECTED AS A MODEL FOR THE ENGLISH CRIMINAL PROCESS

On a number of topics the Royal Commission considered the position in Scotland but declined to recommend a similar rule or procedure for England and Wales.

1. The not proven verdict

At para. 8.75 of the Report the Royal Commission stated that it had considered introducing into England and Wales the verdict of not proven. This is surprising as it is news to most commentators that anyone had seriously suggested that England and Wales should follow Scotland in having two different names for the acquittal verdict. In Scotland this practice continues to cause some confusion and it is difficult to disagree with the Royal Commission's view that if a jury or judge does not convict the accused, the prosecution has failed to make its case and accordingly the accused should be entitled to a verdict of not guilty. Given the unassailable logic of this reasoning, it remains a puzzle to Scots lawyers that the Royal Commission made no recommendation or even examination of the situation in the English criminal process where this basic principle is completely disregarded. This arises where a jury is split in such a way that it cannot return a verdict of guilty. But instead of the defendant being acquitted in this situation, he will receive a not guilty verdict if, but only if, the jury can agree on that verdict. To Scots lawyers it is difficult to reconcile this rule with the principle of presumption of innocence (Maher 1983).

2. The role of the CPS in criminal investigation

The introduction of the Crown Prosecution Service, as a prosecution service independent of the police, has been one of the most important changes to the English criminal process made in recent times. It is therefore easy to understand why the Royal Commission set itself against proposals that the investigative and prosecuting functions should be merged again. The Royal Commission explicitly refused to recommend that the CPS should supervise police investigations or even that the CPS should have a legal power to require police to make further inquiries (though in the second situation it did exhort the police to comply with CPS requests for further investigations to be made).

In both situations the Royal Commission noted the corresponding positions in Scotland but did not see Scotland as a suitable model for English law. The Commission argued that although the theory in Scotland was for the procurator fiscal to supervise police investigations, in practice crime investigation was left entirely in the hands of the police in all but the most serious cases, and that it was unusual for a procurator fiscal to direct police inquiries in full. The Commission also noted that in France it was rare for a *judge d'instruction* to be involved in the investigation of crime.

However the Royal Commission appears to have misunderstood the role of the prosecution agencies in the investigation of crime in the Scottish (and the French) system. Clearly at the initial stage of an inquiry into a reported or discovered crime, virtually all of the work is carried out by the police, for that is where their expertise lies. But the Royal Commission's views on the CPS not being in charge or supervising police investigation is flawed by a failure to draw a distinction between two stages of the criminal process which are sometimes more formally demarcated in some legal systems. This is a distinction between the investigative stage properly so-called and the stage of *instruction*. The investigative (pre-*instruction*) stage is where a crime has been reported to some official body and investigation is carried out to discover whether in fact a crime has been committed and who was its perpetrator. The closing-off of this phase can be marked when someone has been brought into the criminal process as a likely perpetrator (though systems will vary as to the degree of suspicion or likelihood in question). The pre-trial (or *instruction*) stage is where the details of a case against the particular suspect or accused are made more certain and a case is built up against him in preparation for a trial.

Of course, investigation continues once the stage of perpetrator identification has been reached but these investigations are focused not so much on the offence but on building a case against that particular person. Now there is a crucial difference between a prosecutor intervening in police investigations of a crime where there is no suspect and prosecution supervision of further police investigations whose purpose is to build up, but possibly also to weaken, a case against a particular suspect. In many of the actual miscarriages of justice which led to the establishment of the Royal Commission fatal errors occurred at the *instruction* stage by leaving further investigations solely within police hands. It is true that in many legal systems, including the Scottish, the judicial or prosecuting authority which now supervises police investigation at the *instruction* stage were established before the development of a specialised investigating police force, and the relationship between police and prosecution may be for that reason less problematic than would arise if a similar practice were introduced in England and Wales. But it does seem that the Royal Commission's proposals on these issues have given too much weight to police interests and these will do nothing to help build up the role and authority of the CPS.

3. Corroboration of confessions

One area where the Royal Commission divided in its views was whether it should remain possible in England and Wales to convict a defendant solely on the basis of confession evidence. The majority of the Commission rejected proposals made by a number of organisations that confession evidence should require supporting evidence but accepted that a warning should always be given to a jury about accepting confession evidence and that where there was no supporting evidence the warning should refer to a variety of different factors (paras 4.77, 4.87). Three members of the Commission, by contrast, favoured a requirement that a confession must always be supplemented with independent supporting evidence to allow a conviction (para. 4.86).

Somewhat surprisingly the Royal Commission devoted only brief attention to the position of Scots law on corroboration. In Scotland corroboration is a general requirement of proof of an accused person's guilt, and not simply in relation to confession evidence against him. A similar rule requiring corroboration of the essential facts in civil cases was finally abolished in 1990 but there has been no demand in Scotland to abolish the general corroboration rule in criminal cases, and the rule is accepted as firmly established by police and prosecutors. As concerns the application of the corroboration rule to confession evidence, what seems to have influenced the Royal Commission is a development in more recent case-law which has weakened the practical requirement of corroboration, especially where a confession shows 'special knowledge' of circumstances of the crime on the part of the accused (para. 4.59). It is undoubtedly the case that this particular development has had the effect of watering down the principle of corroboration of confession evidence in Scottish criminal practice but this is a trend in the case-law which has caused critical comment among Scottish lawyers themselves (see e.g. MacPhail (1992), at 149–52). On this particular aspect of the law on corroboration it is true that Scots law is inconsistent with its underlying principle and it is to be hoped that the

Appeal Court will take steps soon to restore the proper force of corroboration. However what the majority of the Royal Commission seem to have done is to throw out the baby and keep the bath water, for the general approach of Scots law to corroboration has implications for some of the arguments made about the introduction into English law of corroboration of confession evidence.

The majority identified a number of problems in any proposal for corroboration of confessions, starting with what they called the main argument against it, namely the likely effect that a requirement of corroboration would have on the numbers of people who presently are 'properly convicted' on the basis of genuine confession alone (para. 4.68). To a great extent this argument begs the whole question of what is to count as a proper conviction. Another argument against corroboration is the impact it would have on police resources, as such use of resources would not be matched by increase in a greater number of guilty verdicts (para. 4.72). However Scottish practice indicates that these sorts of consideration are suspect. Police resources there are used to look for corroborating evidence in all cases and not just those where there is an incriminating confession, and this practice has not been seen as a waste or misuse of resources. Furthermore it is true that in Scotland lack of corroboration is sometimes a reason for a prosecution being dropped (Moody and Tombs (1982), 61) but where this situation occurs there has been a *saving* of prosecution and court resources. Savings of resources also takes place where there are guilty pleas, and the existence of evidence against an accused, other than his own confession, is a factor which might lead to a guilty plea being made.

Consideration might also have been given to Scottish civil procedure on this point. In 1968 the requirement of corroboration was removed in respect of actions of damages for personal injuries and in 1990 the rule on corroboration was abolished for all civil actions. However the civil courts have reacted to this change by developing a rule that if corroborating evidence was available but had not been adduced by the pursuer, he would not succeed in his action; in other words there is an onus on a pursuer to explain the *absence* of corroboration in his case. This is a rule or practice which could be modified or adapted to apply to a criminal process which stopped short of having a general principle of corroboration of the prosecution case.

7. The Politics of Criminal Injustice: The Irish Dimension

Paddy Hillyard

I INTRODUCTION

It is some thirteen years since many of us were burning the midnight oil expressing our profound dissatisfaction with the last Royal Commission (RCCP 1981) on the criminal justice system. I wrote a paper entitled 'From Belfast to Britain: Some Critical Comments On the Royal Commission On Criminal Procedure' (Hillyard 1981). It criticised the previous Commission for its failure to examine in detail three central topics – the delicate relations between the police and the public, the extent to which the police were currently misusing their powers and the context of police work, particularly the pressures to misuse powers. It then went on to consider a number of the more important proposals in detail, drawing upon, where appropriate, the lessons from Northern Ireland. While a number of the points made have been subsequently confirmed by detailed and expensive empirical research, I think that it is fair to say that the paper itself has been ignored. One reason may, of course, lie in the fact that it was published in a collection entitled *Politics and Power: Law, Politics and Justice* which put it outside the dominant legalistic discourse in which debates about criminal justice have been traditionally located. A second, and much more obvious reason, and this is a point which I have made many times before, is that there has been a long-standing reluctance among academics living in England, Scotland and Wales to examine the situation in Northern Ireland when writing about policing and criminal justice in Britain: intellectual curiosity and the search for understanding has tended to stop at the Irish Sea.

In this paper I do not wish to return to a re-examination of the lessons of Northern Ireland for the British criminal justice system. It is clear, however, that if the recommendations are accepted the form of the criminal justice system in Britain will become closer to that used to deal with political violence in Northern Ireland. Instead, I wish to focus on the so-called 'miscarriages of justice' cases arising out of the IRA bombing campaign in Britain – the Birmingham 6, Guildford 4, Maguire 7 and Judith Ward – in order to contextualise the setting up of the Commission and to draw out some of the more covert political elements in the operation of the criminal justice system in Britain. I will therefore be saying very little about the content of the Commission because I consider its findings to be largely irrelevant to the issues which emerge from an analysis of the Irish cases. A central strand of my argument is that it is important to separate out these Irish cases from other miscarriages of justice cases and not to assume that they all form a homogeneous group.

II THE ORIGINS OF THE ROYAL COMMISSION

While there may be some disagreement about all the various factors which led to the government deciding to set up the Royal Commission in March 1991, few people would dissent from the view that the wrongful convictions of the Guildford 4, the Birmingham 6 and the Maguire 7 were of crucial significance. These seventeen people – all but two of whom were Irish – had been convicted of the most serious offences and had spent in total over 200 years in prison before their convictions were quashed. While there were a number of other important cases in which the convictions were quashed it is most improbable that another Royal Commission would have been established in the absence of the Irish cases.

The Government announced the setting up of the Royal Commission on the very day of the release of the Birmingham 6 and this adds further support to the importance of the Irish dimension. The Birmingham 6, it should be recalled, had been convicted for murders arising from bombs placed in public houses in Birmingham in November 1974. These explosions not only led to their wrongful conviction but to the introduction of the Prevention of Terrorism (Temporary Provisions) Act (PTA) which came into force on 29 November 1974.

The Royal Commission was preceded by a number of separate police investigations into different aspects of the Irish cases. More importantly, Sir John May, who was a member of the Commission, was appointed on 19 October 1991, the day of the release of the Guildford 4, to inquire into the circumstances surrounding the arrest and trial of the Guildford 4 and the Maguire 7. It was not possible for him to embark immediately upon an investigation into the Guildford and Woolwich bombings because police investigations were continuing. Moreover, as the two cases were closely related, it was also impossible for him to consider a wide-ranging investigation of the trial and convictions of the Maguire 7. He was therefore forced to focus only upon the forensic evidence in that case. In July 1990 he published an interim report (May 1990) and recommended that the Secretary of State refer the Maguire 7 case back to the Court of Appeal and stated the grounds on which the appeal should be made. I will return later to the Court of Appeal's decision.

III THE ECLIPSE OF THE GREEN

What is extraordinary about the Commission's Report is that there is no analysis whatsoever of either the Irish cases which were central in the setting up of the Commission or, indeed, of any of the other so-called miscarriages of justice cases. The reader of the Report is informed on the opening page that it was not appointed 'to look into individual cases'. But its terms of reference did require it to examine 'the effectiveness of the criminal justice system' and an analysis of some of the issues which arose from the various reported cases, particularly the Irish cases, was essential to an understanding of the criminal justice system it was attempting to reform.

There were some references to the Irish cases and it is instructive to look at what was said about them. In the introduction the Commission refers to three of the key cases but it does not mention that the people wrongfully convicted were mainly Irish or that the cases arose out of the conflict in Northern Ireland. A second reference to the three cases and that of Judith Ward, whose convictions were quashed after the Commission had been established, is made under a section entitled 'public confidence'. Here the three are referred to in a very revealing and prejudicial phrase as '*the terrorist cases* [emphasis added] where convictions were quashed' and this permits the Commission to go on and make a distinction between these cases and 'a number of cases not connected with terrorism' (para. 22). A third reference is made in the two short paragraphs on the PTA where it is recorded that 'We bore in mind too the fact that some of the serious miscarriages of justice which came to light immediately before we were set up had followed from Irish terrorism' (para. 93). This is the closest it gets to recognising that there was an Irish dimension, but there is no attempt to take this any further. The Commission, therefore, has played a crucial role in writing out through its silences the significance of these cases. They are implicitly assumed to be part of a whole series of miscarriages of justice. As a result the Irish dimension, which played an important part in the setting up of the Commission, is effectively eclipsed, providing another example of the power of official legal discourses to define out issues (see Burton and Carlen 1979).

From a sociological, legal and political perspective there are, of course, a number of differences between the cases arising from the conflict in Northern Ireland and those arising from ordinary criminality. To begin with, most of those involved in violence are carrying out their activities in Ireland or in Britain for a political purpose: to contest the British presence in the North of Ireland. Those involved in ordinary decent crime, on the other hand, are principally motivated by individualistic motives of acquisition or expression. While the authorities continually deny that there is a distinction between the different types of incidents – 'a crime, is a crime, is a crime' in Thatcher's infamous aphorism – they nevertheless accept that there is a need to police and dispense justice for those suspected of political violence very differently from those suspected of ordinary decent crime. As Tomlinson (1980:193) put it in relation to those arrested and charged in Northern Ireland: 'They are considered as political in the courtroom but criminal for the purposes of punishment'.

In Britain similar distinctions are made between those suspected of being involved in political violence connected with Northern Ireland and those suspected of ordinary crime. The police since 1974 have had, under the PTA, very different investigative and custodial powers and suspects detained under the PTA have had far fewer safeguards. The PTA has therefore created a dual track system of criminal justice where Ordinary Decent Criminals (ODCs) (Colville 1991) continue to be dealt with under the ordinary criminal law while those suspected of political violence are dealt with under a system which provides far greater powers and far fewer safeguards (Hillyard 1993b).

Another crucial difference is that the pressure on the police to produce results is likely to be of a very different magnitude following acts of political violence, in contrast to the vast bulk of ordinary crime. Following the Birmingham and other bombings there was considerable political and public pressure on them to capture and convict those responsible.

Finally, there are likely to be significant differences between the way Irish people are perceived by the police in comparison with other ethnic groups or the indigenous population. These perceptions are based on popular prejudices and influenced by policing history. The nineteenth-century prejudices which saw the Irish as an inferior race, typically violent, drunken and dishonest (see Lewis and Curtis 1971; Curtis 1984) continued well into the 1950s and have resurfaced over the last twenty years in the wake of the conflict in Northern Ireland. In addition, ever since the introduction of a police force, the form of policing in Britain has been influenced by the British/Irish problem (Palmer 1988). For example, the Special Branch owes its origins to the use of violence by the Fenians in Britain in the nineteenth century (see Bunyan 1977). These historical features will have an impact on the way Irish people are perceived.

As a result of all these very important contextual and other differences, the factors which lead to the construction of a 'suspect community' under the PTA (Hillyard 1993b) are likely to be very different from those which create a suspect community of ordinary decent criminals (McConville, Sanders and Leng 1991).

IV THE IRISH CASES

There is now a large literature on the Irish cases (see for example, Mullin 1990; Woffinden 1988; Conlon 1990; Hill and Bennett 1990; Bennett 1993; Ward 1993)) and a number of them have been heard in full on appeal. It is therefore possible to draw out some of the methods and techniques which were used to convict the 17 people for crimes which they did not commit. The Birmingham 6 were convicted on the basis of four confessions and forensic evidence. They have consistently argued that these statements were beaten out of them. It emerged during the Appeal that statements were concocted using the so-called 'Reade Schedule' as a template for avoiding contradictions and inconsistencies and that scientific tests were flawed. Judith Ward was convicted on the basis of a confession and forensic evidence. It has since emerged that her confession was produced while she was suffering from a mental disorder. The forensic evidence has also now been discredited. In addition, there was non-disclosure of scientific evidence and 1475 of some 1700 statements. Moreover, the Prosecuting Counsel provided misleading information to the defence and there was criticism of a Senior Prosecutor in the DPP's Office.

The Guildford 4 were convicted solely on the basis of confessions which they always claimed were beaten out of them during the seven days they were interrogated under the PTA. Like the Birmingham 6, they claimed that their statements were concocted after the interviews. Unlike the Birmingham 6 and the Ward cases, there was no full appeal. The Crown requested a hearing with the Court of Appeal on 19 October 1991 to inform the Court that it did not seek to uphold the convictions. It argued that three police officers had misled the court in stating that their notes were made contemporaneously at the interviews when there was prima facie evidence that they were produced together later. It alleged that the three officers had conspired together to pervert the course of justice. The Court agreed and quashed the convictions.

During the hearing the Crown also drew attention to other suspicious documents. For example, it pointed out that the details on the detention sheets did not coincide with the number and times of interviews presented in evidence. In addition, an interview with Hill relating to relevant and significant matters was never submitted in evidence and had not been disclosed to the DPP, leading to the conclusion that the true interview was suppressed and a false version was given to the Court. This was not all. In a comprehensive analysis of all aspects of the case, Ronan Bennett (1993) describes other irregularities which the Crown did not comment upon in Court.

V DAMAGE LIMITATION

Throughout the long campaigns to free the Birmingham 6, Guildford 4, Maguire 7 and Judith Ward, members of the judiciary and politicians took steps to limit the damage which they perceived was being done to maintain the integrity of the criminal justice system. In refusing legal aid for the Birmingham 6 to appeal in 1980, Lord Denning made his 'appalling vista' comment in which he made it clear that the integrity of the system was of far higher importance than justice for the individual. He reinforced his position in an interview in *The Spectator* in which he argued that it would have been better if the Birmingham 6 had been hanged so as to avoid all the damaging campaigns in support of guilty men. In an interview on RTE shortly after the release of the Guildford 4 he was pressed about the Birmingham 6 and he repeatedly made the distinction between the two by pointing out that there was new information in the Guildford 4 case. It was then pointed out to him that four of the six had been interviewed by the West Midlands Serious Crime Squad which has since been disbanded. Did this concern him? He thought that there was room for disquiet but he was against reopening the case.

After the release of the Birmingham 6 and the Guildford 4 there appears to have been a deliberate campaign to suggest that they were not innocent after all. Bennett (1993) describes the 'whispering campaign' in relation to the Guildford 4 which took the form of off-the-record briefings of journalists which did not appear, for one reason or another, in their copy, nevertheless he argues that they had an impact on attitudes towards the case. He also records that the judiciary were prepared to say in private that the four were guilty. One member, Sir James Miskin, went further and, on his retirement, in July 1990 gave his opinion of the Appeal Court's decision in a BBC TV interview: 'That was a mad decision, was it not? They didn't give any thought to the fact that there was a full appeal and there was no suggestion from any source that police documentation showed that the confessions were cooked up'. In a TV interview Lord Hailsham added his views pointing out that he saw no connection between the Birmingham 6 and the Guildford 4 cases. The interview continued:

Hailsham: 'The IRA make us believe that the police have got the wrong people in all the cases. This is highly improbable'.

Interviewer: 'Yes, in the case of the Guildford 4 they have had the wrong people for 15 years'.

Hailsham: 'We don't say that. We say that they obtained convictions by wrongful means and that is the truth. It is wholly indefensible and its lowers confidence in the judicial system.'

VI UNANSWERED QUESTIONS

There are many unanswered questions. Why were only three police officers prosecuted when many more were involved in the case? In any major investigation it is normal practice for senior officers to collate all the information which is being produced by the teams of officers carrying out the interrogations. Did they know about the many discrepancies in the records and non-contemporaneous notes to which the Crown referred in the Appeal? If they knew why did they allow the practices to take place? In 1977 three people in a London Active Service Unit (ASU) admitted to the bombings for which the Guildford 4 were convicted. During their trial forensic evidence showing that the Guildford and Woolwich bombings were linked to a whole series of bombings carried out by the ASU was withheld from the defence. Similarly during the trial of the three police officers the Prosecution did not draw attention to this evidence nor to the confessions which members of the ASU had made to the Guildford and Woolwich bombings. Why? In the Birmingham 6, Guildford 4, Maguire 7 and the Judith Ward cases there were stringent criticisms of the role of forensic scientists and the withholding of information. Yet no one has been prosecuted.

There is another case with connections to the conflict in Northern Ireland about which there are also many unanswered questions. This is the less well-known case of Kevin Taylor. His case differs in a number of respects from the others: the trial took place in the mid-eighties, the case was dismissed and Mr Taylor was English and not Irish. However, there was a strong Irish connection: Kevin Taylor was a friend of John Stalker who was removed from the investigation into a shoot-to-kill policy in Northern Ireland (see Doherty 1986; Taylor 1987). In his own account of the affair, Taylor (1990) alleges that he was framed as a means of removing Stalker. There were certainly a number of extraordinary aspects to the case. Although he was charged with conspiracy to defraud a bank, the bank never complained! Orders of access to his bank accounts and those of his businesses are alleged to have been obtained by deceit and the judge persuaded that it was in the 'national interest' to place the information in a sealed envelope. Search warrants obtained to investigate the fraud were used to take away family photograph albums containing photographs of Taylor and his wife with the Stalkers. During the trial, which lasted 16 weeks, it emerged that witnesses had been coerced into making statements, crucial information was withheld from the Prosecution, files were conveniently lost and two police officers were pulled up before the judge for contempt. The case was eventually dropped but Taylor, once a millionaire, is now a ruined man.

What conclusions can be drawn from this brief analysis of police and prosecution practices in these cases? Given the catalogue of methods used by various authorities sometimes alone or in combination, the commonly used phrase 'miscarriage of justice' appears to be a singularly inappropriate description implying a mistake, an error. The methods and practices in all the cases appear to be systematic, deliberate and intentional.

VII EXPLANATIONS

The explanation typically put forward by the authorities to account for these methods and practices lays the blame on a few deviant and bent police officers – the so-called bad apple theory. The focus is on the individual characteristics of the police officers and may include good qualities such as their over zealousness or bad such as psychopathic tendencies. In prosecuting only three of the many officers involved in the Guildford 4 case, the authorities gave further credence to this theory of police malpractice.

Another explanation has been put forward by McConville (1989) which I would like to call the bad barrel theory. He argues in a detailed comment on the Guildford 4 case that what happens in miscarriages of justice cases is that the police quickly fix on some suspect and then work up a belief in guilt. Once evidence is available which is consistent with this everyone, he suggests, then loses their ability to make an independent judgment or fails to provide the necessary scrutiny. All those involved in the prosecution team, he argues, shared the assumption that the four were guilty and hence there was no need to call for the original records or to scrutinise police files. The fundamental reason for this occurring is that the prosecution system is in McConville's words 'a police system and one directed towards conviction'.

The problem with this explanation is that it rests on the acceptance of the notion that team or group pressure leads to a situation where people lose their ability to make independent judgements. It is difficult, however, to conceive that many of those involved did not believe that some or all were innocent. Perhaps at some stage they may have genuinely believed that one or more were involved but it would have been impossible to have maintained such a belief in the face of the weight of the contradictory evidence which they subsequently had to go to such pains to conceal, alter or manipulate.

A third and far more contentious explanation, which I would like to label the rotten orchard theory, has been suggested by people within the Irish community. This argues that the majority of those involved in the arrest and subsequent prosecution of the Birmingham 6, Guildford 4, Maguire 7 and Judith Ward knew that the people arrested were innocent but because of the circumstances at the time were encouraged to obtain convictions for two reasons. Firstly, to help defuse the massive anti-Irish hysteria resulting in attacks on the Irish at work, petrol bombings of Irish clubs and public marches. Second, and more importantly, to discourage those who lent support to the IRA campaign by making it clear that the authorities were prepared to arrest and convict the innocent as well as the guilty. In the Taylor case the pressure was of a different order and was associated with the need to remove Stalker.

All the trials are seen as political to the extent that they went beyond the accepted core function of any criminal trial, namely, the affirmation of public order through the instrumentality of the trial. Instead, the trial and subsequent judicial developments appeared to have been used for deliberate political ends and hence to fit within Kirchheimer's definition of a political trial (Kirchheimer 1961:49).

From this perspective, the whispering campaign and the public statements of retired members of the judiciary, the subsequent prosecution of the three police officers and the setting up of the Commission was a carefully planned strategy, perhaps at the highest level, to prevent further damage. In retrospect it is arguable that from the position of the authorities the best outcome has been achieved. All the people are released, there has still been no full and detailed public inquiry into all aspects of all the cases, no police officers or any other person in any of the cases have yet been found guilty of any offences, and there is now considerable public doubt about the innocence of most of those released.

Some supporters of the rotten orchard theory argue that there was a deliberate policy to pervert the course of justice while others argue that there was a coincidence of mutual interests within the criminal justice system as a whole. All would agree, however, that the effect was to subvert justice to political expediency – now a common feature of the treatment of Irish people in the British criminal justice system. For example, within days of the Guildford 4 appeal, the Government announced that it intended to derogate from the European Convention on Human Rights following the European Court's decision in the Brogan case that seven days, detention under the Prevention of Terrorism Act (PTA) violated the Convention. Similarly, on the day after the publication of the findings of the Commission, the Home Secretary used his powers under the PTA to serve an exclusion order on John Matthews after the Crown had dropped proceedings against him.

From the rotten orchard perspective political expediency rather than justice is therefore a dominant feature of the treatment of those drawn into the criminal justice system in connection with the North of Ireland conflict. The problem lies not only in the criminal justice system, as suggested by the bad barrel theory, but in the way political considerations enter into the administration of justice.

VIII CONCLUSIONS

It is perhaps not surprising that the Commission failed to examine the Irish cases. It would have revealed, at best, many questionable methods and practices and, at worst, prima facie evidence of corruption at the heart of the system. Denning's appalling vista would have emerged as an accurate description of the state of British justice. By ignoring the cases, the Commission has, however, successfully reconstructed what was an issue of political injustice into an issue of criminal justice. At the same time, its recommendations will have little impact on the practices and methods identified here. Most involved a violation of existing rules and regulations. More of the same will achieve very little.

In weakening the position of the defence, substantially strengthening the position of the prosecution and leaving the PTA intact, the Commission's recommendations moves the form of criminal justice in England and Wales even closer to the form which has been developed in Northern Ireland to deal with political violence (see Hillyard 1987). Although trial by jury has been totally abolished in the Diplock Courts, the Commission's recommendation that the defendant should no longer have the right to insist on trial by jury in either-way offences, erodes still further the right to be judged by one's peers in Britain (see Harman and Griffith 1979). Second, the recommendations for a system of plea-bargaining, disclosure and the abolition of the right to remain silent after the prosecution's case has been fully disclosed by permitting an adverse comment, will increase the pressure on defendants to incriminate themselves – a long-standing feature of the Diplock Court process. Finally, the overall thrust of the Commission's thinking towards administrative efficiency will, as in Northern Ireland, subordinate issues of justice to the dictates of bureaucracy.

As far as the Irish cases are concerned, only a tribunal of inquiry to investigate the circumstances of the arrest and trial of all the cases examined can get at the truth. Although Sir John May is now free to complete his inquiries his powers are insufficient and, in any event, he is investigating only two of the cases. Moreover, as we have noted, the judiciary and the Government have expressed the view that there is little more to be gained from further investigation. In the absence of a full-scale inquiry the rotten orchard theory, embracing the belief that there has been widespread corruption at the heart of the British criminal justice system, will gain credibility.

8. Criminally Unjust: The Royal Commission and Northern Ireland

Jane Winter

When the Royal Commission on Criminal Justice was announced, we[1] wrote to the then Home Secretary asking him to extend the Commission's terms of reference to include Northern Ireland. The reply we received was classic in its failure to recognise Northern Ireland as anything except a passive recipient of policies made in England. The terms of reference would not be expanded, we were informed, but any useful findings of the Commission would be extended to cover Northern Ireland.

We went ahead and submitted evidence to the Commission anyway, convinced that the fact that so many miscarriages of justice involved cases concerned with the conflict in Northern Ireland, and that Northern Ireland had been the testing-ground for inroads into the right of silence, meant that lessons from there would be perceived as being of burning relevance. We were wrong. The Report of the Commission not only ignores the situation in Northern Ireland, where miscarriages of justice arise on a daily basis, but fails comprehensively to take on board important lessons for avoiding such problems in Britain.

Such myopia, if depressingly familiar, is unsurprising, perhaps particularly in view of the fundamental flaw which lay at the heart of the Commission's terms of reference. The Government asked the Commission to 'examine the effectiveness of the criminal justice system ... in securing the conviction of the guilty and the acquittal of those who are innocent.'

As we pointed out to the Commission, the conviction of the guilty and the acquittal of the innocent are not necessarily compatible aims. If a system of criminal justice is designed to secure the conviction of the guilty, it will put the onus on the defendant to prove his or her innocence and will give the benefit of any doubt to the prosecution, with the result that some people will go to prison for crimes they did not commit. If the system is designed

---

[1] Acting then under the auspices of the Britain & Ireland Human Rights Project, which submitted lengthy representations to the Commission.

to acquit the innocent, it will emphasise the rights of the defendant and require the prosecution to prove its case beyond reasonable doubt, with the outcome that some guilty criminals will go free.   Since neither bias is desirable in a democratic society – miscarriages of justice are not only about the innocent who are wrongly imprisoned, but about the perpetrators who are still at large – a better aim would be the provision of a fair trial to anyone suspected of committing a crime, based on the presumption of innocence and the privilege against self-incrimination, as is enshrined in a number of international human rights instruments to which the United Kingdom is a signatory.[2]

For those arrested under the PTA,[3] the system of criminal justice has been weighted in favour of obtaining convictions, with the result that the right to a fair trial has been seriously eroded throughout the United Kingdom, but most especially in Northern Ireland, where the combination of those provisions with those of the EPA[4] bite particularly deep.   In Northern Ireland, those arrested on suspicion of terrorist involvement are seriously disadvantaged when compared with their counterparts in England in a number of significant respects.

I ARRESTS

First, people in Northern Ireland are far more likely to be arrested under the emergency laws. In 1991,[5] 121 people were arrested under the PTA in Great Britain in connection with Northern Ireland, whereas 1,680 were arrested under the PTA and a further 108 under the EPA in Northern Ireland.   Given that the population of Northern Ireland is only about 1.5 million, its citizens are thus at much greater risk of arrest. Many of those arrested are young Catholic men aged between 17 and 25.   They are arrested and interrogated by police officers of the RUC, a police force which is drawn overwhelmingly from the Protestant community.[6] Detainees are held in one of three special holding centres, designed

---

2   For example, Article 10 of the Universal Declaration on Human Rights and Article 6 of the European Convention on Human Rights.
3   The Prevention of Terrorism (Temporary Provisions) Act 1989.
4   The Emergency Provisions (Northern Ireland) Act 1991.
5   The latest full-year figures available on Northern Ireland at the time of writing. The statistics quoted in this paragraph are from the *Home Office Statistical Bulletin*, Issue 34/92, and the *Northern Ireland (Emergency Provisions) Act Statistics*, published quarterly by the Statistics Branch of the Northern Ireland Office.
6   According to the Fair Employment Commission, 93 per cent of serving police officers in Northern Ireland come from the Protestant community. *Profile of the Workforce in Northern Ireland, Summary of the 1992 Monitoring Returns*, Monitoring Report No. 3, p. 105. The identical proportion of new appointments made in 1992 were Protestants; see p. 111.

specifically for the purpose of holding and interrogating PTA suspects. They are kept in small bare cells without integral sanitation or natural daylight. They are deprived of books, newspapers, radio and television. They cannot receive food or sweets from outside. They are not allowed to make any telephone calls. They cannot associate with other inmates or receive visits from family or religious counsellors. Smoking is not allowed in cells or in interview rooms. In short, they are kept in conditions far worse than those experienced by prisoners on remand or even after conviction. Seventy-seven per cent of those arrested are released without charge, and many detainees report that the main purpose of their detention seemed to be aimed at the collection by the police of low-level intelligence rather than for the lawful purpose of bringing them before the courts.

II INCOMMUNICADO DETENTION

Such detainees can be kept completely incommunicado for up to 48 hours. In both jurisdictions, the police can decide not to inform either the family or the detainee's solicitor of the fact that he or she has been arrested for the first two days of the detention.[7] However, practice differs significantly in the two jurisdictions. In England and Wales, information about the fact of an arrest is rarely suppressed, and most solicitors report that they are normally informed of an arrest within a matter of hours and are usually given immediate and continuous access to their clients. In Northern Ireland, while solicitors are usually informed that their client is in detention, in 28 per cent of cases in 1992[8] access to their clients was deferred for up to 48 hours. During that two days, a detainee will be interrogated by teams of two or four detectives at a time, for sessions lasting up to (and sometimes longer than) two hours, as many as seven or eight times a day. Many a Northern Ireland solicitor has finally gained access to a client only to find that he or she has already made damaging admissions which might not have been made if legal advice had been available from the outset.

---

[7]   Police and Criminal Evidence Act 1984, s. 56 (2); EPA s. 14.
[8]   *Report on the Operation in 1992 of the Northern Ireland (Emergency Provisions) Act 1991*, Viscount Colville of Culross QC. Between 1987 and 1991 the deferral rate was 58 per cent. The dramatic drop in 1992 reflects a series of judicial reviews brought by solicitors challenging the RUC's decision to defer access in a number of cases.

III ACCESS TO LEGAL ADVICE

The provisions on access to a solicitor are different in Northern Ireland from those in England. Not only is initial access more frequently deferred for up to 48 hours but in Northern Ireland solicitors can only consult with their clients, they cannot remain with them during police interviews, whereas in England once solicitors gain access to a client they usually remain with them during police questioning. The reason for this difference is that in England, PACE applies, albeit with modifications, but in Northern Ireland all PACE protections are specifically withheld from PTA detainees.[9]   Furthermore, access to clients, even for the purposes of consultation, can be deferred for further periods of up to 48 hours in Northern Ireland,[10] with the result that a detainee held for the full seven days permissible under the PTA may only see his or her solicitor on three occasions, for perhaps half an hour at a time. Apart from the solicitor and a police-appointed doctor, the only other human beings with whom a detainee will have contact during the whole of the detention will be police officers.

IV LACK OF SCRUTINY

Fourthly, police officers are under minimal scrutiny during interrogation of suspects. There is no video- or audio-recording of police interviews, which are still manually recorded by police officers, although recently they have been obliged to use time- and date-stamped notebooks. This reform was introduced in the wake of the only acknowledged miscarriage of justice in Northern Ireland, when three of the UDR Four were released by the Northern Ireland Court of Appeal after ESDA tests showed that police officers had tampered with statements. It was ironic that it was a 'Protestant' miscarriage which led to this reform, when the majority – although by no means all – of the cases where miscarriages are currently being alleged concern Catholics.

Interrogations are relayed through silent video cameras to a bank of video screens which are watched by a relatively senior policeman who is supposed to intervene if he sees – he cannot hear – anything untoward. We are not aware of a single instance of a police officer being disciplined or prosecuted because of anything thus observed.

In April 1993, Sir Louis Blom-Cooper QC was appointed as the sole Independent Commissioner for the Holding Centres, with a brief to oversee

---

[9]   Article 59 (12) PACE (Northern Ireland) Order 1989.
[10]   EPA s. 45 (6) (b).

observe, comment and report on the conditions under which people are detained there. One quite extraordinary element in his terms of reference is that, 'His appointment is also intended to reassure the public that the police have nothing to hide and that persons detained in Holding Centres are not being ill-treated or denied their rights'. Such prescription sits uneasily with the notion of independence. The Commissioner is not allowed to be present during actual police interviews, and while his visits to the Holding Centres are unannounced, we doubt that they are unexpected.

V DIPLOCK COURTS

Fifthly, if a person is charged with an offence, the trial will take place in a juryless Diplock Court, before a single judge who is the tribunal of both fact and law. Northern Ireland is a small place. Only 11 judges sit in the Diplock Courts. Not only is there a risk that judges will become case-hardened, but barristers, too, may tailor their arguments to what they know of particular judges. Independent observers of Diplock trials frequently express concern that particular points were not put at a trial at first instance, with the result that subsequent appeals or applications to the European Commission on Human Rights are limited in scope. Acquittal rates in the Diplock Courts compare unfavourably with those trying non-scheduled offences.[11] In 1991, 36 per cent of those tried in the Diplock Courts were acquitted, while 54 per cent of defendants in other cases were found not guilty. Similarly, only 16 per cent of appeals from the Diplock Courts succeeded, compared to 29 per cent of appeals from other courts.[12] Experience in Northern Ireland suggests that inroads into the right to trial by jury such as those recommended by the Commission[13] should be resisted strenuously by all those concerned with the right to a fair trial.

VI ADMISSIBILITY OF CONFESSIONS

Standards of admissibility of confession evidence are lower in the Diplock Courts than in the ordinary criminal courts. Under s. 11 of the EPA the defence must adduce prima facie evidence that a confession was obtained by torture or inhuman or degrading treatment in order to challenge

---

[11] 'Scheduled offences' are those listed in Schedule 1 of the EPA.
[12] Source: *Judicial Statistics in Northern Ireland in 1991*, Northern Ireland Court Service, 1992. The figures given here are the percentages of defendants pleading not guilty to counts who were acquitted on all counts.
[13] Recommendation 114.

admissibility. In other courts, the test is the absence of oppression. According to the Haldane Society's 1992 Report on their delegation to Northern Ireland, 90 per cent of all Diplock defendants have made confessions and 75–80 per cent of cases depend on confession evidence alone. The conviction rate in the Diplock Courts is around 70 per cent of all cases. Thus the majority of convictions rely solely on the defendant's confession.

When a confession is contested, as is often the case in the Diplock Courts, the court dissolves into a lengthy *voir dire*, sometimes lasting for weeks, at the end of which the judge must solemnly forget everything he has heard, should he rule the confession inadmissible. The Commission's recommendations for judicial warnings[14] seem rather hollow in this context.

VII THE RIGHT OF SILENCE

One of the most significant disparities between the two jurisdictions is the fact that the right of silence has been abrogated in Northern Ireland[15] to the extent that adverse inferences can be drawn from a suspect's silence during police interviews and from any failure to testify at trial. Adverse inferences can also be drawn from a suspect's failure or refusal to account for the presence of any object, substance or mark upon his or her clothing or person or in his or her possession or presence when arrested, or to account for his or her presence at a place at or around the time when the alleged offence is said to have been committed. Silence in any of these situations can be corroborative, but guilt cannot be decided solely on the basis of inference. Initial judicial caution in applying these provisions has increasingly given way to a tendency to use the exercise of the right of silence, especially if a client does not testify at trial, to make up ever greater deficits in other evidence in order to convict defendants.

While the Commission's majority rejection of the introduction of the drawing of adverse inferences from silence under police questioning[16] is welcome, their recommendation[17] that it should be possible for the prosecution or the judge to comment on any departure from a previously-disclosed defence or any new defence if the defendant declines to comment on the Crown's case after full disclosure by the prosecution is, in our view,

---

14 Recommendations 89 and 90.
15 By virtue of the Criminal Evidence (Northern Ireland) Order 1988, which came fully into force on 15 December 1988.
16 Recommendation 82.
17 Recommendation 83.

ill-conceived. While it is clearly an aspect of the Commission's views on disclosure by the defence (see below), it seems very muddled. If a suspect says nothing upon hearing the prosecution's case, it is difficult to see how that can be compared meaningfully to any defence subsequently led at trial. We agree with Michael Zander's dissenting view that disclosure by the defence is wrong in principle, and would go further: any abrogation of the right of silence is a violation of the privilege against self-incrimination and as such is contrary to international human rights norms.

VIII DISCOVERY

The Attorney General's guidelines on the disclosure of unused material do not apply in Northern Ireland, although the courts there tend to have some regard to them.[18] Defendants in the Diplock Courts fairly frequently seek to contest the admissibility of confessions on the grounds that they were extorted from them by ill-treatment on the part of the police. A recent ruling[19] made legal history when the judge ordered that the defendants' custody and medical records made while they were in police detention be disclosed to the defence *before* they gave evidence on their own behalf in the *voir dire*. Previously, such records were invariably withheld until after the defendants had testified, and used by the Crown to challenge the defendants' version of events. In Northern Ireland, the PACE provision that a detainee is entitled to a copy of the custody record does not apply to those detained under the PTA.[20]

IX MISCARRIAGES OF JUSTICE

Against this background of the differences in regime, it is hardly surprising that allegations of ill-treatment in police custody, retractions of confessions made in holding centres, and complaints of the lack of a fair trial are commonplace in Northern Ireland. Until fairly recently, though, allegations of miscarriages of justice were relatively rare. However, in the past eighteen months RIGHTS WATCH has received around 40 complaints from convicted prisoners in Northern Ireland that they have suffered a miscarriage of justice, and another dozen or so from those awaiting trial who lack all confidence that their trials will be fair.

---

[18] See, for example, *R* v. *McAllister* [1985] NIJB 10.
[19] Ruling of Sheil J on Timing of Disclosure of Documents in *R* v. *Coogan & Ors*, Belfast Crown Court, 21 May 1993, unreported.
[20] PACE (Northern Ireland) Order 1989, Article 66 (12).

The reasons for these allegations are basically fourfold. First, there are a number of cases in which defendants allege that confessions were beaten out of them by, sometimes quite brutal, ill-treatment – some of these cases go back many years. Secondly, there is a more recent generation of cases in which the operation of the rules on the right to silence are blamed. Thirdly, there are cases where it is alleged that convictions were secured on the basis of unreliable evidence. Fourthly, there is a worrying number of cases in which prisoners have asked for original police interview notes with a view to having them subjected to ESDA testing, only to be told that the notes cannot be found. Anyone who has studied the *Guildford, Birmingham*, and *Ward* cases, or any of the other notorious English miscarriages, would find that our dossier of Northern Ireland cases tells an all-too-familiar story. Below we highlight just a few examples.

X ILL-TREATMENT

Since the United Nations Committee Against Torture criticised the regime at the holding centres in November 1991, and Amnesty International issued its first ever 'urgent action' call in relation to Northern Ireland,[21] the incidence of really serious allegations of ill-treatment in police custody has diminished markedly. However, reports of low-level ill-treatment, and of intense psychological pressure on detainees, continue to be common.

Nevertheless, there are a number of cases still working their way through the system where defendants allege that confessions were beaten out of them. One such is Kevin Lynch, accused on conspiracy to murder a police officer, whose trial is due to start in September 1993, after over two years on remand. He alleges severe ill-treatment while in police custody, and his solicitor complained about the alleged ill-treatment while he was still in Castlereagh holding centre. So far as we are aware, there is no other evidence against him apart from his confession.

Others have become stuck in the system, such as Thomas Green, a Protestant, who was convicted of a sectarian murder of Catholic John O'Neill in 1986. He maintains his innocence, and says that he was assaulted, abused and confused by police officers while in Castlereagh to the point that he collapsed and had to be admitted to hospital, where he was found to have suffered an acute drop in his blood sugar level, a reaction associated with severe anxiety. In his statement about his case, he describes how police officers suggested one version of events to him, to which he

---

[21] In the case of Damien Austin.

confessed, and then decided that they had some of the facts wrong, whereupon he says that they obliged him to make a new confession.

XI THE RULES ON THE RIGHT OF SILENCE

Dermott Quinn was arrested in April 1988 on suspicion of the attempted murder of two police officers. He was released after five and a half months on remand when two key witnesses refused to testify. He was re-arrested in July 1990, after the abrogation of the right of silence had been brought in, and convicted on precisely the same evidence, the two witnesses again declining to take the stand. He maintained silence in police custody on both occasions, but testified in his own defence at his trial, when his employer gave him an alibi. He was convicted on a combination of very slender forensic evidence and his silence in police detention. His appeal against conviction was heard in November 1992; judgment is still awaited.

  Kevin Murray was convicted on 18 January 1991 of the attempted murder of a soldier and sentenced to 18 years' imprisonment. The trial judge used inferences drawn from his exercise of his right to remain silent in the police station and from his failure to testify at his trial in order to convict him on purely circumstantial evidence which it is dubious would have formed the basis of a conviction on their own. Kevin Murray has appealed his case all the way to the House of Lords to no avail. Our independent observer at the House of Lords hearing informed us that the court, having heard his case, did not trouble the Crown to put its arguments.

XII UNRELIABLE EVIDENCE

Michael Hillen and Sean Mathers are serving 21 years for conspiracy to murder and other offences, all of which they deny. They were arrested some distance from a bomb which the police alleged they were about to detonate. Their claim that they were innocently on their way to work, confirmed by their employer, was not accepted by the Diplock judge. Although in the written depositions prepared by the prosecution before the trial reference was made to numerous photographs, only one book of photographs was produced at the trial. The two were convicted despite the fact that the judge rejected some of the police evidence as being untruthful. In a disturbing development since the trial, the police have informed their solicitor that much of the forensic and other evidence vital to their appeal has been destroyed.

Forty-one people have been tried to date for the murder of two army corporals, David Howes and Derek Wood, who were killed in Casement Park in March 1988 after they had become involved in the funeral of Kevin O'Brady, who was himself shot at the funeral of the three IRA members who were killed by the SAS on Gibraltar. Although the two soldiers were shot, not one of the accused was said to have fired the gun. Great controversy surrounds the convictions, not least of all because the accused were identified from poor-quality video film shot by an army helicopter flying overhead. Our observers expressed concern that various judges in the Diplock Courts were drawn into becoming identification witnesses during the course of the trials.

XIII ESDA TESTING

Peter Markey was convicted in 1986 of aiding and abetting a murder purely on the basis of a confession which he now says was extorted from him. When he requested his original statements in order to subject them to the ESDA tests, he was told by the police that they are missing without trace.

Seamus Mullan is serving a life sentence for the murder of a policeman. His conviction rested on an uncorroborated confession which he denies ever having made and on disputed vocal identification evidence. He also requested his original statements for ESDA testing. His solicitor was told in July 1992 that the RUC had reservations about releasing his notes because they feared being inundated by such requests. The solicitor supplied further grounds for making the request, as the police insisted, only to be told in October 1992 that the notes were missing and could not be found.

XIV CONCLUSION

The system of criminal justice in Northern Ireland is very severely distorted by the notion that terrorism is a special category of crime. A whole panoply of special measures, all of which diminish basic standards of justice and erode the right to a fair trial, has been put in place predicated upon the assumption that political motivation on the part of perpetrators justifies treating them less favourably than those who are motivated by the greed, ambition or sadism which drives many mis-named 'ordinary decent criminals'. The image of the hardened terrorist, trained to withstand all legal means of police interrogation, who turns his back on the court, is a powerful icon in our criminal courts. It is also a myth. The victims of the system of criminal injustice which pertains in Northern Ireland are more often young, without many educational qualifications, and vulnerable, with, in many cases, a short lifetime's experience of discrimination and harassment on the streets. They are easy meat for a police force drawn almost exclusively from one side of the conflict and operating under no meaningful scrutiny.

The Royal Commission on Criminal Justice, by failing to examine the effect of the PTA on the English system of criminal justice, and by refusing to acknowledge the Irish roots of the miscarriages which gave rise to its being set up in the first place, did a grave disservice to those who are caught up in the system in Northern Ireland. As a result, much of what the Commission has come up with, whatever the merits or demerits of individual recommendations, is simply irrelevant in the Northern Ireland context. It is to be hoped that those who are concerned with the right to a fair trial, and its necessary concomitant, equality before the law, will not let the irrelevancy of the Commission's Report blind them to the lessons for other jurisdictions to be drawn from what has been done to justice in Northern Ireland.

Northern Ireland has long been the testing ground for changes in the English law.[22] The strident lobby in favour of abrogating – if not abolishing altogether – the right of silence in England will not go away. Anyone who wants to gaze into the crystal ball of the future of criminal justice in England need look no further than Northern Ireland. Lessons from there will be ignored at the peril of all of our civil liberties and human rights.

---

[22] The taking of compulsory mouth swabs, for example, has been in place in Northern Ireland for some time – see Recommendation 14.

9. Race and Racism – the Missing Dimensions in the Royal Commission on Criminal Justice

Chris Boothman

I INTRODUCTION

In its submission to the Royal Commission on Criminal Justice, the Institute of Race Relations urged that racism be made a central focus of the Commission's inquiries, arguing that

> many of the specific denials of rights which black people have suffered over the years at the hands of the police and within the criminal justice system have proven to be forerunners of more general problems affecting the community as a whole. In this sense, the prism of race offers a unique perspective through which to expose and evaluate the underlying failings of the criminal justice system as a whole.[1]

In this context, the Institute of Race Relations noted that it was disturbing that race did not gain a mention in the Royal Commission's terms of reference and only one reference, to do with the selection and composition of juries, in the 80-item questionnaire issued by the Commission at the beginning of its inquiries.

Yet, prior to the Commission being set up, there was a considerable body of research on race and criminal justice which at the very least suggested a serious problem. Whether or not it could be proven that there was discrimination, there was a very wide public perception that certain groups were being treated unfairly by the police and the criminal courts. A number of the most serious miscarriages of justice that led to the Commission being established had in fact involved black defendants, including the Tottenham 3, a significant proportion of those who had lodged complaints against both the West Midlands Serious Crime Squad and Metropolitan Police officers based at Stoke Newington police station in North London, the Cardiff 3,

---

[1] Institute of Race Relations, *Memorandum of Evidence to Royal Commission on Criminal Justice*, London, Institute of Race Relations, 1991.

and Ivan Fergus.   These cases at the very least should have led the Commission to question the extent to which racism may have contributed to wrongful arrests and convictions.

Not only was race omitted from the specific terms of reference, but the Commission itself decided early on that its remit did not cover such issues as police use of stop-and-search, arrest powers, police operations on the streets, and police accountability, all of which had long been matters of concern to the black community.   In fact, the Commission was charged with considering the 'conduct of police investigations' and quite arbitrarily decided that, while this might include consideration of wider powers for the police in terms of sample-taking from and questioning of suspects in police stations, it did not cover their operations outside the police station.

Nor did the Commission take its terms of reference as extending to cover the issue of the police's relations with the media during the course of investigations or, indeed, at subsequent criminal trials.   This was another matter raised with the Commission early on by bodies such as the Institute of Race Relations, which pointed to 'the weakness of existing legal safeguards for suspects and defendants in the face of virulent and racist media campaigns against sections of the community or specific black individuals.'   The Institute of Race Relations went on to argue that

> such media prejudice is frequently a product of deliberate action by the police themselves, for example, in leaking selective information to friendly press sources before or during the course of trials.   Moreover, such prejudice can often pre-date the arrest, charging or trial of particular individuals, with the police involving the press and other media representatives directly in their investigatory operations and raids on estates, clubs or homes.   For black people to have their homes and communities violated in special operations of this type is in itself a serious violation of their civil liberties; to have this filmed for immediate television transmission or covered in specially-arranged press reports is to compound this assault on their basic rights and seriously to compromise the fairness of their subsequent treatment and trial.[2]

II THE COMMISSION'S RESEARCH ON RACE

In November 1991 the Royal Commission took on Marian Fitzgerald on loan from the Home Office to assemble the key findings from existing research on ethnic minorities and the British criminal justice system.   Part of the brief was also to provide some indication of the strengths and weaknesses of the studies on which previous findings were based. Interestingly, Fitzgerald's draft report, which was produced prior to the publication of a major study commissioned by the Commission for Racial

---

[2] Ibid.

Equality from Dr Roger Hood, of the Oxford Centre for Criminological Research, was very critical of and cast doubt on the findings of most of the earlier studies on race and criminal justice.[3]

However, when the final version of the Fitzgerald study was released, following publication of the Hood study (and, indeed, the Royal Commission Report itself), its tone had completely changed. Hood's report not only exposed new concerns, especially over the discriminatory sentencing behaviour of some Crown Courts and Crown Court judges, but also reinforced and gave substance to the findings of earlier studies. Thus, Fitzgerald was able to argue that

> The research evidence available when this paper was commissioned did not provide conclusive explanations for apparent differences between ethnic groups dealt with by the criminal justice system. Since then, the Hood report has clarified a number of the issues.[4]

Fitzgerald identified many of the same conditions within the criminal justice system which have been shown to lead to racial discrimination in other social policy fields, including the absence of clear guidelines about the criteria on which decisions should be taken, decisions depending on subjective judgments rather than objective criteria, criteria used that are not strictly relevant to the decisions to which they relate and have a disproportionately adverse impact on certain groups, wide scope for the exercise of individual discretion, the lack of a requirement to record (and still less to monitor) the reasons for decisions, and the strong influence of local and organisational norms and cultures on decisions and patterns of service delivery.

Fitzgerald's review, following the Hood report, also listed the precise areas in the criminal justice system where there is statistically significant racial variation, suggesting racial discrimination. These included the use of stop-and-search powers, the use of cautions and police decisions to take no further action, the overall pattern of charging, the incidence of remands in custody, defendants' decisions on plea and venue and to proceed to trial in the Crown Court, acquittal rates, and the imposition of custodial sentences and use of non-custodial disposals by the courts. Finally, she concludes by setting out a framework for addressing the relevant issues by focusing on discretion, legal variables and social and other factors.

---

[3]   R. Hood, *Race and Sentencing: A Study in the Crown Court*, Oxford, 1992.
[4]   M. Fitzgerald, *Ethnic Minorities and the Criminal Justice System*, London, HMSO, 1993, pp. 10–11.

III IMPACT OF RACE ON THE COMMISSION'S WORK

But if the Commission researchers came to recognise race as a crucial dimension of criminal justice, it hardly appears to have impinged on the Commission's work itself. Out of a total of 352 recommendations contained in the Report, only seven relate specifically to race. These seven recommendations essentially deal with just three issues: ethnic monitoring, multi-racial juries, and interpreters. Recommendations 2 and 3 call for the introduction of ethnic monitoring throughout the criminal justice system in order to ensure 'as far as possible the rules, procedures and practices of the ... system are applied in the same way to all.'[5]

Not only do these recommendations have a smack of tokenism about them, but the wording of the Report suggests that the Commission mistakenly believes that ethnic monitoring is the answer to the problem and will identify anti-discrimination measures. In fact, ethnic monitoring is merely the first step in the process. It is a neutral device and will do no more than highlight areas where discrimination may be occurring. Since the Fitzgerald review had already highlighted a number of areas where discrimination appears to be occurring, it is difficult to understand why anti-discrimination measures were not proposed or at least discussed by the Royal Commission.

One such area where clear patterns of differential impact on minorities have been shown to exist is in relation to the stop, search and arrest practices of the police. As a result of this evidence, these areas of police operations were supposedly made subject to certain 'safeguards' under the Police and Criminal Evidence Act and its codes of practice. But these 'safeguards' in turn rely on adequate monitoring, and the fact that black people continue to be disproportionately stopped and arrested, in what one author has described as 'operational racism',[6] should have served as a warning to the Commission that ethnic monitoring is a completely inadequate response, in itself, to patterns of discriminatory behaviour.

Recommendation 223 calls for the restoration of judicial discretion to empanel a multi-racial jury, in appropriate cases. This discretion was removed by the Court of Appeal in the case of *Ford*.[7] However, the Commission recommended that use of this discretion be limited to exceptional cases, involving a specific racial dimension to the alleged offence, and this is unlikely to inspire much confidence among ethnic minority defendants. Finally, Recommendations 208 and 211 call for accessible, organised and professional interpreter services within the

---

5 Royal Commission on Criminal Justice, *Report*, London, HMSO, 1993, p. 188.
6 Stephen Feuchtwang (1992), 'Policing the streets', in S. Feuchtwang and A. Cambridge (eds) *Where you Belong: Government and Black Culture*, Avebury.
7 [1989] 3 All E.R. 445.

criminal justice system. As important as this is, it is again likely to have only a marginal impact on the general experience of minorities in the system.

IV REINFORCING RACISM IN CRIMINAL JUSTICE

The Royal Commission at one point argues, in relation to the issue of racial discrimination, that their recommendations are 'designed to improve the criminal justice system for all who become involved in it',[8] thereby implying that the issue of race does not deserve separate consideration other than through ethnic monitoring. As we know from other social policy fields, however, such a 'colour-blind' approach to racism runs the risk, if inadequate consideration is given to the potential for racially differential effects of general measures, not just of leaving patterns of discrimination untouched but actually reinforcing them. Nowhere is this more clear than in the Royal Commission's recommendations on mode of trial and its endorsement of formalised sentence discounts and open judicial involvement in 'sentence canvassing'.

All the research evidence points to the fact that black defendants are much more likely to plead not guilty to criminal charges against them and, where they have a choice to do so, to elect for their cases to be heard before a jury in the Crown Court. Although the specific decision-making of black defendants has yet to be systematically investigated, it is likely that this pattern of decision-making, as with other groups of defendants, relates to their distrust of the police and of magistrates' courts, with their image of being 'police courts'.[9] Yet, the Royal Commission rejects such perceptions by defendants, even if backed up by the advice of their lawyers and by clear statistical evidence that magistrates do in fact have a much higher conviction rate for 'either-way' offences than Crown Court, as a rational basis for determining mode of trial. Indeed, the Royal Commission states that they 'do not think that defendants should be able to choose their court of trial on the basis that they think they will get a fairer hearing at one level than another.'[10] Instead, they recommend that decision on mode of trial in such cases should be transferred from defendants to the same magistrates who defendants already appear to distrust to try their cases fairly.

The Royal Commission recognises that such a change may result in up to 35,000 cases annually being transferred from Crown Court to magistrates'

---

[8] *Report*, p. 7.
[9] On this point, see C. Hedderman and D. Moxon, *Magistrates' Court or Crown Court? Mode of Trial Decisions and Sentencing*, London, HMSO, 1992.
[10] *Report*, p. 88.

courts against the wishes of defendants. However, they fail to acknowledge
that, because of the higher conviction rate by magistrates, it could result in
many defendants who are currently acquitted actually ending up being
convicted of fairly serious criminal charges. What is worse, there is no
mention at all in this section of the Report of potentially discriminatory
effects of such a change, given that black defendants currently tend to
exercise their rights of election more frequently and will therefore be more
adversely affected if this right is denied to them in future.

Similarly, the practice of giving a discount for guilty pleas in Crown Court
is specifically identified in the Hood report as having a disproportionately
adverse effect on black people because of their tendency to plead not guilty
more often than their white counterparts. Despite a clear recommendation
from Hood that the sentence discount system be reviewed and certainly not
be given any further impetus until its indirectly discriminatory effects are
more closely investigated, this is precisely what the Royal Commission
proposes in Recommendations 156 to 160, under which a fixed system of
percentage sentence discounts for early guilty pleas would be introduced,
reinforced by more open judicial involvement in the process under a
formalised 'sentence canvass'. It is again only as an afterthought that the
Royal Commission acknowledges the Hood research on this point and calls
for improved ethnic monitoring of Crown Court sentencing. But the tone of
the Report suggests a body that had long since made up its mind to back, on
grounds of efficiency, the sentence discount system (which was not even
covered by the terms of reference) and which was not going to be deterred
from this purpose by any liberal concern over its racially discriminatory
effects.

V CONCLUSION

In these latter respects, it is arguable that the Royal Commission on
Criminal Justice's recommendations would actually serve to more deeply
institutionalise racism within the criminal justice system. More generally,
my view is that there has been an abject failure by the Commission to take
seriously the issue of discrimination in the criminal process. The
Commission's terms of reference, although not specifically mentioning
race, were nevertheless broad enough to enable it, had they the will to do
so, to address many of the points of discrimination at different stages of
criminal justice. And, as its own research study on the subject argued:

action could be taken to prevent unjustified differences – whether actual or potential – without waiting for the results of further studies. For it is already apparent that the criminal justice system has the capacity for both indirect and direct discrimination.[11]

---

[11] Fitzgerald, op. cit., p. 11.

10. Denial, Neutralisation and Disqualification: The Royal Commission on Criminal Justice in Context

Philip Scraton

The 'appalling vista'

I think, too, of my confessions. When I made them I was broken, I had no will left. I agreed to what they said and lost fifteen years of my life. Other people suffered as a result: the police started a ball rolling that did not stop until it had crushed many other innocent victims .... There are times when I cannot help but think that if I had had greater resistance, if I had been able to hold up to the violence and threats, none of this would have happened. (Hill and Bennett, 1990:265)

If the six men win, it will mean that the police were guilty of perjury, that they were guilty of violence and threats, that the confessions were involuntary and improperly admitted in evidence and that the convictions were erroneous. ... This is such an appalling vista that every sensible person in the land would say: 'It cannot be right, that these actions should go any further.' (Lord Denning: Gilligan (ed.), 1990)

These words refer to two of the most spectacular miscarriages of justice in British history. They represent the kind of cases, both in content and process, more typical of British imperialism – the disquieting legacy of 'justice' in the colonies. Yet these cases, along with many others, happened under the noses of a consenting public and an approving media. As Paul Hill of the Guildford 4 reflects on 15 years of continuous fear, intimidation, beatings and 'ghostings', the process of British justice not only failed to protect him, it made him vulnerable, it made him its victim. Lord Denning's now notorious comments, referring to the Birmingham 6, were as accurate as his sentiments were contemptible. That police officers used violence and threats, that confessions were forced, that evidence was falsified, that prison officers meted out summary punishments, that the convictions were unsafe and that the appeals procedure persistently failed to expose or accept these deep-seated injustices, was – and remains – an appalling vista. Worse still, Paul Hill is left to contemplate that perhaps, in some way, he could have resisted the full force of an essentially corrupt criminal justice system.

While Denning was prepared to see the innocent languish in prison in order to sustain the supposedly sound reputation of English justice, this was never an impressive logic, the campaigns mounted and the Irish cases collapsed. Others followed, seriously undermining public confidence in a wide range of convictions certainly not limited to framing Irish women and men. The disbanding of the West Midlands Serious Crimes Squad, with many important documents and records mysteriously destroyed in the process, shook the foundations of policing (Kaye, 1991). While the official accounts cast the West Midlands Squad as an exception, police officers from other forces slept uneasily. As James Morton's (1993) detailed overview of police corruption shows, bending rules, planting evidence, bullying interrogations and physical brutality to secure convictions has a long history and is deeply institutionalised.

With the 'appalling vista' realised the Government had no option but to initiate a Royal Commission. Often used to 'defuse ... embarrassing situations' (Thomas, 1982:40) Royal Commissions acknowledge public concern while demonstrating an apparent willingness to overhaul, through 'independent' inquiry, a system which is discredited. Certainly the Royal Commission on Criminal Justice (RCCJ) faced an uphill task. With several hundred further cases awaiting re-examination, strong representations already made by reform groups and the abject failure of the much vaunted changes within the Police and Criminal Evidence Act to protect suspects, the criminal justice system had become the site of systematic miscarriage. While the highly publicised cases have dominated media attention it is widely recognised that the 'negotiation' of justice at much lesser levels has secured wrongful convictions, doing immeasurable damage to the reputation of the police, the legal profession and the courts. Payouts to those wrongfully arrested, humiliated and brutalised remain a common feature of cases resolved through civil litigations and well-founded doubts about the circumstances of several deaths in police custody or during arrest continue to haunt the police.

Much that has been written in response to the RCCJ, as in this volume, has focused on the specifics of the Report and on particular recommendations. This is both inevitable and, given that certain recommendations will be implemented, essential. Whatever the disappointments, wherever the flaws and however the recommendations emerged, the RCCJ will have an impact on criminal justice over the next decade and it requires critical evaluation in detail. This article is concerned with a broader evaluation and critique of the RCCJ. While it focuses briefly on arrest and custody procedures as they represent the seed-bed of most miscarriages of justice, the greater objective is to question the integrity and legitimacy of the RCCJ by placing it within an analytical framework of official discourse. With this in mind it presents a sceptical appraisal of the RCCJ's capacity to deliver an independent, informed and critical review of the criminal justice system.

It is not unusual to find that the outcomes of Royal Commissions, Home Office inquiries or other official inquiries fail to deal with central issues and often pay little more than lip-service to the circumstances out of which they emerge. Lord Scarman's inquiry into two days of street disturbances in Brixton, for example, was proclaimed as a definitive appraisal of operational policing and became the basis for an extensive review of police–community relations (Scarman, 1981). Yet his Report was far from comprehensive, either in methodology or substance. Two years later his finding that institutionalised racism was present neither in state agencies nor in the police was exposed by more exhaustive, police-commissioned research (PSI Report, 1983). Further, inquiries and Royal Commissions are constrained and defined by their terms of reference. Consequently the claim that they are apolitical, standing free from Government interests or influence, has to be measured in terms of the setting of political priorities.

I THE RCCJ: RESTRICTING TERMS, BALANCING MISCARRIAGES

It is against this backcloth that the eagerly awaited RCCJ has experienced heavy criticism. Despite its apparent substance there is minimal reference in the Report to the cases which gave rise to the RCCJ and the significance of those and other miscarriages is never discussed. As John Mackenzie (1993:1035) states, 'I had assumed in my naive way that the recommendations put forward by a Royal Commission set up to prevent miscarriages of justice might contain the odd recommendation that might prevent a miscarriage of justice. I could find none.' Seàn Enright (1993:1023) was left with the 'abiding impression ... that this Commission was primarily concerned with a ruthlessly effective disposal of criminal business' which consequently failed to address the issue of miscarriages. The Legal Action Group (1993:1) argues that the response of the RCCJ is 'inadequate at a very basic level: its theoretical model of the criminal justice system is flawed, being founded on the concept of co-operation between defence, prosecution and the court ... this denies the major lesson from the recent cases of miscarriage of justice: the system is failing because it is insufficiently adversarial'. Mike McConville pursued this line in a scathing indictment of the political and moral bankruptcy of the RCCJ:

> ... it is not empirically grounded, deploys defective reasoning in support of its recommendations, is based upon a flawed understanding of the organising principles of criminal justice and often amounts to ... little more than opinion and assertion. As a result the Report does not have the intellectual weight and moral authority needed to support the significant changes to the existing system which it advances. (McConville, 1993a:8)

These responses are typical, exposing the considerable inadequacies of the RCCJ.   Given the terms of reference, however, could the Royal Commission have delivered a more critical Report?

The eight terms of reference, supported by an 88-point circular, at first sight appear to generate the broadest of debates.   However the entire project was determined by the RCCJ's statement of introduction: 'To examine the effectiveness of the criminal justice system ... in securing the conviction of those guilty of criminal offences and the acquittal of those who are innocent, having regard to the efficient use of resources ...' (RCCJ, 1993:iii). All that followed, therefore, took-as-given the concepts of efficiency and effectiveness within the constraints of resources and also, most significantly, the presumption that for every innocent person convicted many others are wrongly acquitted. It was meant to be a salutary reminder that 'miscarriage' has two dimensions. Consequently the RCCJ remained restricted in its thinking and, inevitably, in interpreting its own commissioned research.

In discussing the terms of reference immediate weight is placed on the process and means of police investigation, particularly their 'conduct and supervision' and 'the protection afforded to suspects who are held in custody' (ibid.:1). Despite the fact that the RCCJ was set up because of disillusionment with a criminal justice process which had secured wrongful convictions and had then systematically failed to right the wrongs perpetrated in its name, the other side of the political coin was soon revealed:

> It is widely assumed – and we are in no position to contradict it – that the guilty are more often acquitted than the innocent convicted. (ibid.:2)

Whose assumption?   How widely?   Inevitably this crude attempt at 'balancing' the scales, uncorroborated and without empirical reference, reflected a political agenda for the RCCJ. As with so many official inquiries and Royal Commissions it is an agenda of appeasement. It is a warning to the critics of the criminal justice system that 'there is only a handful of cases in which it is possible to be certain, with hindsight, that the jury's verdict was mistaken' (ibid.) and that miscarriages of justice cut both ways: yes, people have suffered many years in prison through wrongful conviction and inadequate structures of appeal but note the guilty who walk free from the courts. The RCCJ, then, approached its task with two guiding principles: the first being that of 'balance' (i.e. wrongful convictions/wrongful acquittals) and second that miscarriages were, and remain, an aberration. Taken together these powerful assumptions redefine the issues and redraw the boundaries. It is in its discussion of the circumstances of operational policing that further principles are revealed.

II OF 'ERROR' AND 'MALPRACTICE': UNDERSTANDING INSTITUTIONALISED CORRUPTION

The evidence, from the multiple cases which gave rise to the appointment of the RCCJ, from the files of organisations such as JUSTICE, LIBERTY and INQUEST, and from the findings of numerous unofficial inquiries, indicates that the police habitually break the rules, commit unlawful acts before, during, and after questioning, and fabricate evidence. Such disdain, even contempt, for procedures sets in train a sequence of responses which together constitute the institutionalisation of unlawful practices. It seems, however, that the Royal Commission was incapable of accepting the full implications of the cases which gave rise to its appointment. 'Malpractice' becomes a euphemism, an acceptable term, for widespread operational behaviours which involve fear, intimidation, threats, sleep deprivation and physical assault. The RCCJ recognises unfair, unreasonable and even discriminatory treatment but it softens the brutal and dehumanising process to that of 'overstepping the mark' or unprofessional behaviour. But more significantly it affirms two significant and familiar caricatures. The first, well rehearsed in David McNee's evidence to the 1979 Royal Commission on Criminal Procedure, is that the rules and guidelines under which the police operate inhibit the pursuit of justice and favour the suspect. Rather than encouraging and achieving stronger sanctions against the rule benders, McNee succeeded in winning greater permissiveness in the rules. The second is that police who overstep the mark do so because they are zealots. In the words of James Morton (1993) these officers are 'bent for the job' as opposed to being 'bent for self'. Their 'malpractice' is simply the result of their occupancy of the higher moral ground in which the end (conviction) justifies the means (malpractice).

The principle of the 'zealot' who is no more than an over-enthusiastic and highly motivated police officer keen to 'get the job done' is compounded by the Royal Commission's concern with procedures. In 1986, under the Police and Criminal Evidence Act, Code C was introduced – ostensibly to ensure that anyone arrested should be interviewed exclusively at a police station under the direction and supervision of a custody officer. What has remained an issue of concern, and this was echoed by the RCCJ, is the 'gap' in time and opportunity between the moment of arrest and the police station interview. However, by placing emphasis on 'so-called "car seat" confessions' while underlining the 'success of tape-recorded interviews', the RCCJ (op. cit.:25) appears at best complacent, and at worst ignorant, of the negotiation of justice which takes place at the station but off-the-record. When it does make reference to 'malpractice' the RCCJ reveals a startling naiveté:

> During our examination of the criminal justice system, we have been struck by evidence of a disquieting lack of professional competence in many parts of it. There is, for example, a clear need for the police to improve their skills in interviewing suspects. (ibid.:6)

What this 'disquieting lack of professional competence' amounts to is no more than over-enthusiastic interviewing. This example illustrates the distance which prevails between the reality of police investigation and the construction of the problem. In March 1993, preempting the publication of the RCCJ, new police interview guidelines were issued following the Lord Chief Justice's criticism of 'oppressive' interviewing. The guidelines state:

> The officer's voice should never be raised nor should he shout. This should be unnecessary from a person in authority. ... Never should abusive language be used in an interview. ... It is not oppressive to tell the suspect that he is telling lies or to refer to different facts. However, to repeat that he is lying or shout that he is lying would be oppressive depending on the degree. (ACPO/Home Office, 1993)

It is as if the realities of incarceration at police stations have remained a closed book to the Commissioners. Inevitably the conditions under which people are held in custody, the often poor protection afforded to them by duty solicitors or by police surgeons and professional complicity in failing to expose the regularity with which those in 'safe' custody are psychologically intimidated and physically brutalised, provide the foundations for false confessions and unsafe convictions. This cuts no ice with the RCCJ.

In discussing the risk of false confessions the RCCJ uses Gudjonsson's (1992) research in proposing that there are four distinct categories: voluntary – reflecting a desire for notoriety, guilt for other actions or fantasy; in protection of another person; 'coerced-compliant' in order to end questioning or secure release; 'coerced-internalised' where people are convinced temporarily that they committed an act. Again there is a failure here to recognise the full impact of fear through intimidation or assault. The Helsinki Watch Report (1991) into abuses of human rights by security forces and the RUC in Northern Ireland chillingly demonstrated how police interrogators secured confessions by acts of violence which amounted to torture. The lines between persuasion, coercion and torture are drawn finely when people under intense pressure, deprived of sleep and subjected to bullying interrogation, lose their grip on reality and their capacity to make sound judgments. This hardly amounts to people 'see(ing) a prospect of immediate advantage from confessing' (RCCJ op. cit.). Rather it is that they are cowed and coerced into submission. How often it is said by those who make false confessions that 'they had me so that I would have signed anything they wanted ...'

The tame, almost apologetic response of the RCCJ to the abuse of power by police officers is well illustrated by the following statement:

> We recognise that police malpractice, where it occurs, may often be motivated by an over-zealous determination to secure the conviction of suspects believed to be guilty in the face of rules or procedures which seem to those charged with the investigation to be weighted in favour of the defence. Police officers must, however, recognise that, whatever the motive, malpractice must not and will not be tolerated. The remedy lies in a better-trained, better-equipped and better-supervised police force, not in the tacit acceptance of procedural rule-bending. (RCCJ, para. 24, p. 7)

Having identified the 'zealot' as the problem it will be remedied by an unbending faith in managerial procedures. This endorsement of the Scarman principle is typical of official inquiries which give the impression that occasional indiscretions can be corrected by a better management of circumstances. Serious miscarriages of justice, each originating in the sequence of events at police stations, are lost in the understatements of 'errors' or 'malpractices'. Redefined as unfortunate aberrations such errors can be identified, regulated and rectified by exposure to improved procedures. Those conducting investigations will receive 'proper' training and adequate supervision, will be provided with improved scientific and logistic aids and will work to set rules and procedures. The latter will protect the interests of both witnesses and suspects while establishing proper systems of record-keeping. This 'new approach to supervision' will prevent 'errors' and avoid 'mistakes' (RCCJ:70). Alongside this is the proposal to introduce video-recording in custody suites (RCCJ:33).

As Roger Smith (1993) comments, the Commission's research into the conduct of police investigations confirmed a 'horrifying picture'. Maguire and Norris (1993) show that in securing results the police are over-zealous and, accordingly, persistently cut corners, bend the rules and operate 'off-the-record' deals. Yet they consider that this can be eliminated by a 'change in occupational culture'. Having established that there is an endemic abuse of power in circumstances which are threatening and intimidating, the solution amounts to no more than the strengthening of managerial and supervisory procedures. This trust in the internal procedures of managerialism, central to Scarman, is precisely what has been systematically abused. Effective procedures of accountability are sacrificed through a myopic vision of efficient managerialism. Consequently the stinging nettle of regularly corrupt and occasionally brutal practices has remained untouched. Further, the introduction of procedural changes is conditional on their potential for obstructing the 'smooth-running' of investigations. The RCCJ (op. cit.:9) concludes, 'a set of safeguards which prevented the police from bringing large numbers of offenders to justice would be unacceptable'.

Through its adoption of these guiding principles the RCCJ neatly sidesteps the central issues. While there is recognition that care is essential in processing the vulnerable, the inadequate, the easily impressionable and the mentally ill there is a failure to accept that the process itself, regularly exploited, has the capacity to induce vulnerability, undermine people's 'adequacy' and inflict mental torment. Wider consideration of the research available, and more imaginative commissioning of research, would have provided considerable evidence of the extent of differential policing, of targeting identifiable groups and of discriminatory practices. There is no reference to institutionalised police racism, ranging from intimidation and aggression on the streets (IRR, 1987; Scraton, 1985) through to the deaths of black people during arrest or in custody (IRR, 1991). There is no discussion of the strategies and their consequences of policing working-class neighbourhoods or industrial disputes (Scraton, 1985; Green, 1990; Farrell, 1992). Two paragraphs are the sum total of the RCCJ's discussion of the Prevention of Terrorism Act (PTA) yet the experience of the PTA within Britain's Irish communities amounts to an abuse of human rights unparalleled in Western Europe (Hillyard, 1993a). Closely associated with the PTA has been the use of strip searches on women, particularly Irish women, as a functioning punishment in its own right. In more general terms gender is neglected by the RCCJ as an issue, despite the growing weight of research that demonstrates its significance in the enforcement of the law and differential administration of justice. Additionally, the entrapment of gay men and the selective use of the law leading inevitably to institutionalised miscarriages are not identified as pertinent issues.

III INTERPRETING OFFICIAL DISCOURSE

In a sharp analysis of the philosophy which informed the RCCJ, Mike McConville, himself a research contributor to the Commission, identifies four elements which together constitute a 'clear ideological agenda which infects the whole Report' (McConville, 1993a:7). He argues that taken together plea-bargaining, the drawing of adverse inferences, and obligations for defence disclosure bring into question the fundamental principles of where the burden of proof lies and what the objectives of the trial system are. Again, the key problems are the RCCJ's inappropriate terms of reference and the assumption that there is persistent failure to convict the guilty. As the RCCJ leans heavily on the categories of 'guilt' and 'innocence', it assumes an 'equivalence of obligations on prosecutor and defence alike' (ibid.). For McConville this promotes not only a rejection of the inquisitorial system but also a rejection of the long-established adversarial system in which the burden of proof lies firmly in the prosecution's court.

> Set up to deal with a system which had miserably let down defendants, failed society as a whole and sullied the face of justice, the commission's bizarre solution is to strengthen the prosecution and weaken the defence by converting the administration of criminal justice into an administrative criminal process. The end result of its effort is a miscarriage of judgment. (ibid.)

While agreeing unreservedly with McConville's scathing commentary it is important to stress that the shortcomings of the RCCJ are not reducible to poor judgment or lack of will. Neither are they expressions of a shift in political value or definition. The RCCJ, like its predecessors, is not simply about the control of crime or about the safeguarding of rights. The history of official discourse is one, as Foucault's (1977) work argued so persuasively, of the institutionalisation of effective strategies which prioritise surveillance, regulation and control. As power centres concerned with the application of 'useful' or 'relevant' knowledge for over a century criminal justice agencies have operated an agenda based on the targeting of 'problem' populations. Throughout that period techniques of surveillance, monitoring, intelligence-gathering and record-keeping have developed and been refined. What the RCCJ emphasises is the more efficient utilisation of procedural and technological strategies and techniques. Rather than providing the system with 'rights', itself a contradiction in terms, it fine-tunes the operational procedures and practices.

Consequently the RCCJ never challenges the validity of differential policing or differential justice. Institutionally these are the means through which identifiable, 'problem' populations or groups are criminalised. In this context miscarriages of justice are the exposed tip of the iceberg. As Cohen (1985) indicates, the discourses of surveillance, regulation and control have come to inform the professional training and operational practices of a range of institutions entrusted with the negotiation of justice and, accordingly, the negotiation of personal freedom. The RCCJ does not stand outside its social–legal and political contexts. It is a necessary and inevitable contribution to official discourse. That is its function.

Burton and Carlen's (1979:51) complex analysis of 'state official publications on law and order' identifies three distinct but related functions: incorporation; legitimacy; confidence-building. Official law and order discourse is constructed, 'in terms of an ideal of distributive justice which cannot admit to the material conditions which render that ideal impossible' (ibid.:95). This summarises precisely the contradiction inherent in the RCCJ. If official discourse is to succeed it has to negotiate (at best) or deny (at worst) the material conditions out of which it emerged. The political purpose is to reaffirm public confidence in a fractured criminal justice system, to reconstruct new forms of legitimacy (operational/procedural) and to secure strategies of incorporation which ostensibly demonstrate a willingness to respond to public concern. To do this the RCCJ employs techniques of denial (viewing miscarriages as aberrations; redefining acts of violence as malpractices) and techniques of neutralisation (balancing convictions of the innocent against acquittal of the guilty; shifting the burden of proof). Further, in its selective commissioning and use of research and its conspicuous neglect of existing research and unofficial inquiries, the RCCJ effectively disqualifies all knowledge but that which is its 'own'. What these three processes, techniques of denial, techniques of neutralisation and the disqualification of knowledge, amount to is a classic deconstruction of criticism through which a new agenda is established deflecting the central issues, confirming legitimacy and reaffirming confidence.

Royal Commissions cannot be viewed simply as sophisticated expressions of political conspiracy nor as subtle instruments of authoritarian states. What they project is an image of independence institutionally standing apart from the social and political conflict of competing interests. Through their membership and their procedures for 'open' consultation they add to the impression that all is well within pluralist society. As Phil Thomas (op. cit.:40) argues:

> The neutral state operating by popular consent requires active illustrations of its commitment to heed public opinion. In a time of crisis a shift towards a more repressive state may occur. This involves the movement of law into more contentious areas ... [Royal Commissions] stand apart from policies and it is within the principles of democratic pluralism that their justification is found.

As Thomas concludes, this interpretation misrepresents conflict as the product of healthy sparring between competing interest groups thus denying the primary significance of structural and material inequalities. It is in their negotiation of the latter that Royal Commissions function as 'devices for social control' (ibid.:40). To explain the spectacular failure of the RCCJ in its neglect of pathways to fundamental reform requires a more coherent and integrated analysis of the structural contradictions, and their consequences for social and political action, within contemporary British society.

The miscarriages of justice which have dominated the last twenty-five years have arisen out of the differential policing of Northern Ireland and Irish communities in Britain, black communities, the unemployed and the poor, political protesters and trade unionists. They have brought deep personal suffering but they are not simply unfortunate aberrations tied to individual cases. Their roots lie in the administration of justice informed and sustained by ideologies which are expressions of structural inequality. For all the current intellectual criticism of 'standpoint' theory, the structural relations of production, reproduction and neocolonialism are powerful determining contexts both in terms of material conditions and the administration of criminal justice and social policy. They are inherently relations of conflict. Using pseudo-scientific justifications of individual and social pathology, the poor, single mothers, black people, Irish people and other 'problem populations' are marginalised, watched, targeted, policed and, therefore, criminalised.

This version of 'justice' is expectant. It waits for what it defines as inevitable and reacts accordingly. When it comes it is a popular and vote-winning reaction appealing to the worst prejudices and assumptions, supported by a sensationalist and irresponsible press and enabling desperate politicians to shoot from the lip at easy targets. The 1993 Conservative Party Conference provided the Home Secretary, Michael Howard, with a platform from which he pumped new life into the folk devils of the previous decade. On the back of vindictive and spiteful addresses to the Tory faithful, however, will come harsher penalties, increased use of imprisonment and further draconian legislation, including withdrawal of the right to silence. The RCCJ, despite its position on the latter, has contributed greatly to a political agenda which will target and regulate 'problem' populations with renewed vigour. It is an agenda within which miscarriages of justice will flourish as police confidence is reaffirmed. Just as the Appeal Courts could not, or would not, accept that gross miscarriages of justice had occurred so the RCCJ failed to accept that they are the visible and incontrovertible manifestation of a social order which sets out to police, to prosecute and to convict on the basis of ideology, at the expense of truth.

PART II

11. The Royal Commission on Criminal Justice System Surveillance

Richard V. Ericson[1]

I CRIMINAL JUSTICE SYSTEM SURVEILLANCE

1. The Old Official Discourse: Crime Control and Suspects' Rights

Prior to the Royal Commission on Criminal Justice (RCCJ), official discourse was constructed in terms of a binary opposition between crime control and suspects' rights. On the one hand there was a need for crime control, for an efficient suppression of crime and punishment of criminals. On the other hand there was a need for protecting suspects' rights, for procedural fairness and due process. Debate centred on whether the 'law and order' advocates of crime control, or the 'civil libertarian' advocates of suspects' rights, were winning the day. Analyses focused on the extent to which legal reforms and practices protected suspects' rights, or intensified state control to the point where 'due process is for crime control' (McBarnet 1981; see also Packer 1968; Ericson and Baranek 1982).

The RCCJ is different in profound ways. It provides a new official discourse of surveillance which displaces the former emphasis on crime control. It also refigures the meaning of justice, further eroding suspects' rights in favour of surveillance system rights. Moreover, rights have not only been shifted away from the accused, they have been disconnected from the state as a central, unitary entity. Rights are increasingly bestowed upon and embedded in the system itself, enabling it to produce, distribute and use whatever knowledge is deemed necessary to conduct efficient surveillance of both suspects and its own criminal justice agents.

[1] Preparation of this paper was funded by a research grant from the Social Sciences and Humanities Research Council of Canada. I am grateful to Kevin Haggerty for his assistance in preparing this paper, and to Joel Bakan, Christine Boyle, David Downes and Robert Menzies for their comments.

2. The New Official Discourse: Surveillance and System Rights

a. Surveillance displaces crime control

The RCCJ is concerned with describing, analysing and improving criminal justice as a surveillance system. Here surveillance does not have its popular sinister connotation of police undercover intrusion to suppress undesirable people and organisations (Marx 1988). Surveillance is the bureaucratic production of knowledge about, and risk management of, suspect populations (Giddens 1985; Dandeker 1990).

The RCCJ depicts criminal justice as a system whose principal coordinating mechanism is knowledge. Knowledge coordinates the risk management of both criminal suspects and suspect criminal justice agents. This emphasis on surveillance for risk management is in keeping with the predominant activity of other major institutions in risk society. Based on an assumption of distrust in human relations, institutions construct risks as threats and then respond to their own constructions through probability calculations for risk management (Giddens 1990, 1991; Beck 1992a, b; Simon 1987; Stehr and Ericson 1992).

There are two meanings of risk. First, there is risk as a threat or danger. This is the meaning of risk that is most salient in the RCCJ Report. The word risk appears *76 times* in the Report, and the risks identified largely pertain to threats to the efficiency of criminal justice system surveillance.

The RCCJ identifies risks created by deficiencies in system organisation, for example regarding financial arrangements, occupational cultures, and specific investigative, pre-trial and trial mechanisms. It also pinpoints risks created by deficiencies in the roles and personal attributes of system agents. For example, the police lie, make errors and produce knowledge too coercively. Prosecutors fail to communicate adequately with witnesses and police, fail to disclose relevant forensic evidence to defence lawyers, and make inappropriate disclosures to defence lawyers that affect the police, informants and commercial security agents. Defence lawyers are often inept, create delays, pressure witnesses and malign victims. Juries suffer from an inadequate capacity to understand and to make appropriate inferences. Judges also make inappropriate inferences, and they are prone to exposing their biases publicly. These are all threats to the capacity of the system to obtain knowledge useful in the risk management of suspect populations. The only solution is to turn surveillance back on to the system itself, to develop new rules, technologies and formats that will foster criminal justice agents' surveillance of each other.

This brings us to the second meaning of risk. Risk is a probability statement. Suspects are made objects of knowledge in order to classify and profile them into risk categories. This profiling increasingly becomes an end in itself for the police and criminal justice system (Ericson 1994). The hard edge of crime control, of maximal prosecution and severe punishment, gives way to having access to and recording knowledge about dubious members of the population. In this respect the police are knowledge workers. They spend most of their time producing and communicating knowledge that serves the needs not only of their own bureaucracy and the criminal justice system, but also the needs of myriad other institutions that require police knowledge for their own systems of risk management and security provision (ibid.; O'Malley 1991).

The RCCJ research studies provide ample evidence to support this view of police as knowledge workers. The vast majority of juveniles (in 1990, 72 per cent of males and 85 per cent of females) arrested are cautioned by police rather than charged and prosecuted in court (Evans 1993a:2–3). They are not scathed by formal prosecution and punishment, only marked on police records. These records are kept for possible police uses in the future, and for distribution to other agencies and institutions. Among adults 'Case mortality is, in fact, the daily experience of routine police and prosecutorial decision making ... in all cases in which disposition was known (n = 1068), no fewer than 49.4 per cent (n = 528) were disposed of without any court action by means of no further action, caution or informal warning' (McConville 1993a:86). Nationally, 'the number and range of cases in which people are cautioned by the police have increased steadily over the years' (RCCJ 1993:82). This tendency away from prosecution and punishment is accentuated in cases of serious fraud and other white-collar crime, which are routinely dealt with in an administrative compliance mode (Levi 1993). It is not that the punishment of white-collar crime is moving closer to the criminal deterrence mode, as some wish it (Pearce and Tombs 1990). To the contrary, the criminal deterrence mode is moving closer to the administrative compliance mode characteristic of white-collar crime regulation.

The RCCJ has not thrown out the 'efficiency baby' with the 'crime control bathwater'. Rather, the concern for efficiency is now focused on the efficient production and distribution of knowledge useful in the risk management of suspect populations. The major concern of criminal justice system surveillance is the efficient formatting and availability of detailed knowledge about people in the hope that it will come in handy in future system dealings with them, or, more often, in the dealings other institutions (credit, welfare, education, insurance, health etc.) might have with them.

b. System rights displace suspects' rights
Priority is given to the system's rights to better knowledge over suspects' rights to due process protections. In both practice (as documented in the RCCJ research reports) and prescription (as recommended in the RCCJ Report), the 'justice' in 'criminal justice' is no longer focused on due process in an adversarial system where each side is given an enabling environment to make its case. Justice is a matter of ensuring that system agents, in particular the police, have the requisite resources to obtain knowledge of suspects.

As elaborated in Part II, these requisite resources are knowledge resources. It is a matter of providing the system with expert knowledge resources to obtain useful knowledge about suspects. The system is already structurally arranged to give the police an enormous advantage in access to legal, scientific, electronic, information system and craft knowledges required to conduct surveillance efficiently. The RCCJ's reform solution is to concretise these structural arrangements even further by creating more system rights to obtain the knowledge it needs.

c. Reform discourse and practice
As I document in Part II, the RCCJ research studies leave no doubt that criminal justice is already a surveillance system. This fact leads to the inevitable conclusion that the RCCJ is an exercise in rationalising surveillance practices that are already firmly in place. The RCCJ is a classic example of reform discourse that does not pave the way for something radically different, but refines what is a *fait accompli* (McMahon 1992). The reform discourse is catching up to and capturing practice. It has arisen out of practice and it will in turn form practice (Valverde 1990). As such the RCCJ does not stand alone as a kind of removed and dispassionate depiction of criminal justice surveillance mechanisms and how they might be improved. The RCCJ is itself a surveillance mechanism, one of the forms of expert knowledge used to constitute criminal justice.

As exhibited in the analysis that follows, there is a disturbing irony in the role the RCCJ is playing in criminal justice system surveillance. The RCCJ was established as an official response to the worst imaginable denials of suspects' rights. In addition, the RCCJ research studies provide a wealth of systematic evidence that arrangements ostensibly in place for the protection of suspects typically end up enhancing the ability of the police to make a case as they see fit. However, in spite of the RCCJ's mandate and research evidence, it makes recommendations that will systematically strengthen the tendencies it was supposed to guard against!

On the one hand it is diabolical that a Royal Commission established as a response to tragic miscarriages of justice, and that offers superb empirical evidence on how injustice is embedded in structural arrangements for surveillance efficiency, ends up making recommendations that undercut suspects' rights and enhance system rights. On the other hand this outcome is predictable in a risk society driven by demands for more certain knowledge useful in the efficient risk management of suspect populations.

II KNOWLEDGE, POWER AND SURVEILLANCE OF SUSPECTS

1. The Five Knowledges of Criminal Justice System Surveillance

The RCCJ is concerned with five basic types of knowledge used in criminal justice system surveillance. *Legal knowledge* is how to make one's case by using legal rules and organisation to control knowledge about the case. *Scientific knowledge* is how to access, interpret and use forensic expertise to make a case. *Electronic knowledge* is how to produce case relevant video- and audio-tapes of criminal justice system activities. *Information system knowledge* is how to classify and present system-relevant knowledge in standardised formats. *Craft knowledge* is practical, common-sense reasoning special to each of the occupational cultures in criminal justice (police, prosecutors, defence lawyers, forensic scientists, judges etc.): it bears *double entendre*, for it refers not only to the special occupational skills that make a particular vocation a craft, but also to the 'craftiness' of practitioners in controlling knowledge to make a case as they see fit.

The RCCJ research reports document with respect to each type of knowledge that power is embedded in the system itself. Both suspects and criminal justice agents are left with little autonomy. The RCCJ Report offers reform solutions that substantially augment this institutionalisation of knowledge and power in the system, leaving both suspects and criminal justice agents with even less room to manoeuvre.

2. Legal Knowledge

a. The legal knowledge system
In principle, the police start from a legally disadvantaged position in the face of the suspect's right to silence. The two rules of law regarding the right to silence are: 1) 'no person, including the suspect, may be required to give information to the police in the course of a criminal investigation';

and, 2) 'a person charged with a criminal offence cannot be required to give evidence in court at any stage of criminal proceedings' (Leng 1993:1). However, this right is all but extinguished by legal knowledge resources provided to the police.

The system advantage begins with the legal use of arrest to produce knowledge of suspicion, as opposed to suspicion being used as the basis for making arrests.

> [C]itizens have moved from a position in which they were asked if they had *anything* to say, to one in which they may be held in detention until the police are satisfied that they have *nothing* left to say (Code C, para 16.1). Nothing could better symbolise the primacy given in policing to arrest over information-gathering, and the subversion of a 'right' to silence into a legal requirement to remain in police detention and interrogation until the police decide that no more can be wrung out of the arrestee. (McConville and Hodgson 1993:202; see also McBarnet 1981)

This development clearly flies in the face of the Royal Commission on Criminal Procedure (1983) and its translation into the Police and Criminal Evidence Act 1984, which was supposed to reduce reliance upon arrest. However, it comes as no surprise in the context of criminal justice system surveillance which consistently gives police the requisite legal resources to produce knowledge about citizens as it sees fit.

Suspects clearly suffer from a knowledge-deficit with respect to their rights. In research by Gudjonsson et al. (1993:17), only a minority of suspects said they read the 'Notice to Detainees' given to them, and only 1 per cent knew they had a right to access their custody record! Their main recollections about rights pertained to their ability to access third parties, who presumably might help them overcome their knowledge-deficit.

Suspects' access to expert knowledge in law is supposed to counteract the increased police powers that have evolved with criminal justice system surveillance. However, legal advisers themselves face a severe knowledge-deficit and they do little to overcome it. For example 'they fail to speak to custody officers in the overwhelming majority of cases ... the person in the custody sheet is almost never consulted ...[and] investigating officers manipulate case-related information by withholding it altogether, releasing it selectively, or using it to undermine the suspect's reliance upon the adviser or the adviser's faith in the suspect' (McConville and Hodgson 1993:192–3). Furthermore, following the Legal Advice and Assistance Regulations (1989), a solicitor can delegate the task of attending a police interrogation to a non-qualified representative in her employ, and most suspects are seen by such representatives. These representatives not only lack training in police station advisory work, they are rarely briefed adequately or subject to close supervision by solicitors. In consequence, 'far from such individuals counteracting excessive police power, many of them, because of their lack of expertise, training and confidence or because of their 'law and order" ideologies, actually add to the imbalance of power against the suspect' (ibid.).

Several research studies document that legal advice to suspects at the police station, whether given by qualified solicitors or their non-qualified representatives, does little or nothing for the suspect but often facilitates policework. Evans (1993a) found that solicitors called to offer expert knowledge to juveniles made a positive contribution in only 1/18 cases, and sometimes provided knowledge or assistance that helped the police turn their suspect into an accused person. Solicitors representing adults in police custody at best see themselves as referees rather than as adversaries, and as often as not they help the police, even to the point of serving as interrogators (Baldwin 1993c; see also Baldwin 1993d)!

Legal advisers are structurally-backed in this role by the Law Society, which directs them to help their clients in police custody 'without obstructing the interview,' and to engage in 'mutual cooperation' with police (Baldwin 1993c:35–6). These directives are followed dutifully, so that in the vast majority of cases legal advisers not only fail to invoke the right to silence, they advise or assume the suspect will answer police questions (McConville and Hodgson 1993:Ch. 5). In keeping with the thesis that criminal justice system surveillance is structured to facilitate police knowledge work, McConville and Hodgson (ibid.:201) observe that 'police station advice ... has been effectively redefined by solicitors in essentially non-adversarial terms, as at best carrying out an administrative 'watching brief' over police interrogations and hardly involving advocacy on behalf of the client at all'.

In criminal justice system surveillance defence lawyers help the police to produce legal knowledge within a Holiday Inn-style 'no surprises' format. Only a tiny fraction of cases proceed to contested trial. Among cases that do proceed, 76 per cent involve defences already fully expressed at the police interview stage, and only 5 per cent involve 'ambush defences' (Leng 1993). Defence lawyers collaborate with the police in turning their clients' right to silence from being a means to protect a vulnerable population against self-incrimination into being a means to protect the system from unreliable knowledge provided by that population. In the light of this conversion of a suspect's right into a system right, the fifty million pounds per annum spent on legal aid to support legal advice to suspects in police custody should perhaps be added to the police side of the criminal justice expenditure ledger, swelling further the 79 per cent market share they have already (cf. McConville and Hodgson 1993:200; RCCJ 1993:5).

The knowledge structure disadvantage of suspects goes well beyond the way in which legal advice is made available to them. The law turns in the peculiar twist that if the suspect has the support of a solicitor during the police interview, this places the parties on even terms. We have already seen that this proposition is fallacious. Nevertheless, it has serious legal knowledge consequences. Without a legal adviser, the suspect who remains silent cannot have the record of interrogation put in evidence; and, if he/she answers selectively, only answered questions can be put in evidence. However, the suspect who has a legal adviser and who answers questions selectively is subject to having the whole of the statement made admissible, not only those aspects where he/she gave an answer. The suspect's reactions to unanswered questions are admissible, and the tribunal of fact can draw adverse inferences from the failure to answer some questions. The law ostensibly gives the suspect access to legal advice as a means of empowerment, then disempowers him/her by allowing adverse inferences to be drawn from his/her every gesture, utterance or silence.

There are additional rewards and sanctions to ensure that silence is rarely maintained, and that confessions and guilty pleas are routinely forthcoming. The main currency offered for suspects' knowledge is leniency in charges and sentences, but the offers often involve consequences that would probably not have followed if the deal was refused. The police play on suspects' ignorance and fear in believing that options are real (Maguire and Norris 1993:90–91). In any case, suspects and their lawyers are usually wise in deciding to confess and plead guilty. Accused persons who elect to be tried at Crown Court are acquitted in only a tiny fraction of cases, and are much more likely to receive custodial sentences and longer periods of custody than if they had remained at the magistrates' court level (Hedderman and Moxon 1992). Most end up pleading guilty in Crown Court anyway (ibid.), which is probably wise given the prevailing 25–30 per cent sentence discount for guilty pleas in Crown Court (RCCJ 1993:110).

Given this panoply of mechanisms to eliminate silence, it no longer seems reasonable to refer to the suspect's right to silence. It is more apt to think in terms of the system's right to legal knowledge of the suspect, a right that is almost never denied.

The Crown Prosecution Service (CPS) does not change the structure of legal knowledge. Except in occasional serious fraud cases (Levi 1993), the CPS does not participate in investigations. It only offers advice to police and helps to take selected cases to trial. Moreover, the police consult the CPS in only a tiny fraction of cases (Moxon and Crisp 1993; McConville 1993a:33), and then largely about the sufficiency of evidence and appropriate charges (RCCJ 1993:72; Baldwin and Moloney 1993:64). The CPS are not allowed to compel the police to make inquiries, and when they do make specific requests of the police they are sometimes rebuked. Relations between the police and CPS are such that there is sometimes specific 'failure to provide evidence when required' (Block, Corbett and Peay 1993:59; RCCJ 1993:74). Along with defence lawyers, CPS lawyers are a convenience to police, helping them to produce and format legal knowledge for criminal justice system surveillance.

In any event, confessions are just icing on the cake. There is no research evidence indicating that suspects who invoke the right to silence are less likely to be charged or less likely to be convicted (RCCJ 1993:53). Furthermore, it is rare for the police to rely upon the confession exclusively in making their case. 'In the vast majority of confession cases (86.6 per cent; n = 264) the confession was supported by admissible evidence from independent sources, such as a civilian witness, a police witness or forensic witness ... confessions are most likely to be made when the suspect is confronting an overwhelming case' (McConville 1993a). As we learn in subsequent sections, the system has other knowledges available to augment its powers of surveillance.

b. Legal knowledge reform

The RCCJ's legal knowledge reforms enhance system rights to ensure that criminal justice is even more summary.

Greater rights to knowledge production are recommended. For example, it is recommended that the Criminal Justice Act 1987 Section 2 powers that *require* suspects in serious fraud investigations to answer the questions of investigators should be extended to police (RCCJ 1993:23). The RCCJ also recommends extension of the ability of the police to question accused persons after charging them (ibid.:17). While the police are thereby encouraged to cast their nets more widely, this is not in the interest of corroboration of confessions. The majority of Commissioners counsel against a corroboration rule even though their own research documents that corroboration is already the rule in practice (McConville 1993a). Not surprisingly they also fail to see the value of an exclusionary rule.

While the police are directed to fish with trawlers, the defence is left with only hook, line and sinker. Defence searches for knowledge are to be curtailed. For example, 'The defence must not feel free to conduct a 'fishing expedition" through large masses of material simply in the hope that something may turn up which will embarrass or obstruct the prosecution ...' (RCCJ 1993:85; see also 92ff.). The Commissioners recommend against a scheme for solicitors to be regularly present at police stations, even though research indicates there would be much greater demand from suspects for legal advice if such a scheme existed (ibid.:37). They also recommend against a rule that a confession is inadmissible if it is not made or at least confirmed in the presence of a solicitor (ibid.:62).

CPS lawyers are also to be excluded from closer scrutiny of police knowledge production. CPS lawyers are to remain as legal experts and advisers to the police, to be called upon occasionally when the police are having particular legal difficulty in making their case (ibid.:71–2).

Recommendations for more defence disclosure and less police disclosure are also made regarding pre-trial processes. For example, it is recommended that defendants be required to disclose the substance of their defence once the prosecution case is disclosed (ibid.:84ff.). To ensure that compliance is forthcoming, it is recommended that adverse comment by the prosecution and direction by the judge be permitted if the defendant introduces at trial a defence not previously disclosed. The Commissioners intend to force disclosure and eradicate ambush defences (ibid.:84), even though their research evidence shows that such defences are very rare indeed (Leng 1993). The Commissioners take advanced defence disclosure in major fraud cases even more seriously. They propose that reluctant defendants be charged with Contempt of Court which 'would allow the court to deal summarily with defendants by imposing a short term of imprisonment from which we would expect them to be released once the requisite cooperation was forthcoming' (RCCJ 1993:115).

While advocating more system rights to force defence disclosure, the Commissioners believe that police and prosecution should disclose less in some areas. They frown upon Mr Justice Henry's ruling in the trial of Saunders and others, which extended the police duty to disclose. They also comment negatively upon what they see as an exacerbation of that extension by the Court of Appeal's judgment in *Ward* (ibid.:92ff.). Their concern is the potential these decisions create for the defence to cause delay or to find something – such as the prosecutor's desire to protect witnesses or informants – that might induce the prosecution to drop the case.

The Commissioners also argue against prosecution disclosure to the defence of adverse findings in disciplinary proceedings against a police officer. The only exception is when those records are relevant to an allegation by the defence about the officer's conduct in the present case. They also state that there should not be disclosure of the fact that a police officer's evidence in a previous case was disbelieved by the jury, resulting in an acquittal (ibid.: 97).

Following the recommendations of Block, Corbett and Peay (1993), the Commissioners urge abolition of committal proceedings and the termination of the accused's right to elect trial in Crown Court in either-way cases. In the latter cases magistrates would decide venue where the defence and prosecution cannot agree. '[D]efendants would no longer have the right to insist, as they do now in over 35,000 cases a year, contrary to the views of magistrates, that their cases should be heard in the Crown Court' (RCCJ 1993:87). Contrary to assumptions of distrust that permeate their Report otherwise, the Commissioners justify this denial of an existing right to a fairer and potentially more advantageous hearing by asking accused persons to trust established practices.

> We do not think that defendants should be able to choose their court of trial solely on the basis that they think they will get a fairer hearing at one level than the other. Magistrates' courts conduct over 93 per cent of all criminal cases and should be trusted to try cases fairly .... Nor in our view should defendants be entitled to choose the mode of trial which they think will offer them a better chance of acquittal. (ibid.:88)

Summary justice is also fostered by recommendations that encourage guilty plea settlements. In order to overcome 'cracked trials' and other problems of efficiency, the RCCJ recommends graduated sentence discounts; the earlier the guilty plea is entered the greater the discount (ibid.:111–12). In white-collar crime cases, regulatory agencies are to be involved in plea-bargaining, helping to structure legal arrangements so that the defendant will agree to a regulatory penalty in exchange for reducing the criminal charge or terminating the criminal prosecution (ibid.:116).

Appeals are to be made even more unappealing. The RCCJ does not recommend any change in the power of the Court of Appeal to order that all or part of the time spent in custody pending the outcome of the appeal should be counted as part of the appellant's sentence. The only recommendation is that the knowledge of this power should be communicated more clearly to prospective appellants! The retention of this power is justified by the perceived need to discourage appeals that have no merit, and by pointing out that it is at least 'a weaker sanction than the Crown Court's power to increase sentence in appeals from the magistrates' courts' (ibid.:167).

While the RCCJ is otherwise obsessed with procedural regularity and technical efficiency, any irregularities or inefficiencies in pre-trial or trial processes are not to be grounds for appeal. The majority opinion is that a person who is 'clearly guilty' should not be 'accorded a retrial merely because there has been some error at trial,' and there is unanimous opinion that 'appellants should not be able to exploit purely technical irregularities in the conduct of the trial' (ibid.:170). Similarly the majority contend that pre-trial malpractice should not be grounds for quashing a conviction unless the Court thinks the confession may be unsafe (ibid.:172).

3. Scientific Knowledge

a. The scientific knowledge system

Forensic science could be mobilised in almost every criminal case. In practice, for reasons of economy it is used sparingly. It is most likely to be used in serious cases in which the police decide to prosecute but lack a confession from the accused and statements from the victim or other witnesses (Roberts and Willmore 1993). Thus forensic evidence becomes especially important in contested cases at the Crown Court, and is estimated to play a role in 30–40 per cent of such cases (Zander and Henderson 1993).

Used selectively and strategically for the big case, forensic science is clearly structured as a police knowledge resource. The leading forensic experts are usually employed in public sector laboratories most accessible to police. Defence counsel can now hire an expert employed by a Forensic Science Service (FSS) laboratory. However, they cannot hire an expert in the particular laboratory that is advising the police on the case. Furthermore, most defence counsel are one-shot or occasional participants in Crown Court contested trials. As such they typically experience great difficulty in ascertaining what type of expertise is required, who can best provide it, and who can be trusted to sustain their obligations (Roberts and Willmore 1993; Steventon 1993). In locating and mobilising forensic expertise the prosecution has close relationships with the FSS and MPFS labs, and the luxury of having the lab experts themselves judge who among them is best qualified to help the police make their case (Roberts and Willmore 1993:23). Even when they turn to private defence experts, defence lawyers cannot escape the hegemony of the FSS laboratory structure. Many private experts are former FSS employees with personal and professional links to FSS personnel and a tendency to take a collaborative approach with the prosecution that can entail disclosure harmful to the defence (ibid.:108ff.).

The defence is disadvantaged in other ways. Legal aid is usually inadequate for hiring defence experts. Defence experts 'go second', meaning that they have access to physical evidence samples and exhibits only after those objects have been selected and analysed by experts working for the police. In the majority of DNA analyses, there is not a sufficient crime scene sample left over after the police expert examination to allow an adequate defence expert examination (Steventon 1993:5–6). If a sample is available, defence experts are required to conduct their work at FSS laboratories using FSS equipment (Roberts and Willmore 1993:86–7). Most of them do not bother but simply interpret the tests produced by the prosecution for the FSS. This knowledge structure disadvantage obviously voids independent assessment (Steventon 1993:41). While defence lawyers are entitled to full disclosure of forensic science evidence from the prosecution, the onus is on them to pursue forensic science evidence which the prosecution has but does not intend to use (Roberts and Willmore 1993:69), and they are occasionally denied access to exact materials because of commercial and copyright restrictions (Steventon 1993:44).

Given their highly selective mobilisation of forensic expertise when other forms of knowledge are unavailable, it is not surprising to learn that the police use the FSS 'to inculpate a suspect, requesting the FSS to confirm or refute an investigative hypothesis which they have already formulated. Potentially exculpatory lines of scientific inquiry may be neither requested nor pursued' (Roberts and Willmore 1993:136; also Ramsay 1988:Ch. 2). Of course this approach is not peculiar to police use of forensic scientific evidence. It is consistent with the way the police generally construe and construct facts to make their cases (Ericson 1993; Miyazawa 1992).

Roberts and Willmore (1993) indicate that the police in effect convert the FSS into their way of producing and formatting knowledge. The police sometimes try to influence the expert report by asking for a definitive opinion, for weight to certain findings, and/or for re-writes (ibid.:48). Scientists are converted from the pursuit of scientific truth through open collaboration and publication into the pursuit of legal truth through selective accounts, rhetorical flourishes and courtroom clashes. Forensic *performance* (Carson 1990; Nelken 1987) takes over, and forensic reports thereby become 'highly selective documents which reflect the scientist's structural position within the justice process, the functions which the report is required to discharge, the organisational and institutional arrangements designed to achieve these goals, and the scientist's personal preferences and stylistic idiosyncrasies' (Roberts and Willmore 1993:42).

Even police surgeons who are called to tend to the therapeutic needs of persons in police custody end up having the knowledge they produce converted to police forensic surveillance needs. Regardless of the purpose of the doctor's visit to the police station, his/her knowledge may be made available to the police and courts for forensic purposes (Robertson 1993:35; in the case of forensic psychiatry, see Menzies 1989).

b. Scientific knowledge reform

The RCCJ Commissioners are explicit in asserting that the forensic science knowledge system is in place to bolster the police and prosecution. The system is so iron-clad in this regard that all reforms will end up perpetuating the scientific knowledge/power advantage of the police and prosecution. 'Whatever reorganisation were to be effected, it seems to us unrealistic to suppose that it would remove the laboratories concerned from identification with the police and prosecution. However forensic science is organised, its results will be used, as they always have been, in support of police investigations and the prosecution case' (RCCJ 1993:147).

The Commissioners are equally explicit in making recommendations that significantly enhance police and prosecutorial scientific powers. For example, in keeping with their 'no surprises' formula for surveillance system efficiency, the Commissioners advocate scientific fact-bargaining sessions akin to plea-bargaining. Where the defence is calling its own expert evidence, there should be a meeting of expert witnesses on both sides to settle their difficulties and get the facts straight. Where the defence is not calling its own expert but wishes to challenge the prosecution's expert, the basis of the challenge must be disclosed early in order to allow the prosecution time to settle the difference and get its facts straight (ibid.:158).

The Commissioners are even more forceful in their recommendations regarding system rights to knowledge about suspects that might serve the ends of science. Where changing scientific knowledge needs require it, the police should be able to remove forcefully from the suspect's body samples of plucked hair, saliva etc. Here justice is *totally* equated with system surveillance needs: 'Given that plucked hair samples may increasingly be capable of providing DNA evidence, we recommend that *in the interests of justice* power to take a sample of hair, other than pubic hair, without consent should extend to hair that is plucked as much as to hair that is cut' (ibid.:14, emphasis added). In order to enhance police power to pluck scientifically useful knowledge from the suspect, the Commissioners recommend the reclassification of assault, burglary and other arrestable offences as being eligible for sample-taking without consent.

Treating the suspect's body as an object of knowledge is deemed just even when DNA evidence is considered irrelevant to settling the particular case! The reason for recommending this particular system right is the apparent value of DNA records in linking convicted criminals to offences and in profiling evidence for scientific purposes. If the person is convicted, DNA samples and data would be retained; if the person is not convicted, the material would still be retained for database purposes by an independent body (ibid.:14). Here the police are constructed as scientific research associates with the power of legitimate force to collect data! While science conducted in universities and other settings is subject to ethical review and guidelines on the use of human subjects, in this scenario humans will be compelled to give up items from their bodies even if the search and seizure is known to be irrelevant to the particular investigation.

Such explicit recommendations for system rights to scientific knowledge led the RCCJ to recognise that it is proposing a shift towards an inquisitorial system. At least as visualised by the Commissioners, the inquisitorial system is a surveillance system. Justice is system rights to efficient knowledge production, and adversarialism is a risk to these rights that must be overcome. 'In ... our approach to forensic science evidence, our recommendations can fairly be interpreted as seeking to move the system in an inquisitorial direction, or at least as seeking to minimise the danger of adversarial practices being taken too far .... We have been guided throughout by practical considerations ... of both justice and efficiency' (ibid.:3)

4. Electronic Knowledge

a. The electronic knowledge system
The Commissioners also embrace electronic means of knowledge production with great enthusiasm. There are two reasons why these technologies are viewed so favourably and invested in so heavily. As we learn in this section, they are a useful means through which the police can refine their surveillance of suspect populations. As we learn in Part III, electronic media also allow the simultaneous surveillance of police officers' activity. In the very moment of using these technologies to conduct surveillance of others, the police create knowledge about their own activities that gives others the capacity to monitor them.

There is no doubt that video-taping and audio-taping have a substantial impact on how the police think, act and organise their work (McConville 1992; Baldwin 1993b, 1993c, 1993d). However, there is only limited use of these electronic records by outside parties to monitor police conduct. For example Baldwin (1993d) reports that audio-taped records of interviews between police and suspects are rarely obtained by solicitors for independent scrutiny. Rather than taking the time to obtain and listen to the entire tape, solicitors rely on written summaries of the tapes produced by the police. These summaries are produced through a 'prosecution prism', being highly selective in favour of the outcome the police judge most suitable.

In the light of the minimal use of these electronic records to directly monitor or challenge police investigators, it is not surprising that the police are favourably disposed towards their use and much more so than defence solicitors (RCCJ 1993:40). The police are enthusiastic because they know that these electronic media are in their hands. They are the criminal justice media producers in the same way that journalists are news media producers (Ericson, Baranek and Chan 1987, 1989; Carriere and Ericson 1989; Schlesinger, Tumber and Murdoch 1991). Just as no one would contend that television or radio news mirrors reality, so it is that police video and audio productions do not mirror reality but are subject to myriad back-stage preparations and negotiations, and front-stage dramatic techniques. The document produced is not a reflection of reality, but rather reflects the cultural and social organisation of policework and the media format characteristics that allow the police to make certain knowledge public.

While the police are obviously aware of their role as electronic media producers, the RCCJ underplays this aspect of police knowledge production. At various points the RCCJ seems to subscribe to a mirror-of-reality hypothesis. For example Baldwin's research is referred to as follows.

[A]nyone is bound to be struck by how real and vivid are the interviews on audio tape ... his project ... constituted a very efficient way of finding out *exactly* how interviews with suspects were being conducted ... [and] enabled a third party to make a confident assessment of the fairness or otherwise of almost any interview'. (RCCJ 1993:39, emphasis added)

When the RCCJ tempers its enthusiasm about the development and extension of audio- and video-recording, it is only in terms of a view that such records cannot be relied upon entirely because they are subject to technical failure, tampering and mis-reading by audiences (ibid.:26). Again, what is missed in this mirror-of-reality view is the role of the police, and of the media formats in which they work, in creating the realities their audiences come to see.

In spite of the prevalence of the mirror-of-reality view in the RCCJ reports, sporadic evidence does indicate that electronic knowledge in criminal justice system surveillance is a police production. Like journalists, the police do off-the-record preparation of their 'sources' to ensure the production quality of what appears on the record (Moston and Stephenson 1993; RCCJ 1993:27). Also like journalists (Ericson, Baranek and Chan 1987, 1989) the police use trickery and deceit to get on the record that which they know their sources would like to keep confidential. For example, in Baldwin's research there were 'three instances in which private exchanges between solicitors and suspects were video-recorded despite the officer assuring both parties that the cameras had been turned off' (RCCJ 1993:12).

Properly staged, electronic media records of police–suspect transactions greatly enhance police knowledge and power. 'The introduction of tape and video records has left the police free to monitor suspects' behaviour for perceived non-verbal cues of guilt. These attempts at identifying 'lie signs" are of dubious value and increase both the accusatory atmosphere of interrogation and the likelihood of suggestible suspects making statements which comply with the wishes of interrogators' (McConville 1993a:194). Far from being of 'dubious value', these cues and signs can be used directly against an accused. As noted previously (pp. 120–1), the suspect who has a legal adviser is deemed to be on equal terms with the police; therefore, when he/she answers questions selectively he/she is subject to having the whole of the statement made admissible in evidence against him/her including non-verbal reactions to unanswered questions. Again it is not surprising that it is the police more than defence lawyers who are most supportive of the routine use of electronic media in transactions with suspects.

b. Electronic knowledge reform

Given both their mirror-of-reality view of electronic media, and strong police support for the use of those media, the RCCJ recommends expansion of system rights regarding electronic knowledge production. The Commissioners urge that, where technologically practical, audio and video recording of transactions with suspects should be extended to all contexts, including for example the period when the suspect is being driven to the police station (RCCJ 1993:26ff.). This raises interesting puzzles about who is a suspect and about the limits to suspicion. For example, one context of police interrogation is the suspect's residence during search and seizure operations (Ericson 1993). Are camera crews to be directed to interrogation contexts such as searches?

Beyond persons under reasonable suspicion of having committed criminal offences are those who are merely offensive, or potentially so. The RCCJ endorses electronic media system surveillance rights over all members of the population who are or might be out of order.

> The police service themselves place great emphasis on equipment which helps them keep suspected criminals under surveillance, including closed circuit television and video recording cameras in public places such as football grounds and shopping centres. We strongly support the use of such devices, whose potential contribution to bringing offenders to justice has already proved its worth. (RCCJ 1993:18)

Meanwhile, back in the police station, the RCCJ recommends annual expenditure of £9 million to ensure continuous video recording of all activities in and around the custody office, and of all passages up to and including the doors of individual cells. System surveillance rights are asserted: 'We see no case for enabling suspects to avoid being filmed; the procedure is for their own protection .... Suspects should be made aware that the camera is on, although failure to do so should not be a breach of PACE or the codes' (ibid.:34). Some Commissioners urge video-recording of all police–suspect transactions, based on the mirror-of-reality argument that the camera reveals more than the tape-recorder (ibid.:40). All Commissioners agree that there should be colour still photographs or video records of all identification parades, regardless of whether the suspect has a friend or solicitor present.

The Commissioners seem to have revised an old adage in the light of the television age: they think that believing is seeing. They believe that criminal justice system surveillance rights should be asserted to enhance the system's vision.

5. Information System Knowledge

a. The information system
The RCCJ documents that criminal justice information systems are under perpetual development and expansion, on the promise of ever more certain knowledge (see generally Ackroyd et al. 1992; Manning 1992a; Ericson and Shearing 1986; Ericson, Haggerty and Carriere 1993; Ericson 1994). For example, the HOLMES system for major investigations is described as providing 'an entire record of the investigation' through 'a set of standardised procedures ... which govern the input, processing and accessing of data, the allocation of work and the review of information within the system' (Maguire and Norris 1993:57, 68). Information systems devised to meet special surveillance needs are also described. The following description of a 'prostitute squad' nicely illustrates the role of police information systems in both enhancing surveillance of suspect populations and framing how police officers classify and act in relation to those populations.

[The squad] of over 40 detectives ... [was] established to trace and interview 300 prostitutes who worked in a particular locality. A database was compiled from all existing police sources and a questionnaire devised to be administered to all known prostitutes. The aim of the questionnaire was to determine any knowledge of the victim, full details of each woman's whereabouts at the time of the murder, whether they had been to the victim's house, and so on. Each prostitute interviewed had a detailed PDF filled in on her. In addition all prostitutes found on the street were questioned to ensure that their names were included on the list. It is important to note that such inquiry teams have clear terms of reference and standardised procedures ... [they are] akin to piece workers, operating within fixed parameters and with limited discretion. (ibid.:60)

All areas of policework are subject to tightening communication formats which de-skill police labour into 'piece work'. For example, witness statements are 'designed ... to establish certain evidential points necessary to meet the technical requirements of proving guilt of a particular criminal offence' (ibid. 50). A package that includes a 55-page 'Guide to Interviewing' and a 28-page 'The Interviewer's Rule Book' offers a standardised format for interviewing suspects. Police interviews with suspects are also formatted in terms of the detailed 'Notice to Detained Persons' (Clare and Gudjonsson 1993). Tape-recorded interviews with suspects are summarised on a standard form; this knowledge work alone is said to absorb approximately 1 per cent of the entire police force establishment, the full-time equivalent of 1,300 to 1,500 police officers (RCCJ 1993)!

Expert knowledge used by police in making cases is also subject to tighter information system formatting. For example, Administrative or Operational Support Unit officers specialise in packaging the detective's case file for submission to the CPS (Maguire and Norris 1993:36). New formats and writing conventions for the FSS have been introduced, streamlining further a process in which it is mainly the 'expert's black and white report' rather than his/her 'shades of grey' courtroom testimony that is relied upon (Roberts and Willmore 1993:121).

b. Information system reform

The RCCJ prescribes various types of information system reform. There are recommendations for additional technological hardware, such as computer terminals for all investigators who make use of HOLMES (RCCJ 1993:19). There are recommendations for the development and implementation of computer and paper formats that will further standardise and tighten the classification system. For example, there is a need for a national standard to 'prescribe the minimum acceptable form and layout of all custody records' because 'some of the forms which we observed in use were not as clear in design and appearance as they might be [and] the forms also vary from force to force in ways which seem inconsistent with the need to observe rules that are of national application' (ibid.:32–3).

In some instances the proposed reforms are designed to facilitate system rights to information from the defence. For example, it is proposed that new requirements for disclosure by the defence could be facilitated by a standardised form that is simply checked off by the defendant's solicitor. 'Standard forms could be drawn up to cover the most common defences, such as 'accident', 'self-defence', 'consent', 'no dishonest intent', 'no appropriation', 'abandoned goods', 'claim of right', 'mistaken identification'' and so on. There will be complex cases which may require the assistance of counsel in formulating the defence' (ibid.:99). This is clear recognition of the fact that most defences are treated as routine and formulaic, reducible to a simple fixed-choice checklist.

The RCCJ also supports the development of information technologies that protect the system from suspects who are prone to offering troublesome information. For example, the research by Gudjonsson et al. (1993), entitled *Persons at Risk During Interviews in Police Custody: The Identification of Vulnerabilities*, is in part concerned with risks to criminal justice system surveillance caused by people with clinical problems. 'The characteristics studied are those that are considered relevant to the potential vulnerabilities of suspects to giving erroneous or misleading information to the police during interrogation' (ibid.:23). The researchers are in essence developing a risk assessment technology that might help give the system a cleaner record.

6. Craft Knowledge

a. The craft knowledge system
The RCCJ research reports make frequent reference to craft knowledge, especially as it is developed and used in police cultures. Craft knowledge is depicted as practical, common-sense knowledge learned on the job, filling in gaps where expert knowledge, systems and training are lacking (e.g. Baldwin and Moloney 1993:70). Typical of this view is McConville and Hodgson's (1993:197) observation that 'the overwhelming majority of officers are untrained and lacking in interviewing skills, and are forced instead to rely on crude techniques acquired from other long-serving officers or imported from their own common-sense understandings of how an interrogation works.'

Craft knowledge is improvisational. It is 'crafty knowledge' of the ways and means to get the job done (Irving and Dunningham 1993). It is not simply knowledge of how to interpret rules creatively, or how to make rules up to fit a situation, as is so often depicted in studies of police culture (e.g. Manning 1977; Punch 1985; Reiner 1992: Ch. 5). It is also figurative, making use of tropes to recall what was done in similar situations in the past as a referent for what might be done in the immediate case. The basis of craft knowledge is a 'vocabulary of precedents' (Ericson, Baranek and Chan 1987; Shearing and Ericson 1991) that allows the translation of legal, scientific, electronic and information system knowledges into the common sense of the particular occupational culture.

The fact that craft knowledge is improvisational does not mean that it lacks systemic qualities. It is the system of the occupational culture and the precedents for practical action of that culture. It produces its own forms of knowledge, its own truths, through its particular genre capacities and formats of presentation. For example, the truth produced using police craft knowledge involves constructing a case against an 'obviously' guilty person rather than searching for truth through the testing of alternative propositions (Maguire and Norris 1993; Evans 1993a; Roberts and Willmore 1993; McConville and Hodgson 1993; see also McConville et al. 1991). As such, craft knowledge is used to patrol the facts, to keep certain things secret and confidential and to make public only those things that will help the police to make their case.

b. Craft knowledge reform

While craft knowledge is crucial for efficient social organisation (Manning 1992b), it is under increasing administrative scrutiny and intervention in all social institutions because it is seen as too arbitrary (unsystematic) and as allowing members of the craft to escape accountability. The RCCJ is in keeping with this trend towards greater scrutiny of craft knowledge. While it seeks to enhance legal, scientific, electronic and information system knowledge, it recommends the curtailment of craft knowledge in many contexts. Moreover the attack on craft knowledge is to be effected through the refinement of legal, scientific, electronic and information system mechanisms.

Both individual research reports and the final Report stress the need to attack criminal justice occupational cultures and their craft knowledges. Police culture and knowledge in particular is singled out. For example Maguire and Norris (1993:109), under the heading 'Attacking the "culture"', advocate training young detectives to ensure that they will not be 'sucked into' the 'traditional "detective culture" ('macho" and "elitist" attitudes, the belief that 'rules are made to be bent", excessive secrecy and suspicion of outsiders, and so on)'. Similarly the Commissioners assert that the remedy for police malpractice 'lies in a better-trained, better-equipped and better-supervised police force, not in the tacit acceptance of procedural rule-bending' (RCCJ 1993:7) that is seen to be the essence of police craft knowledge and its 'Ways and Means Act'.

The RCCJ proposes an elaborate system for surveillance of its criminal justice agents aimed at limiting their craft knowledge. Characteristic of risk society (Giddens 1990, 1991), this surveillance is justified and promoted in terms of an assumption of distrust. Typical is Baldwin's (1993d:23) recommendation that both CPS and defence lawyers listen to police tape-recorded interviews with suspects rather than rely upon police written summaries of those interviews because it is 'the only way of avoiding the high risk strategy of taking the records of interview on trust – and the odds at present are greatly inferior to those that apply in Russian Roulette'. Similarly, Maguire and Norris (1993:115) advocate system rights to independent random checks on detective investigative activity by pointing to trusting relations between detectives and their supervisors as being *the* problem: 'Trust ... is a weak guarantee of compliance and, given that trust is largely a private contract, is open to abuse. To overcome this problem, we suggest that a system of 'quality control' is required, whereby integrity can be demonstrated rather than assumed'.

The *demonstration* of integrity requires surveillance mechanisms that monitor criminal justice agents routinely and systematically. We now turn to how the RCCJ proposes to effect this monitoring.

III KNOWLEDGE, POWER AND SURVEILLANCE OF CRIMINAL JUSTICE AGENTS

1. Monitoring Criminal Justice Agents

a. Police

Traditionally police supervision has been personal and retrospective,with an emphasis upon the *appearance* of complete investigations (Punch (ed.) 1983). '[T]he focus of supervisory attention has largely been concentrated upon the *product* of policework rather than the activity itself: in a nutshell, the first priority has been to ensure that 'the paperwork is right' (Maguire and Norris 1993). However, police supervision is changing rapidly, and the RCCJ recommendations clearly reflect the change. Supervision is increasingly *prospective* because it is built into information systems and technologies. The computer and reporting formats for presentation of police knowledge provide classifications that fundamentally influence how the police think and act. Supervision is prospectively embedded in the formats rather than retrospectively in supervisors' checks of filed reports.

A number of RCCJ recommendations provide for instant monitoring of police. For example, the recommended computerisation of the custody record process includes a monitoring component: 'The risk of falsification may be further reduced if the computer has an integral time clock and a print-out can be made of the record at the time the entries are made. The print-out can be given immediate verification by the suspect's signature at the time' (RCCJ 1993:33). Tampering with evidence recorded in police officers' notebooks is to be dealt with by only issuing notebooks that contain fixed pages numbered sequentially (ibid.:22). There are to be new standards and auditing procedures aimed at offering prospective '*guarantees* that records are properly kept [and] mistakes so far as possible detected' (ibid.:9, see also 153). Where technology is not enough, the RCCJ stresses that supervisors must be put in place to guide investigations prospectively. For example Maguire and Norris (1993:112) recommend that 'best practice' in major inquiries should include

the principle that interviews should be conducted by someone other than the Senior Investigating Officer; the appointment of an independent 'PACE Officer' (rather like an *ad hoc* custody officer, but with a wider brief) to oversee and advise upon procedural correctness; regular and thorough reviews of the state of long-running investigations, preferably by a senior officer from another force, as well as a careful de-briefing at the end; and encouragement of advice from the CPS once a clear suspect has emerged.

Knowledge of occupational deviance is always elusive. Therefore the RCCJ recommends whistle-blower protections for police employees who act as informants, and communication lines that facilitate their capacity to inform on fellow employees.

There is a real risk that police officers and the civilian staff employed by police forces may be deterred by the prevailing culture from complaining openly about malpractice. We are strongly of the view that they should be able to voice their concerns without fear of reprisal, whether open or covert. We recommend accordingly that all forces should put in place, if they have not already done so, a 'helpline' scheme ... in addition, since some officers may be reluctant to report alleged misconduct to someone in the same force, it should be possible to make such reports, on a wholly confidential basis, direct to the Inspectorate. This might in turn lead to a specific audit by the Inspectorate of an ongoing investigation. (RCCJ 1993:22)

In keeping with the demise of suspects' rights and the rise of system rights, the RCCJ proposes new legislation to deal with police wrongdoers. The proposals include the recommendations that a police officer acquitted in the criminal court should still be subject to disciplinary proceedings on the same facts, and the disciplinary tribunal should have the power of dismissing the officer from the force; hearings should be even less formal and more summary than criminal proceedings, including a lower standard of proof; and, in a civil suit against a police authority resulting from alleged malpractice of a police officer, that officer should be eligible for disciplinary proceedings notwithstanding the pending civil proceedings (ibid.:48). In other words, the RCCJ proposes to add the double jeopardy of disciplinary proceedings to criminal or civil proceedings, and to have less due process in the disciplinary proceedings.

The risks of police deviance are also to be profiled systematically. Thus the Commissioners recommend a national system of data on police disciplinary matters, including breaches of PACE (ibid.).

b. Other criminal justice agents

While RCCJ recommendations for monitoring criminal justice agents are mainly directed at police, there is considerable attention to other agents. Again the concern is the efficiency of these agents' surveillance mechanisms as they articulate with the needs of criminal justice system surveillance.

Lawyers for both the defence and prosecution are to participate in a new format for pre-trial reviews (RCCJ 1993:102ff.). This format includes new forms for declaring guilty or not guilty pleas, for disclosure, and for giving notice regarding preparatory hearings, all of which are subject to time restriction. While it is assumed that these new formats will have a supervisory influence on lawyers – ensuring that they will make timely presentations of their cases – disciplinary mechanisms are recommended just in case they do not comply. Failure to complete the necessary forms properly or on time, or requests for preparatory hearings that are deemed frivolous, are to be subject to 'comment by the court, to cost sanctions and, if necessary, to disciplinary action by the Bar Council' (ibid.:106).

The Bar Council is also urged to extend its reach into chambers by establishing rules of conduct that require briefs to be read or reassigned within a specified time. This regulation of the internal management systems in chambers is recommended in the name of speed and efficiency as core values in criminal justice system surveillance. The system has for too long been 'wedded to delay and to the last-minute preparation of cases' (ibid.:109), whether caused by poor management of lawyers' work or too much of an emphasis on using delay strategically to protect the interests of accused persons. The system should now reward surveillance efficiency, and sanction those lawyers who impede it.

We can see no reason for lawyers refusing to do the work necessary to ensure that the system operates as effectively and efficiently as possible, *whatever grounds* there may be for seeking more time to prepare in any individual case. The judge should have a range of sanctions against poor performance or limited cooperation ... [including] a report from the judge on the competence of the lawyer to the taxing officer dealing with his or her fees; or a report to the barrister's head of chambers or to the leader of the circuit or to the Bar Council; or a wasted costs order. (ibid.: emphasis added)

Above specific new forms, and disciplinary procedures for ensuring the efficient production of knowledge by lawyers, the RCCJ urges general mechanisms of surveillance. For example the Law Society should use its 'research unit' to look into 'such questions as consumer satisfaction, efficiency and operational problems in the system' (ibid.:139).

Forensic scientists also require monitoring of their monitoring procedures. It is recommended that a Forensic Science Advisory Council (FSAC) should be established 'to keep under continuing review the performance and efficiency of forensic science provision' (ibid.:144ff.). The word 'Advisory' should perhaps be replaced by 'Regulatory' or even 'Disciplinary,' since the call is for external inspection and assessment of forensic science work and reporting to the Home Secretary on 'the performance and standards of ... [police in-house] laboratories as well as the large public sector laboratories and the firms and experts in the private sector' (ibid.: 151). Indeed, in spite of acknowledged difficulties in establishing an enforceable code of conduct regarding forensic science work, the RCCJ nevertheless recommends codification and suggests the possibility that the FSAC be given regulatory powers (ibid.).

The RCCJ envisages a changing role for judges. At least in more complex cases, judges are to be given responsibilities as case managers, aided by court administrators and new computer systems such as CREST (ibid.:142). Far from being only impartial umpires in an adversarial justice system, judges are to become partial managers of an efficient surveillance system. 'Our recommendations will require a more informed and decisive control of trials by judges and their training and performance in this enhanced role must be regarded as essential matters' (ibid.:137). Naturally, the judge-as-case-manager must also be monitored. Towards this end it is recommended that presiding and resident judges serve as monitoring agents. They should 'attend trials so that they can assess the performance of judges in their courts. Alternatively or additionally, recently retired judges could fulfil this function' (ibid.:141). These monitors would also collaborate with the Bar in establishing systematic opinion surveys of members of the Bar regarding the performance of judges (ibid.). However, unlike other criminal justice agents who are to have their peculiarities and wrongdoings widely know, judges will keep the knowledge gained to themselves. The monitors 'findings should be made known to the judge being assessed and possibly to the presiding judge. The findings should be kept within the judiciary, in order not to put at risk their independence' (ibid.).

Legal Aid Officers (LAO's) in prisons are also to be monitored regarding their monitoring capacities. An entire research study (Plotnikoff and Woolfson 1993) is devoted to documenting the shoddy performance of

LAO's in the past and recommending surveillance mechanisms to regulate their conduct. Indeed the language, emphases and recommendations of this study exemplify the RCCJ's thrust towards more surveillance of criminal justice agents. For example, it is recommended that 'controls should be introduced to regulate the performance of LAOs. Terms of reference should be drawn up and procedural standards produced ... these should be kept under continuous review. Line management responsibility should be identified and performance of LAOs should be monitored and evaluated' (ibid.:123). Control should also come from within. Therefore it is recommended that LAOs should have formal re-socialisation in 'i. communication skills, ii. coping with the problems of inmates with special needs, iii. maintenance, organisation and transfer of records' (ibid.:123). Knowledge of risks, communication skills and good records: this is the official trinity of criminal justice system surveillance.

2. External Agencies of Criminal Justice System Surveillance

In addition to myriad proposals for improving the monitoring of criminal justice agents, the RCCJ advocates a number of new agencies above and beyond the present system.

From above, a new independent body to consider miscarriages of justice is visualised (RCCJ 1993:180ff.). This proposed Authority would have a close working relationship with the Court of Appeal. It would receive cases when appeal rights have been exhausted; or, alternatively, the Court of Appeal could refer cases to it before an appeal is decided and the Authority would be required to investigate. The Authority would have powers of investigation, directing and supervising the police and deciding whether or not to refer the case to the Court of Appeal in the light of the investigation. The Authority would be the final investigator of system deficiencies in the highly exceptional case, underpinning the normal efficiency with which criminal justice system surveillance operates. As such it is to function as an over-arching monitor and regulator of criminal justice system surveillance capacities and efficiencies.

From beyond, there are recommendations for new information systems that will provide ongoing monitoring of risks created by the decisions of criminal justice agents. For example, 'ethnic monitoring' is recommended as a means of ascertaining 'how minorities are treated and thus to identify the measures which are needed to ensure as far as possible that the rules, procedures and practices of the criminal justice system are applied, and seen to be applied, in the same way to all' (ibid.:7–8).

Of course the Commissioners themselves have commissioned a large number of excellent empirical studies that also provide a surveillance function. Increasingly, criminology has an influential role in surveillance of criminal justice agents (Ericson and Carriere 1994). Indeed, it relies on the same knowledge resources – legal, scientific, electronic and information system – as criminal justice agents to effect its monitoring tasks. For example, video- and audio-tapes of police-suspect interviews prepared by the police also allow social scientists to monitor the legal propriety of police and solicitors in terms of systematic data. Criminology texts connote this criminology-as-surveillance function, for example McConville and Shepherd (1992), *Watching Police Watching Communities*. No knowledge can be outside criminal justice system surveillance. Surveillance mechanisms are there to ensure that all potentially relevant knowledge is made available for system purposes.

IV CONCLUSIONS

The thesis of this paper is captured in the phrase 'criminal justice *system* surveillance'. In the RCCJ, criminal justice appears more than ever before as a system. Practitioners, policy officials and academic criminologists have long fretted that it is not a system. They have complained about the lack of coordination among people and subunits even within a particular component of the system, such as the police, let alone among police, prosecutors, defence lawyers, judges, prison officers, probation officers and so on. However, the RCCJ research studies make it evident that criminal justice is a system, coordinated by knowledge, communication and surveillance mechanisms. The RCCJ recommendations urge that it be even more systematic. The promise is that enhanced legal, scientific, electronic and information system powers will both ensure more certain knowledge of suspects, and curtail the influence of craft knowledge among criminal justice agents.

In order to accomplish *system* surveillance, previously dominant values and emphases in criminal justice have had to be displaced and new ones substituted. First, there is no longer an expressed commitment to efficient control of crime. Crime control is displaced by surveillance, the efficient production of knowledge useful in the administration of suspect populations. This reflects the de-centring of the State itself: as the system ascends, the State as a central unitary entity recedes. Second, there is no longer a primary emphasis on suspects' rights in an adversarial system. Suspects' rights are displaced by system rights. Justice becomes a matter of just knowledge production for the efficient risk management of suspect populations.

This emphasis on surveillance for risk management, and on system rights to maximise surveillance capacities, is by no means peculiar to the criminal justice institution. It is characteristic of all major institutions in risk society. Social institutions increasingly construct risks as threats, underpinned by an assumption of distrust in human relations. Social institutions increasingly respond to their own constructions through probability calculations, through knowledge systems for efficient risk management of those threats.

Given its context of reporting to a risk society, it is perhaps inevitable that the RCCJ does not exhibit much imagination. As official discourse, the RCCJ could only articulate and rationalise the prevailing institutional arrangements of risk society. This is not to say the RCCJ offers nothing new. It does signal official recognition of the fact that crime control and suspects' rights are on the way out and that surveillance and system rights are taking their place.

12. Thinking About Criminal Justice

Andrew Sanders

I ESTABLISHING GUILT AND INNOCENCE

Most of the 'official' legal rhetoric about criminal justice in the UK and USA broadly echoes Packer's familiar 'due process' values.[1]

1. Due Process

In such a system, which requires a) proof beyond reasonable doubt; and b) proof on the basis of evidence secured in accordance with lawful procedures, a distinction needs to be made between truth in fact and legal truth. Beliefs about the former are less important than proof of the latter. Legal guilt and actual guilt therefore do not always coincide in a due process system. Some 'factually' guilty people, who might be convicted were the threshold of guilt a balance of probabilities, should be acquitted.

2. Crime Control

In a 'crime control' system (the polar opposite to due process in Packer's scheme) there is a presumption of guilt which need only be proven on a balance of probabilities. Any relevant evidence may be thrown into the balance, however it was secured. Legal guilt is established when there is sufficient actual belief of guilt. This means that the 'legally guilty' category expands to take in a larger proportion of the actually guilty than in due process systems, but at the expense of some people who are actually innocent.

---

[1] H. Packer *The Limits of the Criminal Sanction*, 1968. The use of these models in this paper does not imply their endorsement, either descriptively or normatively. For a critical assessment see e.g. Ashworth, 'Criminal Justice and the Criminal Process' *BJ Crim* (1988) 28:111 and M. McConville, A. Sanders and R. Leng, *The Case For the Prosecution*, 1991, Ch. 9. One of the many problems of these models is their inability to incorporate any coherent notion of victims' rights.

The aims of both systems are ostensibly to ensure that legal guilt and actual guilt are as close together as possible, while accepting that neither will ever produce a perfect match. They are different ways of attempting to secure the same broad objective.

3. Formality and Reality

These formal propositions need to be treated with caution. First, contrasting 'actual' with 'legal' guilt and innocence assumes that guilt and innocence exist independently of their legal context. This is a difficult assumption to maintain, for the legal elements of criminal offences are themselves legal constructs. Examples include intention, provocation, offensiveness, and dishonesty. As the criminological labelling theorists taught us 30 years ago,[2] criminal behaviour is a product of social labelling as much as the behaviour which gives rise to the label.

Second, it assumes that law enforcement agencies will behave in the same ways regardless of the rules under which they operate. In reality, we would expect police and prosecution agencies in systems with tough evidential thresholds to secure more evidence than in more 'crime control'-oriented systems. The result of the former might not therefore be more acquittal of the guilty, although there would be other knock-on effects (e.g. more expensive investigative procedures). On the other hand, attempting to control the police through tough evidential hurdles may *fail* to secure desired changes in police behaviour if that behaviour is not actually aimed at securing evidence intended to secure convictions. Both models make legalistic assumptions that all stops, arrests, interrogations, and so forth are aimed at the conviction of individuals.

As we shall see, police behaviour may instead, or additionally, aim to control whole sections of society in general, rather than in respect of specific acts of criminality. This requires us to consider another model which I shall call the 'repressive' model.

II THE ROYAL COMMISSION, CRIME CONTROL AND REPRESSION

At a Conference on 27 July, 1993 sponsored by *The Times* and LSE, Michael Zander directed participants to the terms of reference printed on p. i of the Report. They require the Royal Commission to 'examine the

---

2   E.g. H. Becker, *Outsiders*, 1963, Free Press.

effectiveness of the criminal justice system' in securing the conviction of the guilty and the acquittal of the innocent, 'having regard to the efficient use of resources'. The Commission saw its duty as being, he said, to balance these three objectives. Is the result a balance between crime control and due process, or a wholesale adoption of the crime control agenda?

The crime control model elevates efficiency in prosecution and conviction above all else. Hence, for instance, its acceptance in trial of illegally obtained evidence. Efficiency, though, does not mean as many convictions as possible, regardless of guilt and innocence. As I have argued, the crime control model attempts to make the actually guilty and legally guilty correspond as closely as possible. Advocates of the crime control model argue that its essence is fact-gathering, 'seeking data which will help prove or disprove' guilt.[3] This is for at least two reasons: a) an arbitrary and grossly inaccurate system would lose its deterrent effect; b) every time an innocent person is convicted a guilty person remains free, and so arbitrariness leads to failure in crime control, as well as in due process, terms. Thus efficiency requires the most utilitarian balance between protecting the innocent and convicting the guilty. Securing this balance requires some protections for suspects, so no crime control-based system could be totally without such protections.[4]

A repressive system, by contrast, tries to control oppositional, disruptive or 'subversive' sections of society by breaking up street gatherings, searching houses in force, and making mass arrests. Legal procedures are side issues in such systems, but they can be used to provide superficial legitimacy. This is the role of stop–search, arrest, detention and so forth in such systems. Whether those on the receiving end of such powers are actually 'guilty' or 'innocent' really does not matter much: 'efficiency' is not measured by such criteria, and who or what one is or believes – not what one does at any specific time and place – constitutes guilt.

I am not suggesting that the Royal Commission subscribes to this repressive model of criminal justice. However, I do believe that this model accurately describes elements of the British (and American) systems i.e. that this is what happens at some times and in some respects to oppositional groups, or those perceived to be such, especially (but not exclusively) when those groups are working class or black.[5] This is

---

3 J. Walkley, *Police Interrogation, A Handbook for Investigators*, 1987, p. 5
4 Such a system would probably be regarded as not 'legal' by most jurists as it would not have any 'natural law' content.
5 This is my reading of works such as Institute of Race Relations, *Policing Against Black People*, 1987, and E. Cashmore and E. McLaughlin (eds), *Out of Order?*, 1991, regarding black people. See more generally P. Scraton (ed.), *Law, Order, and the Authoritarian State,*

especially true at times of riot, disorder, and in major strikes.[6] This may
be true of the legal system's approach to the 'Irish problem' since the start
of the Troubles, and it may be a contributory factor in the 'Irish' group of
miscarriage cases which gave rise to the appointment of the Royal
Commission. The problem with the Royal Commission is not that it
endorses this model but that it ignores it (presumably because it would not
accept that it could describe even one element of our current
arrangements). We shall see that this failure to understand the nature of
our system has unfortunate consequences.

It also means that the Royal Commission can portray itself as 'balanced'.
In a crude sense it is. But the balance is between due process and
repression, rather than between due process and crime control. The next
section will show that the 'balance' of the Royal Commission is in fact
consistent with the crime control model.

III THE ROYAL COMMISSION AND 'BALANCE'

Does it matter whether we characterise the Royal Commission Report as
'crime control', 'due process' or something in between? Isn't it the likely
effects of the specific recommendations which matter? The answer is no,
because the only way to judge their likely effects normatively is in the light
of their purposes. And as we have seen, the purposes of legal rules in
crime control systems (to convict as many guilty people as possible
without convicting even more innocent people) are different from their
purposes in due process systems (to protect as many innocent people as
possible).

1. 'Efficiency' versus Fairness

The Report regards equally seriously the risk of the 'innocent defendant
being convicted or a guilty defendant being acquitted' (see e.g. Ch. 1, para.
5). For the Royal Commission both are 'miscarriages of justice' (para. 9).
This is a negation of the presumption of innocence: as LAG points out in
its response to the Report,[7] the presumption of innocence means that if
guilt is not *proved* the factually guilty *should go free*. When this happens
we might say that there has been a failure of efficiency, but from a due

---

1987, for the UK and I. Balbus, *The Dialectics of Legal Repression*, 1973 for the USA.
6   See eg., B. Fine and R. Millar (eds), *Policing The Miner's Strike*, 1985; R. Vogler, *Reading
    the Riot Act*; D. Cowell et al., *Policing the Riots*, 1982.
7   *Preventing Miscarriages of Justice*, 1993.

process point of view there will not have been a miscarriage of justice. The Report goes on to say that 'mistaken verdicts can and sometimes do occur and that our task is to recommend changes ... which will make them less likely in the future.' (para. 9). Clearly the intention is to make mistakes less likely whether they be mistakes as to guilt or to innocence. The crime control goal of efficiency is paramount.

The Commission's recommendations follow this path with remarkable consistency. Where it argues for a balance of rules it is not generally in furtherance of a balance of purposes, but in furtherance of the efficiency purpose alone. Very few of its recommendations are based on the due process principle of integrity. In this short paper, this will have to be demonstrated through just two examples.[8]

First, take police malpractice which helps to produce evidence used to convict a defendant, for example oppressive interrogation producing a confession, or unlawful denial of a solicitor leading to the absence of an independent check on whether an alleged confession was really made. The majority view on the Commission argues that the Court of Appeal should not quash convictions on the grounds of the malpractice alone, but only if the conviction is or may be unsafe (Ch. 10, para. 48). Even if quashing was an appropriate punishment for malpractice, it argues, it would be ineffective and criminals should not walk free (para. 49): classic crime control arguments. At first sight this appears to recommend no change. However, The Court of Appeal does sometimes quash convictions because of the sheer scale and nature of police malpractice, although it does so inconsistently.[9] Thus the Commission recommended a move *away* from due process, which was, ironically, castigated by Michael Zander in his 'Note of Dissent' primarily on the grounds of principle.[10]

> The moral foundation of the criminal justice system requires that if the prosecution has employed foul means the defendant must go free even though he is plainly guilty. (para. 68)

Secondly, take Chapter Two, on police investigation. It intelligently identifies some of the ways in which criminal justice works: for example,

---

[8] Some of its recommendations are neutral and technical in character. Some are as consistent with due process as with crime control, and a few appear to be due process oriented, but the overwhelming majority are crime control driven. This small element of inconsistency is not surprising in a report so desperate to avoid explicit theory and clear principles.

[9] See, for instance, *Samuel* [1988] QB 615; *Canale* [1990] 2 All ER 187. Bevan and Lidstone's discussion of the PACE s.78 cases well captures the complexity and inconsistency: *The Investigation of Crime* (1991), p. 476–84.

[10] 'Ironic' because, with one exception (the recommendation in Chapter 6 that, if the defence fails to disclose its defence to the court, adverse inferences could be made) Zander accepted every one of the crime control recommendations proposed.

the police failing to seek exonerating evidence as well as incriminating evidence (para. 7), the police and courts ignoring failures by witnesses to identify defendants as well as positive identifications (para. 11), and aggressive interrogation techniques (para. 18–23). However, the concern of the Commission is not with the poor treatment of suspects *per se* or with these failures to presume innocence until otherwise proven. Its concern is to protect the innocent and to ensure 'that fewer guilty people are acquitted because the evidence against them fails' (para. 7). Similarly, 'oppressive interviews are liable to be inaccurate.' (para. 24).

What if these features were not, in the Commission's judgment, to lead to the acquittal of the guilty and inaccurate interview data? Consistent with the Crime Control approach, it would presumably not be concerned. The Commission's Crime Control logic could lead it to recommend literally anything if it thought it sufficiently efficient. Fortunately, the Commission accepts (para. 4) that there will always be some risk of error or malpractice by the police. The due process response to this and to such specific issues as identification and interrogation would be to require corroboration, judicially supervised identification and interrogation, and so forth. The Commission's response, though, is to recommend

> ... a reasonable balance between the need to protect the suspect and the need to leave the police free to do the job they are called upon to do. A set of safeguards which prevented the police from bringing large numbers of offenders to justice would be unacceptable. (para. 2)

So corroboration and judicial supervision are not recommended. Instead, 'the police should see it as their duty ...' (para. 7), 'the jury should be warned...' (para. 11), and 'training should ... be given' (para. 23) in relation to exonerating evidence, identification, and interrogation respectively. The Commission puts the onus of change on the police itself. This self-regulation approach is central to crime control, for outside regulation would have aims additional to the maximising of accurate identification of guilt (such is the accurate identification of innocence!). The 'balance' recommended by the Commission is therefore not a balance of approaches, but a balance consistent with Crime Control. This approach also incorporates two assumptions which are *at no point* identified or questioned. The first is the ability of the police to be so efficient. The second is its desire. But before dealing with these assumptions about police efficiency let us look at another false balance.

2. The Interests of the Community versus the Interests of Suspects

The Report of the Royal Commission contains very little general discussion of principles, and no discussion of theories, models or concepts. This makes it difficult at first sight to grasp the rationale of its recommendations, and perhaps explains why Zander dissented on principle in respect of just two out of dozens of recommendations all with the same underlying rationale. One clue to the rationale is given at the end of Chapter 1, in paragraph 27:

> ... there is a potential conflict between the interests of justice on the one hand and the requirement of fair and reasonable treatment for everyone involved, suspects and defendants included, on the other. ... Our recommendations serve the interests of justice without diminishing the individual's right to fair and reasonable treatment.

Taken literally, this makes little sense. For what can the 'interests of justice' encompass over and above everyone being treated fairly and reasonably? This appears to be a false dichotomy. Reading between the lines, it seems to hark back to the Royal Commission on Criminal Procedure, whose terms of reference enjoined it to have:

> regard both to the interests of the community in bringing offenders to justice and to the rights and liberties of persons suspected or accused of crime ...[11]

This is only superficially coherent. For persons 'suspected or accused' have as much interest as anyone else in bring actual offenders to justice, just as it is in the interests of justice to treat suspects fairly.[12] For all members of the 'community' are potential suspects. The question which requires consideration is whether the community as a whole should be subject to the interference with liberty which crime control powers involve, especially bearing in mind that they are not exercised against all sections of the community equally.

Who is to weigh up the competing demands of detection versus liberty? The law is made and implemented primarily by the white, middle-aged middle classes, while those who are stopped and searched, for instance, are primarily black, young and poor. One section of society makes the laws and reviews the policies (for the two Royal Commissions have been almost exclusively white middle aged and middle class too) which bear down on the other. It is easy for the decision-making community to decide that it is in 'society's' interests for suspects to have their liberty compromised when

---

[11] RCCJ *Report*, 1981, p.vi.

[12] From a due process point of view. The Royal Commission, though, was not thinking on due process lines.

those suspects are mainly drawn from the non-decision-making community. Only if it is true that stop–search, for instance, is part of a wider repression model of policing do these apparent dichotomies begin to make sense. In other words the 'balance' between 'interests of justice/community' and 'rights and liberties' either makes sense, in which case the repression model does accurately characterise one strand of British criminal justice; or it does not make sense, in which case the rationale on which both Commissions' recommendations are built crumbles away.

IV POLICE EFFICIENCY OR POLICE REPRESSION?

There is no space here to systematically examine police efficiency. However, almost any research or official report on the police will undermine any residual belief one might have in the forces' efficiency in investigating crime. This is so whether measured in terms of the proportion of stops and searches which lead to arrest (less than 14 per cent of *recorded* stops),[13] the proportion of arrests which lead to detections (less than 50 per cent)[14] the proportion of time actually spent investigating crime, and so forth. This should not be surprising. As the police themselves argue, bureaucratic demands (especially in the wake of PACE) leave them little time for investigative work. However, much police error is avoidable. The police often fail to follow up obvious witnesses to the detriment of their own as much as the case of the suspect,[15] their cases are often obviously weak,[16] they are spectacularly poor at identifying (or officially noticing) vulnerable suspects,[17] they often fail to observe the rules on cautioning,[18] and they still often breach PACE Code of Practice C (on detention and questioning) in relation to reading suspects their rights and interviewing outside the police station.[19]

To say all this about the police is not to single them out as a particularly

---

[13] Most stops are unrecorded, and a very low proportion indeed of unrecorded stops lead to arrest or summons. See W. Skogan, *The Police and Public in England and Wales*, 1990, HMSO.

[14] M. McConville, A. Sanders, R. Leng, op. cit.

[15] Ibid.

[16] B. Block et al., *Ordered and Directed Acquittals in the Crown Court*, Royal Commission Study No. 15, 1993, HMSO.

[17] G. Gudjonsson et al., *Persons at Risk During Interviews in Police Custody: The Identification of Vulnerabilities*, Royal Commission Research Study No. 12, 1993, HMSO.

[18] R. Evans and T. Ferguson, *Comparing Different Juvenile Cautioning Systems in One Police Force*, Home Office, 1991.

[19] D. Brown et al., *Changing the Code: Police Detention under the Revised PACE Codes of Practice*, 1992, HMSO.

corrupt or self-seeking organisation, as organisations go. What organisation is so efficient and philanthropic that one would sensibly provide it with extensive powers and allow it to regulate its exercise of those powers itself? It is generally recognised that when, for instance, corporations, dentists, and lawyers – to name a few at random – are unregulated, patients and clients always suffer. Yet despite the fact that there is no good reason to believe the police to be any different, the Commission apparently does so believe, despite much of the research cited here being commissioned by itself or by the Home Office.

The reasons for these failures of efficiency and breaches of various rules include lack of ability, care and time. Much of this means that the police are not very good at catching criminals. Even in crime control terms, the Commission's judgment is poor. However, much of this can be explained by the police's desire to pursue other goals. This takes us back to the repressive model. As we said earlier, repressive systems use legal forms such as stop–search, arrest, interrogation, and so forth as much to intimidate, control and maintain surveillance as to build specific cases against specific individuals. In countries like Britain repression is not general, but directed against certain groups identified earlier. It is against these groups that those 'inefficient' stops and arrests are disproportionately made.[20]

Take as another example suspects' rights in police stations. These are 'inefficiently' provided by the police, albeit less so now than before PACE. One puzzling feature of this is that many suspects obstructed by the police still exercise their rights.[21] To some extent this is because the case against most suspects is insufficiently important for the police to take their obstruction far. Then why obstruct them at all?[22] It seems to me that this stems from the police's more general contempt for suspects as a class (bearing in mind the class from which most suspects are drawn), and their belief that those presumed guilty do not deserve such expensive state resources. Legal advice and the whole panoply of due process rights recognises the legitimacy of suspects as citizens, something which policing – based as it is on the crime control model at best – routinely denies and has to deny, in order to justify the gross violation of rights which the police

---

[20] Although not discussed in these terms, the recent study of Norris et al., 'Black and Blue: An Analysis of the Influence of Race on Being Stopped by the Police', *BJ Soc* (1992) 43:207 shows that this phenomenon has survived PACE. This is not surprising from my perspective, but it ought to surprise those who deny it.

[21] Brown, op. cit; Sanders et al., *Advice and Assistance at Police Stations*, Lord Chancellor's Department, 1989.

[22] The half-heartedness of these ploys, as we call them, has led to some dispute about how frequent ploys are and whether most obstruction and obfuscation can properly be called 'ploys'. See Brown, op. cit.

engage in when suspects refuse to recognise police authority. The police view suspects in the way society views convicted persons: as having forfeited all but the most basic rights. In anticipating the future status of most suspects the police can justify to themselves treating them as if they were already convicted.[23]

An illustration of this police view of society is provided by McConville and Shepherd. They were discussing with an officer a 'Neighbourhood Watch' scheme in a middle-class area which was surrounded by working class communities. Asked whether the new scheme would spread into the surrounding areas the officer replied, 'No, it's them that the scheme is protecting members from.'[24] When commentators talk about such tactics as stop–search alienating 'the community' and thus impairing police efficiency they miss the point that there are two (or more) communities. There is the 'police and community' which is hardly policed and which voluntarily provides information for crime control, and there is the policed community from which information is involuntarily extracted through crime control.

In other words much 'error and inefficiency' is often no such thing. Much malpractice arises not from failed attempts at crime control but from pursuit of the repression model. Had the Royal Commission been prepared to view the police in this way it might not have been so willing to trust them to carry out their ostensible crime control tasks with so little restraint.

If we accept this analysis we should not rest with undermining the Royal Commission alone. Commentators who argue that the police should be subject to more constraints in order to pull the system more towards due process (and I am, or have been, one of them) make exactly the same mistake. First, it is naive to think that just because the rules are there the police will adhere to them. Second, we have to ask what the nature of those constraints are or would be. Exclusion at trial of illegally obtained evidence? This is no use if the illegal acts were not aimed at producing evidence to be used in court. Abolish stop–search laws? What is to stop the police stopping suspects on the streets anyway, as they always used to? Putting faith in the power of law to enforce due process is as naive as the Commission's faith in the power and desire of the police to control crime.

Whereas traditionally the argument against the power of law is bureaucratic, the argument here is structural: the police have a set of political roles, as well as their law enforcement roles, and only in different political conditions will those roles, and thus police behaviour, be

---

[23] For a fascinating insider/outsider account which conveys this viewpoint, albeit in anthropological terms, see M. Young, *An Inside Job,* Oxford, 1991.

[24] M. McConville and D. Shepherd, *Watching Police, Watching Communities,* 1992, p. 140.

markedly different. For it is not the police who decide what to do and how to do it at times of perceived crisis. It is government, through such institutions as the National Reporting Centre. Cop culture, with its portrayal of respectable society as constantly threatened by 'them', is a vital mechanism by which to transmit to the police the paranoia of government about subversion and disorder. But the mainspring of this repressive strand is government and not the police.

V WHERE DID THE ROYAL COMMISSION GO WRONG?

We have seen that the Report is based on the unarticulated assumption that the police (and by extension criminal justice in general) does and should operate according to a balance between crime control and due process. As such, it misunderstands the nature of both those models and the empirical reality. It only advocates the maintenance or strengthening of suspects' rights where that is judged to be more efficient in truth-finding. So what it is in fact advocating is a further lurch towards a crime control framework.

What it will lead to is a further capability to engage in legal repression. This is because, first, this crime control belief in police and criminal justice ability is naive: professionals are just not that clever. Second, it rests on a simplistic notion of unconstructed 'facts' and 'truth'. Third, even were the above not so, the police could only be trusted with self-regulatory powers and reduced rights for suspects if they were to use their powers to pursue the 'truth' (as prescribed by the crime control model). This is only tenable if we ignore the repressive functions of the police which are not geared to finding facts to build cases but which have a *wider* social and political purpose.

13. Gatekeeping and the Seamless Web of the Criminal Justice Process

Mike Brogden

Constable to street urchin 'Move on!'. Child 'Why?'. 'I don't know. You're just to move on.' (Dickens *Bleak House*)

I STRUCTURING THE 'PROBLEM' – THE ABSENCE OF 'NORMAL' INJUSTICE

The Royal Commission properly noted the absence from its mandate of several key areas of the criminal justice process. Excluded from the enquiry were investigations into the legal definition of criminal offences, into police powers of arrest, into sentencing and sentencing policy, and into the granting of bail. All of these matters have a bearing on the crisis in the criminal justice process, and it is legitimate to ask why such matters were subject to a new form of exclusionary rule. In particular, the Commission was not required to investigate what has been a major area of public contention for two decades, police powers of stop-and-search. Coupled with the focus on the Crown Court experience at the expense of the magistrates' courts, the Commission failed to deal with the 'normal' experience of the vast majority of recipients of criminal justice in England and Wales.

It is in that latter context in which injustice is both least newsworthy but perhaps the most important. Poor justice for poor people is compounded – even state research ignores your plight in its preference for high-profile cases. The dramatisation of the Crown Court miscarriages at the expense of 'normal' injustice, is of course not unique to the State's perception of the faults of the criminal justice process. Much 'left idealist' polemic has been addressed to the same focus. On both sides, there has been a general failure to deal with the routinisation of injustice. Cumulatively – for every one person whose case is concluded in the Crown Courts, ten are laid to rest in the magistrates' courts – and relatively – the wrongful conviction for a minor offence blights for the young person a future career – there is a rather different cause for concern.

This selectivity stems from the apparent belief by the Home Office that it had laid to rest via PACE many 'minor' matters. Conversely, where it recognised a problem at the lower end of the scale – as in the concern with the role of the Custody Sergeant – the Commission brief reflected police rather than public disquiet. That circumscribing decision indicates some of the influences determining the Commission's work. If there is police resentment, such as in the perception of the 'bureaucratic' completion of quintuplicate forms in the case of the Custody Record, the matter falls within the Commission's mandate. If there is public disquiet, the continuing concern with police street practices, the matter is deemed, often, not of sufficient importance to be relevant to the enquiry.

The tragedies of Guildford, of Birmingham and of related miscarriages, should not distract attention from the routine 'public order' inequalities perpetuated in the 'Police Courts' of England and Wales. Convictions are often a formality. In those cases, the determinant of the conviction is the weight given to the patrol police officer's account of the event. Street practices, police function and inevitable partisanship, structure the initial components of the career.

II STREET POLICING AS THE CATALYST FOR CRIMINALISATION

This failure, of government rather than of Commission, is important for several reasons. *Stops* (and stop-and-searches) as a principal form of police practice, are a critical gatekeeping part of the criminal justice process. Street policing is the device by which many suspects commence their career in the criminal justice process. Stops are critical as a threshold factor.

Secondly, stops themselves are only part of wider police gatekeeping practice. At one end of the continuum are the 'move-ons', the colloquial, historical, term for normal police harassment. At the other end, are the arrests under the permissive public order charges for offences such as obstruction. Stops, move-ons, and public order arrests, are collectively the way policing is experienced by the majority of those whose territory is typically constrained by the street – the young, the unemployed and those itinerant categories with no fixed abode of home or work. Selective culling, with all its arbitrary injustice, of the lower social strata is an insufficient problem for those who determine the research agenda.

Further, the encounter is an unequal power play. The officer has the 'knowledge' and the power, legal and physical, often strengthened by potential peers in uniform, to determine a partisan outcome. Police discretion informed by culture and by force goals, structures the interaction. In the one-to-one encounter in the street, as in the magistrates' court, where the police officer is often the only prosecuting witness, the invisibility of the stop from wider scrutiny ensures that specific forms of selectivity determine police practice and the elements of the future 'criminal career'.

Fourthly, this medley of street practices is the factor which effectively frames official accounts in later stages of the process. Later judgements and dispositions are formulated by that initial subjective account. The image of the defendant is fabricated through the street encounter lens. Conversely, the reputation of the criminal justice process and of its functionaries is initially constructed in that context. For many young defendants and suspects, the criminal justice process is read as a seamless web, framed by experience with the street police. While a minority of defendants have accrued wisdom about the legal construction of criminal justice and its formal stage, many, especially young persons, have no idea of either the limitation of police powers within the street encounter nor of how the stop relates to later court processes. The suspects are of course not dummy players who react like robots to police actions. Police behaviour is sieved through structural and personal experiences and reactions mediated accordingly.

In that confrontation, police practices are crucial. Legal categories and limitations of process obfuscate sociological perceptions.

Finally, given the peculiarity of the (unfortunately-named) 'strike' rate – the proportion of stops without a career outcome (commonly in the 12:1 ratio) – reflects the number of people who unjustifiably experience policing without proceeding through the formal process. Alienation from the state police is commonly an indirect product of the stops – an experience that the recipient might regard as harassment. Attitudes to policing and to the formal criminal justice process are produced through the unfair stop. Treated commonly by the functionary as a non-event, it conveys more significant meaning to the suspect.

This is peculiar given that the street experience is characterised in terms of power relations to which no other part of the criminal justice process is accustomed. It allows maximum discretion on the part of the police. If no search is conducted, there is no public recording of it – it is open to denial. It occurs regularly against an established suspect group. It is the context most informed by sub-cultural practices. It is the most difficult context to guide by external rules.

More importantly, and a factor not recognised by the relative restrictions of PACE, it occurs under a variety of legislation. Legal discourse confines the 'control' of stops to one aspect of the criminal justice process – the encounter on the street under the mandate of PACE – and ignores those events which do not fit within that legal capsule. More stops occur under, for example, the Road Traffic Acts than are recorded under PACE. Even obscure legislation like the Wild Birds Act potentially subject particular populations to what are, sociologically, stop practices. Increasingly evident in the last decade have been the powers of stop-and-search under the Misuse of Drugs Act. None of these are covered by the limited controls of the PACE legislation.

In any case, where police practice is 'hindered' by law, there are two responses by that institution. There is creative reconstruction of those powers to allow old practices to continue within a re-interpretation of the rules. Imaginative recording and lack of corrective supervision have allowed ingenuity free rein in recording a search. *Post facto* rationalisations have dominated the written records. Secondly, new powers are invoked to avoid the use of those now relatively restricted. Thus when the old 'sus' power was challenged, an alternative street power, the 'stops', appear, to have taken its place (Brogden 1984). In invoking such alternative powers, police officers were not only imaginatively finding other ways to practise control on the streets. They were acting in accordance with the structural power to operate policing as intended – to confine street populations to particular practices and locations on behalf of a more 'legitimate' audience of policework.

III THE FALLACY OF ORGANISATIONAL RESTRAINTS ON STOPS

PACE has failed to control stops because it has dealt only with one of the reasons for stops – the crime control function. The Codes of Practice and their supervision have had minimal effect on practice. Although most of the research on stops pre-dates PACE, given the comparative material from overseas there is little suggestion that legislation or codes of practices have any significant effect in preventing the targeting of those unique groups distinguished by the factors of age, ethnicity and class (see amongst many others, Brogden, Jefferson and Walklate 1988).

The PACE powers have been ineffective for several other reasons. The stops are a function of occupational rather than criminological practice. In any tedious job, incumbents find ways of relieving the monotony. In Smith's words 'A considerable number of stops are carried out mainly for something to do' (Smith 1984:55). Throughout British police history, with its tradition of beat policing, there has been a continuing search for ways of interrupting the monotony of the night-time patrol (Brogden 1991). Stops are a strategy of independence in a work context in which police officers can exercise relative autonomy, one in which police officers bored by a ritual practice can be most creative in dealing with boredom. It has personal, occupational, dividends, in altering the uniform nature of practice. Attempting to constrain the stops without dealing with the occupational factors that may give rise to its use, is to confuse cause with effect.

Secondly, the restrictions have failed because they have stayed within the legal discourse of what constitutes a stop. They have ignored the stops under other legislation and the reasons for which they are carried out. Road traffic officers, for example, suffer from the same problem of occupational boredom, and from cultural, and structural pressures as does the patrol officer.

Rule-making devices which seek to deal with only one cause of a particular phenomena inevitably fail. The PACE Codes attempted to constrain discretionary action by the device of monitored recording. But sanctioning social practices by such constraining devices fails to account for the other factors which create the motivation for the stops, dealing with only one item on the agenda. Hence controlling stops is not just a means of rule-making in terms of correcting crime control practice. Action must include dealing with the larger factors of organisation but also of culture and structure.

IV A STRUCTURAL VIEW OF POLICE STREET POWERS

Most police potential confrontation with the public occurs on the street, whether it be through the activities of the patrol officer dealing with a putative suspect or a road traffic officer perceiving a possible traffic infringement. The stops are, however, the tip of the iceberg. More commonly, as much historical evidence demonstrates, police hostile interaction is characterised by the 'move-on' phenomenon. 'Move-ons' are important for analysis not just because of their direct confrontational character but rather because they signify more graphically than do the stops, the structural character of street policing and its practices.

Since before the founding of the Peelite police, the mandate of those various bodies concerned with street patrol – from the Night Watch to the New Police – was to move on anyone deemed to be suspects in the eyes of conventional society. The move-on phenomenon, because it does not fall into a legal category and because it relatively rarely results in a formal legal charge, is ignored by the constrained analysis of the criminal justice process. 'Move-ons' having no legal explicit legal mandate have not been subject to empirical study by researchers from within orthodox research. Move-ons have the specific function of demonstrating the police right to determine who shall occupy the street. The stops may have a limited crime control purpose. But the move-ons are the naked expression of police powers and illuminate in their practice the more complex role of the stops.

As the tip of a legal iceberg which includes both move-ons and public order arrests, the stops feed into the larger process but remain unconnected in the Royal Commission mandate. More importantly, the analysis of the stops has been largely commuted to factors that ignore larger structural determinants. The expansion of the stop practice has failed to take into account the larger social control function of policing and has limited itself to a perception that the stops, like the move-on phenomenon, is limited to one of crime control.

Norris (1992) has provided a useful summary of the research which seeks to explain both stops and arrest practices. Three categories of decision-making influences are outlined. There are individual factors, under which heading, Norris (curiously) lists the age, sex, race, social class, educational achievement, and length of service of the officer. Situational factors also contribute. Officer decisions are said to be affected by the location of the event, its perceived legal seriousness, the personal characteristics of the suspect, the presence or absence of bystanders, and whether the police are acting proactively or reactively. Finally, the decisions are said to be influenced by a medley of organisational features – the style of policing in the area, the nature of the patrol organisation and the nature of supervision.

Norris has argued that this categorisation ignores at least one major factor. In particular, those approaches fail to appreciate the extent to which street police decision-making is shaped by a cultural lens. Street practice, he argues, is guided not by station supervision but primarily through the imperative of the occupational culture. Front-line supervisors do not see it as their job to guide practice in the street and are rarely in a post long enough to affect its practices. In the place of that supervision, peer group advice and loyalties become the major determinants. Arrests, stops, and move-on practice, may be influenced by the factors listed above. However, the principal constraint is that of the peer group.

While Norris's synthesis is a little like re-inventing the wheel, his analysis ignores one general factor that is crucial to evaluating the gatekeeping role of the stops and of more general street practice. It ignores the structural location of policing in two ways. Historically, the primary function of policing has been social control not crime control. Secondly, to see the police culture as being somehow a variant from those organisational goals is to make a major theoretical mistake. The gatekeeping role of the stop, as with other police street practices, needs to be understood not in terms of its efficacy or inefficacy with regard to the strike rate and the organisational, situational, and interactional factors that may affect it, but rather within a wider structural framework. The seamless web of the criminal justice process is predicated on a notion of crime control when the historical function of policing has been social control.

Crime Control versus Social Control

We have listed elsewhere the fallacy of debating the effectiveness of stops in terms of their apparent crime control function (Brogden 1985). There is no substantive evidence that the stops have any significant effect on the level of crime in a particular area. Most of the charges that accrue from stops under the PACE provisions result in public order charges – that is they are generated by the stop. The stops are counter-productive in several ways as a strategy of crime control. An initial public order charge leads to permissive criminalisation, which as Gill first documented nearly twenty years ago (Gill 1977), then precipitates possible later conviction for personal violence and property offences. The data of convictions produced by the stops gives the *appearance* of effectiveness without the substance – being produced by proactive policing, offences arising from the stops have a high but artificial clear-up rate. More generally, the stops are counter-productive in the longer term leading to wider alienation from the criminal justice process amongst those stopped and their peers and, in some cases, to criminal careers from within that group (Brogden 1985).

Historically, crime control grew slowly out of undifferentiated social control (Rock 1983). Eighteenth-century England, with its medley of 'policing' apparatuses was geared towards those idlers and vagabonds who disturbed their betters on the highways and byways of Hanoverian and Georgian England. The arrival of the New Police, whatever the Chadwickian arguments about the rationale for their development, ended up as being primarily engaged in the culls of the street population (as summarised in the 'watching St Giles to guard St James' aphorism). The very nature of the organisation of policework as beat work demonstrated a primary concern to clear the streets of those who disputed Victorian social order. Police crime powers were insignificant as compared with, for example, the medley of public order powers developed under such legislation as the Town Police Clauses Act. In the early twentieth century, street practice – the reification of the beat system – was reinforced by law and in practice by a moral order that saw 'its' police as being concerned, as did their Victorian ancestors, to separate out and police in their habitat the lower classes of the cities (Brogden 1991; Dixon 1991). In move-on practice, in the use of stop-and-search powers, and quantifiably in the number of cases that appeared in local magistrates' courts under public order charges, public order rather than crime control was the reality. Crime control was a miasma, a chimera, that beguiled an external audience that the police were somehow concerned with crime.

V POLICE CULTURE AS SYSTEMIC IN DIRECTING STOPS

Further, Norris's recognition of the influence of police culture on street practice in insufficient. Police culture itself has a direct structural connection. Orthodox approaches to police culture as the determinants of street practice have portrayed that phenomenon as a distraction from the real goals of policing. Police culture in informing the stops by peer group guidance has been portrayed as aberrant, sabotaging the true mission of policing. In its various manifestations, police culture was represented in those accounts as antithetical to 'proper' policework.

However, during the 1980s, a quite different perception of police culture arose, one that saw police culture not as aberrant but rather as expressing – albeit in a different form – the essential mission and objective of police organisation and the state of which their organisation was a part (Shearing (1981). This approach recognised, like that of interactional sociology, that the practice of policework was often different from that desired by those in command positions. However, this latter approached posited not an oppositional relationship between culture and organisational goals, but a convergence.

No chief officer ever wished his junior to use violence against suspects. Given the classic contradictions in policework – for example, between the requirements of law and the demand for social order – police officers as guided by the culture inevitably carried out practices deemed inappropriate by those on top. However, while the culture might provide alternative strategies for achieving the goals, it shared with the larger organisation and its client audience, the same general objectives.

A vivid example of this apparent contradiction concealing the larger shared imperative, was in the demand for confessions produced in the Maguire case. State and society wanted convictions. In the absence of appropriate evidence, police culturally-guided deviance produced 'guilty' parties. A Nelson's eye was turned to the interrogation tactics. In the event of the recognition of that violence, the Surrey police officers were effectively absolved. In this case, police deviance as guided in practice by the culture, succeeded in achieving organisational goals and those of the 'legitimate' consumers of police services. No formal disapproval was expressed through the judicial process of those deviant strategies which had appeared to be serving legitimate goals.

This second perspective clarifies the further connection between police practices on the street operating as gatekeepers, to the wider structural imperatives determining policework on the street. The organisational and state imperatives combine to determine police practice. Although the nuances of the stops, as with move-ons, and public order arrests, clearly owe something to local exigencies of organisation, of situation, and of interaction, the imperatives compelling such policing in its restraint of the lower social orders, stem from wider structural factors. The wider public, the 'legitimate' consumers of police services require, desire visible action against crime (as epitomised by the recurring demand for 'bobbies on the beat'). Police stop practices, like move-ons and public order arrests, furnish a cultural resolution for a structural problem. Pragmatic, peer-guided devices, partially satisfy that demand both in the visibility of police 'doing their job' on the street and secondly, in conducting the historical mission of sanitising the main thoroughfares and shopping precincts of those deemed to be non-respectable.

In other words, while the practice of the stops appears superficially aberrational, in the 'realistic' context of street policework, they are regarded by patrol officers as 'the best way of getting the job done'. The gap between command rhetoric and the realities of street policing is spanned by officers, as informed by the police culture, creatively bending the rules to implement formal policies. The lack of formal sanctioning of deviance in the justification for the stops, furnishes further evidence of this convergence between structure and culture. Apart from the normal problem of colleague loyalty in covering up the deviance of peers and juniors in policing, the evidence of the *lack* of condemnation of aberrant stops, as required by PACE, suggests that senior officers agree with their juniors that stop practices, while often formally regarded as out of order, represent realistic ways of getting the job done. As such they are not to be countermanded but treated permissively. The stops reflect therefore a hidden recognition of the relationship between wider demand on the police institution and police command, and the real practice of stopping and searching on the streets as the primary phase of social control through the criminal justice process.

VI CRIMINAL JUSTICE AS A SEAMLESS WEB

We have argued that there are a range of problematics missing from the rubric of the Royal Commission. Critical amongst those areas are typically the stop-and-search powers of street policing, powers which affect many more people than do the later legal categorisations of the criminal justice process.

The stops are interconnected with the wider criminal justice process in two ways. They are linked laterally to other police powers – to the move-on and to public order arrests, in rendering a proactive entry to the process. They are linked vertically as representing the first step for many future offenders, into long-term, criminal careers and the subsequent blighting of legitimate external opportunities.

Those powers and the rationale for their invocation, often frame the later career of a defendant through the process. As such, they are subject to evidential gross partisanship in their implementation. The central problematic of the Royal Commission, that it analysed police and judicial practices in terms of their crime control relationship, misses the wider social control function of which crime control is only one element.

Attempting to modify the wider image and processes of the criminal justice process requires attention to the importance of this gatekeeping area. It cannot be assumed that the PACE Codes of Conduct have resolved the problem as a major cause for concern. Legal categorisation and discourse have wrongly constructed street practices as outside the Commission's frame of reference.

14. Understanding the Long-Term Relationship between Police and Policed

Satnam Singh

Many suspects find themselves in a long-term relationship with the police which is imposed by the police, structured by policework norms and attitudes, based on a demand for deference, and maintained by the threat, and at times the actuality, of physical violence. To understand an encounter between the police and a member of the policed community, it is necessary to be aware that the behaviour of both parties is shaped by the norms and expectations of this long-term relationship.

The argument presented in this paper is drawn from research conducted with the Midsouthern Police over a three-month period in 1992. The field-work was carried out in two police stations, Nasherford and Grimeston, situated in small neighbouring cities in the south of England. In addition to interviewing 80 defendants about their experiences of arrest, detention and interrogation, I spent long hours observing proceedings in the custody room, and talked to police officers about their job.

I TARGETED POLICING

The police complained that they dealt with 'the same dross', 'the same losers' again and again. This was supported by the findings of the study: 89 per cent (n = 71) of those respondents said that they had been the subject of police suspicion in the past, and most of them (n = 65) had actually been arrested and detained at the station on previous occasions. This situation arises because policing is targeted against a narrow section of the public, namely the lower-working class and, to use the words of the Policy Studies Institute, those 'whom the police tend to lump with them on other grounds' (PSI Report 1983, p. 166).

Almost 80 per cent of the defendants said that they were unemployed, and a minority (n = 10) indicated that they were living on the streets or in night shelters (see also Skogan 1990, p. 31; Walker 1992, p. 268). The way in which these individuals are often policed has more to do with police perceptions of worth and worthlessness than with the criminal law. The following extract provides an example of views which I regularly heard from police officers:

Field-Note (Nasherford)
An elderly man, shabbily dressed and slightly drunk, was led into the custody area by a PC. The Custody Officer was informed that the man had been arrested for being 'drunk in a public place'. The man's details were taken, he was searched and placed in a cell. From talking to the PC it emerged that the man had been asleep on a park-bench, the officer had awakened him and arrested him. I told the Custody Officer the circumstances of the arrest and asked him whether he considered it worthwhile to spend public money processing such trivial cases. He replied, 'Of-course it is! I mean just look at him ... he's more than just a blot on the landscape, he's taking up a park-bench where members of the public may want to sit .... Would you want to walk through the park with your wife and kids with the likes of him around?'.

The contempt of this Custody Officer was not aimed solely at the individual arrested, but 'the likes of him' generally. Similarly, a sergeant at Grimeston explained that the force would not tolerate any pedlars or beggars on the streets: 'Where', he demanded to know, 'would we all be if everyone started begging?'. It was imperative, he explained, that 'the public' should not be 'intimidated by these people'.

Empirical studies have also shown that young black males are far more likely to be stopped and searched than individuals from other ethnic groups (Brogden 1981; Willis 1983; PSI Report 1983; Skogan 1990). Blacks are also over-represented in the arrest figures. Although they accounted for only 5 per cent of London's population in 1986, 17 per cent of those arrested in the capital were black (Home Office 1989), and although only 3 per cent of the city's population in Leeds, blacks accounted for 7 per cent of all those arrested (Jefferson et al. 1992, p. 141).

Some of the non-white defendants whom I questioned were firmly of the view that they were targeted by the police because of their colour. The sample included 23 non-whites (11 Asians and 12 blacks) and 39 per cent of them (5 Asians and 4 blacks) stated that they were treated unfairly on the streets by the police because the police were racist. Some 50 per cent of blacks and 45 per cent of Asians complained of past unfair police treatment on the street, as compared to only 25 per cent of whites. The following interview extracts provide examples of the conviction on the part of blacks and Asians that they are subjected to differential policing.

Case 52 Grimeston
Def: Everywhere that us Asians or blacks go, we get picked up by the police. They

won't let us live in this town; even when we go into town just to do a bit of shopping they just come up to us and start saying 'What you doing?', 'Where you going?', 'What you been nicking?' If you go out after about eight in the evening, they'll just come and start searching you, and if you question what they do, they throw you around and arrest you, they'll just make something up, burglary or something. Then they'll let you out five hours later and say there was no evidence and you can go.

Case 49 Grimeston
Def: The uniform must go to their heads: they're violent, they're rude and harass for no reason. It's a fact, a fact that I have discovered through personal experience and from what my friends have told me – and they've always been non-white.

The complaints of black and Asian suspects are given credence by the fact that racist attitudes within the police force are widespread. (See Lambert 1970, p. 190; Cain 1973, p. 119; Reiner 1985; Southgate 1982, pp. 9–15; Gordon 1983, p. 71; Holdaway 1983, p. 66; PSI Report 1983, p. 109; Foster 1989, p. 144; and McConville and Shepherd 1992, p. 166.)

In the present study, when discussing general problems of law enforcement, police talk was permeated by negative stereotypes of blacks. Officers at both stations commented that those locations which had a large West Indian population were 'problem areas', and that one would 'never go up there without back-up'. These views were voiced more frequently at Grimeston than at Nasherford, but this was most likely due to the larger non-white population of the former city. I was informed that 'most blacks' were engaged in organised crime and drug dealing, and possessed a propensity for violence. The following extracts provide an illustration of some of the views which were voiced:

Field-Note Extract (Grimeston)
PC: What the West Indians do is that they have white girlfriends for show, and black ones for keeps. This is because they get the white girls to go out and do all the cheque book fraud, because it looks less suspicious. We get a lot of cases with these girls being beaten up by these guys when they get caught.

Field-Note Extract (Grimeston)
PC: We get a lot of guys for possession, but we never get the big black guys at the top. The little guys are too scared to talk because I mean these guys are not to be messed with – I mean they'd probably get knee-capped or something.

In addition to targeting particular ethnic communities, the police have a tendency to concentrate their activities against those who have been the subject of suspicion or criminal proceedings in the past (PSI Report 1983, p. 345; Skogan 1990, p. 31). A third (n = 26) of the defendants whom I questioned complained about the way in which they were constantly stopped and searched, and routinely arrested for trivial matters because in their view, their face was known to the police:

Case 7 Nasherford
> Def: If I'm stopped on the street and they CRO me and find that I've got a criminal record, I'm a criminal whether I am or not ... there's a lot of discrimination in that way .... You're guilty whether you are or not. All they want at the end of the day is another body – if they've got a body to charge they're happy.

Case 48 Grimeston
> Def: You walk the streets, yea? And the copper will say, 'Where you come from?', 'Why you running?', 'What you running for?' Then they turn your pockets out ... these fucking coppers, they nick you 'cos they wanna get promotion ... once you're a criminal yea, you don't count for *nothing*. (original emphasis)

It was a common theme in conversations with police officers that those with 'previous' were more than likely to be 'at it', and therefore good policing required that a close watch be kept on them (McConville et al. 1991, p. 24). Anyone falling in this category stands in danger of achieving the status of 'permanent suspect', and becoming the subject of continued scrutiny even after having left the police station.

II THE RULES OF THE POLICE-POLICED RELATIONSHIP

The norms and expectations of the police-policed relationship are shaped by police attitudes and working practices. Much has been written about police work-culture, but it is the strands of 'action' and 'authority' in police culture which have most utility in explaining the nature of many police citizen encounters.

Most officers feel that their job should entail 'action' and 'excitement' (Reiner 1985, p. 89). This collective quest for action is held by an institution noted for its ethos of machismo (PSI Report 1983, p. 91) and is combined with the fact that the police possess, in the last resort, a monopoly on the legitimate use of force. The result is that for many officers the possibility of violence is a positive attraction of the job,[1] and the overwhelming majority of relief officers 'want the core of policing to be aggressive, action-centred encounters with citizens' (1992, p. 149).

During the course of the field-work I came across some officers who certainly viewed the possibility of being involved in a violent confrontation with what can only be described as glee:

---

[1] PSI Report, ibid., at p. 87: 'We find that the idea of violence is often central to the conceptions that police officers have of their work ... many officers see violence as a source of excitement and glamour.'

Field-Note Extract (Grimeston)
(Speaking to a custody officer (CO) about policing and the stories of violence officers
had recounted to the researcher, the following exchange took place.)

Researcher: All this confrontation can't be good though, can it? I mean it increases the
risk that officers are placed at.

Custody Officer: Oh, they can try it! Yes, sir! They can't knock us down, we've got the
biggest gang around here: there's more than three thousand in our gang.

Field-Note Extract (Nasherford)
CO: These boys, they're our support group. They don't take no shit. I mean if I'm on
the street and someone says something to me, I just ignore it. But these boys, they won't
wear it. They'll go up and ask 'em what they said, and if they get any mouth, they'll
drag 'em in.

This quest for excitement leads some officers not simply to 'want'
aggressive confrontation, but to *create* it. Almost one-third of arrestees
complained of unnecessary or excessive police violence outside the station,
or of attempts by the police to provoke a violent reaction.

Case 33 Grimeston
(Defendant stated that he had been at a football match where one of his friends had been
arrested. The police had used unnecessary violence and numbers to effect the arrest, and
he and his friends objected to this.) One of the coppers said, 'If you feel hard enough,
have a go ... '. They just wanted us to start so they could have a bit of fun, and then
make us do time.

The authors of the PSI Report found that in addition to the glamour of
violence, the 'central meaning of the job for most officers is the exercise of
authority' (PSI Report 1983, p. 87; see also Bittner 1967, p. 708; Lambert
1970, p. 192; Lee 1981; Foster 1989; McConville and Shepherd 1992).
Foster was explicitly told by officers that they expected respect to be
forthcoming and would not condone any challenge to their authority. This
was seen to result in some officers adopting a tone and stance demanding
submissiveness, and Foster observed that where the police complained of a
lack of respect 'the provocation often came from the officers themselves
setting the tone of the encounter by their attitude and stance' (p.134).
    Officers can seek to impose their authority by either demanding that their
requests for information be unquestioningly complied with, or by simply
treating people in an off-hand and cursory manner. This left some
individuals with a sense of powerlessness and humiliation.

Case 61 Grimeston
(Defendant said that he was returning from the DHSS when he was approached by two
policeman who had alighted from a panda-car. He said that one of the policeman took

hold of his arm and started asking him where he had been and where he was going. The defendant, being in a bad mood due to problems with his unemployment benefit, told the policemen that he didn't see why he should answer their questions) I couldn't see how it was any of their business ... I just said 'leave me alone, alright.' They said 'Right, you're going down the station *now*'. I said I didn't see any reason why I should be arrested, and he punched me in the balls. I pushed him off ... Now, there I was humiliated for no reason, punched in the balls in front of ordinary people going about their business, and I had to resort to force to defend myself. (He said he was arrested, placed in the cells for some hours and then released without charge.) The guy assaulted me and got away with it.

The situation is further exacerbated by the fact that the police find it difficult to accord any respect to those whom they regard as 'the world's dross', 'losers', 'toe-rags' and 'obnoxious shits'. The essential worthlessness of those brought to the station was a constant theme in police conversation, and legal rights were seen by most officers to attach only to those individuals who have 'worth':

Field-Note Extract (Nasherford).
Custody Officer: And the other thing which really gets my goat is the amount of money we spend on these, these – these (contemptuously) 'persons' with solicitors, doctors, meals and all that!

The view constantly put forward by officers was that the law attached too much significance to the rights of suspects. Being arrested, searched and placed in the cells for hours on end – these were events, I was informed, which may cause distress to 'someone like you or me', but were everyday occurrences in the lives of 'these people' and *did not bother them.*[2]

The police section-off not only particular defendants or groups as worthless and innately criminal, but write-off entire districts of the city in a similar fashion (McConville and Shepherd 1992, pp. 165–6). Officers at both stations stated that certain areas of the city containing a significant non-white population, were 'lawless', inhabited mainly by 'losers' and 'social security scroungers', and that these areas contained a significant 'obnoxious' element which hated the police. I was informed that because some of these areas were 'sensitive' (i.e. prone to erupt in anti-police riots), it was important for the police to enter them in large numbers and make a show of force. Some of the residents of these areas, however, viewed the police as adding to their problems, not solving them.

---

[2] Bittner discovered a similar attitude amongst American patrolmen: 'It is difficult to overestimate the skid-row patrolman's feeling of certainty that his coercive and disciplinary actions towards the inhabitants have but the most passing significance in their lives' (Bittner 1967, p. 713).

Case 19 Nasherford

Father of defendant: What you have here is a situation like South Africa. These kids can go to work, but they can't go out in the evening. They've got to stay in the township, and the riot van comes round to keep them in the township ... there's no reason why they should 'move on' – it's their estate and they can stand around, there's nothing else for them to do. One of the coppers once said to me, 'you *keep* him in!' I mean, what can you say to that?[3]

The police see themselves as representing 'Authority', and those whom they have categorised as the 'scum' and 'losers' embody all that which is anti-authority. Many of the interactions which take place between the police and suspects revolve around police efforts to neutralise the anti-authority elements in society by forcing them to accept 'the authority of the cloth'. By forcing the 'obnoxious' to tolerate uncivil, unreasonable and provocative behaviour, officers reassure themselves that their 'gang' still reigns supreme.

The police station must be placed in the context of this relationship. Once this is done it becomes clear that, in addition to helping the police construct a prosecution case, the police station provides them with the means to inflict summary punishment. Those who are regularly policed state that they are approached by the police with a clear presumption of guilt. They must answer whatever questions the police decide to ask. Those who challenge the 'right' of the police to behave in this fashion are carted off to the 'punishment block'. The power to arrest and detain at the station allows each officer to extract the submissiveness which he feels is his due.

Once inside the station, defendants are routinely humiliated through being rendered powerless. They are told when to stand and when to sit down, when to talk and when to remain silent (Holdaway 1983, p. 27). They must behave with complete submissiveness, hand over their property on demand, tolerate abuse and threats of physical violence if not its actual infliction, and suffer incarceration in sometimes appalling conditions. Those who in any way sought to question the 'usual procedure' were shouted at and verbally abused. I observed cases where the police resorted to the use of force when, in my view, such force was unnecessary or excessive. The police have power over such matters as search of the defendant's premises, strip-searches, the speed with which to process the defendant, whether or not to charge, the choice of charge, whether or not

---

[3] The remark allegedly made by the officer in this case is reminiscent of that made by David McNee, then Commissioner of the Metropolitan police, who, when asked by a reporter what action he was taking regarding the large number of complaints that had been made against SPG officers, replied: 'If you keep off the streets and behave yourself, you won't have the SPG to worry about'! (reproduced in Rawlings 1985).

to grant police bail and whether or not to recommend a remand in custody when the defendant is presented before the court. The result is that defendants are locked into a system of rewards and punishments: rewards for the 'good as gold' and punishments for those who decide to be 'obnoxious' or whose 'obnoxious' status is permanent because they have been less than deferential on previous occasions.

The majority of defendants to whom I spoke knew the 'rules' of the police station, and said that it was best to go along with police wishes because otherwise matters would be made worse:

Case 54 Grimeston
Def: I've been treated fine in the past, I've been treated good 'cos I've never been any hassle to them ... because when I come down here I know there's no point, yea? I just stand there and say 'Yes sir, Yes sir, Yes sir.' And they put me in a cell and let me go when they want to let me go.

Case 59 Grimeston
(The defendant said that he did not want to be questioned. I asked him why, that being the case, he answered police questions) I mean the way I look at it, if you don't talk to 'em they aren't gonna let you go, they'll keep you here for the full 48 hours, or whatever it is now.

Interrogation allows the police to set up a situation in which they can ask the suspect *any* question they want, and in any *manner* they want, regardless of whether it relates to the original suspicion (McConville and Hodgson 1993, p. 185). Suspects in my sample were asked about their personal relationships, asked where they got their new clothes from and how they paid for them, asked about their immigration status and asked about why they were claiming state benefits, even where the questions had no connection whatsoever with the original reason for the arrest.

The police are under no obligation to charge or to justify to anyone why they thought it necessary to bring the 'suspect' to the station. Large numbers of those who are taken to the police station are released without charge, whilst nearly a third of those who are cautioned never admit to any offence. This situation is explained by the fact that in a large number of cases policing is geared, not towards the enforcement of the criminal law, but towards the achievement of police-defined objectives. Police actions, both inside and outside the station, are designed to send a message to certain communities, groups and individuals. The message is that challenge, resistance and a lack of respect will always incur punishment, even if it has to be imposed through an informal, police-administered system of 'justice'.

III THE RECOMMENDATIONS OF THE ROYAL COMMISSION

The RCCJ has decided to examine the criminal process after the point of arrest (para. 1.5). It has put forward its recommendations on the assumption that all arrests are lawful and that the purpose of 'processing' is to select for prosecution those who are 'legally guilty' and to discard the remainder. In making this assumption it has ignored a wealth of research findings which demonstrate that this view of arrest and processing is extremely problematic.

Although it is true that many suspects are arrested and processed in the manner envisaged by the legal rationality model of criminal justice, in a significant minority of cases the rules of legal rationality do not apply. In these cases arrest takes place despite the lack of reasonable suspicion, and the purpose of the post-arrest process is to create the suspicion necessary to justify the arrest (McConville and Hodgson 1993, p. 188). This happens because of policework methodologies, which are in turn informed by police views of particular individuals and groups. It is difficult to see how the Commissioners can seek to 'regulate' police station procedures without understanding the functions of the police station, and this they cannot do without understanding how and why particular individuals are drawn into the process.

In 'processing' suspects the police are not always interested in prosecuting the guilty and weeding out the legally innocent. 'Processing' may be aimed at the denigration of a particular individual, it may serve institutional goals in helping the police to assert their authority, or it may have a social purpose in sending a message to a certain community or locality. These wider policing objectives may in fact be given priority over the assumed sole objective of selecting the guilty and discarding the innocent:

Field-Note Extract 35 (Nasherford)
The defendant was arrested for swearing at an officer whilst the officer was in the processing of arresting someone. The colleague of the arresting officer explained the facts to the CO.

CO: So he got arrested for telling PC X to 'fuck-off'?
PC: Well, that's about it.
CO: So what does he (PC X) want to do about it?
PC: I think he wants him, Sarge, he was really annoyed.

The youth was eventually brought out and charged, not only with 'using insulting and abusive language', but also with 'assaulting a police officer in the execution of his duty'.

Far from seeking to encourage the police to operate on the basis of individualised reasonable suspicion, the Commissioners endorse policing practices which aim to control suspect populations:

> The police service themselves place great emphasis on the equipment which helps them keep suspected criminals under surveillance, including closed circuit television and video recording cameras in public places such as football grounds and shopping centres. We strongly support the use of such devices ... (para. 2.47)

Rather than examining the causes of police deviance, the RCCJ has sought refuge in yet more regulation as a solution to the problem of PACE violations. For example, now that the research has persuasively shown that custody officers are not in fact independent of investigating officers, a concept central to the protective scheme introduced by PACE, the Commissioners recommend that they in turn be supervised by station managers (para. 3.29). This recommendation is farcical in view of the fact that all the research indicates that the reality of policing is forged by the work-culture of the lower ranks.

Regulation cannot stop the police from treating some individuals less favourably than others, and so long as the police can do this their power to inflict arbitrary punishment remains unfettered. For example, by extending police powers to take samples (paras 2.33–4) the Commissioners have increased the ability of the police to punish those whom they have defined as 'obnoxious'.

The Commissioners have recommended that there be continuous video-recording, with soundtrack, of all custody blocks, corridors and stairways within the police station (para. 3.54). This will undoubtedly encourage officers to think twice before physically assaulting suspects, but as the following extract demonstrates it is important to appreciate that the camera will portray only a partial and possibly distorted picture of the police-policed encounter.

Case 73 Grimeston
> Whilst the defendant was being searched, the police informed me that he hated the police and was an 'obnoxious' individual who ought to be locked up for good. When I interviewed him, the defendant said that the police hated him, and had on one occasion run him over and caused permanent damage to one of his legs. He accused them on this occasion of taunting and mocking him: 'They were baiting me left, right and centre; they were offering me the chance to have a roll, they wanted me to start ...'

The point is that the suspect may have suffered humiliation and provocation at the point of arrest, or in fact the whole history of his relationship may be one of police persecution and harassment. Remarks made by the police to the defendant in front of the camera may make no sense to an outsider, or may appear to be petty and insignificant, and yet such remarks may be designed to wound and provoke the defendant by reviving memories of previous 'defeats' or humiliations. Unless those viewing the film are aware of those previous dealings, they may interpret the defendant's response to such remarks as being unreasonable and blameworthy.

Rather than seeking to bring in yet more regulation, the RCCJ should have used the opportunity presented to it to reconsider the purpose of arrest and detention. Arrest should be used only for the purpose of putting a stop to continuing criminal behaviour and/or to ensure attendance at court. By failing to consider the variety of reasons which may underlie the police decision to arrest and detain, the Commissioners have implicitly endorsed the police practice of using these powers for the purpose of inflicting summary punishment.

IV CONCLUSION

In common with most writing on the criminal justice system, the RCCJ Report is based on the myth that policing is directed towards *individuals* whom the police have *reasonable suspicion* to believe have committed a criminal offence, and that persons are arrested because the police wish to gather the evidence required for a *prosecution*. The dynamics of police–suspect encounters will not be altered until there is recognition in official circles that much of policing is aimed at *social control*, targeted against specific *communities*, initiated on the basis of *prejudice*, and frequently prompted by the desire of the police to impose their *authority* on groups who are seen to challenge 'respectable' notions of normality.

15. A Recipe for Miscarriage: The Royal Commission and Informal Interviews

Roger Leng

The admissibility of confessions[1] is traditionally founded upon two pervasive assumptions: that a confession is particularly likely to be true; and that police officers are to be trusted.[2] These twin assumptions have been subject to cumulative erosion traceable to the crisis of confidence in criminal justice following the *Confait* case (Fisher, 1977). Thus it is increasingly recognised that some individuals are highly suggestible under interrogation and that the oppressive circumstances of even lawful interrogations may induce false confessions (Gudjonsson et al., 1992;1993). Modern research indicates the prevalence of bargaining as a means of inducing confessions (McConville et al., 1991, pp. 60–65; Maguire and Norris, 1993, pp 45–48) and the notorious miscarriage of justice cases coupled with the West Midlands Serious Crime Squad scandal have demonstrated the inclination of some groups of police officers to collaborate in manufacturing confessions (Dennis, 1993; Kaye, 1991).

Modern scepticism in relation to confessions is reflected in the provisions of the Police and Criminal Evidence Act 1984 (PACE) and Codes, which regulate detention and questioning and require interviews to be tape-recorded, and which provide for the exclusion of confessions which are unreliable, or obtained unfairly or by oppression. A consequence of PACE is that it would now be virtually impossible to fabricate a confession in formal interview and have it admitted as evidence. Similarly, bargaining or bullying in the course of interview is likely to lead to the exclusion of any

---

[1] The term confession is used throughout the paper to include other admissions (statements wholly or partly adverse to the maker), which are governed by the same rules of evidence: Police and Criminal Evidence Act 1984 s 82(1).

[2] The practical effect of this assumption is normally bolstered by having two officers present during interview.

173

resulting confession.

A probable consequence of tighter regulation of police interviews is a shift of emphasis in investigations from formal interview to informal exchanges. Research indicates that such a switch of emphasis occurred following the introduction of tape-recording of interviews in Scotland (McConville and Morrell, 1983). Although there is insufficient pre-PACE data to determine conclusively whether there has been a similar shift of emphasis in England, it is significant that, with one exception (Irving and McKenzie, 1989),[3] all of the major post-PACE studies have found substantial evidence that informal interactions have a significant role in police investigations (McConville et al., 1991, pp. 58–65; Bottomley et al., 1991, pp. 157–60; Maguire and Norris, 1993, pp. 45–8; Brown et al., 1992, pp. 80–90; Evans, 1993a, pp. 28–9).

Informal interactions may be significant in the investigation in three major ways.

1. The informal interaction may influence the exercise of procedural rights by the suspect. Whereas some of the procedural rights under PACE are absolute (for instance the right not to be held beyond the prescribed time limits), others depend upon an election by the suspect and may therefore become a subject of negotiation between police and suspect (Sanders et al., 1989).
2. The informal interaction may influence the content of the formal interview. The police may use informal discussions to gain the confidence of the suspect, to offer inducements or threats, to suggest appropriate terminology for the interview or to dissuade the suspect from raising a defence.
3. The informal interaction may be a source of evidence. A confession is admissible evidence against the maker, provided that it does not fall foul of any specific exclusionary rule.

I THE RE-DRAFT OF CODE C

Concern about the prevalence of informal interviews (among other things) led to the re-drafting of PACE Code C on detention and interrogation in 1991 (Wolchover and Heaton-Armstrong, 1991). The revised Code

---

[3] Irving accepts that these findings relating only to Brighton in 1986–7 were not typical (personal communication July 1993). His most recent research includes a discussion of the scope for the police to bring pressure to bear on suspects outside the formal interview (Irving and Dunningham, 1993).

provides that: 'Following a decision to arrest, a suspect must not be interviewed about the relevant offence (subject to limited exceptions) except at the police station' (para. 11.1). In *Cox* [1993] 96 Cr App R 464, the Court of Appeal underlined the prohibition on informal interviews by ruling inadmissible a partial confession allegedly made during questioning on arrest.

However, whereas the Code reserves evidence collection for the police station, it necessarily retains a power to question outside the station, not least because otherwise the police might arrest needlessly where suspicion might be dispelled by a simple question. Thus whereas 'interviewing' a person regarding his involvement in an offence is outlawed:

> Questioning a person only to obtain information or his explanation of the facts or in the ordinary course of the officer's duties does not constitute an interview for the purpose of this Code. Neither does questioning which is confined to the proper and effective conduct of a search. (Code C, Note 11A)

Thus, suspects' answers to permitted questioning, as well as spontaneous utterances, continue to be a legitimate source of evidence. For this reason, the Code requires that the police make a timed and signed written record of such utterances at the earliest opportunity. The suspect must then be invited to read the record and to either sign it as correct or to indicate in what respect he/she considers it inaccurate (Code para. 11.13). Recent cases indicate that the courts will exclude alleged informal admissions where no adequate opportunity to verify or deny has been given.[4]

Although the revision of Code C signals a serious attempt to tackle the evidential problems caused by informal interactions between police and suspects, its effects will necessarily be limited. The only real sanction for breach of the Code is exclusion of a resulting confession.[5] There will be no incentive to abide by the Code where the purpose of the interview is not to obtain an admissible confession, but rather is to bargain with or influence the suspect.

II THE ROYAL COMMISSION'S RESEARCH

As well as sponsoring research on informal interviews by Moston and Stephenson (1993), the Commission also relied upon Brown's study for the Home Office (Brown et al., 1992) which assessed the effects of

---

4 *Chung* [1991] 92 Cr App R 314; *Joseph* [1993] Crim L R 206.
5 Research indicates an absence of supervision of investigating officers (Maguire and Norris, 1993; Baldwin and Moloney, 1993). No post-PACE study has found evidence that officers responsible for breaches of the Codes of Practice are disciplined.

revising PACE Code C.

Both studies found substantial evidence of questioning outside the police station. Brown et al. found that the police reported questioning outside the station in 10 per cent of cases (as opposed to 19 per cent prior to the Code revision). Moston and Stephenson found that some form of offence-related exchange took place outside the station in about 35 per cent of cases. They also noted a high correlation (82 per cent) between interviews outside the station and admissions in formal interview, although the research design did not permit exploration of the nature of the relationship.

For the purpose of shedding light on the incidence and significance of informal exchanges with suspects, these studies are of limited value. Both focus on exchanges outside the police station and therefore miss informal exchanges within it. Neither study attempts to assess the extent to which informal exchanges produce admissible confessions where suspects do not confess in formal interview. For both studies data collection was by police officers who reported on their own dealings with suspects. Although both research teams seek to dismiss this possibility, it seems very likely that officers would tend to classify their conduct into legally acceptable categories and that this would result in an under-recording of informal police–suspect exchanges.

III INFORMAL EXCHANGES WHICH INFLUENCE THE CONTENT OR CIRCUMSTANCES OF THE INTERVIEW

The Commission's approach to informal exchanges which may influence the formal interview has three strands. First, it adopts and seeks to clarify the Code C restriction on interviews outside the station. Secondly, it cautiously recommends 'carefully researched progress' towards greater use of tape-recorders outside the police station. Thirdly, it recommends continuous video-recording of the environs of the custody suite to both deter and record informal exchanges within the station.

Whilst approving the objective of restricting interviews outside the station, the Commission recognises that Code C fails to distinguish clearly legitimate and illegitimate questioning because 'questioning in the ordinary course of the officer's duties or to obtain information or the explanation of facts' may also be 'questioning regarding his or her involvement in a criminal offence'. The semantic problem arises from a conflict between two interests: on the one hand questioning on the street may prevent unnecessary arrests; on the other hand such questioning side-steps PACE safeguards. Striking a balance involves difficult questions of principle and practicality. The Commission's recommendation: 'that the apparent confusion should be clarified when Code C is next revised' (p. 27) abdicates the responsibility for striking the correct balance to the Home Office, and wrongly implies that purging the confusion involves a mere drafting issue.[6]

The Commission notes a current experiment in Essex on tape-recording outside the police station and hopes that greater use will be made of tape-recorders if this is shown to be feasible. Recording from the point of arrest would certainly reduce opportunities for the police to influence the suspect's decision-making or to prescribe the content of the formal interview. For this reason it may be resisted in some quarters of the police. Those who recall the debates surrounding the introduction of tape-recording for formal interviews, will recognise the need to scrutinise carefully any objections to feasibility raised by the police (Baldwin, 1985a).

As the Commission realistically accepts, tape-recording could never remove all grounds for argument about what occurred before a suspect reached the police station, and it should not be an objection that tape-recording cannot provide complete guarantees of propriety. It follows that whereas a recording might operate as a shield for the accused, by demonstrating for instance that an inducement was offered, it should never operate as a sword for the prosecution since the recording could not conclusively prove a negative, that a threat or inducement alleged by the suspect had never been made.

The Commission also suggests that tapes would enable supervisors to monitor the conduct of junior officers. Whilst this is technically correct, it suggests naiveté about the inclination of senior officers to supervise, and an ignorance of research which demonstrates the failure of internal police supervision as a regulatory mechanism (Bottomley et al., 1991, pp. 42–4; Baldwin and Moloney, 1993; Maguire and Norris, 1993).

In response to concerns about illicit visits to suspects in their cells (McConville, 1992) the Commission recommends continuous video-recording of custody suites, extending to the cell door, but not into individual cells. This is arguably the most important of the Commission's recommendations in terms of securing the integrity of the formal interview. However, it may be queried whether it goes far enough. Brown found significant disparities between the duration of recorded interviews and the

---

6   Commentators have noted the extent to which the Royal Commission abdicates important issues of principle to other bodies (Baldwin, 1993a; Evans, 1993b). For a reply see Zander (1993).

times booked out for interviewing on custody records (Brown et al., 1992, p. 90). This indicates that there are opportunities for informal exchanges in the interview room while the tape-recorder is not running. If it becomes more difficult to conduct off-the-record discussions elsewhere in the station, interviewing officers may be tempted to make greater use of these periods. This suggests that in order to be effective, continuous video recording should extend to interview rooms as well as the corridors of the custody suite.

IV INFORMAL INTERVIEWS AS A SOURCE OF CONFESSION EVIDENCE

The Commission's approach to confessions made outside formal interview has three main strands:

i) informal confessions are seen as a valuable form of evidence which should be admissible;
ii) because of doubts about reliability, measures are proposed for recording, authenticating and verifying such confessions;
iii) but, doubts about reliability are not so substantial as to require special rules of evidence to protect the accused, apart from a general judicial warning about the dangers of relying on confession evidence.

1. Verification and Authentication

The Commission recommends that an alleged confession should be put to the suspect at the beginning of the taped interview for confirmation, denial or comment.[7] The Commission does not accept, however, that the risks of fabrication, misunderstanding, selective recording and misrecording, are so substantial that the confession should not be admitted in the absence of verification.

The proposal to give the suspect an opportunity to confirm or contest an alleged confession is superficially attractive, but perhaps deserves further consideration. One problem is that the alleged confession will effectively set the agenda for the interview and may place the suspect on the defensive. This may inhibit the suspect from fully developing his or her

---

[7] Moston and Stephenson examined the transcripts of interview in 19 cases in which a suspect was interviewed both outside and inside the police station. The formal interview contained reference to the earlier interview in only five of the cases (1993, p. 38).

story.[8] Further, a suspect who contests the confession at trial may be prejudiced by the dramatic impact of the alleged confession at the beginning of the interview.

The Commission also favours the adoption of a procedure operating experimentally in the Metropolitan district by which written records of conversations with suspects are stamped with the date and time at which the officer presented the record in the custody office. Whereas this procedure could not prove that a statement had actually been made it could establish the stage in the investigation at which the alleged statement emerged. This would offer some protection against an officer retrospectively fabricating a verbal confession in order to make good a failure to obtain a confession in formal interview. It would not prevent a corrupt officer anticipating that problem.

This proposal adopts the PACE technique of presenting a recording procedure as a safeguard. McConville et al. (1991, Ch. 5) have argued that recording procedures function not as safeguards for the accused but rather as a means of legitimising police conduct and of officially denying alternative accounts. In the present context, if the risk involved is that officers may fabricate confessions, it can hardly be a safeguard to invest such officers with a mechanism for self-authentication.

2. Safeguards by Rules of Evidence

Many who gave evidence to the Commission pressed the case for special rules of evidence to guard against false confessions. For recorded confessions, falsity may result from manipulation by the police or others, or from psychological factors (Gudjonsson, 1992). For unrecorded confessions there is the further risk of fabrication by the police. Although, the Commission acknowledged the need for 'effective safeguards against false confessions being believed' (p. 57), it ultimately rejected any new special rules of evidence. It is argued below that the Commissioners' reasons for rejecting special safeguards are neither logical nor satisfactory in principle. However, perhaps the most astounding feature of their reasoning is that it fails to distinguish between recorded and unrecorded confessions and therefore fails to address the real risk of fabrication where the only evidence of a confession is a police officer's word.

---

8   It is not suggested that current interview techniques are conducive to the suspect developing his or her story. Research suggests the contrary for some cases (Irving and Hilgendorf, 1980; McConville et al., 1991, Chapter 4; Baldwin, 1992; Evans, 1993a). ACPO/Home Office guidance on interviewing issued in 1993 would, if followed, improve opportunities for suspects to put their case in interview (Central Planning and Training Unit, 1992).

3. Tape-Recording

The first safeguard to be considered was a rule which would exclude confessions unless recorded or repeated on tape. Such a rule is rejected on the basis that spontaneous remarks uttered on arrest are often the most truthful (p. 61). This may or may not be true but it is beside the point. Where a spontaneous confession is alleged, the issue is not the credibility of the suspect but rather the credibility of the officer who claims to have received the confession. A belief that spontaneous confessions are reliable does not assist a court to determine whether such a spontaneous confession was actually made.

For the Commission, the fact that many suspects would refuse to confirm on tape an alleged spontaneous confession, is an argument for admitting the earlier confession. This is puzzling because the refusal is essentially ambiguous. For instance, the suspect might refuse to confirm because the confession was fabricated. By ignoring this possibility, the Commission betrays twin working presumptions: that police suspects are guilty and that police officers do not fabricate confessions. An alternative approach, proceeding from the presumption of innocence, would be that an alleged confession followed by a refusal to confirm it, is not sufficiently probative either way to warrant admission as evidence.

4. Presence of a Solicitor

The Commission also considered whether confessions should be inadmissible unless made or confirmed in the presence of a solicitor. The thrust of this proposal would be to guard against improper pressure rather than to simply verify that the confession had been made. In rejecting the proposal the Commission pointed out that many suspects did not wish to have a solicitor present and that research indicated that the presence of a legal adviser did not guarantee propriety (Baldwin, 1993b; McConville and Hodgson, 1993). It was also argued that such a rule might lose prosecution evidence because a suspect who had made an earlier confession might refuse to confirm it before a solicitor. Again, the Commission appears to be blind to the possibility that refusal to confirm casts doubt on the credibility of the alleged confession.

The final ground for rejecting the proposed rule is that a solicitor's presence at formal interview would not prevent improper pressure being applied beforehand. Thus, the prospect of improper pressure becomes a reason for *not* imposing a safeguard. It is hard to conceive of more perverse reasoning.

5. Corroboration

Following the exposure of wrongful convictions based on confession evidence alone, a substantial body of opinion has favoured the introduction of a rule barring conviction on confession evidence unless supported by other evidence linking the accused to the crime (Pattenden, 1991; Thornton et al., 1992). In research conducted for the Commission, McConville demonstrated that 7.8 per cent of cases would fall foul of a corroboration requirement if the police made no changes to existing investigative practices. However, if the police were to utilise as evidence more of the information already in their hands and exploited further opportunities for investigation, the proportion of convictions lost as a result of a corroboration rule would be less than 4 per cent.

In rejecting a corroboration rule,[9] the Royal Commission argues that it would lead to a number of guilty defendants walking free, and that this would be acceptable only if the introduction of the rule provided significantly greater safeguards against wrongful convictions than are now available. This argument assumes that of the group of offenders who would be acquitted under a corroboration rule, a substantial number would be guilty. But this cannot be demonstrated. Indeed, the whole basis of the argument for reform rests upon the view that guilt cannot be satisfactorily established where the defendant denies the offence in court and the only evidence is a confession.

The Commission's reasoning is also odd in that it implies that it is possible to separate the issue of defendants walking free through lack of evidence from the issue of safeguards against wrongful convictions. The prime safeguard against wrongful conviction has always been the defendant's right to walk free if guilt cannot be satisfactorily proved.

The Commission's second argument against a corroboration rule is that it would not provide safeguards against wrongful convictions resulting from 'fabricated confessions and the production of evidence obtained by improper means'. This is a ludicrous argument. It has never been suggested that a corroboration rule could protect defendants against determined and sophisticated efforts to frame them. The point of a corroboration rule would be to protect defendants against conviction on confession evidence alone because of the intrinsic unreliability of such evidence.

Perhaps the weakest aspect of the Commission's treatment of corroboration is the fact that it ignores the huge qualitative difference

---

[9] A minority of three members of the Commission recommended that a conviction should never be possible on confession evidence alone, in the absence of supporting evidence (p. 87).

between recorded and unrecorded confessions. Stated baldly, the Commission proposes that a criminal conviction can be based on a police officer's assertion that the defendant confessed, where the defendant denies this and where there is not a shred of further evidence.

6. Warnings

The Commission considered two proposals to introduce special judicial warnings relating to confession evidence. The first of these, inspired by the Australian case *McKinney and Judge* ([1991] 65 ALJR 241), would have required a special warning about the dangers of convicting where the only evidence is a confession made in police custody.

The fundamental argument for such a warning is that the natural inclination of some jurors to trust police testimony is at odds with the propensity of some groups of police officers to fabricate confessions. However, the Commission was unhappy about 'singling out all police officers in a judicial warning to be given in every case' (p. 60). The dominant concern here seems to be to avoid offending police witnesses. Whereas it is important that witnesses should not be deterred from giving evidence nor harmed by doing so, this interest is normally subordinated to the need to place all relevant evidence before the jury. The departure from principle embodied in the Commission's reasoning can be justified only if the police are viewed as a particularly vulnerable group of witnesses deserving special protection.

The Commission however, does recognise the need for a general warning about confession evidence. It proposes that judges should be required to give a warning tailored to the facts of the case, outlining possible reasons for false confessions, drawing attention to any reasons advanced by the defence and emphasising the need for care before convicting on a confession alone (p. 66).

7. Reliance on General Safeguards

Whilst reluctant to erect any special barriers to convictions on the basis of informal confessions, the Commission places great reliance on general safeguards to prevent wrongful convictions. The Commission also proposes a new judicial power to halt a case where the prosecution case was demonstrably unsafe or unsatisfactory or too weak to be put to the jury (p. 59). This would reverse the courts' self-imposed bar on usurping the function of the jury, imposed in *Galbraith* [1981] 1 WLR 1039.

It is not clear that the Commission's faith in general safeguards to weed out unsafe cases is well founded. The belief that prosecutorial or judicial discretion, or the exclusionary rules would be effective to prevent wrongful convictions is dependent upon an assumption that it is possible to identify those cases in which an uncorroborated confession is unreliable. However, in the absence of other evidence it is difficult to see how this could be done. If it is accepted that some uncorroborated confessions are not a reliable basis for conviction, but that these cannot be identified, the only proper course is a rule of evidence barring conviction in all such cases.

Neither the police nor the CPS are likely to weed out unreliable cases, or to require further investigations, where as a matter of strict law evidential sufficiency is satisfied (McConville et al., 1991, Ch. 7). Thus, McConville found that in 60 per cent of cases in which a conviction was obtained on confession evidence alone, the police either had access to further evidence or could have conducted further enquiries to get it (McConville, 1993b, p. 85). From the point of view of the police, struggling to respond to high crime rates with limited resources, it is entirely rational to prosecute less serious cases on the minimum evidence required for conviction.

The Commission's vision of a new era of judicial activism founded on the reversal of *Galbraith* may also be optimistic. The notions that convictions can be founded on confession evidence and that the judge should leave issues of fact to the jury have similarly deep roots in the criminal justice system. Neither is likely to be dislodged by simply extending the powers of the trial judge.

The judges have been active in excluding confessions under sections 76 and 78 of PACE where breaches of Code C are established.[10] However, the potential for excluding alleged verbals is limited. Thus, there would be no ground for exclusion where the police allege that a confession was spontaneous or resulted from permissible questioning, and that the verification procedures had been complied with.

V THE POLICE WITNESS

Where a confession is received in evidence the testimony is that of the police officer who allegedly heard the confession. In relation to interviews conducted under PACE, credibility is normally settled by the tape-recording of an interview. Where the prosecution tender an informal confession as evidence, credibility depends upon whether the officer

---

[10] *McGovern* [1991] 92 Cr App R 228; *Chung* [1991] 92 Cr App R 314; *Cox* [1993] 96 Cr App R 464.

correctly understood and recalled what had been said and is telling the truth. Under present law and under the Commission's proposals, a case may be tried in which the only prosecution evidence is an alleged informal confession. In such cases, the truthfulness of the officer is the central, and perhaps the only, issue at trial.

In an important recent case, *Edwards* ([1991] 93 Cr App R 48), the Court of Appeal held that where it is alleged that a confession had been fabricated, the police officer who testifies to the confession could be cross-examined about other cases in which he had given evidence of a confession in which the defendant had been acquitted. The officer might also be cross-examined about previous criminal convictions or proven disciplinary offences, but not about any pending criminal or disciplinary charges.

Discussing *Edwards* in the context of the prosecution's duty to disclose information, the Commission suggested that the decision went too far. In the Commission's view, the prosecution's duty to disclose should relate only to an officer's criminal convictions or disciplinary findings: the prosecution should not be obliged to disclose details of other cases in which an acquittal suggested that the officer had been disbelieved (p. 97). This recommendation would effectively emasculate the *Edwards* rule since limited defence resources would normally preclude investigation of previous malpractice by a police witness.

The Commission's rationale for undermining the *Edwards* principle is that because juries do not explain their verdicts, it would be impossible to attribute an acquittal to disbelief of the officer's evidence. But this is surely disingenuous. Where the only evidence is a confession testified to by an officer, the explanation for acquittal must be that the officer was disbelieved.

This issue is of central importance to the evaluation of prosecution evidence and the avoidance of wrongful convictions. It is unfortunate and discreditable that it should have been considered in a part of the Report which is primarily concerned with husbanding prosecution resources. It is shocking that the Commission appear more concerned with protecting police witnesses than with ensuring that police evidence is properly tested.

If the Commission had been serious about avoiding wrongful convictions and committed to the doctrine of proof beyond reasonable doubt, would they not have extended rather than curtailed the *Edwards* principle (Pattenden, 1992)? In practical terms, if a defendant stands accused on the evidence of a single police officer, should not the jury be told if that officer has been charged with perjury, has serious disciplinary charges pending, or has been accused of fabrication and disbelieved at other trials?

VI CONCLUSION

The Royal Commission offered an opportunity to re-think the primacy of confession evidence in the criminal process, to dislodge institutional beliefs about the provenance and reliability of confessions, and to incorporate modern psychological and sociological insights about why people confess and about the police role in generating confessions. These issues are acknowledged, and are reflected in valuable proposals to video-tape custody suites and to instruct juries on the inherent risks of relying on confession evidence.

In contrast, the Commission's recommendation that an uncorroborated confession should remain a sufficient evidential basis for conviction, is rooted elsewhere. The dominant influence on the Commission's thinking appears to be a paralysing fear of losing convictions, bolstered by a willingness to countenance some instances of miscarriage of justice, in the interests of effectively convicting the guilty. This policy is illuminated by the twin recommendations: that an unsupported informal confession should be sufficient for conviction; and that grounds for doubting a testifying officer's credibility should be hidden from the defence. This is a recipe which has generated miscarriages of justice in the past, and if the Commission's recommendations are accepted, will do so again.

16. Defence Services: What Should Defence Lawyers do at Police Stations?

Ed Cape

If the Report of the Royal Commission on Criminal Justice discloses an underlying philosophy it is that the two parties to the criminal justice process join adversarial battle on equal terms. Although there is no analysis of the respective resources and powers of defence and prosecution, it is a convenient philosophy. It enables the Commission, for example, to recommend certain restrictions on the duty of the prosecution to disclose evidence, but to significantly increase the duty to disclose of the defence. This 'redresses the balance', whilst conveniently ignoring the fact that the defence have a small proportion of the resources and none of the powers available to the prosecution. The rationale for the prosecution's burden of proof is lost in the search for managerial solutions to the 'problems' of criminal justice.

This 'equality' philosophy is also evident when the Commission considers the issue of legal advice at the police station. Legal advice is regarded as a safeguard for the suspect – it is dealt with in Chapter 3 under the heading 'Safeguards for Suspects' – which, the implication is, places the suspect on an equal footing with the police. This is also convenient for, once the role of the defence lawyer is properly understood (both police and lawyers are encouraged to 'understand' the lawyer's role better) (Royal Commission on Criminal Justice, *Report* (RCCJ Report), HMSO, London, 1993, pp. 36–7), equilibrium is secured. No matter that, however good the defence lawyer is, the police determine the course of events during a person's detention and no matter that there is very little the defence lawyer can do in terms of enforcement.

Indeed, the issue of power, or more particularly the disparity of power as between the defence and the prosecution is hardly recognised at all (as noted by Baldwin 1993a, at p. 1197). The failure to take account of the structural imbalance between the two parties leads to a complete failure to deal with an issue that is fundamental both to police detention and to the provision of defence services at the police station; that is, what is the true purpose of police interrogation of suspects. It has recently become popular to characterise the purpose of police interrogation as being a search for the truth. Whilst Code C Note for Guidance 11A provides that an interview is 'the questioning of a person regarding his involvement or suspected involvement in a criminal offence or offences', the *Guide to Interviewing* (a document recently produced under the direction of a joint ACPO/Home Office Steering Group, and issued with Home Office Circular 7/1993 *Investigative Interviewing: National Training Package*) describes the aim of an interview as being to establish the facts of the incident under investigation (ACPO/Home Office, 1993, p.1). This is a neutral description of the activity which nicely accords with the equality principle. However, there is ample evidence, including evidence from the Commission's own researchers, that the police use interrogation of suspects as a mechanism for constructing a case against the suspect, which may well involve inducing an admission or a confession (McConville et al., 1991). This is even recognised, in part, in the *Guide to Interviewing* which, having defined the interview in neutral terms goes on to state that the interviewer must have a clear understanding of the legal points to prove. The interviewer is also given guidance on, amongst other things, the use of silence to prompt an interviewee to speak.

The problem here, and it is one that the Commission ignored completely, despite being prompted by the Law Society (The Law Society Memorandum of Evidence No. 4 to the Royal Commission on Criminal Justice, p. 7), is of defining the true purpose of interviewing and then, having defined the purpose, setting out what the police are or are not permitted to do in pursuing those objectives. Given that the process is adversarial, which it must be since any information obtained by the police can be used in the process of prosecuting the suspect, it is not honest or adequate to say that the purpose is simply to secure information about the facts of the case. To take one practical example which is a daily problem for both police and defence, if interviewing really is a neutral fact-finding exercise, then once a suspect has stated that s/he does not wish to answer police questions there can be little reason to interview him/her. Interviewing such a suspect only becomes explicable or justified if the purpose is to seek to persuade him/her to talk. However, once this is accepted, the question arises of how far can the police go in such persuasion. Code of Practice C makes it clear that a suspect's unwillingness to answer questions is not a reason for an interview not taking place. *The Guide to Interviewing* endorses this and advises that silence 'coupled with eye contact' can amount to 'a powerful tool to prompt an interviewee to speak' (ACPO/Home Office, 1993, p. 57). However, there is plenty of evidence, of which the Commission was clearly aware since some of it has been produced by its own researchers,[1] that some people, or most people in certain situations, are peculiarly prone to falsely confessing if placed under any kind of pressure, such as silence or repetition of the same question. The fact is that there is probably no interrogation technique designed to persuade a guilty person to make admissions that will not also induce an innocent person to do the same. Whilst the *Guide to Interviewing* makes some gesture towards this problem in that it advises that silence of the interviewer should be used 'with discretion', the Commission ignores this fundamental problem. This is perhaps inevitable given its reluctance to grapple with the issue of the purpose of interrogation of suspects.

How is this relevant to legal advice for the suspect? The Commission was faced with two fundamental contradictions. The first is between the implicit characterisation of prosecution and defence as being on equal terms when this patently is not the case. The second is between the implicit acceptance that police interrogation is a neutral, fact-finding process when, as the Commission specifically endorses (RCCJ Report, op. cit., p. 3.), the police clearly perform an adversarial role. Thus, for example, the Commission purports to strengthen the position of the defence by recommending that Code C be amended to encourage the police to inform the suspect's solicitor of 'at least the general nature of the case and the *prima facie* evidence against the suspect', whilst ignoring the fact that such provisions of the Codes are largely unenforceable. However much 'encouragement' is given, in the absence of some mechanism for enforcement,[2] adversarial interests will remain paramount.

It is within the context of these unresolved contradictions that the Commission approached the question of the proper role of the defence lawyer at the police station. Recently a debate about the role of defence lawyers has been developing, prompted by the growing body of evidence that most lawyers' performance is very limited in practice. The Commission, despite noting its own research by Baldwin and by McConville and Hodgson on the inadequacies of legal advice, firmly decided not to join that debate. Rather it contented itself by noting the lack of clarity about the lawyers' role and endorsing the Law Society's view as set out in its booklet 'Advising the Client at the Police Station' (The Law

---

[1] In particular G. Gudjonsson, who undertook two research studies for the Commission.

[2] The Legal Action Group, for example, submitted that PACE should be amended so as to exclude evidence obtained as the result of a serious or substantial breach of PACE or the Codes of Practice.

Society, 1991). The Law Society's view is not without difficulty. Baldwin (1992, (2), p. 36), criticised the second edition of the booklet for its timidity and lack of assertiveness. The emphasis, he says, was 'not upon confrontation but upon 'mutual cooperation' with the police, ensuring fair play and generally doing whatever was required to look after the physical welfare of the suspect'. The current, third edition, Baldwin accepts is less conciliatory. Nevertheless, the booklet describes the purpose of legal advice at the police station as being 'to maintain the balance between the powers of the police when investigating whether a criminal offence has been committed and the protection of the rights of the suspect'. ('Advising a Suspect at the Police Station', op. cit., p. 1). Whilst it does contain useful advice to the defence lawyer, it fails to provide it within the context of an explicitly adversarial setting. The conduct and control of the police interview is firmly left with the interviewing officer, so that practical involvement of the lawyer in the interview is dealt with under the heading 'Interruptions by solicitors' (ibid., p. 28).

Code of Practice C is even less encouraging to the assertive lawyer. The Code says nothing of the role of the defence lawyer generally but defines his/her role in a negative sense in the police interview by stating that a solicitor 'is not guilty of misconduct' if s/he takes certain actions such as challenging an improper question or advising the suspect not to answer a particular question (Code of Practice C, Note for Guidance 6D). As Baldwin remarks 'It is clear, therefore, that lawyers in England are not expected or encouraged to intervene frequently or forcefully at police interviews.' ((2), 1992, p. 36).

The Royal Commission's response to this malaise is largely, as noted above, to ignore it. Since Baldwin's research for the Commission makes the point quite strongly, the Commission can hardly ignore the issue altogether. Thus it does accept that the role of the lawyer contained in Note for Guidance 6D 'could be put more positively' (RCCJ Report, op. cit., p. 37.) At present, continues the Report, 'it suggests that a solicitor is an unwelcome obstruction to police enquiries and to be tolerated only as far as necessary'. At this point, however, the Commission appears to run out of ideas, and so offers no more positive alternative. In its view, the Law Society's views as set out in the booklet are adequate, and the answer to the lack of clarity of role lies in more training for both lawyers and police officers (RCCJ Report, op. cit., pp. 36 and 38).

One might have expected the Royal Commission to have been more forthcoming about the role of defence lawyers given both the research evidence it obtained and the fact that defence lawyers are clearly regarded as a safeguard for the suspect in other parts of the Report. Again, one reason for this omission lies in the Commission's failure to accept the adversarial nature of the process. The Commission rejects a change to a more inquisitorial system because, amongst other reasons, it would result in a fusion of the roles of police and prosecution. Separation of these roles 'offers a better protection for the innocent defendant' (ibid., p. 4.).What it fails to acknowledge is that the roles of prosecution and police, at least in so far as they relate to the securing and use of evidence against the suspect, are one and the same.

The classic general statement of the lawyer's role is that s/he should act in the best interests of his/her client. Within the context of the police station, embodying as it does the adversarial features of the criminal justice system, this also provides an adequate statement of the role of the defence lawyer. It is the interests of the suspect, not those of the police and not those of the public generally, that are to be protected as far as possible. This simple statement of purpose does not appear in the Law Society's booklet although it is a principle that any civil lawyer, or non-contentious lawyer, would readily understand. If Nuclear Electric, for example, wishes to buy a piece of land on which to build a nuclear power station, the lawyers it employs to conduct the purchase will ensure that the land is bought for the negotiated price and unencumbered by any unwanted restrictions. The lawyer will not seek to increase the price because s/he has sympathy with the poor farmer who is having the land compulsorily purchased, or delay the purchase because s/he has sympathy for the demonstrators camped outside the site. If a lawyer is acting for a company that is being taken to an industrial tribunal for unfair dismissal, s/he will not advise the company to settle without making any effort to find out how strong the case against the company is. And when attending a conciliation meeting, s/he will not remain silent whilst the former employee makes all the running. And s/he certainly would not join in and endorse the demands made by the former employee.

Yet in the context of the police station this is exactly the kind of behaviour on the part of defence lawyers that was observed and identified by the Commission's own research (in particular, by Baldwin and by McConville and Hodgson). Faced with this, and again given the weight place by the Commission on the provision of legal advice, one might have expected the Commission to seek to understand why this occurs. In trying to understand why it is so, the Commission may have been prompted to make suggestions as to how it might be dealt with. As it was, the Commission confined itself to suggesting that the Law Society produce a training video and, 'in the longer term', review the training, education, supervision and monitoring of legal advisers (RCCJ Report, op. cit., p. 38).

As Baldwin has said, there is 'a pervasive air of superficiality about the discussions in this chapter'.(Baldwin 1993a, op. cit., p. 1194).

It is worth considering here why defence lawyers at police stations frequently do not perform their task in accordance with the principles that govern the profession generally. A partial explanation may be found in terms of resources, and the Commission did consider this in fairly general terms although it made no specific recommendation (RCCJ Report, op. cit., p. 38). McConville and Hodgson, in their research for the Commission, expressed doubt that higher payment for police station work would lead to an improvement in quality (1993, p. 200). As they point out, earlier research by Sanders et al. (1989) had shown that despite the fact that duty solicitors were paid one-third more for attending police stations in unsocial hours than 'own' solicitors, they gave advice by telephone only in far more cases than did 'own' solicitors.

A more satisfactory explanation may be found in terms of defence lawyers' own perception of their role, although as noted below, this is likely to be greatly affected by other, structural, factors. There are here three possibilities: solicitors do not recognise or accept the role as set out above; they are confused about their role; or they do accept the role but for a variety of reasons do not follow it in practice.

Lawyers may not recognise or accept the role of the lawyer acting in his/her client's best interests for a number of reasons. Some lawyers may simply accept the values of the police which, for these purposes, may be described as crime control values. From this point of view, whilst they are formally required to act in the best interests of their clients there are other, competing, values some of which may in practical terms be more significant. Having a good relationship with the police, a desire to see 'criminals' successfully prosecuted, a lack of sympathy for the kinds of people arrested by the police, a desire to do their work as quickly or as easily as possible, may mean that crime control values are more attractive to them. The problem of identification with police values is all the more likely where the lawyer is an ex-police officer. McConville and Hodgson found that nearly 50 per cent of the firms in their study employed ex-police officers for their police station work (ibid., p. 17).

For other lawyers, it may be that the role they implicitly adopt depends upon their view of the particular client, adopting an adversarial role where they have some sympathy for the suspect, but rejecting it where, for example, they believe the suspect to be guilty or where they are accused of a serious or repugnant crime.

Some lawyers are unclear about their role, as the Commission accepts (RCCJ Report, op. cit., p 38). According to Baldwin, 85 per cent of the lawyers in his study for the Royal Commission regarded their role as being 'first to advise their clients as to their position *before* questioning commenced, and, secondly, to act as a referee in the interview to ensure that fair play was observed' (emphasis added) (Baldwin 1992, op. cit., p. 49). The limitations of professional guidance was referred to earlier. McConville and Hodgson found that as much as 60 per cent of advice at the police station was provided by people who were neither solicitors nor articled clerks (McConville and Hodgson, op. cit., p. 17), and that such staff were relatively rarely given any training other than attending the station with another clerk on a couple of occasions (ibid., p. 28). Solicitors and articled clerks may hardly be in a better position. Substantive criminal law is frequently only studied in the first year of a law degree, and the Law Society Finals course has not until now included police station advice in its syllabus. 'Own' solicitors are not required to attend training courses on police station work, and even police station duty solicitors are not required to attend a course prior to initial selection if they already have substantial experience.[3] Of course, as the research evidence implies, substantial experience does not necessarily equate with expertise. Ironically, when the new provisions for the training of criminal clerks are introduced in October 1993,[4] clerks may be better trained than solicitors for police station work.

The third possibility is that the lawyer does accept the adversarial role but does not, or does not all of the time, feel able to give it practical expression. This may relate to the lawyer's own difficulty of squaring professional duty with moral concern. Thus the lawyer may exaggerate the mitigation benefits of admitting an offence in order not to be faced with a situation where s/he otherwise has to advise a client s/he knows to be guilty to remain silent in the police interview and thus deprive the police of the means of establishing guilt. Alternatively, the lawyer may be affected by pressure resulting from the crime control values of the police. Whilst not necessarily accepting those values s/he may nevertheless have difficulty in resisting them. The lawyer is on police territory and is subject to the power of the police to control the course of the investigation and to control the flow of information. The police may themselves employ tactics explicitly or implicitly designed to put pressure on the lawyer; emphasising the serious nature of the allegation, exaggerating the strength of the

---

[3] Legal Aid Board Duty Solicitor Arrangements 1992 para. 35(3). Oddly, if the solicitor is subject to the Law Society's post-admission training requirements, s/he must have attended the equivalent of at least one day's training in the previous 5 years before re-selection as a duty solicitor. See para. 42.

[4] A system of training and accreditation is being introduced in October 1993, and as from 1 October 1994, the Legal Aid Board will not pay for police station work done by an 'own' solicitor's representative who has not been accredited.

evidence, bringing in extra personnel or utilising the police hierarchy if tensions develop.

If the problem of the lawyer's role was simply one of perception, the recommendations of the Commission might be sufficient. Perceptions could be altered by greater clarity of purpose and standards could be improved by training. The Commission might, on this view, have said something disapproving about the employment of recently retired police officers as clerks, but essentially they would have struck the right note. However, perceptions and attitudes do not emerge from nowhere. They derive from real experiences. They derive from a professional history which, as Baldwin observes, leads solicitors to be passive in the police interview room ((2), 1992, p. 52). Perhaps most importantly they derive from the structural context within which police detention and interrogation is located. This structural context both explicitly and implicitly places the police in firm control. Lawyers are, in the end, allowed into police stations on sufferance. Lawyers in police stations have almost nothing but their powers of negotiation and advocacy to assist them. Some examples will help to illustrate this.

In order for a lawyer to be able properly to advise a client in the police station, s/he will need to obtain information from the police not only about the reason for the arrest, but also about the evidence the police have and the detention itself. McConville and Hodgson found that advisers relatively rarely tried to secure information from the custody officer (McConville and Hodgson, op. cit., p. 41). Lawyers did ask the arresting or investigating officer for information more frequently, but still in nearly half of cases no enquiry was made. As significant was the police response. Custody officers gave extensive details to the lawyer in just over 1 per cent of cases, and extensive details were given by the arresting or investigating officer in under 15 per cent of cases. McConville and Hodgson explain this largely in terms of the functional benefits to the police of information management. Withholding information 'is no accident but is embedded into the way in which the police seek control of the suspect and to become 'dominant persuader' (ibid., p. 44). This is perfectly understandable given the adversarial context and given that the true purpose of detention and interrogation is to secure evidence against the suspect. It may be, therefore, that lawyers do not ask for information because they do not expect to get it. Even if they are given information, how will they know that it is truthful or complete? Giving limited information, which may delude the defence into believing that the evidence is weak or flawed, and then releasing further information during the course of the interview, can be a very effective method of interrogation as McConville and Hodgson recognise (ibid., p. 46).

At present, the defence lawyer cannot look to PACE or the Codes of Practice for assistance. There is no requirement in PACE or the Codes of Practice for the police to provide such information to the defence. Indeed, the defence do not even have the right to see the custody record whilst the suspect remains in police detention.[5] Further, it is highly unlikely that a court would throw out a confession because it had been obtained following the selective release of information. The court is likely to regard it as a legitimate method of interrogation. Faced with an unwillingness by the police to supply information, about the only thing the defence lawyer can do is to advise his/her client to remain silent in interview (McConville and Hodgson, op. cit., p. 194).

The Commission's response to its own research in this respect is timid. It is recommended that solicitors see and 'if possible' be given a copy of the custody record on arrival at the police station, and that they be able to hear any tape-recorded interview already held (RCCJ Report, op. cit., p. 36). There is no mention of how this might be enforced. It is not even suggested that it be embodied in the Codes of Practice. Further, police officers are told by the Commission that they 'should see it as their duty to enable solicitors to advise their clients on the basis of the fullest appropriate information'. It explains that it is in the interests of the police to make available such information. It is unclear where this novel idea came from, but it was not from its own research. The Commission recommends that Code C be amended 'so as to encourage the police to inform the suspect's solicitor of at least the general nature of the case and the *prima facie* evidence against the suspect (ibid., p. 36). So the police are to be 'encouraged' to do something that will frequently be directly contrary to their interests. However, even if the recommendation were implemented, it need not cause too much concern to the police since it is well recognised that this kind of provision in the Codes of Practice is largely unenforceable.[6]

A second example relates to the impact a lawyer might have on the control exerted by the police over the suspect whilst in detention. In truth, although the criminal justice process may be described as adversarial in form, the police have many inquisitorial powers. In the first instance, the police, in the form of the custody officer, decide whether a suspect is to be detained. Although PACE s. 37 sets out criteria that have to be satisfied in

---

[5] The right only arises when the suspect leaves police detention or is taken before a court (Code of Practice, C para. 2.4).

[6] It was for this reason that the Legal Action Group, in its submission to the Commission, proposed that significant breaches of the Codes should lead to exclusion of evidence so obtained.

order for detention to be authorised, they are so broad as to enable such authorisation to, in the words of McKenzie et al. (1990, p. 33) amount to a 'rubber stamping decision'. Although authorising detention is the first step into an inherently coercive interrogation process, the Commission did not obtain research and had nothing to say about it in its Report.

The grounds for detention must, according to PACE s. 34, continue to prevail throughout detention prior to charge and to help ensure that this is the case, a person in police detention must have their detention reviewed by a senior officer at regular intervals (PACE s. 40). At review, s. 40(12) provides that the suspect or his/her lawyer (if available) must be given an opportunity to make representations. There are similar provisions if authorisation is sought to detain the person without charge beyond 24 hours.

An important indicator of the extent to which the police control detention, and the impact defence lawyers can have, would be how often reviews result in the suspect being charged or released as opposed to being further detained. The Commission did not secure research evidence on this. Indeed there appears to be no research evidence on reviews and representations, and the Commission made no mention of it in its Report. This is convenient, since it is likely that research would show that the requirement to review detention and to listen to representations from lawyers has little impact on the detention process. Research evidence, such as it is, suggests that lawyers do not affect length of detention.[7] Feldman refers to anecdotal evidence that the efficacy of making representations at review is doubtful (1990, p. 460). Bottomley et al. have reported that the review procedure 'tends to be routinized and insubstantial' (Bottomley, K. et al., 'Safeguarding the Rights of Suspects in Police Custody', unpublished paper presented to the British Criminology Conference, Bristol, July 1989, at p.11).

Again, the legal context is significant. It was noted above that PACE s. 40(12) requires the review officer to seek the views of the lawyer, if they are available, before making a decision. However, it is framed in terms of giving the lawyer the 'opportunity to make representations', a very undemanding requirement which does not even require the reviewing officer to take them into account. In any event, since the police are under no duty to disclose information to the lawyer, the officer can quite legitimately discount representations made on grounds that are entirely

---

[7] If anything, legal advice correlates with longer detention, but the question is fraught with methodological difficulty since there are so many variables. See, for example, Brown D., *Detention at the Police Station under the Police and Criminal Evidence Act 1984*, HMSO, London, 1989, p. 64, and Maguire M., 'Effects of the PACE Provisions on Detention and Questioning', (1988) 28 *British Journal of Criminology* 1, p. 27.

unknown to the lawyer. It can be argued, therefore, that the legal rules regarding reviewing detention are almost entirely presentational.

The length of detention of a suspect is also governed by the point at which the police decide to charge the suspect, and if they do, the decision whether to grant bail pending the first court appearance. With regard to the latter, although under PACE s. 38 there is formally a presumption of bail which is only to be displaced if certain criteria are satisfied, the custody officer making the decision is not even under a duty to listen to defence representations let alone under a duty to take them into account. The decision to charge is governed by PACE and Code of Practice C which, in effect, provide for a two stage process. First, Code C para. 11.3 makes it quite clear that it is for the interviewing officer to make a decision to terminate an interview, which s/he need not do until satisfied not only that a prosecution should be brought, but also that there is sufficient evidence for the prosecution to succeed. The wishes of the suspect or his/her lawyer are irrelevant since it is only after the officer has reached this stage that s/he is required to ask the suspect if s/he has anything further to say. Once the officer is so satisfied the suspect must then be taken before the custody officer who must then make a decision about charge (PACE s. 37(7) and Code of Practice C, para. 16.1). Again, there is no duty on the police officers concerned to seek representations from the defence, let alone take account of any representations made. The defence lawyer, therefore, will find little or no assistance in the legislation or the Codes to support a contention that an interview should come to an end or that a decision should be made about charging the suspect or, indeed, the nature of that charge. In these circumstances, it is not possible to maintain that suspect and police are on equal terms. In practice the police dictate the detention process from beginning to end, and the law provides more or less complete support for this.

One further example concerns the police interview itself. The Commission lamentably failed to deal with police interrogation of suspects and some of the real problems that arise. However, since this paper is concerned with defence services I will concentrate on that aspect. It is clear from the research carried out for the Commission that lawyers intervene in police interviews relatively infrequently (see McConville and Hodgson, op. cit., Ch. 9 and Baldwin 1992, op. cit., p. 28). It is also clear the police officers regard it as 'their' interview and that lawyers are often in agreement in this respect. As one lawyer put it, talking of the police interviewer, 'It's his interview' (McConville and Hodgson, ibid., p. 170). In many respects this is, of course, true. The suspect would not be there if the police officer did not want to interview him/her and had not detained him/her for that purpose. This view also reflects the fact, not admitted by the Commission, that the purpose of the interview is to secure a confession or, at the least, to secure evidence *against* the suspect, as the research by McConville and Hodgson informed them (see especially McConville and Hodgson, op. cit., pp. 197–9) We have already seen that the lawyer's role in interview is currently viewed in Code of Practice C in an essentially negative fashion. It has also been noted that the Commission did make some comment upon this. However, it failed to come to terms with the fact that if a lawyer is to act as a safeguard for the suspect the law must provide both support and legitimacy for this to happen. It is true that the Court of Appeal, in *R* v. *Miller* ((1992) *The Independent* 17 December) has recently expressed approval of intervention by lawyers in police interviews in certain circumstances. In the words of Lord Taylor, solicitors must discharge their function 'responsibly and courageously'; but not many police officers read Court of Appeal decisions.

However, neither the legislation nor the courts have laid down any firm guidelines. It is not clear, as Baldwin has written (Baldwin 1993a, op. cit., p. 1195), whether officers can shout or swear at suspects, or whether they can lie to or mislead them as to the evidence. It is not known to what extent they can exert pressure on the suspect, particularly pressure on a silent suspect to talk. It is not known how long a suspect should have to endure repeated questions of the same kind. It is not clear how far the police can seek to control the suspect in interview. Is it legitimate, for example, for them to tell the suspect to 'look at me when I'm speaking to you'? To what extent can the police themselves use silence to try to secure an answer? Can the police force the suspect to go to an interview room if s/he does not wish to answer questions? The courts have found relatively few forms of behaviour to be oppressive within the meaning of PACE s. 76. The Commission leaves both the police and lawyers no clearer about these crucial issues.

The uncertainty does not end with what the police may or may not do. Although the Law Society offers some guidance on when a lawyer should intervene, the advice is partial. Should the lawyer intervene to stop a 'control' question? How long should the lawyer wait before intervening in a 'no comment' interview? How much pressure should the lawyer allow to be put on the suspect? Can the lawyer ask his/her own questions of the suspect in order to bring out matters s/he knows should be said? Should the lawyer allow the police to determine where the suspect and the solicitor sit? It is becoming clear that in many police forces action is being taken in a concerted manner to marginalise lawyers in the police interview. One mechanism is for them to direct the lawyer to sit in the corner, out of sight of the suspect. In some cases, seats are even bolted to the floor in this position! Are the police allowed to do this? Does the lawyer have the right to take action against it?

If the lawyer does intervene, what status does this intervention have? Research for the Commission showed that intervention by the lawyer may be given short shrift by the interviewing officer (see, for example, Baldwin 1992, p. 34.).   What then is the lawyer to do?   Code C para. 6.9 provides that a solicitor may only be required to leave the interview if his/her conduct is such that the officer is unable properly to put questions to the suspect. Note for Guidance 6D further provides that it is not misconduct if the lawyer seeks to challenge an improper question or the manner in which it is put. However, as was seen above, it is not clear what improper questions are nor is it clear what style of questioning will be improper. So a lawyer persistently challenging what s/he regards as improper questioning puts him/herself at risk of being ejected. It is significant that there is no provision in the Codes that a police officer acting improperly can be ejected from the interview! As important, since the police regard themselves as being in control, a view as we have seen which is not disturbed by the legislative provisions, they can make it very unpleasant for the lawyer who is, in their view, challenging the prevailing power structure.

Evidence in the hands of the Commission showed that legal advice to people detained by the police is, in general, completely inadequate. Those who actually provide legal advice are often poorly trained, are doing work that is not generally valued, are often unclear about their role, and do not advise their clients adequately. Perhaps most significantly, they do not advocate on behalf of their clients with the same adversarial dedication as that displayed by the police. Although the Commission was presented with the evidence, it has not sought to understand why this should be. Tinkering with the Codes of Practice and exhorting the police to understand the role of the defence lawyer is hardly a sufficient response. Encouraging the Law Society to improve lawyers' own understanding of their role and to improve training, although useful, will have limited effect. What is needed is for defence lawyers to change their attitude to police station work. In order for this to happen, the adversarial role of the defence lawyer and the privileged position of the police has to be recognised by the legislative provisions governing police detention. One method of starting this process would have been for the Commission to have accepted the submission of the Legal Action Group that only confessions made in the presence of a lawyer would be admissible. This would have ensured that the police had an incentive to secure the attendance of a lawyer, and may have concentrated minds on what is legitimate behaviour on the part of both police and defence lawyers in the interrogation process.

17. No Defence for the Royal Commission

Jacqueline Hodgson

The Royal Commission on Criminal Justice was set up in the wake of a string of miscarriages of justice, though more were to follow. The announcement was made on the afternoon of 14 March 1991 after the Court of Appeal's decision to quash the convictions for murder of the six men held responsible for the Birmingham pub bombings. The then Home Secretary, Kenneth Baker, told the House of Commons, 'the aim of [the Commission] will be to minimise so far as possible the likelihood of such events happening again.'[1] Despite the extent of the malpractice uncovered in these cases, the common plea from the Government is that they 'represent only a tiny proportion of the work that is carried out to very high standards' (ibid.) and that they would be unlikely to happen now because of legislative reforms which have taken place, such as the Police and Criminal Evidence Act 1984 (PACE). This is clearly not so, as cases such as the 'Birmingham 6' and the 'Guildford 4' would be dealt with under the Prevention of Terrorism (Temporary Provisions) Act 1989 (PTA) which affords the suspect fewer safeguards than PACE and gives the police wider powers of detention. In addition, we have witnessed the continuation of miscarriages of justice, despite PACE, with cases such as the 'Tottenham 3', the 'Cardiff 3' and many of those associated with the now disbanded West Midlands Serious Crime Squad.

The source of these wrongful convictions has been a failure on the part of both police and prosecuting lawyers to play by the rules. Suspects have been coerced into confessing by physical and psychological abuse; confession and other evidence has been fabricated; relevant material has been withheld from the defence. Yet, the structural flaw of placing contradictory pressures upon the police has been spelled out time and again. In his report on the Maxwell Confait affair, Sir Henry Fisher[2] pointed to the

---

[1]   14 March 1991, Hansard p. 1109.
[2]   Fisher, H. (1977) *Report of an inquiry into the Confait case*, London: HMSO.

dangers of an investigative body whose primary purpose was to assemble evidence to convict, rather than to conduct a wider-ranging enquiry which may eliminate the suspect. Legislation following the Royal Commission on Criminal Procedure's proposals in 1981, establishing the Crown Prosecution Service and a range of new measures to regulate the treatment of those detained in police custody, including the creation of the custody officer, has done little to resolve this conflict.[3] Independent research examining the efficacy of other safeguards implemented under PACE indicates a reluctance on the part of the police to accept the value of these measures and the necessity to adhere to them.[4] Rather, the message is if police officers can get around them they will – be it a requirement to record the stopping and searching of an individual or informing the suspect of his/her right to legal advice without seeking to dissuade him/her from taking it up.[5]

Given this background and the nature of the malpractice in cases such as the 'Birmingham 6', a thorough review of the role played by both police and prosecutors was clearly called for. Missing from this debate, however, has been any thorough evaluation of the function of the criminal defence lawyer. As someone who does not exercise coercive powers over the suspect, but on the contrary, is there to assist him/her, the role of the defence adviser has been neglected by researchers focusing on the power imbalance between state and citizen. However, the criminal defence lawyer has come to play an important role in the criminal process as a huge expansion in the provision of legal aid in the 1970s and 1980s has meant that the vast majority of criminal defendants are now represented. This has brought functional benefits to the courts with the establishment of duty solicitor schemes[6] and the introduction of 'paper' committals. But more importantly, along with the custody officer and the recording of interrogations, the criminal defence lawyer has come to play an important and integral part in the protection of suspects held in police custody. Placing the suspect's right to custodial legal advice on a statutory footing provided a crucial counterbalance to the extension of police powers under

---

3 See for example, McConville, M., Sanders, A. and Leng, R. (1991) *The Case for the Prosecution*, London: Routledge.
4 See for example, Dixon, D., Bottomley, K., Coleman, C., Gill, M. and Wall, D. (1990) 'Safeguarding the rights of suspects in police custody', *Policing and Society*, 1, 115. Sanders, A.F., Bridges, L., Mulvaney, A. and Crozier, G. (1989) *Advice and Assistance at Police Stations and the 24-Hour Duty Solicitor Scheme*, London: Lord Chancellor's Department.
5 C.f. the view of the Royal Commission on Criminal Justice (1993) London: HMSO at Ch. 3 para. 2.
6 See Bankowski, Z. and Mungham, G. (1976) *Images of Law*, London: Routledge. Also, Parker, H., Casburn, M. and Turnbull, D. (1981) *Receiving Juvenile Justice*, Oxford: Basil Blackwell.

PACE.[7] However, whilst the functions and duties of those such as the custody officer are set out in PACE and the Codes of Practice, the function of the defence lawyer in 'advising' and 'representing' his/her client is more nebulous, and a question of professional skill and judgment. The potential breadth of interpretation which such a remit allows, makes the defence lawyer a key individual for inspection, as the protection of the suspect rests with a competent defence as much as with a fair prosecution. In addition, the presence of a defence lawyer brings with it a number of expectations about the benefits that will accrue to the suspect. These are effectively claimed by the profession through its official rhetoric which portrays solicitors as exercising their legal skills in an adversarial way to the benefit of the client and they are clearly assumed by the courts in evaluating the position of the suspect and the admissibility of evidence.[8]

The project we were commissioned to carry out examined the role of the criminal defence lawyer at the police station and the suspect's exercise of the right to silence, within the context of the interrogation strategies employed by the police.[9] Discussion here is limited to the first of these, the role of the defence.[10] Our research covered only suspects detained under PACE. Despite the Home Secretary's statement that the PTA was within their remit,[11] the Commission disqualified itself from considering it.[12] As many of the wrongful convictions which gave rise to the Commission's existence were conducted under the PTA, this was a missed opportunity for research and re-evaluation which disappointed many.[13]

The vulnerable position of an individual detained in police custody was clearly expressed by the Royal Commission on Criminal Procedure (RCCP) 1981:

---

[7] See PACE sections 58 and 59.
[8] See for example, *R* v. *Chandler* [1976] 3 All ER 105 and Hodgson, J. (1992) 'Tipping the Scales of Justice: the Suspect's Right to Legal Advice', *Criminal Law Review*, 854.
[9] McConville, M. and Hodgson, J. (1993) *Custodial Legal Advice and the Right to Silence*, London: HMSO.
[10] For a wider consideration of this across all aspects of the defence case, see McConville, M., Hodgson, J., Bridges, L. and Pavlovic, A. (1993) *Standing Accused*, Oxford University Press.
[11] 14 March 1991, Hansard p. 1113, 1117.
[12] See the Commission's Report (supra note 6) Ch. 3 paras 93–5.
[13] This is particularly surprising given the Commission's willingness to take up things not specified in its remit, such as the defendant's right to trial by jury.

He is unlikely to be properly aware of the legal intricacies of the situation, to understand, for example the legal concept of intent or the application of the laws of evidence to his case, or the full implications or the desirability of exercising his right to silence, or to know what the penalty is likely to be for the offence for which he is suspected. Only an experienced lawyer can give him this kind of information and advise him how best to proceed.[14]

Section 58 PACE gave broad effect to the RCCP's recommendation by providing that, 'A person who is in police detention shall be entitled, if he so requests, to consult a solicitor privately at any time'.[15] In addition, duty solicitor schemes were established in order to ensure that requests for custodial advice could be met at no charge to the detainee. Although the expectation was that the scheme would be serviced by admitted solicitors, limited use of 'representatives' was contemplated, but only after the individual had been approved by the local duty solicitor committee and each case considered personally by the solicitor before delegating it. Where a firm of solicitors is called upon in their capacity as 'own solicitor' these restrictions do not apply. Given the exacting nature of the provision of custodial legal advice and the importance attached to the presence of an adviser, both for the protection of the suspect and the court's subsequent determination as to the admissibility of evidence, one would expect solicitors to exercise their professional judgment in favour of only careful and limited delegation to trained and experienced staff.

The pattern of the provision of custodial legal advice wholly contradicts these expectations. Solicitors attended clients in custody in less than a quarter of the 180 cases in our sample. Instead, a variety of individuals – trainee solicitors, former police officers, legal executives, non-qualified clerks, secretaries – are sent to advise suspects detained in police custody. In-house rotas were established to service demand on a 24-hour basis and several firms regularly contracted out work to agencies or individuals on a piece-work arrangement. Nearly half of the firms in our sample employed former police officers. This widespread use of representatives confirms the concerns expressed in earlier empirical studies conducted by Sanders et al. (1989) and Dixon et al. (1990) (see note 5).

The delegation of tasks to non-qualified staff will not always result in the client receiving an inferior service. Non-solicitors who are experienced and trained in the provision of custodial legal advice may perform better than solicitors unfamiliar with this type of work. However, we saw little evidence of the existence of such individuals. Those attending the police

---

[14] RCCP (1981) *Report*, London: HMSO, para. 4.89.
[15] PACE, s. 58(1).

station were for the most part inexperienced, untrained and unable to provide anything which might be termed 'advice' to their clients. Neither was work delegated to representatives; there was no grading of tasks nor any filtering system allowing personal consideration of cases by the solicitor responsible. Instead, the structure of criminal defence practices is organised so that police station attendances and the bulk of case preparation, including proof taking and briefing counsel for the Crown Court, is automatically handled by non-qualified staff, freeing solicitors to 'front' the firm at the magistrates' court.

The dangers of heavy reliance upon non-qualified staff were clearly demonstrated when we accompanied them to police stations. Most were in no better a position than the suspect described above by the RCCP. They lacked legal expertise of even the most basic nature and together with their inexperience this resulted in them lacking confidence and being unable to challenge police decisions or represent the interests of the client with any vigour. In the absence of any legal training or an appreciation of the necessary role to be played by the defence adviser in an adversarial process, non-qualified staff exhibited serious role conflict which was usually resolved in favour of over-identification with the police.

However, it must not be assumed that the presence of a solicitor will necessarily bring any greater benefit to the client. Although most solicitors understood the legal constituents of the offence and the rules relating to the admissibility of evidence, they lacked any adversarial ideology that would spur them on to use these skills to the benefit of the client. Instead, police station work was considered unrewarding, unimportant and essentially non-adversarial. The passive role played by the defence advisers both inside and outside the interrogation contrasted sharply with the highly adversarial behaviour of the police, who were reluctant to reveal details of the case against the suspect, sought to control the lawyer's access to his/her client and employed a range of strategies during interrogation designed to secure a confession. Whilst the absence of legal training and experience will prevent the provision of competent custodial legal advice, the presence of these features alone will not guarantee it.

THE COMMISSION'S RESPONSE

Chapter 3 of the Report contains a number of recommendations aimed at reinforcing the suspect's right to legal advice. Suspects should be asked to confirm on tape that they do not require legal advice and to give reasons for their decision. Those declining legal advice should be given an opportunity to speak to the duty solicitor on the telephone. Other recommendations require the police to be more receptive to the presence and function of defence advisers. A copy of the custody record and access to tapes of earlier interrogations with the suspect should be made available to solicitors. Code C of the codes of practice issued under PACE should be amended: firstly, to encourage the police to inform defence advisers of at least the prima facie evidence which exists against their client; and secondly to include a more positive description of the role of the defence solicitor. These recommendations, together with those requiring better training of custody officers and the continuous recording of custody suites, may curb the sometimes overly-adversarial behaviour of police officers holding individuals in detention for interrogation. But on the whole, they are designed to encourage better adherence to the existing safeguards and pale into insignificance alongside the more radical proposals to strengthen the prosecution's hand: greater powers to take intimate samples without the suspect's consent; the power to question after charge; a limited obligation to disclose prosecution material conditional upon the defence demonstrating its relevance to their case.

And what of the defence, whose commitment to safeguarding the position of the suspect in custody has been found to be lacking in the majority of cases? The Commission reports that the findings of our study are 'disturbing'.[16] Other researchers focusing on the police interrogation have commented upon the passive role played by legal advisers even in the face of questioning which is overbearing and oppressive.[17] Our own study, whilst confirming these findings, sought to go much further in exploring the arrangements in place for attending clients held in police custody and uncovering the key variables which influence the provision of that advice. We found that the arrangements for advising suspects at the police station were not uniform across all defence practices, and the quality of service provided depended upon the nature of the individual firm or sometimes of particular individuals within a firm. The interests of the client are defined in different and contradictory ways by the legal profession. Yet, the Commission has ignored the complexity of these issues and made a series of recommendations which appear to prescribe more of the same. It has

---

[16] Ch. 3, para. 59 of the Report (see note 6).

[17] See for example Evans, R. (1993a) *The Conduct of Police Interviews with Juveniles*, London: HMSO. Baldwin, J. (1993b) *The Role of Legal Representatives at the Police Station*, London: HMSO. This has been noted in earlier research such as that of Sanders et al. (1989) supra note 5 and McConville et al. (1991) supra note 4. A recent example which has come to the courts' attention is that of one of the 'Cardiff 3' whose solicitor sat silently through the interview, including that part held to be oppressive by the Court of Appeal. See *R* v. *Paris, Miller, Abdullahi* (1992) *The Times*, 24 December.

failed to address why it is that only 10 per cent of defence advisers asked to see the custody record; why advisers frequently failed to ask police officers for details of the case against their client; why advice to clients during the private consultation was poor; and why lawyers failed to protect their clients during interrogation. In short, why solicitors organise their defence practices in a way which relies almost exclusively on non-qualified and inexperienced staff to advise clients and to prepare the defence case.

It seems implausible that the Law Society is ignorant of the situation, or that solicitors have not read the Society's booklet 'Advising the Client at the Police Station'. Equally unlikely and unsupported by empirical research[18] is the assumption that duty solicitors and their representatives are a breed apart who consistently provide advice of a different nature to 'own solicitors' and are able to fulfil the protective role which they are assigned under PACE.[19] It is unrealistic to expect that the same regulating body and the same mechanisms which are currently in place and which have demonstrably failed to ensure the provision of a professional service will begin to do otherwise.

In their defence, solicitors point to falling levels of remuneration, claiming that this places them in a position where they are forced to delegate aspects of defence preparation. Although a factor in the equation, and one which does not encourage good practice, it does not account for the overall structure of criminal defence practices and the ideologies of solicitors and their staff. Improvements in criminal legal aid rates are unlikely to be forthcoming, nor would such a move necessarily alter current practice. The rates of pay for police station attendance are among the highest for legal aid work and account for over one-quarter of the total amount received for representation of defendants in all stages of magistrates' court proceedings. Despite enhanced payments one-third higher than those made to other solicitors attending the police station at anti-social hours, research[20] indicates that duty solicitors provide telephone advice in far more instances than do 'own solicitors'.

Delegation is not a recent phenomenon in the provision of legal services. While legal aid was expanding rather than declining, Bridges et al. (1975)[21] noted the tendency for firms to expand by employing a higher ratio of non-qualified staff to solicitors. Neither is the delegation of defence work

---

[18] Indeed, despite enhanced rates of remuneration, duty solicitors continue to provide only telephone advice at a higher rate than 'own solicitors'. See Sanders et al. (1989) supra note 5.

[19] These recommendations are contained in Ch. 3, paras 59–64 of the Report (see note 6).

[20] See Sanders et al. (1989) supra note 5.

[21] Bridges, L., Sufrin, B., Whetton, J. and White, R. (1975) *Legal Services in Birmingham* University of Birmingham: Institute of Judicial Administration.

something which is forced upon solicitors. Official spokespersons are obliged to recognise the undesirability of this practice, as it clearly contradicts the professional rhetoric of providing a quality service, with standards guaranteed by self-regulation through the Law Society, in exchange for a monopoly on legal services relatively free from external scrutiny. By contrast, a striking feature of the ideology of the majority of criminal defence solicitors is that this routine delegation of defence work is not seen as problematic. Rather, it is the view of police station advice, and indeed much of the defence case preparation, as low-grade work which is the crucial factor in determining the division of labour. This is highlighted by the way in which those firms who considered police station advice as crucial to the construction of the defence case were able to ensure the attendance of experienced and qualified staff.

Poor rates of pay and the pressures of the court bureaucracy do not make the defence lawyer's task an easy one, but they are not the overriding determinants of legal practice. Instead, it is the solicitor's firm which is the site where practice and values are learned and working ideologies develop. The profession's own rhetoric of adversarial practice, uniform standards of quality and professional ethics is of no relevance to the majority of criminal lawyers whose practices centre around a high-volume caseload and a central belief in the guilt of their clients. Whilst some firms form notable exceptions to this trend, this is through an individual or firm-based commitment to the notion of providing an effective and adversarial defence service. There is no external regulation preventing those who do not possess this ideal from employing staff with no legal training to perform the bulk of fee-paying work.

In conclusion, the Commission's proposals seem unlikely to bring an improvement in the provision of defence services or to strengthen the position of the individual who must increasingly rely upon defence advisers to safeguard his/her rights in the criminal process. The Commission's failure to address many of the key issues in the protection of the suspect at the police station is compounded by the host of other recommendations which serve only to weaken the position of the defendant. Proposals for an open system of plea-bargaining militate towards increased pressure on the accused to plead guilty at the earliest possible moment. The adversarial nature of the defence, together with principles of oral argument and the testing of the prosecution case in open court, are undermined by making prosecution disclosure conditional upon the defence demonstrating its relevance through disclosure of the defence case. Given the organisation and context of the majority of criminal defence practices which are unable to protect the suspect as the rhetoric of the law expects and assumes, both at the police station and subsequently, the Commission's proposals give us little hope that they will 'minimise so far as possible the likelihood of such [miscarriages of justice] happening again'.[22]

---

[22] Kenneth Baker, Home Secretary, supra note 1.

18. DNA Profiling and the Law:
A Critique of the Royal Commission's
Recommendations

Jane Creaton

I INTRODUCTION

DNA profiling is a technique which enables comparisons to be made between the unique genetic codes extracted from different sources of biological material. The forensic applications of the technique were quickly appreciated, and DNA profiles have been used in criminal casework since the mid 1980s. It has been argued, however, that the legal framework governing the taking and storage of body samples and the use of expert evidence is no longer appropriate in the context of the new technology. The recent report of the House of Lords Select Committee on Science and Technology concluded that four particular issues call for urgent resolution:

1. Do the courts accept the validity of the science behind DNA evidence?
2. Under what circumstances may body samples be taken for DNA analysis? Under what circumstances may samples taken be retained?
3. Under what circumstances may the results of analysis (a 'DNA profile') be retained, either identified or anonymous, on a computer database? Who should have access to such data, and for what purpose?
4. How do the statements of probability derived from DNA analysis relate to the legal concept of 'reasonable doubt'?... (1993, para. 5.3)

Issues 1 and 4 are not explicitly addressed by the Royal Commission's Report, but the general recommendations relating to forensic science and other expert evidence are obviously of some relevance. However, specific proposals are made to reform the law relating to the taking and storage of samples for the purposes of DNA profiling, and it is with an analysis of these recommendations that this paper will be primarily concerned. Its purpose is to examine the extent to which the proposals would clarify the law in this area, but also to consider whether the desire to exploit and the need to control the technology would be satisfactorily reconciled.

II THE TAKING OF BODY SAMPLES

1. The Current Law

The powers of the police to take samples from a suspect's body are governed by sections 62–65 of the Police and Criminal Evidence Act 1984 (PACE). Section 65 distinguishes between an intimate sample, defined as 'a sample of blood, semen or any other tissue fluid, urine, saliva or pubic hair, or a swab taken from a person's body orifice' and a non-intimate sample defined by the same section as '(a) a sample of hair other than pubic hair; (b) a sample taken from a nail or from under a nail; (c) a swab taken from any part of a person's body other than a body orifice; (d) a footprint or a similar impression of any part of a person's body other than a part of his hand'.

An intimate sample may only be taken with the written consent of a person in police detention, where a senior officer has reasonable grounds to suspect that the person is involved in a serious arrestable offence and that the taking of the sample will tend to confirm or disprove the involvement. Where the person does not consent, section 62(10) permits adverse inferences capable of corroborating any other evidence to be drawn at a subsequent trial.

A non-intimate sample may be taken from a person in detention where he or she refuses to provide the appropriate written consent, provided that a senior officer authorises the procedure. The officer must reasonably suspect that the detainee is involved in a serious arrestable offence, and have reasonable grounds to believe that the sample will tend to confirm or disprove involvement.

2. The Commission's Proposals

a. The classification of samples
The Commission proposes that plucked hair (other than pubic hair), saliva, and mouth swabs should be classed as non-intimate samples, and hence may be taken without the consent of the suspect (paras 2.28, 2.29). The purpose of these recommendations is to facilitate the taking of DNA profiles from suspects, as DNA can be obtained from cells in hair roots and the lining of the mouth. Section 65 already includes non-pubic hair in the

definition of a non-intimate sample, but does not differentiate between plucked, combed or cut hairs. The Commission notes (para. 2.28) that the right to take plucked hair without consent has been challenged in recent cases, and thus recommends that the law be clarified to confirm that it is a non-intimate sample.

The Commission also recommends that saliva should become obtainable without consent by the simple expedient of reclassifying it as a non-intimate sample. This would enable a mouth swab to be taken without the consent of the suspect, and bring sampling powers into line with those available to the police in Northern Ireland under schedule 14 of the Criminal Justice Act 1988. The justification given for the reclassification of saliva and mouth swabs as non-intimate samples in that jurisdiction was that both terrorist and non-terrorist suspects in the province are markedly hostile to attempts by the police to collect forensic evidence. The Commission does not suggest that suspects in England and Wales have become similarly belligerent in countering police investigations; it simply accepts the police service's contention that 'the provision has worked satisfactorily there' (para. 2.29). Yet no evidence is presented to show how the provision has operated, and no attempt is made to define what is meant by satisfactory in this context.

In establishing the framework now embodied in PACE, the Report of the Royal Commission on Criminal Procedure (RCCP, 1981) did not attempt to analyse in detail the philosophical and ethical underpinnings of the intimate/non-intimate distinction that was proposed. However, the current categorisation of samples does have a certain coherence. Intimate samples are those that involve invasive procedures, either the taking of tissue from below the skin (such as blood or internal swabs) or the collection of internal bodily fluids (urine or semen). The reclassification of saliva and plucked hairs as non-intimate samples disrupts this rationale.

In order to obtain a DNA profile from either of these sources the Forensic Science Service (FSS) requires a minimum of 20 plucked head hairs with visible root material or at least two swabs which have been rubbed around the inside of the mouth. It may, perhaps, be argued that the infringements involved in these procedures are justified by the projected impact on clear-up rates, but this was not a balancing exercise that the Commission sought to engage in. The fundamental point here is that, if the law is not to be arbitrary or inconsistent in its application, an attempt must be made to develop a coherent set of principles upon which investigative procedures in respect of the person are made.

b. Sanctions for non-cooperation

The current law does not enable an intimate sample to be taken from a suspect, even with consent, where the offence is not a serious arrestable one. The Commission recommends that a suspect should be permitted to supply a sample in these circumstances, particularly as the resulting profile may prove the suspect's innocence. There can be no objection to facilitating cooperation from suspects, provided that consent to provide the evidence is freely given and fully informed. Yet Recommendation 18 provides that where a suspect does not supply an intimate or non-intimate sample in cases other than serious arrestable offences, the court may draw inferences from that refusal capable of corroborating any other evidence.

The effect of these two provisions is not simply to enable suspects to cooperate in providing a sample, but to exert powerful pressure upon them to do so. It may be the case that it is desirable to exert such pressure in serious crimes. However, that such pressure should be considered appropriate for detainees suspected of any criminal offence is, in my view, unacceptable.

Furthermore, the notion that adverse inferences may amount to corroborating evidence in a criminal trial can be criticised in principle. There may be many reasons why a suspect refuses to consent to sampling, including, for example, a mistrust of scientific tests, a desire not to cooperate with the police or an unwillingness to submit to the procedures involved. Convictions based on inference rather than probative evidence are likely to increase the risks of a miscarriage of justice.

c. The definition of a serious offence

Recommendation 19 further extends the power to take non-intimate samples by reclassifying certain offences (assault and burglary) as serious arrestable offences for the purposes of tissue sampling. The RCCP recommended that the power to take samples without consent should be limited solely to grave offences, on the grounds that forcible invasion of bodily integrity could only be justified by reference to the interest of the community in convicting the perpetrator of a serious crime (1981, paras 3.10, 3.137). In this context the addition of assault and burglary to the category of serious arrestable offences is a curious one. Under section 116 of PACE any arrestable offence is serious if it leads to, is intended to lead to or is likely to lead to substantial financial gain, serious financial loss or serious injury to any person. The Royal Commission is therefore proposing that the power to take non-intimate samples without consent should be granted to the police in order that DNA profiles may be performed on suspects held on charges of minor assault and small-scale burglary. In such cases where biological material is available for analysis, the police may not consider a costly and time-consuming DNA profile to be the most efficient use of resources. It is unlikely, therefore, to have any significant impact on the clear-up rates for these offences. However, the potential capacity to exercise the power over the suspect would be a potent bargaining chip with which the police could exert pressure on other issues. Moreover, the notion that offences can be classed as serious for one purpose and not serious for another, is an incoherent one. As was noted in the discussion on the definition of samples, the desire to exploit this technology should not preclude a more principled approach to reform of the criminal justice system.

d. Extension of sampling powers

The final recommendation in relation to sampling is that the police should be empowered to take non-intimate samples without consent from all those arrested for serious offences, even where DNA evidence is not relevant to that particular offence. DNA profiles obtained from the samples will be maintained on an offender database if the suspect is subsequently convicted. The police service argued that this power is necessary as many people who are arrested for sexual offences have previous convictions for other serious offences, such as burglary (para. 2.34). This, it appears, is the rationale for the reclassification of burglary and assault as serious arrestable offences; an assertion by the police service that it is 'not uncommon' for sex offenders to have committed such offences earlier in their criminal careers. Again these recommendations are at variance with the principles developed by the RCCP. It argued that:

> [t]he use of coercive powers cannot be justified unless there is certainty or suspicion based upon reasonable grounds that a crime has been committed or may have been committed, is being or is about to be committed ... (1981, para. 3.4)

This Commission, in effect, considers that coercive powers are justified where a crime may be committed at some unspecified time in the future. No reference is made to any evidence of a correlation between a conviction for a sex offence and a prior criminal record. This is yet another example of the failure of the Royal Commission to justify a proposal which has enormous implications for civil liberties.

3. Assessment

The Royal Commission's recommendations, if implemented, would substantially increase the sampling powers available to the police under PACE. However, this increase is not balanced by a strengthening of the safeguards available for the suspect. The current framework simply requires authorisation by a senior officer of the taking of a non-intimate sample without consent. The Commission's recommendations would release the officer from the requirement that he or she reasonably believe that the taking of a sample will confirm or disprove the suspect's involvement in the offence for which he or she has been arrested. The contrast between this position and the authority required for the search of property has been highlighted by Gelowitz:

> It seems odd that Parliament would require impartial judicial authorisation for the search of a man's home, but not for the forcible search of the inside of a man's mouth. (1989 p. 201)

The requirements that reasons be given for authorisation and recorded where appropriate are also unsatisfactory safeguards for the suspect. The Commission itself recognises the shortcomings of any system of written records in failing to reveal the context in which they are made (para. 3.35). The proposal to videotape the custody suite at all times may resolve this particular problem, but other essential safeguards are absent. There is no requirement, for example, that suspects be reminded of their right to legal advice before providing a non-intimate sample. Nor must they be told of their right to refuse to provide an intimate sample, or that such a sample may not be taken without consent.

III THE STORAGE OF SAMPLES

1. The Current Law

PACE requires that intimate and non-intimate samples taken from an offender in the course of an investigation should be destroyed if the suspect is cleared of the offence or cautioned. There is no provision for the destruction of profiles taken from the samples.

The FSS already maintains a database containing profiles of material from unsolved crimes, from offenders convicted using DNA evidence and from suspects awaiting trial whose profiles match that from a scene of crime sample. Searching of the database is automatically undertaken against any profiles obtained from an undetected offence. Other searches can only be conducted if suspects consent to the search, or if their profile matches a stain from the offence for which they were arrested.

2. The Commission's Recommendations

The Commission recognises the need for legal regulation of the storage of DNA samples and profiles, although it does not consider that it was within its terms of reference to make detailed proposals on the issue (para. 2.38). Broad recommendations are made for two different types of database. One would contain profiles from convicted offenders, and would be used to search for a match with profiles from material found at the scenes of unsolved crimes.

The other would contain profiles of any samples taken during the course of police investigations. The purpose of this proposal would be to provide information on the distribution of genes in the population, thus enabling the probabilities of random matches to be calculated. The identities of the individuals from whom the profiles are obtained would be known to the independent authority maintaining the database, to ensure that duplication does not occur. Other (unspecified) strong safeguards would prevent these identities from being revealed to the police or prosecution (para. 2.36).

In its discussion of this issue the Commission uses the terms sample and profile interchangeably. The recommendations refer to the retention of data and samples. It is not clear if this is a result of confusion about the way in which the information is stored, or whether the Commission is recommending that both the tissue sample and the profile obtained from it be retained. Retention of the actual sample would overcome problems arising from future developments in DNA profiling. The establishment of any database of profiles entails the risk that the technology will become ossified at that point, or that profiles obtained from new procedures will be incompatible with earlier ones. However, retention of the samples raises other difficulties. Presuming that sufficient quantities of the sample remain, additional genetic analyses can be performed in the future. Whilst fears that such information may be obtained by insurance companies to identify high-risk individuals may be exaggerated, the prospect of a central authority retaining identified samples with such potential is a disturbing one.

a. The offender database
As has been noted above, a database of profiles from convicted offenders already exists. This recommendation would allow much greater use to be made of the database, enabling a DNA profile taken from a suspect to be checked against all existing profiles. There would be no prior requirement that a match be obtained with a scene of crime sample, or that the suspect consent to the searching of the database. Where the suspect has been arrested for a serious arrestable offence, a profile may be taken and checked

against the database, regardless of whether DNA profiling is relevant to that particular offence.

As with the proposals relating to the taking of samples, the impact of these recommendations will be limited by the budgets available to police forces. The profiling of all those suspected of serious arrestable offences and all suspects who permit a sample be taken would require a huge expenditure. However, as the technology advances and the market for forensic science becomes more competitive, extensive testing may become a more cost-effective proposition.

The establishment of an offender database would enable more matches to be made between suspects and material from unsolved crimes. Nevertheless, some caution should be exercised. It must be remembered that, unlike fingerprints, DNA profiles are not unique. Current technology examines only a few sites along the DNA molecule, and the resulting profile may be shared by other individuals. Where there is additional evidence linking a person with the offence, then a positive DNA profile may be near conclusive proof of guilt. However, where the only evidence against the suspect is a DNA profile, the safety of a subsequent conviction would be in doubt. There is a danger that the onus will be upon the defendant to show that the profile may have come from another source, in effect reversing the burden of proof.

b. The frequency database
As has been explained above, DNA profiling examines only a few sites of genetic variation in the DNA molecule. Where DNA profiles do not match it is impossible that the samples came from the same source, but where a match is obtained this is not conclusive proof that the same individual is involved. The likelihood of individuals who did not commit the crime having the same profile must be considered. The purpose of frequency databases is to compile data on genetic variations in the population, to enable this likelihood to be calculated.

It is this calculation which has been one of the most controversial aspects of DNA profiling. The standard method is to select a random sample of the population, estimate the frequency of each genetic variation at the sites which will be profiled, and then determine the probability of each variation arising. If the profile has been obtained by examining four sites on the DNA molecule, the probabilities of the variation occurring at each of the four sites will be multiplied together to give an overall probability of the match occurring (the 'product rule').

For a frequency database to give an accurate estimate of this probability it is essential that the database contains an appropriate number of profiles.

Without a sufficiently large sample, estimates of frequency of genetic variations will be inaccurate, particularly where the variation is rare. It is this particular problem that the Commission's proposal seeks to overcome. Yet scientists in the Forensic Science Service have claimed to perform accurate calculations on the basis of databases of a few hundred individuals (Evett 1992). The Commission cannot have it both ways. Either the current databases are perfectly adequate, in which case no further data is needed; or they are not, in which case the probabilities produced in previous casework are open to challenge.

Even if the sampling error is adequately compensated for, other factors may affect the accuracy of the calculation. The distribution of particular genetic traits is not uniform. Genetic disorders, such as sickle-cell anaemia and Tay-Sachs disease are more common among Afro-Caribbeans and East European Jews respectively, than among the rest of the population. Ethnic variations may well be present at the sites that are used for DNA profiling. This fact is already recognised by the FSS and the Metropolitan Police Forensic Science Laboratory, both of which maintain separate databases for Asian Indians, Afro-Caribbeans and Caucasians. However, it has been argued that such classifications are too crude, and that finer distinctions as to ethnic sub-grouping should be made (Lander 1989, p. 146).

Where an appropriate ethnic database has been selected for the offender, there is still a danger that the samples within that database may not be a random selection. The Commission's proposals would broaden the scope of the current database by including in it all profiles obtained in the course of police investigations. A truly random element, however, cannot be established without taking random samples from people who have not been suspected of any criminal offence. The ethical problems of such a procedure are obvious.

A final criticism that can be made of the probability calculation, is that it assumes that the population from which the samples are drawn is homo-genously mixed. However, experience suggests that there is considerable stratification in the population, that is, that people tend to mate within their own ethnic or cultural sub-groups. This tendency is particularly evident in some ethnic groups in which marriage between relatives is common. It has been argued that an injustice may be done where a matching profile is obtained from someone in a such a community. Calculations may show the probability of another person having committed the crime to be very low, where in fact the suspect shares the profile with a 'nugget' of other individuals (Webster 1992, p. 1712). The assumption that the whole of the population is randomly mixed conceals such pockets of similarity.

Given these considerations, the proposals to introduce a frequency database are not entirely satisfactory. For while a wider pool of DNA profiles is to be established, there is no guarantee that it will be any more representative than the current database.

3. Assessment

If these databases are to be established, rigorous safeguards are required. The Royal Commission does not consider what these may be, beyond the fact that an independent authority should oversee the frequency database in order to prevent unlawful identifications being made. Safeguards must be implemented to prevent other misuses of the information stored therein. A DNA profile identifies only a few sites of genetic variation, none of which have yet been associated with susceptibility to particular hereditary diseases or other attributes. But the Commission seems to be suggesting that the samples themselves should be retained from individuals on both the frequency and the offender databases. In view of the potential misuse of information that may be derived from such samples in the future, this proposal should be resisted.

IV CONCLUSION

There is no doubt that the potential value of DNA profiling in criminal investigations is considerable. Nevertheless, as has been outlined above, a number of questions can be raised as to the methods by which material for sampling is obtained and the potential uses to which such samples should be put. The need to balance conviction of those guilty of criminal offences against protection of the civil liberties of suspects is a recurrent theme throughout the criminal justice system. However, the very high degree of individual-specificity which the technique purports to deliver, coupled with the potential misuse of genetic data, makes DNA profiling the focus of particular concern.

The recommendations made by the Royal Commission do little to assuage these anxieties. Indeed, the framework proposed would substantially increase powers to collect and store genetic material, without protecting the suspect from the abuse of such powers. It may be that the implementation of the Commission's recommendations will facilitate some criminal convictions, although, as has been shown, the impact on clear-up rates is not expected to be substantial. More importantly, the price to be paid in terms of infringement of civil liberties and potential miscarriages of justice will be too high.

19. The Royal Commission and the Forensic Science Market

Mike Redmayne

I INTRODUCTION

When the Court of Appeal freed the Birmingham 6 in 1991 a number of problems relating to forensic science evidence were highlighted. In particular, the case showed how the prosecution could build a case around flawed scientific evidence while the defence lacked the ability to challenge such evidence successfully. The Royal Commission's proposals on forensic science evidence fail to give an adequate response to these problems, partly due to the Commission's acceptance of market forces as a suitable means of regulating scientific evidence.

This paper examines the Commission's proposals on the provision of forensic science services to the prosecution and the defence in the context of the emerging forensic science market in England and Wales.

II THE 1991 CHANGES

It is important to see the Commission's proposals in the light of recent changes to the Forensic Science Service. In April 1991 the Home Office-run Forensic Science Service (FSS) became an executive agency. Executive agency status meant that the FSS gained a substantial degree of autonomy from the Home Office and was encouraged to support itself financially. This was accompanied by a change in the way that the police paid for forensic science services. Since April 1991 police forces have had to pay for evidence referred to the FSS on a case-by-case basis ('direct charging') rather than by paying a lump sum each year, an arrangement which had previously enabled them to use the service as often as they liked. The FSS and its use by the police are now broadly subject to market forces.

The 1991 changes had been initiated by a 1987 review of the service by Touche Ross Management Consultants and had also been approved by a majority of the Home Affairs Committee in 1989. The move to agency status and direct charging reflected the Government's fondness for 'next steps' agencies but there were also two specific problems that the changes were meant to solve:

i) The problem of regulating 'selectivity'. Selectivity is the principle that the police should select only certain items to be sent for scientific examination. It was introduced in the early 1980s as a means of preventing the police from overburdening the FSS. Direct charging was seen as a way of encouraging selectivity.

ii) The problem of funding the FSS. The question of how much money should be spent on the FSS had always been a difficult one, and for some time the FSS workforce had only been expanded in relation to police numbers rather than in relation to the increasing possibilities for forensic science analysis. Direct charging was seen as a way of funding the FSS in relation to how much the police were prepared to spend on it.

It was also hoped that the introduction of a vendor–client relationship between the police and the FSS would make the two bodies more responsive to each other's needs.

III POLICE USE OF FORENSIC SCIENCE SERVICES

The initial police decision as to which items to send for forensic science analysis and which tests to request is a vitally important one (Peterson, 1986). Decisions made at this stage may affect the rest of the investigation, both in the way the police approach it (confessions were only extracted from the Birmingham 6 after the police had been told that scientific tests pointed to their guilt), and in the way the defence respond. The defence may not have access to the scene of the crime until some considerable time after it has been discovered. By this time any physical evidence may be used up, degraded or contaminated. The defence thus tend to play a reactive role, criticising the scientific evidence of the prosecution (for example by suggesting that it should be interpreted in a different way) rather than initiating their own scientific investigations (Roberts and Willmore, 1993, p. 67).

It is important, then, that the initial decision to send evidence for scientific analysis is taken on objective grounds, as a means of revealing information about an offence, rather than as part of a process of case construction against a particular suspect. Research before the change to agency status showed that there was a tendency for the police to use forensic science evidence as a corroborative rather than investigatory tool: 'The FSS were not asked to reveal 'who-dunnit', but to corroborate suspicions already well-formed' (Ramsay, 1988, p. 12). More recent research has not undermined this conclusion (Roberts and Willmore, 1993, p. 26). Indeed, the advent of direct charging means that this tendency may well be exacerbated: if the police have to pay for every single item of evidence that is sent for analysis then they are even less likely to send items that may exculpate a suspect. Furthermore, if forensic science evidence is more inherently reliable than other types of evidence, such as confessions or eyewitness testimony, then a move that will make the police less likely to use forensic science evidence when it is available is one that should not be welcomed.

A further danger in the police's new-found position as customers in a forensic science market is that they may simply look for the cheapest forensic science evidence, rather than the most reliable. In practice this has meant that the police are increasingly using their own in-house scientific services, and in some circumstances turning to independent forensic science laboratories which do not have the expertise or the quality control procedures of the FSS (Select Committee on Science and Technology, 1993, para. 4.9).

Faced with this situation the Royal Commission's Report shows some confusion over what the long-term effects of the market are likely to be on the quality of prosecution forensic science evidence. At one point it suggests that competition may lead to high standards (9.14),[1] but eight paragraphs later it reveals fears that undue competitiveness may lead to a diminution in standards (9.22). Overall, however, the Commission takes the view that charging and market pressures are beneficial, ensuring that 'the services offered meet the customer's needs' (9.22). It is submitted that this is too simplistic a view of the police's position within the forensic science market. The Commission suggests that if the police use non-FSS laboratories then it is their duty to assure themselves that the evidence is of a high standard (9.19). Yet, as customers, the police are unlikely to be worried about the quality of the science that they are purchasing, unless the poor quality of that science will lead to failure of their case at a later stage in the process.

As to the number of exhibits sent by the police for scientific analysis,

---

[1] Numbered references in the text are to chapters and paragraphs of the Royal Commission's Report.

there is evidence that the introduction of charging did deter the police from sending exhibits to the FSS. In the early part of the first year of direct charging there was a dramatic decrease in the number of referrals, though the amount did pick up towards the end of the year. The FSS has portrayed the situation as one of teething troubles: police forces need to get used to the proportion of their annual budget that they should set aside for referrals. This analysis is supported by the fact that police use of the service has risen during the past year, passing pre-1991 levels and approaching pre-selectivity levels (FSS, 1993, p. 9). However, a rise in the number of referrals is to be expected, given that new scientific techniques with forensic applications are continually being developed (e.g. DNA profiling and methods for detecting latent fingerprints).

For its part the Royal Commission has decided that there is no need to change the charging system; if the police have to make difficult choices about money: 'this is as it should be, so long as the choice is made on the basis of which [laboratory] is best suited to provide the scientific advice that is needed in the particular case' (9.23) (a view which again ignores the fact that this may well not be the police's priority). The paragraph continues: 'If police budgets are so constrained that the money cannot be found to pay for the advice at all, that is a problem stemming from the allocation of resources to and by police forces, not from charging by the FSS.' This statement can only be described as naive. Direct charging was brought in in the first place as a means of enforcing selectivity, i.e. to stop the police from overburdening the FSS. The question of which items should be sent for examination cannot be separated from the question of the cost of that examination. It is also surprising that the comments in this part of the Report conflict with the Commission's 'concern', in the chapter on police investigations, over evidence that budgetary constraints may deter the police from making referrals to the FSS (2.45; see also comments at 1.17).

It is also remarkable that the Commission makes no attempt to lay down guidelines on the sorts of cases in which forensic science evidence should, as a rule, be sought. For example, the role of confession evidence in miscarriage of justice cases is well known, indeed, 56 paragraphs of the Commission's Report are devoted to the problems of confession evidence. Even though the Commission rejects a corroboration rule (4.85), it might have suggested that in cases where there is an uncorroborated confession the police should seek forensic science evidence as a means of 'double-checking' the confession, even in cases (such as burglaries) which would not normally be seen as serious enough to merit the expense of a forensic science referral.

The police are placed in the position of customers in the forensic science market, searching for the best forensic science 'buy'. There will be only two real checks on the quality of forensic science evidence purchased by the police: the defence expert (if there is one) and the proposed Forensic Science Advisory Council.

IV THE FORENSIC SCIENCE ADVISORY COUNCIL

The establishment of a Forensic Science Advisory Council (FSAC) is the only major change proposed by the Commission in the area of forensic science services. For the Commission the FSAC would operate like a magic wand: wherever there is a problem relating to forensic science services it is envisaged that the FSAC would make the problem disappear. Yet despite the importance of the FSAC to the Commission's plans for the regulation of forensic science services, the membership and powers of the new body are left unclear. The Report does not even specify whether or not the FSAC would be independent from the Home Office. The Commission does, though, identify several functions that the new council would perform.

The 'main responsibility' of the FSAC would be to report annually on the state of forensic science in England and Wales (9.34). More specifically, it would look at the extent to which the needs of the defence are catered for (9.55), advise the police on the role that in-house laboratories should play (9.33), and encourage research (9.34). As to the standard of scientific evidence being used in the courts, the FSAC would oversee an external examination of FSS practices (9.29), and oversee a system of accreditation of individual experts if such a system is developed (9.36). It would also make sure that undue competitiveness does not lead to poor standards (9.22).

The role sketched out for the new council, then, is one of advising and scrutinising. Whether or not it would play a 'policing' role and what powers of enforcement it would have are unclear, but it does not appear that the creation of a body with strong powers is favoured by the Commission. Similarly, the development of rules to exclude from the courts evidence given by poorly trained experts or evidence based on unreliable scientific techniques is not considered by the Commission. Such problems are to be dealt with by the increased scrutiny of the forensic sciences rather than by exclusionary rules of evidence.

The 'soft' approach of the Royal Commission can be seen in relation to the issue of accreditation of individual scientists.[2] One of the recommendations of the recent Report of the Select Committee on Science and Technology (1993, para. 3.52) was that individual scientists should be accredited. Accreditation would act as an indication of expertise in a particular field, though non-accredited experts would not automatically be prevented from giving evidence in court. The employment of 'cowboy' experts by the prosecution or the defence is a danger inherent in the existence of a forensic science market and individual accreditation is one means of preventing it (especially as the courts have not developed a strict test of expertise: under *Robb* anyone but 'a quack, a charlatan or an enthusiastic amateur' may give expert evidence ([1991] 93 Cr App R 161 at 166)). The Royal Commission is ambivalent about an accreditation scheme, hinting that one might be developed in the future and recommending that the various professional bodies draw up lists of those of their members who are sufficiently qualified to give expert evidence (9.75–6).

V DEFENCE ACCESS TO FORENSIC SCIENCE EXPERTISE

As the Commission does not embrace individual accreditation as a means of regulating the forensic science market, and because the powers and the ability of the FSAC to prevent poor scientific evidence being given in court are unclear, the primary means of testing the quality of prosecution forensic science evidence would continue to be a challenge in court (or in pre-trial conference) by the defence. It is therefore important that the defence have access to well-trained forensic scientists not only so that they can prepare their own case, but also so that the prosecution's evidence will be subjected to scrutiny.

Research for the Royal Commission showed that difficulties in gaining access to scientific expertise were among the main problems faced by defence solicitors in cases involving forensic science evidence (Roberts and Willmore, 1993, pp. 73–81; Steventon, 1993, pp. 18–20). This was due to the difficulty of locating suitable defence experts and the lack of reimbursement through Legal Aid.

The Commission was aware of the problems faced by defence solicitors,

---

[2] This approach, whereby the reliability of evidence will be left to the discretion of judge and/or jury, can be seen in other parts of the Report: e.g. rejection of a corroboration rule for confession evidence; rejection of a rule whereby the Court of Appeal would automatically quash convictions based on police malpractice.

claiming that: 'We pay particular attention to the needs of the defence' (9.3). Their main solution to the problem is that the FSS and the Metropolitan Police Forensic Science Laboratory should be available to provide expert evidence to the defence (9.24). This again shows a remarkable lack of insight. One of the expected outcomes of the FSS's change to executive agency status in 1991 was that it would earn money by providing a service to the defence, but an FSS defence service has not really materialised: in 1992–93 95 per cent of FSS business was still for the prosecution (FSS, 1993, p. 10). This may be due to the reluctance of defence solicitors to employ people who are, rightly or wrongly, perceived as 'prosecution-minded' (Roberts and Willmore, 1993, pp. 71–3). It may also be due to the fact that the FSS is already overburdened in providing a service to the prosecution (there is considerable support for this in the evidence given to the Select Committee on Science and Technology). Whatever the reason, the lack of FSS provision for defence needs remains a reality, and one that the words of the Commission are unlikely to change.

There are also reasons of principle for not attempting to develop the FSS into a defence service. If FSS resources are already stretched, provision of a defence service might lead to the de-prioritisation of work for the prosecution. As argued above, it is important that the police should not be constrained in their access to forensic science expertise: the FSS's primary responsibility should be to help the police in the investigation of crime (Stockdale, 1991). Further, even though the Commission proposes that defence work would be carried out at a different laboratory to the one dealing with prosecution work on the same case, one should be sceptical of the ability of the FSS to challenge the evidence of its own employees, especially as one ground of challenge might be that a technique used by the FSS is unsuitable. In the cases of the Birmingham 6 and the Maguire 7, FSS evidence and techniques were necessarily challenged by 'outsiders' rather than by 'insiders'. More recently, challenges to FSS DNA evidence have come from independent experts rather than from those conducting the tests for the FSS.

If the FSS is unable to help the defence in a particular case, then the Commission proposes that it should help the defence to locate forensic science advice elsewhere (9.26). The question remains whether there will be adequate expertise elsewhere, and this depends on the existence of funding for the 'defence sector'.

The Commission believes that there should be 'a thriving private sector of forensic science firms to which the defence should have access if they so wish' (9.55). One factor that has so far prevented the development of a thriving defence sector is that defence firms are reliant almost entirely on

Legal Aid, the precariousness of which has threatened to drive some firms out of business. Solicitors have to negotiate with Legal Aid authorities for permission to instruct an expert, and may find that the money allotted is insufficient for the full range of tests that they wish to have carried out. Alternatively they may be asked to seek a cheaper expert (Woffinden, 1991). Research for the Royal Commission showed one case where the prosecution had DNA evidence against a suspect and the defence were refused funding to instruct their own expert (Steventon, 1993, p. 18). Even when funding is secured, payments can be considerably delayed, and this again discourages solicitors from instructing experts (Roberts and Willmore, 1993, pp. 78–81).

The Commission's proposals on the funding of defence experts are that Legal Aid payments should be made promptly and that there should be clear rules that will allow solicitors to know in advance what forensic science analysis they can commission.

These proposals are welcome but it should be noted that they put the Legal Aid authorities in a critical position because the rules that they make will tend to create a ceiling price for each type of forensic science analysis. The rules are also likely to set out the sorts of cases in which solicitors will be allowed to instruct an expert. Will a defendant against whom there is confession evidence be allowed the luxury of forensic science evidence? It is to be hoped that the proposed FSAC would have some input into the rules drafted by the Legal Aid authorities.

These difficulties apart, there remains the question of whether Legal Aid alone will be sufficient to fund a 'thriving' defence sector, especially one which must compete for defence clients with the FSS (which has the advantage of a steady income from prosecution cases and an existing investment in staff and equipment).

VI RESEARCH AND DEVELOPMENT IN FORENSIC SCIENCE

For forensic science evidence to be reliable it must be grounded on sound science. Because science is a continually evolving discipline, this means that there must be continuous research leading to the refinement of forensic science techniques. Databases, which allow the accurate interpretation of results and in which the courts put faith (*R* v. *Abadom* [1983] 1 All ER 364), must exist and need to be kept up to date.

The Select Committee on Science and Technology received considerable evidence that the FSS had cut back on research and development since gaining agency status in 1991, concentrating almost entirely on research on DNA profiling. It is obvious that, with the FSS expected to cover its costs each year, the income generated from case-work may not be sufficient to fund research, which provides little immediate income.

The Royal Commission's only proposal on research is that the FSAC should 'encourage' research in the universities and in both public and private laboratories (9.34). Again, this proposal would be ineffective unless there is funding to back it up, because the forensic science market itself provides little stimulus for research. As the Select Committee on Science and Technology recommended, there should be central funding for research 'for the benefit of the whole forensic science community' (1993, para. 2.48).

The Commission's only recommendation on statistical databases is that a DNA frequency database should be set up, overseen by an independent organisation (2.36–7). This is welcome, because it is only by the development of such a database that the interpretation of the results of DNA profiling can be anything other than speculative. However, it is remarkable that the Commission does not extend this recommendation to other databases, such as those on the refractive index of glass and on the dyes used in fabrics. Such databases are crucial to the interpretation of trace evidence, and need to be continually updated. The existence of accurate databases should no longer be reliant on the ability of the FSS to fund them. Databases should be centrally funded and should be available to all forensic scientists (at present defence scientists do not have access to FSS databases).

VII CONCLUSION

Recent appeals have shown that forensic science evidence used by the prosecution in several cases in the 1970s was flawed. However, since the Clift affair in 1981, the FSS has done much to put its own house in order, introducing quality assessment schemes and working with the police to improve standards at scenes of crime. There are, though, still many problems with forensic science evidence, stemming primarily from the position of the police as customers in a forensic science market and from the inability of the defence to challenge FSS evidence. Although the Commission was aware of these problems, it has put too much faith in the ability of market forces to provide sufficient high-quality forensic science services in England and Wales. It has not realised that there is a gulf between market forces and the requirements of justice.

Charging is not a suitable method for regulating the relationship between the FSS and the police, both because 'the criminal justice "market" may not be an efficient purveyor of messages to the police' (Roberts and Willmore, 1993, p. 21) and because it may encourage the police to seek cheap, poor-quality forensic science assistance. Although the proposed creation of a Forensic Science Advisory Council is to be welcomed, the Council will need to be independent and to have strong powers if it is to regulate the market. There should also be adequate funding to enable the FSS, or other bodies, to carry out research and to compile databases.

One result of the Commission's proposals on pre-trial conferences and defence disclosure of any challenge to the prosecution's expert evidence (9.56–9.69) will be that the defence will have an even greater need for high-quality forensic science assistance. The defence should not have to go to the FSS to get this, nor should defence laboratories have to rely entirely on Legal Aid in order to develop into a credible check on the quality of prosecution forensic science evidence. There should be a certain amount of direct government funding available to the defence sector, at least to enable scientists to buy equipment, the expense of which would otherwise have to be borne by increased charges. Access to such funding could be made conditional on the accreditation of the scientists applying for it.

20. Testing the Truth: The Alliance of Science and Law

Edward Phillips

Both scientific and legal institutions draw inspiration from belief in a law-like reality which can be controlled by proper observation and analysis.[1]

Wider appreciation of the intrinsic fragility of scientific knowledge when placed in a sceptical social environment, of a kind so well illustrated by adversarial legal practice, will not of itself provide solutions.[2]

The Report of the Royal Commission on Criminal Justice and its recommendations are long overdue. The debate engendered by the Report is also welcome. This is despite the fact that the recommendations do not go far enough and often appear hesitant, especially in the context of the root causes of wrongful convictions as opposed to 'wrongful' acquittals. It is strange that this should be so, given that the concern with forensic evidence formed part of the impetus behind the setting up of the Commission. The Commission, moreover, had the benefit of valuable research on forensic evidence through the commissioned Research Series as well as the Report of the House of Lords Select Committee on Forensic Science.[3] It is disappointing that so little of this found its way into the Report. There is also a certain complacency in the notion that piece-meal reforms, for instance in the Police and Criminal Evidence Act 1984, have eliminated the causes of concern. This ignores the abuses revealed by cases such as that of the 'Tottenham 3' and the 'Cardiff 3' which have occurred since the introduction of that Act. Little acknowledgement is paid to the other critical inquiries into this area, as in the 'Preece' and 'Confait' cases, and the proposals that were made at that time, appear to

1 Smith and Wynne (eds), *Expert Evidence: Interpreting Science in the Law* (Routledge, London, 1989) p. 1
2 Smith and Wynne, ibid. p. 8.
3 Steventon, *The Ability to Challenge DNA Evidence* (Research Study 9); Roberts and Willmore, *The Role of Forensic Science Evidence in Criminal Proceedings* (Research Study 11); HL Select Committee on Science and Technology, *Report on Forensic Science* (HMSO, HL Paper 24, 1993).

have been ignored.[4]

A more serious failing is the lack of attention paid to the particular problems posed by the use of psychological and psychiatric evidence in the proof of *mens rea*.[5] As the Ward case[6] reveals this is an area beset by conflicting judicial pronouncements and the opportunity has been lost to deal efficiently with the complicated issues that arise.[7] By the same token, attempts have been made to address some of the more obvious shortcomings in the manner by which forensic evidence is utilised without tackling some of the more basic conceptual issues concerning the adversarial method of adducing such evidence and the best system of ensuring its reliability and credibility when it is adduced.

Fundamental to this are the rules of evidence. The Royal Commission has nothing to say on this subject as far as forensic evidence is concerned. The indictment must also include the failure to address what might be termed the 'ideology of scientism' and its peculiar effect upon decision-making which arises whenever forensic evidence is relied upon, particularly by the prosecution. This will in the long run undermine some of the Royal Commission's more worthwhile recommendations.

I THE ALLIANCE OF SCIENCE AND LAW

It is part of the culture of science and of scientific experts to make claims regarding objective, rational and logical rules. It is equally part of the culture of the law and of lawyers to apply a healthy scepticism to these claims. It is imperative that procedures be evolved in the criminal courts so that this scepticism is given a more important and structured role to play. It is this scepticism which is lacking in the Report.

The alliance of science and law in authoritative decision-making, through the reliance on forensic evidence, creates a formidable obstacle for any challenger or critic. This is especially the case for any hapless defendant who seeks to mount a challenge in the appellate courts and where the nature of the challenge involves recourse to fresh forensic evidence or, as is often the case, to a more critical evaluation of the evidence adduced at

---

4   Report of the Parliamentary Commissioner for Administration (HC 191, Session 1983–84; Fisher, *Report of an Inquiry into the Confait Case* (HMSO 1977); see also Appendix 5 of the HL Select Committee on Science and Technology, *Report on Forensic Science*
5   The term 'forensic evidence' is used throughout as referring to any scientific evidence used in connection with the investigation, proof or disproof of criminal activity. No distinction is drawn between 'scientific' and medical/psychological/psychiatric evidence.
6   [1993] 2 All ER 577.
7   See *Gunewardne* [1951] 2 All ER 290; *Lowery* [1973] 3 All ER 662; *Masih* [1986] Crim LR 395; *Everett* [1988] Crim LR 626; *Raghip* (1991) *The Times*, 9 December.

the trial. Here, the science–law relation presents a forensic totality that is generally greater than the sum of its individual parts. This combination is made all the more insidious since the natural legal scepticism that surrounds the fact-finding rules of the law of criminal evidence and procedure is often offset, in the minds of lawyers and judges no less than the layman on the jury, by the apparently certain forensic truth of scientific fact-finding: lawyers, judges and juries being apt to consider that the subjectivity of the law and its judgments being more than compensated for by the objectivity of science. To quote Lord Justice Glidewell:

> For lawyers, jurors and judges a forensic scientist conjures up the image of a man in a white coat working in a laboratory, approaching his task with cold neutrality, and dedicated only to the pursuit of scientific truth. It is a sombre thought that the reality is somewhat different.[8]

This has, perhaps, been due to the failure to recognise that science shares with the law at least one essential characteristic; both are inherently open-ended and 'incomplete'. As the House of Lords Select Committee on Science and Technology put it: 'Science has this much in common with the law, that it approaches truth by a process of dialectic in which thesis and antithesis are deliberately set in opposition.'[9]

In consequence, the scientific expert has often been given a prominence out of all proportion to the probative value of the evidence he presents, sometimes with disastrous results for the defendant in criminal trials. This is precisely the point that the Royal Commission does not adequately address. Leaving aside the IRA miscarriage of justice cases, mention may be made of the convictions in the older Confait case which first came to trial in 1972. One of the concerns raised in that case related to pathological evidence as to the likely time of death. This was of crucial importance due to the alibi defence that was raised.

In 1975 the Court of Appeal quashed the convictions on the now-familiar ground that the evidence upon which those convictions had been obtained was unsafe. The subsequent inquiry revealed that the forensic evidence did not include a reading of rectal temperature nor describe with certainty the extent of *rigor mortis* and concluded that such evidence 'might well have altered the whole course of the case'.[10] As one commentator on the case put it: 'This was an occasion on which critics concluded that the looseness of expert evidence, exploited by prosecuting counsel, helped

---

[8] *R v. Ward* [1933] 2 All ER 577, 627 CA.
[9] House of Lords Select Committee on Science and Technology, *Report on Forensic Science* (HL Paper 24, February 1993) para. 5.15.
[10] Fisher, *Report of an Inquiry into the Circumstances Leading to the Trial of Three Persons on Charges Arising out of the Death of Maxwell Confait* (HC Paper 90, HMSO, 1977), p. 21

secure false convictions.'[11]   It is a sad indictment of the criminal justice system that more than 15 years later this comment would be echoed not once but many times, by the Court of Appeal.

To prosecuting counsel forensic evidence may seem a universal panacea to help bolster up a weak case; to defence counsel forensic evidence may seem an insurmountable obstacle that may even lead to an effective 'abandonment' of the defence.   Nonetheless, the recent series of decisions by the courts have demonstrated two main points.   First, that the alleged certainty of forensic science is a fallacy and, second, that challenges to the duality of science and law, if properly mounted by scientifically-literate lawyers, may be successful.[12]

The cases also illustrate the consequences of scientifically-ignorant lawyers who, while being badly briefed and in awe of scientific experts, are only too ready to succumb to the mythology of the existence of autonomous, unambiguous and objective scientific knowledge.   However, the tenor of the Report is such as not to recognise this.   There is little evidence of concern with the defendant who is wrongly convicted due to the fallacy of forensic certainty.

In this context the Royal Commission's recommendation on 'the need for lawyers who practise at the Criminal Bar to be familiar with forensic science' appears, at best, inadequate.   So also is the pious hope that 'This familiarity should be prompted by interdisciplinary exchanges involving barristers, solicitors and experts.'[13]   Given the practical realities involved and the current difficulties over vocational training it is difficult to see how this 'interdisciplinary exchange' is ever to occur.

II THE EXPERT WITNESS

The problematic issues which arise when a forensic scientist is required to testify in court are neatly summarised by the House of Lords Select Committee on Forensic Science:

> We perceive a fundamental clash of cultures between science and the law.   The process of the courts seeks definite answers to questions posed by counsel who are required to be learned only in the law; these answers are delivered *extempore* in an adversarial setting before a jury unlikely to contain anyone with relevant scientific knowledge.   The

---

[11] Smith, 'Forensic Pathology, Scientific Expertise and the Criminal Law', p. 64, in Smith and Wynne (ed.) loc. cit.

[12] See the summary of the miscarriage of justice cases in Appendix 5 of the House of Lords Select Committee Report on Forensic Science *op. cit.* Note in particular *R* v *Maguire* [1992] 2 All ER 433; *R* v *Ward* [1992].

[13] See Ch. 9, para. 79.

scientist, on the other hand, is accustomed to dealing with conclusions which, to satisfy standards of scientific precision, must often be qualified by limits of probability. These may have precise statistical meanings; but they are not easily understood by the non-scientist, and the values will change as knowledge and techniques advance. It may therefore be that the best scientist will appear the most prevaricating witness.[14]

The Royal Commission pays insufficient attention to the *expert* who is called upon to adduce forensic evidence. The crux of the problem is that the Royal Commission considers some of the issues involving forensic evidence without acknowledging that the miscarriage of justice cases had as much to do with the expert forensic *witnesses* who testified in those cases. In consequence the Report says virtually nothing about necessary qualifications, proper expertise, admissibility of evidence and the role, limited or otherwise of the expert's opinion. It appears that these issues seem not to have troubled the Commission even though they had been raised in the cases, in the previous enquiries and in the Research Studies.

III QUALIFICATIONS AND EXPERTISE

Under the common law rules who is an 'expert' and what constitutes expertise is for the trial court to decide, guided by precedent. The courts have traditionally adopted a liberal attitude in this respect.[15] Whether this should continue to be the case is perhaps open to question. Given the immense advancement in all branches of science it is not feasible to accept that a 'general practitioner' of the area of science in question is sufficiently an expert. To mention one example:

> ... at one time an academic practitioner of forensic medicine would be competent to give reliable evidence, based on the state of knowledge then available, on problems in the fields of morbid anatomy, toxicology, the examination of blood, of hairs and fibres, and of some stains caused by biological fluids. But now the disciplines of morbid anatomy and toxicology have moved a long way apart, and the knowledge available in the area of blood grouping, serology, immunology and genetics has expanded vastly, and as a consequence has produced several separate specialities.[16]

It is possible to speculate that the wrongful conviction in the John Preece case, for instance, would not have occurred if the trial court had inquired into Dr Alan Clift's qualification to give expert testimony on matters as diverse as bodily fluids, blood, hair and fibres. This especially so as the

---

[14] House of Lords Select Committee on Science and Technology, *Report on Forensic Science* (HL Paper 24, February 1993) para. 5.14.

[15] See for example *R v. Silverlock* [1894] 2 QB 766; *R v. Oakley* (1979) 70 Cr App Rep 7

[16] Gee, 'The Expert Witness in the Criminal Trial' [1987] Crim LR 307

internal inquiry by the FSS Birmingham found that he was guilty of 'grave technical incompetence'.[17] The recommendations made by the Royal Commission would have been strengthened by a reiteration that the trial judge has a positive duty to ensure that the forensic expert is properly qualified and competent in that particular area of expertise.   A commentator may be forgiven for concluding that the Royal Commission was seeking to put forward, implicitly, a civil justice model whereby the trial judge may be content to leave such matters to the individual parties.

The Research Study on *The Role of Forensic Science Evidence in Criminal Proceedings* considered the task of locating the right forensic expert and rightly concludes that here the prosecution is at an advantage due to its traditional relationship with the forensic science agencies. Moreover, the prosecution need not concern itself with the task of choosing the best qualified expert as this is a matter that can be left to FSS internal case allocation. All the more reason, therefore, for the courts to insist upon rigorous standards of qualification and expertise.

When it comes to the defence, matters are not so simple. The Research Study referred to above found that defence solicitors may encounter problems in locating an expert of the necessary expertise.[18] In such cases the trial judge need not be expected to rigorously insist upon proper qualifications and experience; the burden of proof is, after all, on the prosecution.

The matters upon which the expert may testify is also a matter for the trial court. There is an obvious danger in allowing questions of 'common sense' to be monopolised by expert witnesses[19] and the Royal Commission would have faced an impossible task if it had tried to list the matters on which expert forensic evidence could properly be admitted. The Royal Commission does give its approval to the Court of Appeal's judgment in *Silcott, Braithwaite and Raghip* that expert psychological and psychiatric evidence be admitted on the question as to 'whether the defendant suffers from mental impairment or other mental disorder severe enough to affect the reliability of confession evidence.'[20] The Commission, however, says nothing as to the extent to which expert forensic evidence is admissible so as to prove questions of the defendant's mental state relating to *mens rea*, beyond the bland statement that such evidence 'can be crucial'.[21] Does

---

[17] See Appendix 5, HL Select Committee, *Report on Forensic Science*, loc. cit.

[18] Ibid. para. 3.2.

[19] See the oft-repeated *dicta* in *Turner* [1975] QB 834, 841: the 'fact that an expert witness has impressive scientific qualifications does not by that fact alone make his opinion on matters of human nature and behaviour within the limits of normality any more helpful than that of the jury themselves.'

[20] Royal Commission on Criminal Justice, loc. cit. p. 161 para. 77.

[21] P. 152, para. 39.

this amount to an approval of cases such as *R* v *Lowery* where forensic evidence was admitted to show which of two defendants was psychologically more likely to lead the other in a murder?[22]   The issue may arise in many different contexts, ranging from the question as to the admissibility of so-called psychological profiles to expert testimony of the 'slow-burn' reaction of battered women.[23]

IV FACTS VERSUS OPINION

The classic formulation of the role of an expert witness is that the 'expert may give his opinion upon facts which are either admitted, or proved by himself, or other witnesses in his hearing, at the trial, or are matters of common knowledge; as well as upon an hypothesis based thereon.'[24]   It is crucial to this formulation that while there may be a distinction between 'fact' and 'opinion', facts do not speak for themselves.   The expert has to interpret the facts for the court.

The distinction often breaks down as much expert opinion is in a probabilistic form, that is, expressed in terms of probability.[25]   This is the form that evidence about DNA or blood grouping takes.   This is complicated by the fact that probability evidence may merge with weaker evidence which can only be equated with likelihood and which can only ever be treated as opinion.   Probabilistic evidence, moreover, may well be accorded the status of factual evidence.   On the other hand, it may well be that an expert who testifies as to probabilities is met with the charge of uncertainty and his testimony discredited even though the probability evidence he present may meet the requirements of his field of expertise as amounting to virtual certainty.

> I mean the p value may be less than .0000001, but it's still a probability; and so they say 'ah, you can't be certain', and of course this is ... used by the opposite side very effectively and unless you are actually prepared to stick your neck out – (and of course sometimes for the sake of justice we do).   But this is ... a matter where it rather hurts our scientific integrity to say things we don't really believe in.[26]

As far as forensic evidence is concerned, it is submitted that the distinction

---

[22] [1974] AC 85; see also Sheldon and MacLeod, 'From Normative to Positive Data: Expert Psychological Evidence Re-examined' [1991] Crim LR 811.
[23] See *R* v. *Ahluwalia* [1992] 4 All ER 889.
[24] *Phipson on Evidence* (14th edn) para. 32.14.
[25] Eggleston, *Evidence, Proof and Probability*, 2nd edn Weidenfeld & Nicolson (1983) London.
[26] Interview with a forensic pathologist, quoted from Smith, 'Forensic Pathology, Scientific Expertise and the Criminal Law' loc. cit. p. 69.

between fact and opinion should be as follows: a fact is a conclusion that
would receive near-unanimous agreement from experts in that particular
field; an opinion is a conclusion that would not receive this degree of
acceptance.

In a 1983 article in the *Law Quarterly Review* Professor Kenny posed the
following questions:

> How, and by whom, is it decided when an expert in a scientific discipline is expressing
> an opinion on matters within his science? Who decides when he ceases to do so, and is
> expressing no longer an expert opinion but merely the opinion of an expert? How and by
> whom *should* these questions be decided in a rational system of jurisprudence?[27]

These questions are not raised, much less answered by the Royal
Commission.

V EXPERT EVIDENCE IN THE COURTS

The production of forensic evidence primarily involves a two-stage
process. The first involves a determination that the scientific process or
technique has received acceptance and recognition by the scientific
community. The second involves a judgment as to whether the process or
technique and, more important, the interpretation of facts through that
process or technique is to be recognised by the courts as constituting
validly admissible evidence. One crucial difficulty to be faced is that of
reducing the complicated range of issues involved in the first process
(ascertaining the validity of scientific procedures) into one, or a series of,
narrow and precise legal questions to be used in the second process
(determining admissibility). It also raises the question of whether the
'neutral' consensual presentation of scientific knowledge can ever be
reconciled or even successfully utilised in the adversarial procedure of
criminal trials.

Smith and Wynne put forward the argument that,

> The ... integration of forensic expertise with the law is such that forensic experts have
> learnt to reconcile themselves to the regular adversarial scepticism of legal processes,
> while maintaining the normal consensual discourses of scientific expertise.[28]

In the light of the recent miscarriages of justice and the damaging judicial
pronouncements on the scientific experts involved, this contention can no
longer be acceptable. There is little doubt that these cases illustrate that

---

27 Kenny, 'The Expert in Court' (1983) 99 LQR 197, 200.
28 Smith and Wynne op. cit. p. 15.

the 'consensual discourses of scientific expertise' had been subsumed by the prosecutorial imperative, resulting in the unholy spectacle of scientist turned prosecutor.

Credibility must be established to the criminal standard of proof, i.e. proof beyond reasonable doubt. The consequence of this is that expert 'knowledge' must be seen to satisfy an artificial standard of probity. This in effect means that if the expert's testimony is rejected, for whatever reason, the evidence he has produced for the court's scrutiny ceases to be 'knowledge'.

VI NOVEL FORENSIC EVIDENCE

All these issues come to a head when reliance is placed upon new or novel scientific tests. In effect, the court is turned into an arena for testing scientific validity. In other words, for testing scientific, not legal, truth. The Royal Commission offers no guidance as to how to deal with the resulting problem. It is true that something may be made of the pre-trial phase but this may well be insufficient. The ongoing debate as to the reliability of DNA evidence demonstrates this only too well.

The Royal Commission, it is submitted, should have re-considered the propriety of the flexible and liberal attitude of the English courts when admitting novel scientific techniques. This approach is in stark contrast to the position in the United States where most jurisdictions follow a rule of automatically rejecting testimony based on novel scientific techniques until and unless that technique has been subjected to stringent scrutiny. The procedure, in practice, is to convene what has come to called a *Frye* hearing, after a 1923 decision of the District of Columbia appellate court in the case of *Frye* v. *United States*.[29] The District Court there stated:

> Just when a scientific principle or discovery crosses the line between the experimental and demonstrable stages is difficult to define. Somewhere in this twilight zone the evidential force of the principle must be recognised, and while the courts will go a long way in admitting expert testimony deduced from a well-recognised scientific principle or discovery, the thing from which the deduction is made must be sufficiently established to have gained general acceptance in the particular field in which it belongs.

Given the continuous development of new forensic tests, the advantages of a *Frye*-type procedure are obvious. An important consequence of the Frye hearing and its attendant procedure is that it harnesses the stringent institutional processes and procedures of the law in determining the

---

[29] *Frye* v. *United States* 293 F. 1013 (D.C. Cir 1923).

validity and efficacy of a novel scientific process as far as truth-proving is concerned.

One rationale is that the test ensures a more informed analysis of the merits of scientific testimony. In effect, the test delegates the decision on the admissibility of the testimony to the scientific community. The proponent of the testimony must show that most specialists within the relevant scientific discipline accept the theory. The *Frye* test effectively assigns the admissibility decision to those expert specialists.[30]

On a superficial analysis, the *Frye* hearing is a contradiction in terms; the subjection of scientific expertise and scientific knowledge to the 'unscientific' scrutiny of courtroom procedure. In particular, sceptical legal scrutiny which exposes the intrinsic fragility of scientific knowledge may serve no purpose other than to deprive the courts of an important fact-finding and fact-interpreting tool.

Nonetheless, the hearing confers the advantage of limiting expert conflict and uncertainty and focusing it on a disagreement surrounding a specific issue, which is further refined by placing it within a 'legal' context. Moreover, on a purely pragmatic level, it dispenses with the necessity to develop any 'theory' of expert scientific knowledge in legal settings.

The *Frye* hearings are, admittedly, not ideal. In particular, an astute and well-briefed defence counsel may utilise the requirements of the criminal burden of proof (lying on the prosecution) and the criminal standard of proof (beyond reasonable doubt) to ensure the judicial rejection of a novel scientific technique. It is submitted, however, that it is no bad thing that when science is applied to legal decision-making that it should do so, and only be allowed to do so, in a forum that applies more complex and rigorous criteria then the scientific community itself operates. If this is not done then we will be treated to yet more instances of the tragic incarceration of innocent defendants convicted on the basis of evidence that is later discovered to be of doubtful reliability; the use of the now-discredited tests for the presence of nitroglycerine being a case in point.

In many ways the *Frye* hearings represent a union of the adversarial and inquisitorial methods of judicial investigation, utilised in the adjudication of expert knowledge in a legal context. The present discovery and disclosure procedure might work well enough in those well-established areas where there is sufficient consensus. However, in the newest areas of expertise, there is room for the greatest of legitimate disputes. It is this area, therefore, that requires the *Frye* hearings the most.

---

[30] Imwinkelried, 'The Evolution of the American Test for the Admissibility of Scientific Evidence' *Med.Sci.Law* (1990) Vol. 30, No. 1, p. 60 at p. 61

VII THE CONFLICT OF EXPERT TESTIMONY

The Royal Commission ignores the patent fact that expert testimony often involves both internal and external 'cultural' and ideological conflicts, embedded interests and values within the field of a particular expertise.

Expert conflict which may result is a function of the differences in perspective between different traditions of observation and explanation. It is not merely a matter of empirical imprecision or defective logical analysis.[31]

One issue which arises concerns the question as to whether conflicts of expert witnesses should be encouraged or neutralised. One consequence of the evidentiary reforms which permit an increasing use of documentary evidence and a corresponding reduction in the use of oral evidence is that expert conflict is reduced. This may be counterproductive. Open expert conflict in the court room, aided by examination and cross-examination, may in fact represent an essential component in the hidden 'negotiation' that produces expert consensus.

Another issue concerns the question as to whether there is, in fact, a real conflict. Different experts may give testimony that differs only in balance and emphasis. This may create an appearance of inconsistency that is deceptive. Nonetheless, this appearance of inconsistency may be manipulated by counsel to ensure that the evidence is rejected as unreliable.

VIII THE NEUTRAL EXPERT

Legal understanding of the workings of science obviously affects the way in which scientific expertise is treated in the legal context. Three dangers become immediately obvious. First, it is tempting to assume that the expert's conclusion is objective. This is an illusion. The expert may well be operating from a theoretical or intellectual base which involves predetermined conclusions; scientific knowledge, like other forms of knowledge, does not exist in a political or institutional vacuum. This may involve methodology as well as ideology.[32] Moreover, the conclusions

---

[31] Smith and Wynne op. cit. p. 17.

[32] 'Ideology' refers to the set of related beliefs, ideas and attitudes that exist within a particular professional group and which is used by that group to interpret their findings and work experiences. This may be illustrated by the divergent conclusions of medical experts regarding the nature, origins and symptoms of mental illness: see Smith, *Trial by Medicine: Insanity and Responsibility in Victorian Trials* (Edinburgh University Press, 1981). Additionally, this may also involve untested conventions, for instance, conventions about what amounts to competent laboratory practice.

drawn may involve interpretative value judgments.

Even if this does not affect the scientific *process*, it may well affect the application of that process to the facts of the instant case. Coupled with this is the real possibility that the expert is more prosecution-minded or defence-minded, something which has a significant impact on the evaluative component of the testimony.

The second danger involves the elevation of the expert's opinion (which is essentially a statement of putative 'knowledge') into a legal conclusion (a statement of established judicial 'truth').[33] Third, it must also be borne in mind that science, unlike law, does not proceed on the basis of decisions carrying hierarchical authority. The reverse is, in fact, more likely to be true. The danger here is that the lay outsider who is the 'recipient' of a scientific finding may conclude that it is in fact based upon and shaped by an authoritative consensus; consensus may in fact exist amongst some experts but this does not necessarily bear the imprimatur of hierarchical authority. Recent cases make the point only too well that these dangers affect not only the lay-jury but also trial judges and counsel.

The professional and academic integrity and standing of the expert who testifies in court represents something in the way of a hidden agenda quite separate from the issue of establishing the guilt or otherwise of the defendant. Too little consideration is given to the fact that a judicial decision, or caustic judicial comment, is likely to have implications regarding employment or research funding to the expert witness. This is especially true when a novel method of interpreting evidence is involved. To take one example, the standing of the experts who testified as to the probative value of DNA evidence and the credibility of the technique itself, was boosted immeasurably by the judicial decisions that accepted its validity in courts of law. It also led to an increase in research funding, both by the Home Office as well as by other institutions. There can be no doubt that the reverse would have been the case had the courts refused to accept that the technique of extracting DNA had as large a role, or indeed any role, to play in determining the crucial issue of guilt. The decisions on admissibility also had considerable commercial implications, especially for companies such as Cellmark Diagnostics whose experts testified regularly in these cases. This must raise the question of whether a scientific expert in this position can ever be said to be engaged in the same enterprise as that which is taxing the court before which he testifies.

---

[33] Even in those instances when scientific fact may be regarded as truly objective, a legal fiction may subvert it. For instance, the 'fact' of the normal gestation period of 270 days has been subverted by legal fictions regarding proof of paternity by the 'legal' father: *Wood* v. *Wood* [1947] P 103; *Preston-Jones* v. *Preston-Jones* [1951] 1 All ER 124.

IX CONCLUSION

Searching for an image of law as rational, precise and certain leads to the dangerous over-reliance on science. This has to be checked. It is contended that when science is subjected to detailed and meticulous scrutiny, its possible procedural imprecision and inconsistency become apparent. The now-discredited tests for nitroglycerine provides the classic example of a test, previously taken to be definitive within the scientific community, which were demonstrated by informed legal examination to be full of unstated limiting conditions and unwarranted suppositions. It must be the function of the law, at the point when science and law intersect in the trial court, to mount this scrutiny. The American courts have shown one method by which this is done. This method, or perhaps a quasi-legal variant, should be adopted in the courts of the United Kingdom as a matter of urgency. Only if this is done can science perform its proper, and only, role in the criminal justice system: to enhance the factual basis of legal decision-making.

While the Royal Commission has made some useful recommendations, it is submitted that its failure to address the deeper issues concerning the proper limits to forensic evidence leaves open the possibility of further injustice. The critic is entitled to ask whether there is anything in the Commission's proposals and recommendations on forensic science that will prevent the occurrence of cases such as the recent Berry case[34] where the Court of Appeal freed a defendant after a twelve-year campaign on the grounds that the wrongful conviction had been obtained as a result of highly suspect forensic evidence. Will there need to be many more miscarriages of justice before there is an acknowledgement that, in the final analysis, the Royal Commission has failed in its task of putting forward adequate recommendations to prevent wrongful convictions based on faulty forensic evidence?

---

[34] *The Times*, Wednesday, 29 September 1993.

21. Miscarriages of Justice: Pre-Trial and Trial Stages

John Wadham

I INTRODUCTION

The purpose of this paper is to assess the likely impact of the recommendations of the Royal Commission on miscarriages of justice and the rights of the suspect and, in particular, to look at those recommendations that affect the pre-trial and trial stages. Inevitably it is not possible to do 'justice' to all of the recommendations and only some have been selected for consideration. I have not looked at those areas which are the subject of other detailed contributions: defence services, plea-bargaining, forensic evidence and the criminal justice system in Northern Ireland, all of which are of great concern to Liberty. This paper therefore very much represents a list of the problems that can be identified from Liberty's human rights perspective and not a theoretical critique of the project as a whole.[1] Obviously Liberty is particularly concerned to ensure that in any future changes rights are respected and the chances of new miscarriages of justice are reduced.

First some more general issues. Liberty was very concerned about the terms of reference of the Commission particularly:

1. the fact that they prevented the consideration of the jurisdictions of Northern Ireland and Scotland;

2. the implication that the conviction of the guilty, acquittal of the innocence and the cost of the process should be considered of equal importance;

---

[1] Liberty's evidence to the Royal Commission, *Let Justice Be Done*, November 1991, sets out its recommendations for change in detail. Detailed consideration of the right to silence (including defence disclosure), confession evidence and miscarriages of justice is provided in Thornton et al., *Justice on Trial*, Civil Liberties Trust, 1992.

3. questioning the continued existence of the right to silence; and

4. the lack of any concern with the large number of cases which are not prosecuted following arrest and detention.

We were also concerned about the membership of the Commission and wrote to the Home Secretary requesting that at least one member should have real experience of miscarriages of justice. This was apparently ignored.

The Commission does not appear to have accepted the view that there are some fundamental rights that must be preserved or incorporated into any criminal justice system. Not only is there little or no discussion of the common law principles; there is also no mention of the duties of the Government in respect of international treaties. Perhaps the most important and well known is the European Convention on Human Rights. For example this provides in Article 5 for the liberty of the subject. The Commission fails to mention that the lengthy detentions under the Prevention of Terrorism (Temporary Provisions) Act 1989 (PTA) have been held to breach this article.[2] Perhaps the most important article is Article 6 of this Convention which provides for the right of a fair trial within a reasonable time, the presumption of innocence, the right to be informed about the charge, adequate time and facilities for the defence, legal aid, the right to examination of witnesses and the right to an interpreter. The lack of consideration of this article is all the more unfortunate given that many of the high-profile miscarriage of justice cases have been considered by the Strasbourg institutions.[3]

Finally of course there are other rights in the Convention which are relevant. For instance Article 8, the right to privacy, which is highly relevant to some of the Commission's proposals on increasing powers of search and the taking and retention of samples and other data or Article 14 which is the non-discrimination provision of the Convention.

The other important treaty is the International Covenant on Civil and Political Rights which, in addition to containing many of the rights included in the Convention, also provides stronger anti-discrimination provisions, a specific provision on the right to silence and a right to appeal. Liberty's recent report assessing the criminal justice system against the

---

2   *Brogan* v. *UK* (1988) Series A, No 145B. This unlawfulness remains despite the decision in *Branningan and McBride* v. *UK* (26 May 1993) authorising the Government's subsequent derogation under Article 15.

3   The Birmingham 6 case was ruled as inadmissible, *Callaghan* v. *UK* (9 May 1989) as was one of the Tottenham 3, *Braithwaite* v. *UK* (18 April 1991). The Court itself has only considered one 'miscarriage of justice' case, *Edwards* v. *UK*, *The Times* 21 January 1993.

Covenant indicates real concerns about current breaches of human rights.[4]

These rights would have informed the Commission's deliberations and it is disappointing that they have not been considered. Although there is not space here to develop this it is submitted that some of the proposals may breach these two treaties and if implemented may lead to condemnation by the European Commission or Court of Human Rights and the Human Rights Committee of the United Nations.

The most celebrated miscarriages of justice virtually all involved the wrongful conviction of people from ethnic minorities, primarily Irish people or people from an Afro-Caribbean background.[5] Liberty's work in assisting people who have an arguable claim to having been wrongfully convicted demonstrates that this bias exists not only amongst the more famous cases.[6] The Royal Commission has asked for further monitoring[7] which, although may be necessary, is clearly insufficient on its own. It has taken the welcome step of suggesting that, contrary to *Ford*,[8] the judge should have the power to ensure a mixed panel in exceptional circumstances and where race was an element in the case itself. This does not go far enough. Many black defendants, however, will continue to face an all-white jury in courts where all the other participants are white too. There is also of course no mention whatsoever of the treatment of women in the criminal justice system or that of lesbians and gay men.

The failure of the Commission to make any recommendations on the PTA, given its importance in the terrorist cases that were the reason for the Commission's own existence, demonstrates a clear lack of courage in confronting some of the harder and more politically sensitive issues in the criminal justice system.

Perhaps it is unsurprising but the Commission seems only to have been prepared to support greater protection for the defendant after considerable thought and argument, when it has the support of others and where there is supportive empirical research. Even when all these pre-conditions are

---

4   *Human Rights Convention Report 2: Criminal Justice and Civil and Political Liberties,* July 1993. This is the second report in a series providing an alternative view in preparation for when the Government produces its five-year periodic report to the United Nations Human Rights Committee.

5   For instance: the Birmingham 6, *R* v. *Callaghan and others,* [1992] 2 All ER 417; the Maguire 7, *R* v. *Maguire and others,* 94 Cr App R 133; the Guildford 4, *R* v. *Richardson and others, The Times,* 20 October 1989; Judy Ward, *R* v. *Ward, The Times,* 8 June 1992; the Cardiff 3, *R* v. *Miller, Paris and Abdullahi, The Times,* 24 December 1992; and the Tottenham 3, *R* v. *Silcot, Braithwaite and Rahip, The Times,* 9 December 1991.

6   *Liberty, A Case to Answer: A Dossier of 111 Cases where the Convictions may be Unsafe* (1992); *Further Cases to Answer: A Revised Dossier of 163 Cases where the Convictions may be Unsafe* (1992). Liberty has now investigated over 200 cases where the convictions may be unsafe.

7   Chapter 1, paras 25 and 26.

8   [1989] 3 All ER 445.

present sometimes something else seems to have prevented it from taking the obvious step. However, when it has decided to reduce the rights of the defendant such pillars of support seem to have been unnecessary (see for instance sample-taking in the police station, plea-bargaining and the right to trial by jury).

I think that it is possible to detect at least two strands in the Commission's thinking and to divide the process into three phases. The Commission was very careful to seek opinions on a whole variety of issues. It requested consultees to answer 88 questions[9] that it had carefully drafted and which dealt with the vast majority of areas of concern (though not, for instance, the PTA or racism). Reading these, whilst it is possible to detect the final conclusions as seedlings there, they do in fact disclose a clear concern for the rights of the defendant. One year later and after an election victory by a party traditionally committed to 'law and order' when organisations were being asked to given oral evidence the Commission gave some indications of a different agenda.[10] Although it was unclear how seriously some of the proposals were being treated, tracking the final thinking is much easier.[11]

There was then a phase during which spokespeople for the prosecution and police seemed to regain their confidence. At the same time there appeared to be a gradual drift in the media and amongst 'opinion formers' away from a concern about miscarriages of justice towards crime control concerns, and it is assumed, the Commission was influenced by this. The Commission was finally captured by these new concerns although it never completely gave up its original ideas. This has led, I think, to two reports rather than one. The first one is more considered and well argued (and here I am not merely referring to the parts of the Report that I support); the other one is hardly argued at all but perhaps will have the most significant effect.

The Commission, perhaps partly as a consequence, adopted the tactic common also to the last Royal Commission on this subject[12] which was to abolish or extend rules that are regularly broken by the police and other agencies rather than to recommend increased sanctions. Often, and, incredibly, the fact of the regular breach of the rules is itself used as a reason for the abolition of the rule. The result of this strategy over long

---

[9] Sent in June 1991.

[10] Letter to Liberty and others September 1992 which was 'leaked' to *The Times*, 5 October 1992.

[11] In April 1992 there had been some 350 responses to the Commission, that is six months after the deadline for submissions. By the time the Report was written this had increased to 600. One interesting submission missing from the first list but included in the second is the Security Service, MI5.

[12] The Royal Commission on Criminal Procedure, 1981.

periods is obviously highly problematic as, if anything, it encourages
institutional and personal delinquency.

II POLICE INVESTIGATIONS AND THE RIGHTS OF SUSPECTS

There are a number of proposals which are likely to reduce the number of
miscarriages of justice in the future assuming that they have any effect in
practice.[13] Most of these are designed to tinker with the Codes of Practice
(the Codes) made under the Police and Criminal Evidence Act 1984
(PACE). These proposals do not address the fundamental problem of
ensuring that written rules have an effect on the practice of police officers
and the decisions of the courts. The recommendations rely on the belief
that the current sanctions for breaches of the rules are adequate. This
means relying on supervision by superior officers, the Crown Prosecution
Service (CPS), the courts and the victims of the violations through the
police complaints system. All these remedies will remain inadequate even
if all the Commission's recommendations were implemented without
amendment.

Research, both produced for the Commission and independently,
demonstrates the difficulty of relying on supervision by other police
officers or by the CPS to control malpractice.[14] The civil courts, whilst
having an increased role in awarding damages for malpractice after the
event (often many years after the event) have little apparent effect on
behaviour. In fact even successful cases in the civil courts rarely even lead
to disciplinary action against the police officers concerned.[15]

Both the nature of sections 76 and 78 of PACE and the view taken by the
courts has meant that breaches of either the Codes or PACE itself are
likely to have little or no effect at the criminal trial. Although the new
Lord Chief Justice has had a role in changing the attitude of the Court of
Appeal, which has in turn led to some important decisions,[16] malpractice
and breaches rarely lead to evidence being held to be inadmissible. Of
course many breaches do not have a direct effect on evidence and without
adopting a 'fruit of the poisoned tree' approach the only evidence likely to
be excluded is confession evidence. Even in the case of confession

---

[13] Particularly Recommendations 4 to 8, 11, 12, 25 to 33, 38 to 40, 43 to 47, 49 to 69 and 72 to
81.
[14] Baldwin and Moloney, 1993; Maguire and Norris, 1993; McConville, Sanders and Leng,
1991.
[15] Chris Mullin MP, *The Independent*, 15 April 1993.
[16] For instance see *Ward*, footnote 5, or *R* v. *McKenzie*, *The Times*, 15 September 1992.

evidence the likelihood is that only very substantial breaches of the rules, such as the denial of access to lawyers before interview, will guarantee exclusion.[17]

Interestingly this is one of the few areas that has resulted in public disagreements amongst Commission members and even more rarely led to a minority report.[18] The majority are prepared to allow the Court of Appeal, to assess the guilt or innocence of the defendant once a 'procedural defect' has been found.

> If the procedural defect is such that the Court of Appeal believes that the jury's verdict is unsafe, the conviction should be quashed. If the court believes that in consequence of the defect the conviction may be unsafe, it should in the view of the majority order a retrial where possible or practical. Dismissing the appeal is the right course where the court despite the procedural defect considers the conviction safe.[19]

> In the view of the majority, even if they believed that quashing the convictions was an appropriate way of punishing police malpractice, it would be naive to suppose that this would have any practical effect on police behaviour.[20]

However even Michael Zander seems to believe that it is possible to know for certain who is guilty and on the basis of little evidence says:

> The Commission is unanimous in believing that the Court of Appeal's past practice of allowing many guilty persons to escape their just deserts simply because there has been a defect in the process leading to their conviction requires reconsideration.[21]

Many of the recommendations concerning the police disciplinary process are to be welcomed.[22] In particular the abolition of the bar on disciplinary proceedings following an acquittal of a police officer on a criminal charge. This change will bring police officers in line with all other employees. Also the proposed reduction in the standard of proof in a disciplinary case from the criminal one of 'beyond reasonable doubt' to the civil 'on the balance of probabilities' should result in more police officers being disciplined for malpractice. Unfortunately the acceptance that the system can work effectively whilst it continues to allow the police to investigate themselves will ensure that these recommendations have no fundamental effect.[23]

---

[17] See *R* v. *Samuel* (1988) 87 Crim App R 232 cf. *R* v. *Alladice* (1988) 87 Crim App R 380.

[18] Chapter 10, paras 47–50 and Michael Zander's 'Note of Dissent', paras 62–72 (which is also supported by Yves Newbold).

[19] Chapter 10, paragraph 47.

[20] Para. 49.

[21] 'Note of Dissent', para. 62.

[22] Chapter 3, para. 103.

[23] It is unfortunate that the Commission has recommended that such a fundamentally flawed system as this should be used by the Criminal Cases Review Authority, the body to be set up

It is no surprise that these proposals are very similar to those contained in a consultation paper produced by the Home Office a few months before the Commission reported.[24]

The 'need' for increased powers to take samples from suspects and the need to set up a DNA database have been supported almost unanimously by the Commission.[25]   The only research commissioned on this issue pointed, if anything, in the other direction.[26]

The Commission's argument for recommending that a mouth swab should suddenly become 'non-intimate' has a shocking simplicity: the police asked for it, said it worked 'satisfactorily' in Northern Ireland (without evidence) and said that it could be used to obtain a DNA profile. Similarly extending the law to allow non-intimate samples to be taken in cases other than serious arrestable offences, the proposal that the refusal by a suspect in the same circumstances to give an intimate sample would lead to the possibility of an adverse inference in court, and the recategorisation of some offences as 'serious' for the purposes of giving a greater right to the police to obtain samples, are all accepted without discussion.   The Commission also recommends other increased powers to take samples for DNA purposes on the basis that the police service has pointed out that 'it is not uncommon for persons arrested for sexual offences to have previous convictions for other types of serious offence, for example burglary.'

Note that there is no empirical research, that the 'evidence' originates from the police who will benefit from the new power, that it is not clear what 'not uncommon' means, that it refers not to persons convicted but only arrested (and thus might say more about police practices than sexual offenders) and that lastly there is no attempt to analyse the extent to which previous convictions for other offences is an accurate predictor of subsequent sexual offences.

This all at the very time that there is emerging increased evidence of the reliability of DNA evidence in criminal trials.[27]

The police are not, subject to some narrowly defined exceptions, supposed to continue to question a suspect after he or she has been charged.[28]   The Commission, perhaps conscious of the fact that this is sometimes breached, has decided to abolish the rule.   Again with little or no empirical evidence of the 'mischief' to be addressed and the only support for the measure coming from the police.   From the position of the

---

to investigate miscarriages of justice.
[24] Spring 1993.
[25] Chapter 2, paras 25 on.
[26] Steventon, 1993.
[27] See for instance *New Law Journal*, June 1993.
[28] PACE Code C, paragraph 16.5.

suspect being given an opportunity to speak and answer questions we have moved to the situation where the suspect can be questioned until the police decide that they have wrung everything, including any possible defence, from him or her. The Commission says that detention after charge cannot be justified 'solely' for questioning after charge but the reality is that it will be used in this way. It is an indication of how far the debate has moved that it is now quite difficult to believe that less than ten years ago the right of the police to detain for questioning itself was questioned.[29]   It provides another example of how another fundamental common law right can suddenly so easily evaporate.

III EVIDENCE

The failure of the Commission to recommend a corroboration rule for confessions[30] despite the support from the research[31] ensures that it will follow in the footsteps of the previous Commission[32] which also shied away from taking this necessary step. If there is one failure which will ensure that there continue to be considerable numbers of miscarriages of justice in the future it is this one.

The Commission does not even recommend a corroboration rule for those confessions made outside of the police station which, of course, are even more likely to be unreliable and subject to fabrication.

A judicial warning to the jury in uncorroborated confession cases is likely to have very little effect in preventing wrongful convictions. Is it likely to have prevented the confessions of the Guildford 4 or Tottenham 3?[33]

Despite the evidence from the research[34] on so called 'ambush' defences, the Commission has recommended imposing a duty to disclose the defence case before trial. This will make a large dent in the defendant's right to silence and undermine the principle that the prosecution must be able to prove its case without the assistance of the defendant. Apart from these issues of principle this duty will again tilt the balance away from the defendant and in consequence increase the number of wrongful convictions. In practice once the defence has disclosed its case the prosecution will be able to trim its case to that of the defence and will be able to predict the witnesses that the defence will be likely to call. This

---

29 *Mohammed-Holgate* v. *Duke* [1984] AC 437.
30 Chapter 4, paras 43 on.
31 McConville, 1993b.
32 See footnote 12, para. 4.74.
33 See footnote 5.
34 Leng, 1993.

will allow the police to question these witnesses and in some cases to put pressure on them to alter their evidence or, in extreme cases, to refuse to give evidence. This last scenario occurred in the Guildford 4 case[35] and has happened in other cases. The new duty will obviously allow more prosecutions based on corrupt witnesses to succeed because those witnesses will be more easily able to predict the questions that they will have to meet.

If the defence does not disclose its case, adverse comment at trial will result in convictions based not on evidence of guilt but rather by equating silence with guilt.

IV PRE-TRIAL

It is difficult to treat seriously the proposal that the right to elect trial by jury in either-way cases should be removed and instead be given to magistrates. It is clearly unthought through, wrong in principle, lacking in support from others (even the Magistrates' Association have condemned it), lacking in any empirical basis and unlikely to deal with the 'mischief' intended.

Liberty has been concerned for some time about the gradual erosion of the right to jury trial and believes that as a matter of fundamental principle jury trial should be available in any case serious enough to carry a sentence of imprisonment. The right to jury trial is an important safeguard in criminal proceedings and throughout history has acted as a check on abuse.

Regardless of issues of principle it is worth looking in detail at the Commission's own logic. Magistrates send 64 per cent of cases to the Crown Court of their own volition.[36] Although there is some discussion by the Commission of what should be done to deal with the problems of magistrates sending too many cases to the Crown Court the more fundamental solution is recommended for the smaller 36 per cent of cases 'in order to secure a more rational division of either-way cases ...'[37]

Despite the lack of any research on magistrate's courts 'We do not think that defendants should be able to choose their court of trial solely on the basis that they think that they will get a fairer hearing at one hearing at one level than another. Magistrates' courts conduct 93 per cent of all criminal cases and *should* be trusted to try cases fairly.'[38]

---

[35] Hill and Bennett, 1990, *Stolen Years.*
[36] Chapter 6, para. 5.
[37] Chapter 6, para. 13.
[38] Chapter 6, para. 18, emphasis added. The better alternative, proposed by the Legal Action Group, which would also reduce the number of jury trials but without restricting the rights of

Whilst it is true that in many cases the committal process is unnecessary, the right to apply to have a case discharged is important and this is partly recognised by the Commission. What it has not done is to have kept in a procedure which would allow the court to hear the witnesses at an early stage. Whilst it is clearly true that vulnerable witnesses can be put through the ordeal of having to give evidence twice the Commission fails to consider the virtue of putting an early end to cases in which prosecution witnesses, who have lied on paper, will be not be prepared to lie in court. This is more important in cases where defendants are remanded in custody and will spend long periods in prison before they are acquitted at trial. To suggest that it is sufficient to rely on the CPS to scrutinise weak cases is insulting given their previous record in this regard.[39]

Whilst it is not possible to deal with prosecution disclosure in great detail it is important to note here the two key recommendations by the Commission.[40] The first is that complete disclosure by the prosecution will occur only after the defence has disclosed its case and only when the defence can demonstrate relevance. Now obviously it is impossible to demonstrate relevance if the defence does not know what documents exist or what they may contain. The proposed procedure is also likely to require the defence to reveal more and more of its case in order to establish that relevance. There will be, therefore, an incentive on the prosecution to hold back material. For instance, disclosure of adverse findings in disciplinary proceedings against police officers who are witnesses are only available if the defence intends to make an allegation about the officer's conduct in the case. Despite even these rules and regardless of how much the defence may disclose about its case, it will never be able to obtain documents showing that a particular police officer has been regularly disbelieved by juries.

Interestingly the Commission states that if the court is asked to rule on the issue of prosecution disclosure even after the defence, has disclosed its case and shown the relevance of the documents to that defence the court should do so only after 'weighing the potential importance of the material to the defence.' This is obviously a much higher test than that of merely establishing relevance. The onus of course will be on the defence to establish relevance.

A second concern on prosecution disclosure is the support for the

---

the defendant is to allow the defendant to opt for summary trial on the basis that the court's power to send the case to the Crown Court for sentencing would not exist thus restricting the sentence to that of the magistrates' court.

[39] See Chapter 5 for evidence of this.

[40] Chapter 6, para. 33 on.

position outlined by the Court of Appeal in *Johnson, Davis and Rowe*.[41] Liberty presumes that the origin for the idea came from the police service who made a confidential submission to the Commission on this subject.[42] In this case the nature of documents withheld from the defence was itself withheld by the prosecution and this was sanctioned by the court. Whilst it is understandable that the police may wish to protect the identity of informants and undercover agents such methods of policing have not always been sanctioned by the courts and are a strategy adopted by choice by the police. The fact that such choices might result in problems about disclosure should not necessarily lead to the restriction of the defendant's rights. It could rather lead to a review of the use of these policing methods. In many cases the name and the identity of the informer can usually be protected and of course the option always exists of discontinuing the proceedings.

The alternative adopted by the Commission is that there will be secret hearings without the defence being present and without, at least in some cases, the defence even knowing that a secret order has been made.[43] The judge in such cases will be put in an impossible position. As the Commission has stated, the relevance and importance of the material will change as the trial progresses. Although it is recommended that the judge who made the decision to allow non-disclosure should remain as the trial judge, no guarantees are given and the defence will have to rely on the integrity of the prosecution to raise the issue with any new judge at trial. In any case, but particularly one which involves considerations of national security, this is open to considerable abuse.

It can be argued that public interest immunity applies differently in criminal cases than in civil because of course the liberty of the subject is at stake. However the Commission wishes, to extend the right not to disclose documents beyond grounds outlined by the courts and covered by the concept of public interest immunity to include the concept of 'sensitivity' whatever that may be.

---

[41] *The Times*, 19 January 1993.
[42] Liberty tried to obtain a copy (i.e. discovery) of this submission but this was refused by the police, letter dated 15 April 1992.
[43] Chapter 6, paragraph 45.

V TRIAL

The Commission's view of the trial is very much concerned with speed, efficiency and administration. With the issues of the dispute clarified (partly by defence disclosure), the duty of counsel and solicitors is to assist the judge 'in achieving the proper and efficient administration of justice.'[44] The judge should stop prolix or irrelevant questioning and, prevent bullying of witnesses, there should be limits on speeches and the judge should have the power to reduce the fees of those who breach the rules. These may be important aims but there is no hint that the system is adversarial or that lawyers have a duty to their clients which may conflict with these duties. These changes are clearly aimed at the defendant as the Commission defends them on the basis that they can be introduced 'without sacrificing fairness to the defendant'.[45]

Those without lawyers and who cause delay can be excluded by the judge and an *amicus curiae* appointed instead.[46]

The Commission wishes to allow evidence of the defendant's previous convictions in more cases.[47] The first category in which such evidence should be allowed is where the defendant admits the behaviour but denies the intention. Secondly and of more concern is the suggestion that once an attack on the credibility of a prosecution witness has been made, unless this attack is central to the defence, evidence of convictions can be adduced even where the defendant does not give evidence. I have never really seen the logic of a rule that in practice prevents a person with previous convictions from attacking the credibility of a witness. This change will make it very difficult for persons with convictions to challenge the evidence of witnesses (often police officers) and the protection proposed, where the attack is central to the defence, will be difficult to apply in practice.

VI CONCLUSION

The Commission's Report is likely to lead to an increase in the number of miscarriages of justice. There are many recommendations which could improve the criminal justice system overall although it must be questioned how effective these will be in practice. The more major recommendations

---

[44] Chapter 8.
[45] Chapter 8, para. 14.
[46] Chapter 8, para. 16.
[47] Chapter 8, para. 29 on.

seem to have been reserved to taking away the rights of the defendant and will lead to an increase in the number of cases needing to be reviewed. It is unfortunate that the opportunity was missed to make changes that would reduce the number of miscarriages of justice. It is therefore increasingly likely that the Government will find it necessary to set up another Commission to review the criminal justice system in another ten years' time when new miscarriages of justice cannot be brushed under the carpet any longer.

The Commission's Report demonstrates clearly how easy it is to initiate the abolition of fundamental rights and how important it is to ensure that such rights are structured in a positive way. It provides the clearest arguments possible for the need for a Bill of Rights to protect defendants from such proposals.

The Commission has now given its view and the battle is now on as to which recommendations are implemented and when. Liberty has the obvious concern that not only might the Government select out some parts for implementation and delay or neglect others but might add in ingredients of its own. First amongst Liberty's concerns of course is the abolition of the right to silence in the police station. This must remain under threat despite the evidence and research produced and despite the recommendations of this Commission.

22. Trial by Jury and Alternative Modes of Trial

John Jackson

Any reader of the Report of the Royal Commission on Criminal Justice who has witnessed with concern the increasing lack of public confidence in the English criminal justice system in recent years, is likely to be disappointed in a number of respects. First of all, although the Report recognises that the Commission was established in response to public concern over a number of cases of miscarriages of justice and acknowleges that there is a need to restore public confidence, it plays down the idea that the criminal justice system is in crisis. Indeed towards the end of the introductory first chapter it is asserted that 'the great majority of criminal trials are conducted in a manner which all the participants regard as fair and we see no reason to believe that the great majority of verdicts, whether guilty or not, are not correct' (Ch. 1, para. 23). The Report cites no empirical evidence to substantiate this claim but it is a belief that influences the entire discussion of trial procedures.

Secondly, despite being urged by the Home Secretary, who established the Commission, not to baulk at fundamental reform if necessary (see *The Sunday Times*, 29 September 1991), the Report fails to consider the merits of alternative systems of criminal justice. Research on continental systems of justice was commissioned (Leigh and Zedner, 1992), and the Commission visited Scotland (although not Northern Ireland), but in the end it devotes a bare five paragraphs to a discussion of adversarial and inquisitorial procedures. The reasons it gives for such cursory attention to procedures in other countries are curious. It first of all comments that it has not found anywhere an obvious model of criminal justice to follow, as if it was ever likely that it would find an ideal model. The point of looking at other jurisdictions is surely to see whether they deal with certain issues better rather than expect to find some model that resolves all problems better. Secondly, the Report comments that there is a danger that attempted transplants will fail in the light of the different history and culture that one finds in different systems. This comment applies with less force in systems which have similar roots but even in relation to quite different systems it is somewhat contradicted by its later comment, which is not explained, that 'all adversarial systems contain inquisitorial elements' (Ch. 1, para. 12) and by the claim that certain of its recommendations (notably, those for an independent forensic science service) move the system in an inquisitorial direction.

Although this institutional conservatism is disappointing, it is not altogether surprising. It seems to be the fate of Royal Commissions that they are sparked off by a sense of crisis but when they get down to work they are made aware of the resource implications of any changes they might recommend and they end up suggesting reforms which tinker with the existing system rather than involve any root and branch reform. As the Commissioners point out early in their Report they were required within their terms of reference to have regard to the efficient use of resources and this is likely to have impeded any radical recommendations which might prove difficult to cost. A third disappointing aspect of the Report which is more surprising is that very little attempt is made to discuss what the aims and objectives of the criminal justice system ought to be. In this respect the Report differs quite markedly from the previous commission on criminal justice, the Royal Commission on Criminal Procedure (1981). The RCCP considered that the primary aim of the criminal justice system was to balance the interest of the community in the prevention of crime with the interest of the individual defendant accused of crime, and this balancing metaphor proved quite influential in criminal justice debates throughout the 1980s, although it has been criticised by a number of commentators (Maher, 1984; Jackson, 1990). The present Commission in contrast tends to eschew any discussion of balancing crime control with due process and assumes from its terms of reference that the aim of the system is simply to convict the guilty and acquit the innocent. True, it also refers to the need to treat all who come into contact with the system in a fair and reasonable manner without discrimination, but it makes little reference to the conflicting interests that arise within the system and how these are to be resolved.

If there is any guiding philosophy to be found in the Commission's Report it would seem to be the liberal bureaucratic philosophy which Bottoms and McClean (1976) described some years ago as the model which informed the way professional participants in the criminal justice system acted. According to Bottoms and McClean, this model holds that the need for justice to be done must ultimately override the importance of the repression of criminal conduct but it also takes a practical view that the system has to be run efficiently and that protections must have a limit. So although in the first chapter the Report refers to the importance of treating members of the public fairly, much of the Report is concerned with improving the efficiency of the process and there is little mention of individual rights. Indeed despite the growing interest in the need to ensure that criminal processes adhere to international standards of human rights, there is not one mention in the Report of the European Convention on Human Rights and the need to ensure that at all times standards of justice comply with the standards of Articles 5 and 6 of the Convention.

The Commission's complacency, its institutional conservatism and its emphasis on efficiency rather than fairness are well illustrated by its approach towards the two present modes of criminal trial in England and Wales – trial by jury and trial by magistrates. The Commission gave little recognition to the increasing concern that has been voiced about both these modes of trial. It proceeded on the assumption that these should continue to be the sole modes of trial and its central recommendation that defendants charged with either-way offences (offences triable in either the Crown Court or the magistrates' court) should no longer have the right to elect for jury trial was motivated by considerations of cost rather than of justice.

I THE PRESENT MODES OF TRIAL

Concern has for some time been expressed about various features of the jury system (Findlay and Duff, 1988; Enright and Morton, 1990). The competency of jurors has been a persistent theme of the law and order or crime control lobby ever since the property qualification was abolished in 1972. In 1988 much was made of a survey in *The Times* claiming that professional people were evading jury duty easily with the result that there was a heavy bias in favour of unemployed and manual workers on juries. (see 'The Jury on Trial', *The Times*, 24–27 October 1988). Another concern has been that jurors are intimidated or bribed into acquitting professional criminals. This was the theme of Sir Robert Mark's Dimbleby Lecture 20 years ago and it has been a constant theme of jury critics ever since. Civil libertarians have been more concerned about a number of reforms which they claim have eroded the fairness of the jury system and confidence in it, such as the abolition of the need for majority verdicts, disqualification of persons who have committed offences, jury vetting, and the abolition of the defence right to challenge jurors without cause. Apart from these specific concerns about the jury system, there has also been a growing unease about the trial procedures which operate in the Crown Court. The number of miscarriages of justice have raised questions about the suitability of adversarial procedures as mechanisms for finding the truth (Jackson, 1993). In addition, concern about the treatment which witnesses receive in court raise questions about the basic fairness of such procedures (McEwan, 1992; Rock, 1993).

There has also been concern about trial in magistrates' courts. Part of this has been directed at the disabilities which defendants suffer in this mode of trial, such as the restrictions on legal aid and the restrictions on the disclosure of prosecution evidence. Commentators have also noted an 'ideology of triviality' which pervades much of the work of the magistrates' courts which deters solicitors from taking sufficient time to prepare cases properly (McBarnet, 1981). But part of the disenchantment with this mode of trial would also seem to be explained by a lack of confidence in magistrates themselves. Ashworth (1985) has reported that the decision whether or not to elect for trial at the Crown Court is influenced by a wide range of factors, including a lack of confidence in the thoroughness and impartiality of magistrates' courts. The Commission itself cites the research of Hedderman and Moxon (1992) which found that the main reasons defendants and solicitors preferred Crown Court trial were a belief that the chances of acquittal are higher and that magistrates are 'on the side of the police.' Research has shown that magistrates have a tendency to accept police evidence (Vennard, 1988). Apart from concerns about the close traditional ties between the magistracy and the police and about magistrates becoming easily 'case-hardened', there have also been concerns about the representativeness of magistrates. The appointment of lay magistrates by local advisory committees which advise the Lord Chancellor is shrouded in secrecy. One study concluded that advisory committees operate racist criteria in making selections such as 'being assimilated into the English way of life' as a criterion of suitability for the selection of black magistrates (King and May, 1985).

II THE COMMISSION'S RESPONSE

Although the Commission asserts that the jury system is widely and firmly believed to be one of the cornerstones of our system of justice, it does not offer a defence of the jury system and this is perhaps why it is able to contemplate with such ease its central recommendation that defendants lose the right to elect for jury trial in either-way cases. Short of this, the only important recommendation it makes regarding juries is that a departure from the principle of random selection should be permitted to enable the prosecution and defence to apply in exceptional cases for the selection of a jury containing up to three people from ethnic minority communities. It acknowledges issues of concern about the criteria for the selection of jurors but it felt unable to make recommendations on this because of the lack of information about the way juries operate and it wisely recommends that section 8 of the Contempt of Court Act 1981 be amended to enable research to be conducted into juries' reasons for verdicts. The Commission also makes a number of recommendations designed to guide and assist jurors during the trial. In particular it suggests that jurors are encouraged to ask questions more, but it does not appear to recognise that greater participation by jurors in the course of the trial is difficult to reconcile with present adversarial procedures.

So far as the adversarial procedures that operate in jury trials are concerned, the Commission expresses a general wish to see judges adopt a more interventionist stance in criminal trials. This proposal is largely motivated by a desire to expedite proceedings and prevent time-wasting by counsel, but the Commission also acknowledges the vital role that victims and other witnesses play in criminal trials and believes that judges should be more prepared to check unfair and intimidatory cross-examination of witnesses who are likely to be distressed and vulnerable. It would also like to see judges make greater use of their powers to call witnesses where necessary. This would seem to be a move in a more inquisitorial direction but the Commission fails to recognise the difficulty of greater judicial intervention in the context of present adversarial procedures. It is a necessary part of such procedures that counsel should be able to cross-examine opposing witnesses with some vigour. The dangers of judicial interventionism in adversary trials have been well rehearsed by many commentators (e.g. Frankel 1975; Saltzburg, 1978). Intervention is considered particularly problematic where there is a danger that jurors will become over-influenced by the judge's view of the facts. Even when interventions are limited to restraining counsel's cross-examination, there is the danger that the jury will be misled into believing that the judge is expressing a view about the credibility of the witness being cross-examined. The Commission aims to prevent this by the judge telling jurors in general terms before the trial that he/she will not hesitate to intervene to prevent harassment, but this may not prevent the jury in a particular instance inferring from the intervention that the judge holds a particular view of a witness.

The Commission fails to recognise that there is any problem of fairness in the magistrates' courts and the only comment it ventures about the quality of justice dispensed there is that 'magistrates' courts conduct over 93 per cent of all criminal cases and should be trusted to try cases fairly' (Ch. 6, para. 18), which is a classic *non sequitur*. It is true that the Commission did not set out to examine procedures in the magistrates' courts as it was concerned with serious criminal offences. But this makes its recommendation to abolish the right of election all the more surprising. The effect of this recommendation on the Commission's own reckoning would be to send an additional 35,000 cases a year to the magistrates' court, and these would be serious cases by magistrates' court standards, including offences of theft, assault occasioning actual bodily harm, sexual assaults, criminal damage and arson. That the Commission should recommend such a considerable increase in the magistrates' workload without even considering how justice is dispensed there says something about its priorities. The main reason for the proposal is the Commission's concern, highlighted by research carried out by Hedderman and Moxon (1992), that large numbers of defendants who elect to go to the Crown Court plead guilty and thereby clog up the work of the Court. The proposal appears then to be a simple cost-cutting exercise and it reflects the concern about the increase of cases committed to the Crown Court with the consequent rise in cost and delay which many professionals within the criminal justice system have had for some time.

Not only is the Commission prepared to turn a blind eye on the criticisms of magistrates' courts, it also places little weight on the importance of individual perceptions of justice. Its statement that 'we do not think defendants should be able to choose their court of trial solely on the basis that they think they will get a fairer hearing at one level than the other' (Ch. 6, para. 18) illustrates a misunderstanding of how to restore public confidence in trial procedures. In Chapter 1 the Commission assumes that confidence can be restored by achieving correct outcomes and by ensuring that individuals receive fair and reasonable treatment. But confidence also depends on a perception by individuals who have gone through the system that they received fair and reasonable treatment. Recent empirical evidence suggests that in evaluating the justice of their experiences individuals consider factors unrelated to outcome such as whether they had a chance to state their case and were treated with dignity and respect (Tyler, 1990). In its jurisprudence on Article 6 of the European Convention the European Commission and Court have also put considerable emphasis on the need for individual citizens to be assured that justice will be done. In determining what is meant by an independent and impartial tribunal, for example, the Court has said that the appearance of impartiality is just as important as its reality (see *Piersack* v. *Belgium* 1982 5 EHRR 169, Series A No 153).

Instead of a procedure whereby the defendant may elect for jury trial in either-way cases, the Commission proposes that in future the CPS and the defendant should try to agree on the mode of trial but where they cannot agree the matter should be referred for magistrates to decide. The suggestion that magistrates should make the final decision on mode of trial is hardly likely to inspire confidence in those defendants who wish to be committed to the Crown Court precisely in order to avoid magistrate decision-making! Apart from this, the kind of criteria that the Commission proposes should be adopted by magistrates is also likely to create a sense of unfairness. The Commission proposes that cases where the defendant may suffer loss of reputation are more appropriate for jury trial and that this factor will often be relevant to first-time offenders. This could inculcate an unfortunate class bias into decisions on mode of trial, whereby middle-class professionals with reputations to lose are committed to the Crown Court whilst other defendants are relegated to the magistrates' court.

III ALTERNATIVE MODES OF TRIAL

Had the Commission been more concerned about justice and less concerned about cost, it would not have used the Hedderman and Moxon research as the basis for considering how best to stem the flow of cases towards the Crown Court but instead would have been concerned at the deep unpopularity of magistrates' courts and would have tried to discover why this unpopularity exists and what improvements could be made. At the very least the Commission should have mirrored its call for research into juries with a call for research into other methods of trial, including, but not confined to, the magistrates' courts, instead of consigning large numbers of defendants to an under-researched mode of trial. It could then have considered other forms of trial, short of jury trial, that might be more acceptable. This could have involved alternative modes of trial at the magistrates' level. The Commission argues, without supporting evidence, for more 'judicious employment of stipendiary magistrates on a slightly wider scale than at present' (Ch. 8, para. 103), and it proposes that in either-way cases the defendant should be able to make a submission of no case to answer to stipendiary rather than lay magistrates after the decision has been made to send the case to the Crown Court. But there is no discussion of the merits of the lay or stipendiary magistracy in their own right, nor of the merits of a mixed system.

Various alternatives in the Crown Court could also have been considered. The Commission refers to the Scottish system where the decision on the mode and venue of trial rests with the prosecuting authority and it comments that this does not seem to give rise to any controversy. But there is a greater range of modes of trial in Scotland. In particular the kind of either-way offences which the Commission suggests should normally be tried by magistrates in England are tried in the sheriff's court with or without a jury and presided over by a judge with the equivalent experience and status of a Crown Court judge in England. The point is not that defendants ought always to be able to choose the mode of trial. Rather that the court where the defendant is sent to be tried is perceived to be capable of fairly handling the case in a manner commensurate with the seriousness of the offences charged and at present there does not appear to be enough confidence in the ability of magistrates' courts in England to handle serious either-way cases.

Trial by judge alone is indeed becoming an increasingly common method of trying serious offences in a number of common law countries. It is nowhere mentioned in the Report, for example, that various Commonwealth jurisdictions and many states in the United States have a right to opt for trial by a single judge and this is the preferred option in a number of cases. Closer to home, the Diplock Court in Northern Ireland is also presided over by a single judge. There are a number of disadvantages in this mode of trial from a defendant's point of view. Unlike juries, judges cannot refrain from adhering to the letter of the law in cases where it may be harsh on the defendant to do so or where the law is unpopular. Defendants also do not have the benefit of appearing before a lay tribunal which may view events somewhat differently from a professional judge. Professional judges are commonly thought to develop 'case-hardening' instincts which operate against the interests of defendants. The absence of a lay tribunal may be compensated for by providing for the appointment of lay assessors or jurors to sit with the judge as is the practice in a number of continental countries (Munday, 1993), but it is commonly thought that the judicial figure would tend to dominate the lay participants in any such tribunal. Despite these disadvantages, it does appear that defendants do choose to be tried by judges in preference to juries in certain kinds of cases when this alternative is open to them. This suggests that the 'case-hardening' syndrome need not infect all judges or indeed all types of cases and that the differences that there are in the way professionals approach certain kinds of evidence may not always disadvantage the accused.

Apart from the difference in composition between lay and professional tribunals, there are also certain procedural disadvantages which are likely to flow from the absence of juries unless steps are taken to prevent these. When judges act as the sole trier of fact and law, for example, they become privy to inadmissible evidence just as magistrates do in the magistrates' court. Although this means that they must try to disregard such evidence when they come to act as triers of fact, in practice it may be very difficult to do this. Steps could be taken to reduce this danger by having one judge determine matters of admissibility followed by another who presides over the trial proper. But another question is whether the adversarial character of the trial can remain intact when the jury is dispensed with. The Diplock Commission (1972), which recommended the adoption of the single judge trials in Northern Ireland to deal with the problems of perverse verdicts and intimidation that it perceived there were in cases associated with the emergency, assumed that the substitution of the single judge for the jury was quite compatible with the adversarial trial format, although it believed that collegiate courts were ill-suited to this format. But early observers of these trials have drawn attention to the changing shape of the criminal trial when the single judge is substituted (Boyle, Hadden and Hillyard, 1975), and a study presently under way is aiming to test whether the Diplock procedure has moved away from the conventional hallmarks of the classic adversarial trial in the direction of a more inquest-dominated procedure (Jackson and Doran, 1990). It may emerge that quite apart from the different outcomes that are generated when professionals replace lay persons as the trier of fact, trial by professionals has the potential to be a very different trial *process.*

It is not suggested that the Commission should have embraced these alternative modes of trial with open arms. But recognising the crisis of confidence that has beset the present modes of trial, it is argued that without necessarily examining processes that have emerged from systems with very different legal traditions, it could have considered that there are alternatives emerging within common-law systems and recommended that they be monitored and kept under review. The Commission did not, however, choose to consider trial procedures from the point of view of restoring confidence. Instead its consideration of trial procedures was primarily motivated by a need to cut costs. From this point of view the relegation of large numbers of cases to the magistrates' court may make sense. But it does nothing to avert the mounting crisis of confidence in trial procedures and the Commission's failure to urge a review of all trial procedures only prolongs the day when such a review becomes necessary.

23. Redefining and Structuring Guilt in Systemic Terms: The Royal Commission's Recommendations Regarding Guilty Pleas

Mike McConville and Chester Mirsky

In this article we examine the likely effects of the Royal Commission's proposals for the adoption of a structured system of guilty pleas and its relationship to the embedded concern of the Commissioners for increased 'efficiency' in the handling of criminal cases. Our conclusion is that the proposals regarding guilty pleas, structured discounts, and 'sentence canvasses', are not only lacking in principle and do violence to the adversarial system but overturn traditional understandings of guilt based on the burden of proof and the search for truth. The proposals demonise the presumption of innocence and legitimate an administrative model of criminal justice through claimed savings in time and money. The combined effects of the guilty plea proposals would be officially to transform the criminal justice system from one which sought to determine whether the State had reliably sustained its burden of proof to another which sought to determine whether the defendant, irrespective of guilt or innocence, would be able to resist pleading guilty. In this process, the Commission seeks to redefine the principles underpinning procedures for arriving at convictions through the introduction of a new concept – 'system-guilt'.

I THEORY AND PRACTICE IN THE ADVERSARIAL MODEL

The Royal Commission acknowledged the continuing vitality of the adversary system by advancing its recommendations as beneficial improvements which did not seek to undermine the system's basic tenets except where these were seen as impeding 'a search for the truth' (para. 12,

p. 3). The theory of the adversarial system, however, which receives cursory treatment in the Report, would barely survive implementation of the Commission's recommendations in respect of guilty pleas.

The central protective mechanism of the adversary system is the independent tribunal of fact. At trial, the State must convince a panel of independent individuals beyond a reasonable doubt of the truth of its case through the introduction of reliable evidence of guilt. Jurors, as triers of fact, have no connection with any of the parties and must be free to decide the question of legal guilt without knowledge of or responsibility for issues of punishment. At trial, the State is viewed as an intrusive force which, because it seeks to limit the freedom of individuals, must justify its every act through the introduction of legally sufficient and admissible evidence which persuades to a very high degree of certainty. The State cannot convict defendants and inflict punishment on them without proving, at some cost to itself, that those charged committed each and every element of the offence beyond a reasonable doubt, no matter how minor or inconsequential any component part of an offence might appear. And the defendant may rest, in turn, without offering any evidence by showing that the State has failed to discharge its burden thus requiring the court to enter a verdict of acquittal. The 'burden of proof', as it is commonly called, is weighted in such a fashion because of the disparity of power between the parties and the 'risk of social disutility' which may arise when an innocent person is wrongfully convicted on the basis of any lesser standard of certainty. Thus it is the defendant who is to obtain the benefit of the doubt, and not the State.

Whilst the adversary system described above guards against the possibility that a factually innocent person might be found legally guilty, by placing the burden of proof squarely and solely on the State, this means that the system countenances some inefficiency. Occasionally factually guilty persons may be found legally 'innocent', that is, not guilty, when the State is unable to satisfy the standard of certainty required by the burden of proof. However, the distinction between factual and legal guilt ensures that the innocent are not wrongfully convicted and is at the very core of the adversary system's protections. All its procedures are designed to ensure that questionable assertions of factual guilt do not displace legal guilt as the test whether someone should be convicted of a criminal offence.

Of course, most cases do not conform to this ideal type because they do not go to trial, ending instead in guilty pleas. Under liberal legalism, this circumstance does not contest the foundational principles of the adversary system described above but is fully in line with them. A guilty plea is a judicial confession and can be accepted only if it is a voluntary act of the defendant made in unequivocal terms. As such, the guilty plea itself constitutes reliable 'proof' of guilt. It is equivalent to a conviction after trial and symbolic of the defendant's remorse and repentance for a criminal act, attracting sentencing mitigation through that remorse.

In practice, however, a long line of research has established that guilty pleas have not only replaced trials as the principal method of determining legal guilt but guilty pleas themselves have little, if anything, to do with either remorse or voluntariness. The presence of bids, deals, offers, blandishments and threats actually replace proof of legal guilt with questionable assertions of factual guilt (see e.g. Baldwin and McConville, 1977; Sanders, 1988; McConville, Sanders and Leng, 1991; McConville and Mirsky, 1990). This occurs when lawyers engage in pre-trial discussions and reviews, the object of which is to resolve cases without recourse to trial. These 'amicable' proceedings (see Baldwin, 1985b) are little more than bargaining over charge and sentence discounts. Under these circumstances, the 'facts' that form the basis of the negotiation become a substitute for independent investigation, corroborative evidence and forensic analysis. The 'typical' facts are a by-product of a presupposition of guilt which is attached to the accused and a discourse unencumbered by rules of reliability and guarantees of trustworthiness (see McConville, Sanders and Leng, 1991; McConville, Bridges, Hodgson and Pavlovic, 1993). Such exchanges openly focus the actor's attention on the background and character of the accused and the nature of the offence charged, rather than upon the question of legal sufficiency of the State's evidence. Lawyers, in turn, predict what sentence the judge will impose in return for a guilty plea as compared to a conviction after trial, and thus what risks a defendant will undergo in challenging the State's allegations.

Courts have sought to reconcile the dichotomy between theory and practice by legitimating guilty pleas which result from coercive practices based upon a presupposition of guilt. Whilst the Court of Appeal in *Turner* (1970) was emphatic that a judge, in advance of the plea, should never state that he/she would penalise the defendant for electing trial by sentencing the defendant following conviction after trial to a more severe sentence than that imposed in return for a guilty plea, the Court held that the lawyer's responsibility requires him/her to make such a prediction 'in strong terms' and in 'firm and forceful terms'. Nevertheless, the Court of Appeal in this and subsequent cases condemned 'plea-bargaining' asserting, instead, that sentence discounts were *rewards* only granted to *remorseful* defendants who *voluntarily* acknowledged guilt. However, later, in *Peace* (*The Times*, 28 November 1975) where the defendant had already received a royal pardon following a guilty plea, the Court, in rejecting an application to quash the conviction, defined the term 'voluntariness' to include unpleasant choices that could be made by factually innocent people. The Court stated: 'A defendant who pleaded guilty following advice of the kind given, albeit he did so unhappily and regretfully, could not be said to have lost his power to make a voluntary and deliberate choice'. Hence, a conviction following such a guilty plea would remain intact. Thus, albeit by forced reasoning and an element of hypocrisy, the theory of the system as one reliant upon the burden of proof as a truth-seeking device, either at trial or on guilty plea, was preserved.

II THE DISTORTION OF THE COMMISSION'S GUILTY PLEA RECOMMENDATIONS

The Royal Commission's recommendations concerning guilty pleas institutionalise the Bar's informal practices by systematically coercing guilty pleas, denigrating the importance of the burden of proof, and focusing instead on 'cost-efficient' reasons for not contesting legal guilt.[1] Through the application of structured discounts or 'sweeteners' to a sentence 'canvass' the Commission transforms the meaning of guilt from one based upon an objective assessment of the weight of the evidence in a rational legal environment, to another dependent upon the attribution of guilt through routinised lawyering conducted in a coercive environment and justified in terms of the routinised processing of mass defendants, with the minimum expenditure of time and effort either on the part of the State or of private witnesses.[2] In this officially restructured system of criminal justice, the factually innocent are co-mingled with the factually and legally guilty and treated equally in terms of sentence calibration. Once the factually innocent, through the plea, have adopted a 'posture of guilt' they are eligible for a discount regardless of remorse or voluntariness. In this way, the Commission replaces traditional understandings of what must

---

[1] They are as follows:
  (47) ... A system of graduated discounts might work broadly as follows:
  a) The most generous discount should be available to the defendant who indicates a guilty plea in response to the service of the case disclosed by the prosecution.
  b) The next most generous discount should be available to the defendant who indicates a guilty plea in sufficient time to avoid full preparation for trial. The discount might be less if the plea were entered only after a preparatory hearing.
  c) At the bottom of the scale should come the discount for a guilty plea entered on the day of the trial itself. Since resources would be saved by avoiding a contested trial even at this late stage, we think that some discount should continue to be available. But it should be appreciably smaller than for a guilty plea offered at one of the earlier stages.
[2] See, RCCJ *Report* at p. 111, para. 45.

legitimately precede the imposition of punishment with *system-guilt*, an ideological construct which provides pro forma validation to the initiating actions of the police and eliminates the need for scrutiny of the State's evidence by rendering those charged immediately eligible for punishment.

For its part, the Commission did little more than acknowledge that its cost-savings proposals may be 'held to encourage defendants who are not guilty of the offence charged to plead guilty to it'. The Commission stated that '[t]his risk cannot be wholly avoided and, although there can be no certainty as to the precise numbers ... it would be naive to suppose that innocent persons never plead guilty because of the prospect of the sentence discount' (p. 110, para. 42). Yet the Commission explicitly discounted protections accorded by the burden of proof and, thus, the social disutility of convicting the legally or factually innocent, by concluding that '[a]gainst the risk that defendants may be tempted to plead guilty to charges of which they are not guilty must be weighed the benefits to the system and to defendants of encouraging those of who are in fact guilty to plead guilty' (p. 111, para.45). The Commission denigrated those defendants who might wish to consult a barrister before deciding whether a guilty plea is provident (based on an analysis of the State's ability to sustain its burden of proof) as 'late tactical' pleaders (p. 111, para. 46) and penalised them by contending that they should not 'attract the same discount' offered to early pleaders.

The Commission's recommendations give legitimacy to the Bar's practices by accepting that critical decisions as to whether to plead guilty should be made 'on the papers' and by recommending that pressures be placed on defendants to plead guilty from service of the prosecution file onwards. No justification is offered for the implicit assertions that the prosecution's case papers or statements at the plea 'canvass' are complete and withhold nothing, and that the prosecution's witnesses will appear at trial and testify in accordance with the prosecution's allegations, even though recent notorious cases demonstrate that any such assumptions are unsafe.[3] And as for the state of preparedness of the defence, the Royal Commission is silent. Yet it knew full well that severe deficiencies in the delivery of defence services, resulting in the subordination of defendants, denigration of the burden of proof and routinised and incompetent lawyering (often conducted by lawyer-surrogates), is a systemic problem attested to by research studies conducted prior to the establishment of the Commission (e.g. Sanders et al.,

---

[3] The non-disclosure of expert opinion evidence in the murder case of Antonio Cardoza (*The Guardian*, June 1992); of witness statements, interrogations and expert evidence in the case of Judith Ward (*The Guardian*, 5 June 1992); and of scientific evidence in the case of Stefan Kiszko (*The Guardian*, 18 February 1992) are simply examples of practices which discredit blind belief in the integrity and completeness of the prosecution's case papers.

1989; Dixon, 1991) by research conducted on behalf of the Commission (Baldwin, 1993a; Evans, 1993a; McConville and Hodgson, 1993) and by individual notorious cases (e.g. *Miller, Paris and Abdullahi*, 1992; *Fergus*, 1993, discussed by Lee Bridges in this volume, Chapter 24).

III THE POLITICS OF PLEA-BARGAINING

The Royal Commission recognises the political volatility of a set of guilty plea proposals which, by countenancing the conviction of the factually innocent through the establishment of the concept of system-guilt, can be shown to undermine basic freedoms accorded individuals by common law for centuries. To avoid the backlash, the Report offers a set of justifications. First, the proposals are portrayed as enhancing the fairness of the guilty plea process through the provision of additional information which enables defendants to select more carefully the method by which they proceed – plea or trial (p. 112, para. 48). Defendants would no longer be in the dark with regard to the extent of the discount a court might grant in return for a guilty plea[4] and they would know in advance how much penalty would be extracted should they exercise their right to trial and right to silence.

However, the Commission's own Crown Court survey belies this justification. From the standpoint of legal rationality, it is the *prosecution* and not the defendant who would benefit by the Commission's guilty plea recommendations. According to prosecutors themselves, in 13 per cent of 'cracked trials' (late pleas) 'it would have been difficult to get a conviction' had it not been for the guilty plea (Zander and Henderson, (1993) *Crown Court Study*, Table 5.5, p. 156). In a further 23 per cent of cases the prosecution viewed the obtaining of a conviction as the reason why a guilty plea outcome was, on balance, better than a trial (id.). Furthermore, the notion that fairness would be increased through the provision of certain information about the extent of any discount assumes, of course, that a defendant who pleads guilty is likely to be given a more lenient sentence than that which would be imposed following trial. However, prosecutors said that in 35 per cent of late plea cases the outcome was 'good' because the sentence imposed 'would have been the same even if there had been a trial' (Zander and Henderson, (1993) *Crown Court Study*, p. 156). This

---

[4] Disingenuously, they would not, however, be openly told of the alternative sentence upon conviction after trial as this would confront them with 'unacceptable pressure' (p. 113, para. 50), although with a transparent discount system defendants could actually calculate this themselves.

finding negates the very existence of routine sentence disparity based on plea and the reliability of defence advice which presumes the existence of discounts in the first instance.

Second, the guilty plea proposals are claimed to harm only a *de minimis* number of defendants who may be factually innocent. To justify this assertion, the Commission again relies on its own Crown Court Study in which defence barristers were asked: 'An innocent defendant sometimes decides to plead guilty to achieve a sentence discount or reduction in the indictment. Were you concerned that this was such a case?' The barristers' response, while on its face worrying, indicated that they were so concerned in some 1,400 cases annually. However, the Commission interpreted this response in benign terms, by providing a revisionist explanation, that is that barristers must have 'misunderstood the thrust of the question they were asked' (p. 111, para. 43). Rationalised by the Commission, the barristers' answers were converted to an assurance that only a handful of innocent defendants are ensnared into pleading guilty because most were guilty of some charge even if not of the offence charged and others, while protesting their innocence, were confronted by the weight of the State's evidence.

Third, the Commission accepts that whatever miscarriages of justice may arise as a result of a coercive system of discounts and penalties is, on balance, socially acceptable given savings through a reduction in trials, 'cracked' trials and the costs associated therewith (p. 111, para. 45). However, the Commission's own research showed the dubious nature of almost half (44.1 per cent) of the guilty pleas entered in 'cracked trials' when it tested those pleas by asking prosecutors to assess the chances of defendants being acquitted had such cases gone to trial and the prosecution been required to satisfy its burden of proof. In the judgment of prosecutors had these cases proceeded to trial, each year over 1,000 defendants (n = 1040) plead guilty when they would have a 'good' chance of acquittal, over 2,200 others (n = 2236) when they would have a 'fairly good' chance of acquittal, and a further 2,000 others (n = 2262) when the prosecutor could not reasonably predict the likely outcome (Zander and Henderson, (1993) *Crown Court Study*, pp. 156–7). Moreover, the Crown Court survey also indicated that even in 'cracked' trials, where, on the eve of trial or at its commencement, the defendant chose to plead guilty, 81 per cent of judges said that none of their time had been wasted and court clerks said that no court time was wasted in 69 per cent of such cases (*id.*, pp. 151–2).

Fourth, the Commission invokes the Bar's Code of Conduct as a shibboleth against miscarriages of justice citing that portion which addresses a barrister's responsibilities in counselling a defendant whether to plead guilty:

Where a defendant tells his counsel that he did not commit the offence with which he is charged but nevertheless insists on pleading guilty to it for reasons of his own, counsel must continue to represent him, but only after he has advised what the consequences will be and that what can be submitted in mitigation can only be on the basis that the client is guilty. (p. 111, para. 44)

The Commission contended that, in pursuit of their professional obligation both to the court and to the defendant, barristers should not and normally do not advise clients to plead guilty if they are not guilty. The Code of Practice which the Commission relied upon, however, is designed to protect barristers from claims of duplicity when, having advised against a guilty plea over an assertion of innocence, they nonetheless accept such a plea and base mitigation on false assertions of remorsefulness. Whilst the Commission acknowledged that factually innocent people may plead guilty unknown to the court because of the misleading representations made by the barrister, it denied official responsibility for these inconsistent pleas and instead placed responsibility on defendants: '... that ... decision is one for them' (p. 111, para. 44). Such duplicity has already served the Bar when advancing mitigation on behalf of defendants who assert innocence but who were counselled in 'firm and forceful' terms to plead guilty. The Code which has hitherto acted as a protective mechanism against professional misconduct will now, under the Commission's recommendations, become an operative requirement in a system of structured discounts.

IV CONCLUSION

The Commission began with terms of reference which required it to address three concerns: the conviction of the guilty; the acquittal of the innocent; and the efficient use of resources. The Commission disclaimed a theoretical perspective, resting its approach instead upon pragmatic considerations related to the balancing of the concerns voiced by the terms of reference. Ultimately the Commission proceeded ideologically by accepting the presupposition that those charged should be punished and thus addressing only one concern, that of cost efficiency, to the denigration of the remaining two.

In establishing system-guilt as its preferred method of case disposition, the Commission cast itself adrift from the adversarial system and traditional notions of legal rationality. The definable attributes of a new criminal process based upon system guilt are as follows:

1. the guilty plea is accorded the badge of success whilst the trial is denigrated as a failure of method and a waste of resources;
2. voluntariness is redefined to mean accession to coercion thus severing remorsefulness from the equation and rendering whatever penalty is imposed irreconcilable with rational sentencing theory;
3. criminal procedure is inverted, with sentence considerations preceding the determination of guilt thus institutionalising the presupposition of guilt accorded those charged, and requiring lawyers to convey the results of sentence canvasses rather than to first examine the prosecution's evidence by undertaking an independent investigation into the law and the facts;
4. judicial integrity is compromised in order to paper over the effect that structured discounts have on pleas by factually innocent people and to accommodate misrepresentations by counsel regarding the defendant's reasons for pleading guilty, which are themselves a product of the Commission's own recommendations;
5. racial discrimination in the administration of justice is enhanced because the sentence penalties accorded those who elect trial or plead guilty on the eve of trial will disproportionately affect members of racial minorities who have, for whatever reasons, accepted and acted upon the traditional notion of legal rationality (see Hood, 1992).

By displacing reliance on the burden of proof with system-guilt, the Commission sought to create a mechanism for mass processing of defendants unimpeded by the factual and legal issues arising in the individual case. This process of homogenisation defeats the aspiration of justice for the individual which survives only in the rhetoric of the system as realised in the hollow words of court-room ceremonies where charades of guilt become the only enduring reality.

24. The Royal Commission's Approach to Criminal Defence Services – A Case of Professional Incompetence

Lee Bridges

It is a common complaint of prisoners that they were not given a proper chance to instruct their legal representatives and that the opportunity for consultation was confined to a few minutes in the court precincts before their case came up .... We were told ... that some solicitors engaged on legal aid neglect to prepare their cases adequately and do not interview the client until he reaches the court, while instructions to counsel sometimes consist of nothing more than a copy of the depositions with a back-sheet attached. Prison governors informed us of the mental stress suffered by some prisoners when their solicitors failed to visit them and of the extreme youth of some of the junior clerks who visit the prison to take instructions from prisoners .... Our attention was drawn to the fact that counsel sometimes returns a brief to the solicitor at a very late stage. It is understandable that accused persons may be upset to find themselves defended by a member of the Bar whom they had not expected .... We were told that owing to the way the chambers system works, and the uncertainty of the time of trial, young and inexperienced counsel sometimes appear in cases for which they are manifestly not equipped.[1]

The above quotation is drawn not from the recent report of the Royal Commission on Criminal Justice but from the 1966 Report of the Departmental (Widgery) Committee on Legal Aid in Criminal Proceedings. But it is perhaps a reflection of how little matters have progressed in terms of the provision of criminal defence services in Britain, despite the massive expansion in legal aid during the intervening period, that this statement also represents a fair summary of much of the evidence received on this topic by the recent Royal Commission.

It is commonplace to observe that the main impetus for the establishment of the Royal Commission came from the series of miscarriage of justice cases that, after long years of campaigning and rejected appeals, were finally overturned during 1990 and early 1991, and which continued even as the Royal Commission was sitting. Several of these miscarriages of justice

---

[1] Cmnd. 2934 *Report of the Departmental Committee on Legal Aid in Criminal Proceedings*, London, HMSO, 1966, pp. 81–2.

revealed serious shortcomings in the provision of criminal defence services. Thus, the Birmingham 6 had been represented at their first court appearance by relatively inexperienced court duty solicitors, while two of the Guildford 4, Gerald Conlon and Paul Hill, have subsequently made strong criticisms of their original defence lawyers.[2] More recently in the case of the Cardiff 3 the Court of Appeal was highly critical of one of the defendants' solicitor for 'being gravely at fault for sitting passively through this travesty of [a police] interview' during which his client denied involvement in a murder over 300 times before confessing after lengthy and oppressive questioning by the police.[3] Then, just a fortnight before the Commission issued its Report, a black schoolboy, Ivan Fergus, had his conviction for robbery overturned, the Court of Appeal finding that his original defence solicitors had 'acted in the most flagrant disregard of their duties' in failing to trace or interview named alibi witnesses. Defence counsel was also criticised in the Appeal Court's judgment for a performance at trial that had fallen 'markedly short of the standard to be expected of a member of the Bar', having neglected in particular to call alibi evidence or to invite the judge to withdraw the case from the jury due to several clear weaknesses in the identification evidence.[4]

The Commission was explicitly required by its terms of reference to consider 'the arrangements for the defence of accused persons, access to legal advice, and access to expert evidence'. In fact, the only aspects of the work of criminal defence lawyers (other than their access to expert and particularly forensic evidence) on which the Commission itself funded research were in relation to the provision of legal advice in police stations[5] (which had already been subject to fairly extensive previous research[6]) and, at the other end of the process, on advice to convicted persons on their rights of appeal.[7] Even in the questionnaire sent by the Commission at the beginning of its inquiries to interested parties the only other queries raised

---

2 See Legal Action Group, *Preventing Miscarriages of Justice*, London, 1993, p. 3.
3 *R. v. Miller, Paris and Abdullahi*, Court of Appeal, official transcript.
4 Law Report, *The Independent*, 29 June 1993.
5 See Research Studies No. 3 by John Baldwin on *The Role of Legal Representatives at the Police Station*; No. 8 by Roger Evans on *The Conduct of Police Interviews with Juveniles*; and No. 16 by Michael McConville and Jacqueline Hodgson, *Custodial Legal Advice and the Right to Silence*, all published by HMSO.
6 See A. Sanders, et al., *Advice and Assistance at Police Stations and the 24-Hour Duty Solicitor Scheme*, London, Lord Chancellor's Department, 1989; David Brown, *Detention at the Police Station under PACE*, Home Office Research and Planning Study No. 104, London, HMSO, 1989; David Brown, et al., *Changing the Code: Police Detention under the Revised PACE Codes of Practice*, Home Office Research and Planning Unit, London, HMSO, 1993; and D. Dixon, 'Common sense, legal advice and the right of silence', *Public Law*, Summer, 1991.
7 Research Study No. 18 by Joyce Plotnikoff and Richard Woolfson on *Information and Advice for Prisoners about Grounds for Appeal and the Appeal Process*, London, HMSO.

about defence lawyers concerned whether counsel (not solicitors) might be involved in earlier investigative and preparatory work on cases and the problems arising from last-minute instructions to counsel, changes of counsel, and meetings between counsel and the lay client. It is as if, after the police station, the defence solicitor does not exist, and certainly the great bulk of the work done by solicitors both in magistrates' courts and in the processing of Crown Court cases appears to have been left completely outside the Commission's reckoning.

There was one notable attempt while the Commission was sitting to get it to look in a more comprehensive manner at the work of criminal defence solicitors. This came from the somewhat surprising source of the Law Society, at the height of its dispute with the Lord Chancellor over the proposed introduction of standard fees for criminal legal aid in magistrates' courts.[8] The Law Society argued that the introduction of standard fees would lead to a deterioration in the standards of criminal defence work in these courts and a further reduction in the number of solicitors available to provide criminal defence services as a whole, including police station advice. It therefore proposed that the introduction of standard fees be postponed until the Royal Commission reported and, hopefully, had considered their potentially wider impact on the quality and availability of defence services.

The Commission also had before it a considerable body of evidence indicating that the Cardiff 3 and Ivan Fergus cases were symptomatic of more general problems in the provision of criminal defence services. The studies on police station advice by McConville and Hodgson and by Baldwin not only confirmed earlier research showing that this work is routinely assigned to unqualified and often inexperienced and untrained staff but also that the approach of all types of defence advisers, including solicitors, towards police station visits and interrogations tended to be non-investigatory, non-interventionist, passive and for the most part geared towards co-operation with police objectives rather than the adversarial assertion of suspects' rights. The research by Plotnikoff and Woolfson showed that about a third of convicted defendants received no immediate advice at the end of their cases on rights of appeal and 90 per cent no written advice, and that over half of solicitors themselves misunderstood the Court of Appeal's legal powers to increase sentences on appeal.

As for all the intervening stages of the criminal process, the memorandum submitted by the Law Society relating to fixed fees contained more than a

---

[8] Law Society, *Memorandum on the Future of Criminal Legal Aid: Evidence to Royal Commission on Criminal Justice*, London, Law Society, 1992.

hint of the systematic lack of proper preparation of cases by defence solicitors:

> Very few criminal practitioners are short of work. The great majority have as much as or more than they can efficiently cope with. They are already under pressure to reduce preparation in order to cope with the volume of clients they have.[9]

The Law Society went on to portray a situation of an impending crisis in the provision of defence services through private practice operating under a financially-constrained legal aid scheme:

> The low level of remuneration for criminal legal aid is already leading many solicitors to abandon it .... For those who remain, the pressures to reduce preparation ... will be exacerbated by additional pressures to take more clients arising from the reduction in the number of practitioners doing this work. It seems inevitable that this must have a detrimental impact on the standards of work in the criminal field.[10]

The Commission also received more detailed evidence of the poor standards of preparation and representation provided by defence lawyers, both at magistrates' and Crown Courts. A summary of the findings of an extensive research study on criminal defence lawyers conducted by McConville, Hodgson, Pavlovic, and myself[11] was made available to the Commission. This indicated that, beyond the specific failings of defence solicitors in police stations, the general provision of representation for defendants was characterised by routine and ad hoc delegation of case preparation to largely unsupervised and unqualified staff, with 'work being organised on the basis of who is available', 'insufficient linking with what has happened at the previous stage', and 'investigation ... generally left to the client'.[12] The study also noted the tendency for defence advisers to disbelieve defendants 'when they deny police allegations or make allegations about the way they have been treated by the police' and, more generally, to gear defence work towards 'the routine production of guilty pleas'. These shortcomings in pre-trial preparation were found generally not to be rectifiable at court, while 'advocacy in mitigation of sentence in magistrates' court tends to be routine and based mainly on what the solicitor gets from the social enquiry report.' Finally, solicitors were shown to 'play little role in the Crown Court', generally leaving 'the matter to counsel attended by a clerk'.

---

[9] Ibid., p. 3.

[10] Ibid., pp. 5–6.

[11] *Standing Accused: The Organisation and Practices of Criminal Defence Lawyers*, Oxford, OUP, forthcoming.

[12] These and following quotes are taken from a summary of the findings of the research prepared for the Commission by one of its members, Professor Michael Zander.

This latter point was more than confirmed by the findings of the Commission's own Crown Court study,[13] conducted for it by one of its own members, Professor Michael Zander. This involved the circulation of questionnaires to all the participants in Crown Court cases over a two-week period in February 1992. The report of the study notes that problems were anticipated

> as to who from the [defence] solicitors' firm should fill out the Commission's questionnaire. If we asked the partner in charge to do it, he would frequently know little or nothing as to what had happened. If we asked the firm's representative at court to do so, he would often be a clerk who would not necessarily know what had transpired at earlier stages. (Moreover it was not even certain there would be a solicitors' representative at court in every case.)

> Our instruction to solicitors was that, if the case was a full trial, the questionnaire should be filled out by the person who had *instructed counsel*. (emphasis added)[14]

Of the defence solicitors' questionnaires returned,[15] only 31 per cent were completed by a solicitor, 21 per cent by a 'legal executive', 9 per cent by an 'articled clerk', 31 per cent by an 'other clerk', 5 per cent by a 'secretary' or 'other' in the firm, and 4 per cent by persons 'contracted by' or 'not directly employed by' the firm. As the report notes, this indicates, 'the extent to which crown court work for solicitors' firms is done by staff who are not solicitors (known in the profession as 'unadmitted staff').'[16]

The Crown Court study also indicated numerous other shortcomings in defence work at this level. In *contested* cases, no pre-trial conference was held (even on the day of the hearing) in 29 per cent of cases for which there was a defence solicitor reply and 40 per cent of those where defence barristers responded.[17] In contested cases and 'cracked trials', defence solicitors who responded reported that no barrister had seen the client at all before the hearing in no less than 43 per cent of cases, and in a total of 59 per cent of these cases the defendant only met the barrister on the day of the hearing.[18] Over three-quarters of those attending pre-trial conferences in contested cases on behalf of defence solicitors were not themselves

---

[13] Research Study No. 1 by Michael Zander and Paul Henderson, *The Crown Court Study* London, HMSO, 1993.

[14] Ibid, p. 193.

[15] In fact, there was a problem with poor response rates in the survey, especially on the defence side. The report of the study actually over-estimates the response rates for various categories of participant (see Appendix 1), as these are calculated against the number of cases for which at least one participant (other than a jury member) returned a questionnaire, thereby ignoring the estimated 14 per cent of cases (mostly guilty pleas) for which no replies whatsoever were received. The true response rate for defence barristers was 56 per cent, for defence solicitors 37 per cent, and for defendants just 16 per cent (8 per cent for defendants in guilty plea cases).

[16] *The Crown Court Study*, op. cit., p. 194.

[17] Ibid., p. 52.

[18] Ibid., Table 2.15, p. 55.

solicitors, including 47 per cent classified as 'unqualified' or 'other'.[19] There was a change of barrister, according to defence solicitor respondents, in 48 per cent of cases,[20] and of returned briefs 59 per cent were notified to the defence solicitors after four in the afternoon the day before the trial.[21] A quarter of defence barristers in contested cases who responded received their briefs after four in the afternoon the day before the trial[22], and a similar proportion reported that their brief was inadequate in some respect.[23]

It is instructive to note how the Commission presented and reacted to some of these research findings. As for *The Crown Court Study*, this was not published in full until just a week before the Commission's Report, and in the accompanying press release some of the findings on late delivery of briefs and last-minute conferences with clients were noted. But these were set against the findings of the survey relating to the *opinions* of defence personnel and judges that, on the whole, defence barristers had adequate time to prepare and to get to know the case. Even worse, the press release reported, without qualification, that

> more than four out of five defendants, including nearly three quarters of those found guilty, thought the barrister's work was 'good'; more than four out of five, and nearly seven out of ten of those found guilty, thought their solicitors' work was 'good'.[24]

Given that the study itself acknowledged that the response rate from defendants was 'statistically "too low"',[25] this statement represents a gross misrepresentation of the survey's findings. Indeed, the extent of this misrepresentation can be shown by correctly restating the relevant data from the survey:

> Approximately 13 per cent of defendants thought their barrister did a 'good' job, 2 per cent an 'adequate' or 'poor' job, with 85 per cent of defendants not returning a questionnaire or replying on this point; 13 per cent of defendants thought their solicitor did a 'good' job, 3 per cent an 'adequate' or 'poor' job, and 84 per cent either returned no questionnaire or did not reply on this point.

---

[19] Ibid., Table 2.14, p. 53.
[20] Ibid., p. 48.
[21] Ibid., Table 2.16, p. 55.
[22] Ibid., Table 2.2, p. 30.
[23] Ibid., p. 33.
[24] Royal Commission on Criminal Justice Press Release RC014/93, dated 24 June 1993.
[25] *The Crown Court Study*, op. cit., p. xiv. It is unclear what the quotation marks around the words 'too low' in the original were intended to signify, other than perhaps to suggest to the uninformed that the statistical unreliability of the response rate could somehow be disregarded as a technicality.

The reaction within the Commission to the summary of findings from our more general study of defence lawyers' work[26] was even more interesting, as it provoked a point-by-point rebuttal from one member, Sir John Wickerson, a past president of the Law Society. The Wickerson memorandum proved to be predictive of the contents of the Commission's own Report in a number of respects. It certainly foreshadowed the main Report's tendency to elevate professional opinion, supposition, and mythology to the status of 'fact', even in the face of conflicting empirical research and evidence:

Advisors have no right to see the 'in custody record' [at the police station] and accordingly it is sensible not even to make the request [to see it].

In many cases the competent advisor [at the police station] can find out sufficient in ten minutes to enable sufficient advice to be given, and I do not believe this is a remarkably short time.

The advisor at the Police station is not investigating matters at that time. It is impossible to do so. The facts on which decisions are made at the Police station [by defence advisers] are bound to be those which the Police have.

It cannot be right for a solicitor to agree to the client being interviewed if he has no knowledge of what the client might say. As mentioned above, I have no reason to suppose that a competent advisor could not get instructions within ten minutes in most cases.

Most suspects are well advised to cooperate with the Police.

Of course, defence work is largely reactive. In a large number of cases there is nothing to investigate. The client is guilty, accepts the facts, pleads guilty, and is dealt with.

I have never personally had a case where a client has made such allegations [of police misconduct] which is capable of being true, where it has not been put as part of his defence. I do not believe that there is any difference in any other firm.

I have seen no suggestion anywhere in any research that defendants who want to plead not guilty are made to plead guilty because of some routine production line. All the evidence points to the fact that people plead not guilty who should plead guilty.

The real question is whether there are substantial shortcomings in pre-trial preparation and whether as a result injustice is done. Whilst, of course, this must happen from time to time, I have no reason to suppose it is widespread.[27]

Despite wanting to deny that shortcomings in defence preparation might be 'widespread', Sir John Wickerson also wished to place the blame for any

---

[26] *Standing Accused*, op. cit.

[27] Undated memorandum by Sir John Wickerson, received from Royal Commission on Criminal Justice, September 1992.

such inadequacies elsewhere than on the profession. In seeking to do so,
however, he (like the Law Society) put forward an argument that pointed to
poor defence services as being a structural feature arising from the market
conditions which apply under the combined effects of criminal legal aid and
private practice:

> There is no doubt that the Lord Chancellor and the Legal Aid Board believe that the
> appropriate way to provide legal advice on criminal matters is to have a volume turnover
> paid for at the lowest possible rate and which rewards most the firm which delegates
> most work .... Partly as a result of the turnover requirement and partly as a result of the
> historical context Legal Aid in criminal matters has always been the poor relation. The
> profession has become far more proficient at keeping records of costs earned by
> individual partners and fee earners. The records are routinely seen at partners' meetings
> and where there is a mixed practice there is no doubt that the partner doing criminal work
> brings in less than the partner doing civil Legal Aid work, and substantially less than the
> partner doing private client work .... The pressure on partners dealing with criminal
> Legal Aid work is immense. They are working under considerable pressure and at
> unsocial hours and in an unpleasant environment. The pressure is to do the work in the
> shortest possible time and at the lowest possible level ....[28]

Sir John Wickerson's 'solution' to this dilemma was to look to the same
Lord Chancellor and Legal Aid Board, who he alleged to have a 'high
volume/low quality' policy towards criminal legal aid, to reverse this
position, so as to insist on and pay for higher standards of training for
defence services:

> There is a particular problem about 'own solicitor representatives'. I believe the
> Commission should recommend that training and tests of training should be required for
> anybody who is attending the Police station or dealing with criminal work. The Legal
> Aid Board will have to play its part in providing the framework because it will be the
> paying party. If the standard of training of those who attend Police stations and deal with
> criminal work is to be improved so must the payment available for the work. The
> ultimate decision will be by the Treasury, but if the Treasury continue to require the Lord
> Chancellor to pay less for criminal Legal Aid than for other work ... then the system will
> not improve.[29]

As we now know, this is precisely the line which the Commission ended up
taking in its recommendations relating to criminal defence services and

---

[28] Ibid. In this latter respect Sir John Wickerson was able to take some comfort in the fact that
most of the research he was criticising 'relates to firms who do a large amount of [criminal]
work. I believe that they do work differently from the firms which have a general practice
where part of it is criminal Legal Aid.' However, the Commission also had available an
analysis, based on patterns of payment of criminal legal aid, showing that magistrates'
criminal legal aid work is heavily concentrated among a limited number of firms, so that just
over 100 solicitors' offices receive nearly 20 per cent of total payments and approximately
1,000 offices (about 1 in 13 of the total doing criminal legal aid work) take up 60 per cent of
payments. See L. Bridges, 'The professionalisation of criminal justice' *Legal Action*, August
1992.

[29] Sir John Wickerson memorandum, ibid.

police station advice. In other words, although the research available to the Commission showed that there were deficiencies in the *general* standard of criminal defence services available through private practice operating under the constraints of legal aid, and also that long-standing professional guidelines on such matters as the types of personnel and standards of work required in police stations had been *systematically* neglected in practice, the Commission has proposed that these same structures and mechanisms – private practice, criminal legal aid, the Legal Aid Board, and standards of professional practice and training promulgated by the Law Society – should be utilised to improve the situation. All that seems to be needed is greater professional vigilance, a stricter approach by the Legal Aid Board about who should receive payments for police station work in particular, and above all higher rates of remuneration under legal aid.

The inadequacies of the Commission's recommendations on the role of defence advisers at police stations have already been documented in the papers by Cape[30] and Hodgson[31]. One additional point to be noted in this respect is that, following the line set out by Sir John Wickerson, the Commission bases its recommendations for immediate action in this area on the assumption that it is the work of 'own solicitors' and their 'representatives' that is especially problematic. Thus, it is proposed that steps be taken 'to make "own" solicitors and their representatives subject to the same standards as apply to duty solicitors and their representatives',[32] and only in the longer term to review the 'training, education, supervision and monitoring of all legal advisers who operate at police stations'.[33] In fact, although research has shown that duty and own solicitors provide *different* patterns of advice to suspects in police stations, it does not follow that duty solicitors offer a higher standard of service than own solicitors. The former have been shown to restrict their services to telephone advice only in a far higher proportion of cases (a difference that has persisted

---

[30] Ed Cape, 'Defence Services: what should defence lawyers do at police stations?', Conference papers, reprinted here as Chapter 16.

[31] Jacqueline Hodgson, 'No Defence for the Royal Commission', Conference papers, reprinted here as Chapter 17.

[32] Royal Commission on Criminal Justice, *Report*, London, HMSO, 1993, Recommendation 66. To the credit of the Law Society and the Legal Aid Board, the training package and accreditation standards currently being devised for 'representatives' providing advice at police stations go well beyond the very limited requirements currently placed on duty solicitor representatives and seek to draw more extensively on the results of research and on the lessons of cases such as the Cardiff 3. It is not yet clear whether articled clerks (let alone solicitors) will be made subject to these new requirements. There is also a risk that the result of imposing higher standards of police station advice on private practice will be to reduce significantly the number of solicitors' firms available to undertake this work, thereby limiting even further the availability of legal advice to suspects. Again, the Commission does not address this dilemma, other than to recommend generally higher rates of remuneration under criminal legal aid.

[33] *Report*, Recommendation 68.

despite efforts by the Legal Aid Board to impose a specific performance target on duty solicitors to reduce their reliance on telephone advice) and also fail to be present at interrogations more often than own solicitors or their representatives.[34] The Commission's recommendations are likely to extenuate this differential in service between duty and own solicitors, since it is proposed that even where suspects do not request the presence of a solicitor, they should be alerted specifically to the opportunity to consult over the telephone with the duty solicitor.[35] It is not clear what purpose the Commission expects to be served by this, although it is bound to increase the alienation of solicitors from duty solicitor schemes by increasing the occasions on which they are disturbed in the middle of the night by what they regard as 'trivial' cases.

But this is not the only, nor the most important respect in which the Commission's recommendations will increase the pressures on both suspects and solicitors' firms providing police station advice. Most significantly, the Commission has recommended that police questioning of suspects should be allowed to continue after charge.[36] This proposal is put forward in an almost casual, common-sense manner on the basis that

> Few people would nowadays regard the role of the police as being confined to arrest and questioning leading to a charge. The police are plainly also involved in preparing the case for prosecution after charge which may involve many kinds of further inquiries. We believe that, subject to appropriate safeguards, this could include further questioning of the suspect.... We therefore recommend, provided that the usual caution is repeated, and the person charged has the opportunity of consulting a solicitor free of charge before any interview and of having that solicitor present at the interview, that the questioning of suspects after charge should be permissible.[37]

It is perhaps a sign of how much efficacy the Commission places on the 'safeguard' of legal advice in this context that they give no consideration, despite the proven inadequacies of the profession in providing even pre-charge advice to suspects under interrogation, to the extra burdens implementation of this recommendation would place on solicitors or

---

[34] See Sanders, et al., op. cit., pp.
[35] *Report*, Recommendation 59.
[36] *Report*, Recommendation 22.
[37] *Report*, paras. 41 and 42, p. 17. One interesting fact to emerge from the Commission's Crown Court Study with regard to the 'safeguard' of the 'usual caution' is that in no less than 4 per cent of cases in which the police responded, they admitted that the suspect had not been cautioned about his/her 'right of silence' and in a further 12 per cent of cases the police respondent did not know whether the caution had been administered. The report of the study seeks to downplay this finding by noting that, 'When the category of Don't knows was eliminated, *only* 5 per cent were said not to have been cautioned' (emphasis added) (p. 2). However, even 5 per cent of those suspects who eventually have their cases committed to the Crown Court would amount to 5,000 instances each year in which the police fail, on their own admission, to administer this most basic of safeguards.

whether these could be met under current arrangements. In particular, solicitors presently can operate in the knowledge that the period during which they risk having to attend police stations will be limited by the point of charge, whereas under the Commission's proposal it will potentially extend throughout the period while the suspect is held in custody awaiting his first court appearance (e.g. at weekends potentially over a number of days/nights). It is equally irresponsible of the Commission that it makes no reference to the implications of this proposal for detention time limits or in increasing the risks of false confessions due to the prolonged police questioning of suspects that it will encourage.

More generally, the thrust of the Commission's proposals on police investigatory powers is actually to marginalise the significance of legal advice in the police station rather than to enhance it. It is one thing to require that the PACE codes of practice define a more 'positive' role for defence advisers in formal police interviews.[38] It is another to greatly extend the police's powers to obtain admissions and other evidence from suspects *before* they are given the opportunity to obtain legal advice. Yet, the Commission proposes that the practice of on-the-street and back-of-police-car questioning of suspects be legitimated, by extending the codes of practice to cover them and also possibly introducing on-the-spot tape recording.[39] (After all, 'spontaneous remarks made on arrest are often the most truthful' and to ban such practices would mean that 'some reliable confessions might be lost'.[40]) Similarly, the suspect will be at risk of having anything he/she says or does immediately on arrival at the police station recorded on video and presumably able to be used in evidence against him/her[41] and will be at risk of forcible searches of his/her mouth and the taking of samples in a wider range of offences.[42]

Looking beyond the police station, the Commission's recommendations seem designed, on the one hand, to further downgrade and subordinate the position of defence solicitors in the criminal justice process and, on the other, to make all defence lawyers over formally, from their theoretical position as independent advisers and advocates on behalf of the accused, into agents for enforcing defendants' cooperation in their own prosecution. The Commission has signified the importance it attaches to defence solicitors' work by largely ignoring it and also through such recommendations as the abolition of committal proceedings.[43] These, we

---

[38] *Report*, Recommendation 64.
[39] *Report*, Recommendations 38–40.
[40] *Report*, para. 50, pp. 60–61.
[41] *Report*, Recommendations 50 and 51.
[42] *Report*, Recommendations 14, 15 and 19.
[43] *Report*, Recommendation 116.

are told, serve 'no useful purpose'.[44] This may be true viewed from the prosecution and court's interest in the expeditious processing of cases through the system, but the Commission has failed to consider what role even a 'paper' committal might play as a 'trigger' for defence investigations and preparation. Since so much of the work of defence solicitors has been shown to be geared around court appearances, the abolition of committal proceedings, even as a formality, is likely to have the effect of putting back defence preparation of cases even further. And, of course, abolishing 'old-style' committals will deprive defence solicitors of one of the few opportunities they currently have to engage in serious and sustained criminal advocacy.

Nor would the introduction of 'preparatory hearings' at Crown Court provide an adequate replacement as a bureaucratic spur to defence preparation, since they are intended to be held in only a small minority of less than 6 per cent of cases.[45] In these cases the aim appears to be to place control over the conduct of the case – and of the client – in the hands of the barrister from an earlier stage, presumably because s/he will be further removed from the client and more susceptible to regulation by the Court.[46] It is true that the Commission makes strong criticism, nominally in the interests of defendants, of the late delivery of briefs to counsel and of general last-minute preparation of Crown Court cases.[47]   But these criticisms must be seen in the context of the Commission's desire to deny even more defendants the right to elect Crown Court trial or to induce them to plead guilty and its neglect of poor standards of defence preparation at earlier stages in the process.

Indeed, when it comes to the majority of cases before the Crown Court (let alone those restricted to magistrates' courts), the Commission actively endorses the routine and standardised nature of much of criminal defence practice.   Nowhere is this more evident than in the Commission's recommendations for introducing a requirement for advanced defence disclosure. Defence disclosure will not only leave the defendant open to adverse comment at trial if a different line of defence is then developed, but it will also be crucial to determining what material from the prosecution is to be made available to the defence in advance. How, then, does the Commission expect that this crucial stage in the defence case will be handled? The answer is that:

---

44 *Report*, para. 25, p. 90.
45 See *Report*, para. 17, p. 105.
46 See *Report*, para. 21, p. 106.
47 See *Report*, paras 32–36, pp. 108–109.

In most cases disclosure of the defence should be a matter capable of being handled by the defendant's solicitor .... Standard forms could be drawn up to cover the most common offences, with the solicitor having to tick one or more of a list of possibilities, such as 'accident', 'self-defence', 'consent', 'no dishonest intent', 'no appropriation', 'abandoned goods', 'claim of right', 'mistaken identification', and so on.[48]

It is only 'complex cases' that 'may require the assistance of counsel in formulating the defence'.[49] Otherwise, the disclosure of the defence, which will in turn restrict both the further material to be made available by the prosecution and the scope of the defence case at trial, is portrayed as just one more bureaucratic step in the processing of cases. And, given the evidence that the Commission had before it as to the absence of defence solicitors from much of the preparation of cases for Crown Court, one might have anticipated that it would have at least commented on the level of staff within the solicitors' firm to whom this task should be assigned. But the Report is silent on this point, as it is on most other aspects of delegation of defence work outside the police station to unqualified staff.

In summary, the overall effect of the Commission's proposals would be to reinforce the routine nature of the processing of the vast majority of criminal cases, including by the defence, towards guilty pleas and/or conviction. This will happen by restricting far more defendants to having their cases dealt with in magistrates' courts, where the Commission tells us we must, against the evidence of higher conviction rates and widespread deficiencies in defence practices, trust that cases will be handled fairly.[50] Others will be induced more readily to plead guilty at Crown Court by an open system of sentence discounts and 'canvassing' even if, as the Commission acknowledges, this results in some innocent persons being convicted.[51] Defence lawyers are to be more closely integrated into the bureaucratic rationality of this system, as conduits through which 'sentence canvassing' will be conducted or in their being required first to make routine and then disclose their clients' defences in advance to the State.

In its introduction, the Commission states that during 'our examination of the criminal justice system, we have been struck by the disquieting lack of professional competence in many parts of it.'[52] That judgment can be applied with equal validity to much of the Commission's own work, not least that on defence services. As we have seen, it has been partial and elitist in its interpretation of its terms of reference and negligent in its lack of attention to the fate of the vast majority of defendants in the system. So

---

[48] *Report*, para. 68, p. 99.
[49] *Report*, ibid.
[50] *Report*, para. 78, p. 88.
[51] *Report*, para. 42, p. 110.
[52] *Report*, para. 20, p. 6.

far as the Commission has shown any real concern for avoiding the risk of innocent persons being wrongfully convicted, this has been confined to that small minority of cases (which the Commission hopes to be further reduced) that result in full jury trials in the Crown Court. The Commission has also ignored or misrepresented research it has received or produced and has discounted research findings in favour of opinions, suppositions and prejudices garnered from its discussions with the system's professional 'insiders'. It has put forward conclusions and recommendations that are inconsistent, and many of its most controversial proposals – to increase police powers, restrict defendants' rights, and to place new burdens on the defence and defence lawyers – are based on minimal inquiries and consideration of their potential for increasing the risks of innocent persons falsely confessing or pleading guilty or for the capabilities of defence lawyers to cope with the new demands on them, let alone improve the standards of their practices. A Commission that was established, by a reluctant Prime Minister, as the first such body for over a decade, in order to restore confidence in the criminal justice system, has ended up discrediting the process of rational inquiry itself.

25. Miscarriages of Justice: The Appeal Process

Madeleine Colvin

The Court of Criminal Appeal was established in 1907. Its introduction was the product of one of the longest and hardest fought campaigns in the history of law reform. Between 1843 and 1906 no less than 31 abortive Bills were introduced to extend rights of appeal. All were strenuously opposed on the grounds that these would interfere with the finality of the trial and the courts would be swamped by appeals on questions of fact.

In practice, it appears that similiar concerns still operate to influence appellate decisions. Both JUSTICE's own research (*Miscarriages of Justice: Defendants Eye View*, JUSTICE, June 1993), and that undertaken for the Royal Commission (*Review of the Appeal Process*, Research Study No. 17. The Royal Commission on Criminal Justice), show that the Court of Appeal has limited its function to technical questions of law and procedural irregularities rather than the substantial issue of justice. This narrow interpretation limits its ability to be effective in reviewing and correcting miscarriages of justice.

Based on its long experience of working on individual cases, JUSTICE was uniquely placed in submitting evidence to the Royal Commission on the workings of the appellate process: the immediate post-conviction procedures, the practices of the Court of Appeal and the role of the Home Office in section 17 cases. Much has been heeded in the detailed practical recommendations of the Commission's Report and these are to be welcomed. On more substantial issues of principle, such as the function of the Court of Appeal as guardian of the criminal justice system, the Commission has eschewed substantial debate. The cornerstone of its proposals in remedying miscarriages of justice is the creation of an independent, investigatory review body, but factors crucial to its success – such as the criteria for accepting a case – have been only superficially explored. This chapter looks at some of these issues in detail.

I ADVICE ON APPEAL

Research carried out for the Royal Commission shows the hurdles and pitfalls that convicted persons face in attempting to appeal. (*Review of the Appeal Process*, Research Study No. 17). These are designed to ensure that only a small minority succeed. The sifting process of having to gain preliminary leave to appeal excludes large numbers of potential appellants. In 1992, of the 14,661 people convicted in the Crown Courts, 1,552 put in applications for leave to appeal. Only 36 per cent were successful in gaining leave. The overall picture as described by the Commission is that few defendants make the application to appeal and of these, few are successful.

The role of lawyers in this process is crucial. For example, they effectively carry out an initial sift prior to the single judge. Around half of convicted prisoners who did not appeal gave as one of the reasons the fact that a lawyer had advised them not to do so. Those who appeal despite contrary legal advice are unlikely to succeed; the research shows that applications for leave to appeal both to the single judge and renewals to the full Court are far less likely to succeed where the applicant is unrepresented.

The decision on whether or not to appeal is also significantly affected by the perceived risk of serving extra time in prison. The same research survey found that 21 per cent of prisoners did not appeal because of this reason. This is despite the fact that the 'time loss' rules are more effective in myth than reality. But this is offset by a high degree of ignorance amongst lawyers on the powers of the Court in this area: 52 per cent of solicitors mistakenly believed that a sentence can be increased on appeal.

JUSTICE welcomes the Royal Commission's detailed recommendations aimed at improving practices during the immediate post-conviction period – particularly as regards the nature and quality of advice received by convicted persons from their lawyers and within the prison. On the time loss rules, the recommendation is for a Court of Appeal practice direction which sets a maximum of 90 days loss. It is arguable that the Commission should have gone further in support of statutory criteria, setting out both standards and the point of application of such a rule. For example, there are grounds for arguing that the rule should apply only at the renewal stage of the leave application on the grounds that there should be one level of appeal which is risk free.

Possibly of most significance is the question of legal assistance for applicants through the two-tier system of leave to appeal. Although recognising that there is a serious issue of unrepresented applicants being at a disadvantage, the Commission declined to accept that, on a point of principle, a convicted person should have the right to legal assistance in preparing and presenting an appeal. Instead, it recommends extension of legal aid in certain circumstances. For example, the initial entitlement for those on legal aid should also include advice on whether to renew the application if rejected by the single judge. Legal aid should also always be available for representation before the full court on a renewed application where counsel has advised in writing in favour of renewal. At the same time, the Report endorses the Criminal Appeal Office practice of granting legal aid in limited instances for a changed barrister in cases with special features.

In putting forward these limited reforms, the Commission fails to address adequately the particular problem of a convicted person complaining of defence errors as an element of an unsafe conviction. By the very nature of such allegations, the defendant is unlikely to have the support of trial counsel in appealing. Applicants are then thrown back on an own-grounds application which is less likely to succeed. JUSTICE's recent research confirms the view that errors of defence lawyers contribute significantly to miscarriages of justice (Plotnikoff and Woolfson (1993), *Information and Advice for Prisoners about Grounds for Appeal and the Appeals Process,* Research Study 18). It is essential therefore that legal aid be available for a different barrister to advise further in circumstances where grounds of appeal raise serious allegations of defence error which go to the safety of the conviction.

To what degree the leave process demands that broad rules of natural justice apply in favour of the applicant is not clear. For example, there is presently no general duty on the court to provide reasons for a decision, although it seems appropriate that reasons should be given when the single judge or full court denies an application for leave. Whilst the practice is that the single judge does provide brief reasons on paper, an applicant to the full court may only hear whether the appeal has been allowed or refused. Thus whilst justice may be done in the refusal of an application, it is not seen to be done by the applicant. This situation does not appear to have changed significantly since 1964, when the same criticisms were levied by the JUSTICE Report on *Criminal Appeals.* Regrettably the Commission has failed to tackle this issue and that of the considerable delay in cases being heard by the Court of Appeal.

II AT APPEAL

Much of the evidence submitted to the Royal Commission concerned the role of the Court of Appeal and its reluctance to use its powers in a number of areas: for example, to admit fresh evidence, to order re-trials, to question the decision of the jury and to accept defence errors as a ground of appeal. Despite having wide powers, the Court has shown itself to be less concerned with substantive issues of justice than with narrow and technical questions of law.

The present powers of the Court of Appeal are statutorily prescribed by section 2(1) of the Criminal Appeal Act 1968. The Court shall allow an appeal where:

a) Under all the circumstances the conviction was unsafe and unsatisfactory; or
b) there was a wrong decision of any question of law; or
c) there was a material irregularity in the course of the trial.

A proviso to the section allows the Court to dismiss an appeal even though grounds may be made out if it considers that no miscarriage of justice has actually occurred.

The Court also has the power to order the production of documents or exhibits and order a compellable witness to attend Court (s.23(1)). In relation to fresh evidence, s.23(2) states that the Court *shall* receive evidence unless it is satisfied that the evidence would not afford a valid ground of appeal. The evidence must be likely to be credible and be admissible at trial. The Court must also be satisfied that there was a reasonable explanation for the failure to adduce the evidence at the trial. The 1988 Criminal Justice Act extended the Court's power to order a re-trial in all cases where it allows an appeal.

Research undertaken for the Royal Commission concludes that despite the Court of Appeal's wide powers, it performs, in practice, a relatively limited function (*Miscarriages of Justice: Defendants Eye View*, JUSTICE, June 1993). Most of the Court's time is taken in assessing errors in law or irregularities in procedure at the trial – for example, whether the trial judge's summing up was adequate, whether there was a misdirection to the jury, whether evidence was wrongly admitted. It is rare for the Court to consider the existence of fresh evidence, to apply the 'lurking doubt' principle or order a retrial.

Though it now appears that the Court is developing a more positive and broad application of its powers, research evidence continues to show a failure to develop any discernible criteria governing the application on the ground of 'unsafe or unsatisfactory' (*Review of the Appeal Process*, Research Study No. 17). For example, the JUSTICE research study of 78 appeal transcripts showed that this ground was frequently raised but only succeeded in five cases. In none of these did the Court state any principles attached to its application. In cases where it was rejected, the Court showed an over-cautious view of the sovereignty of the jury decision.

The Royal Commission also was critical of the Court's interpretation of its powers: 'the Court of Appeal seems to us to have been too heavily influenced by the role of the jury in Crown Court trials'. It found section 2 of the 1968 Act to be confusing and to contain overlapping powers. The Commission's main proposal therefore is to redraft the statutory provisions.

The Commission split as to what form the new powers should take. The majority favoured creating a single broad umbrella ground of appeal, under which a conviction would be quashed if it 'is or may be unsafe'. On this formulation, there would be no need for the s.2(1) proviso to operate, and it would be abolished. A minority of three Commission members dissented from this view. They argued that there is an important point of principle in the ability to challenge trials which are seriously flawed by errors of law or procedure which do not necessarily render the conviction unsafe.

As part of this continuing debate, JUSTICE, in its report *Miscarriages of Justice* (1989), favoured a more detailed statement of the Court's powers, rather than a unitary ground of appeal. The formula proposed by JUSTICE would require the Court to quash the conviction, as now, for an error of law or material irregularity, but additionally, where:

- they are themselves doubtful upon the evidence whether the appellant is guilty of the offence of which he has been convicted; or
- the verdict of the jury is on any other ground unsafe or unsatisfactory.

JUSTICE believes that more specific and detailed redrafting will encourage the Court to look at the facts of a case and overcome some of its reluctance to disturb a jury verdict. The broadening of the Court's powers by inclusion of the 'unsafe or unsatisfactory' formula in 1968 has not proven to be sufficiently effective in curing wrongful convictions on appeal. At the same time, JUSTICE believes that a more detailed formula will assist in persuading the Court to heed the consensus view that there should be a broader approach to 'fresh evidence' and defence error cases, with increased use of the power to order re-trials.

The differences of opinion among members of the Commission on central aspects of the role of the Court of Appeal reflect the fact that significant issues of principle remain largely unresolved. For example, to what extent is Professor Zander correct in contending that the moral legitimacy of the criminal justice system must be a higher objective than the conviction of any individual? Putting it another way, is it the Court of Appeal's function to act as a constitutional guardian over the process which goes beyond the guilt or innocence of an accused person? At the same time, there are issues of principle concerning the extent to which jury decisions are considered as sovereign. This is central to the question of how fresh evidence should be treated by the Court and the use of re-trials.

III THE CRIMINAL CASES REVIEW AUTHORITY (CCRA)

Unsurprisingly, the Royal Commission recommends a new body to consider allegations of miscarriage of justice, to supervise or conduct investigations into them and to refer cases back to the Court of Appeal. This body would replace the present work of C3 Division of the Home Office. The Report details some of the features of this investigatory body, its relationship to the courts and to Government, its powers of investigation and referral. Unfortunately, on other crucial areas such as criteria for selection of cases, the Report is short on detail apart from being critical of the present narrow criteria operated by the Home Office.

As discussion at a recent seminar hosted by JUSTICE emphasised, there are numerous other important points of detail which will ultimately determine the success or otherwise of this new body. The danger is that such a body will be overwhelmed by the sheer number of complaints. Resources to sift cases effectively and fairly, including providing assistance for the initial preparation of cases to be presented to the CCRA, must be forthcoming. Accountability and openness are vital to ensure consistency and fairness. Full reasons for turning down an application either before or after investigation need to be given and made subject to judicial review proceedings. At the same time (and contrary to the Commission's recommendation), there must be a presumption in favour of disclosure of all material gathered by the CCRA in the course of its investigation. Procedures which can fairly challenge the withholding of documents on public interest immunity grounds need to be adopted.

At the end of the day, however, it will be a question of political will how this body is to operate. It cannot succeed if it is merely transposed on to the top of a system which itself requires reform. The normal forum for remedying a wrongful conviction must be a reformed Court of Appeal; the CCRA can only ever be seen as a long-stop. In order to carry out its investigatory function effectively it must be realistically resourced from the start. The timing of its introduction is likewise important. A commitment is now required to have it up and running within the very near future.

PART III

26. Looking Forward

Roger Smith

The verdict of posterity on the Runciman Royal Commission on Criminal Justice looks likely to be much the same as on the Benson Royal Commission on Legal Services. For the next decade, students will hone their critical skills by castigating its complacency; ravaging its methodology and ridiculing its findings. Already, however, within a few months of publication of the Commission's Report, we have to be aware that the battle has moved on. Debate has now to be conducted with one eye on a Government currently looking weak in what used to be its home territory of law and order. If you thought the Royal Commission was bad, wait till you see the Criminal Justice Bill that will implement the Government's response.

The job of chronicling the inadequacies of the Royal Commission is important in order to destroy its credibility as any kind of compromise that will carry those concerned with the interests of both prosecution and defence. It is clear both that the Commission intended to take what it saw as a middle ground between these two pressures and, equally, that it has been unsuccessful in this regard. Libertarians, defence lawyers and most academic commentary has been hostile to the Report, as is shown by the contributions to this book.

We must not, however, lose sight of the main political issue. This remains the multiple failures of the criminal justice system that led the Government to establish the Commission in the first place. As he stood outside the Court that ultimately accepted his innocence, Paddy Hill said, 'I don't think them people in there have got the intelligence or the honesty to spell the word justice, let alone dispense it.'[1] That accusation stands. In responding to it in the political world in which we live after publication of the Commission's Report, we must look to take what is helpful.

---

[1] *The Guardian*, 15 March 1993.

I THE PROBLEM

The current wave of miscarriages has overwhelmingly concerned police malpractice, sometimes complicated by later prosecution collusion or defence incompetence. Cases of mistaken identity, a feature of earlier concern as a source of miscarriages of justice, have been few. There is much in the Royal Commission's own research studies that confirms the extent of the problems with police discipline. For instance, the picture that emerges from the study of Michael McGuire and Clive Norris is horrifying. CID officers admitted taking suspects on 'scenic routes' back to the station so that there was longer time for a confession to be encouraged. Their conclusion, with their italics, was that 'What is needed is a change in managerial culture so that *as much emphasis is placed upon ensuring procedural and legal compliance as upon securing results.'*[2]

Here, as elsewhere in the Commission's research reports, there is much honest and useful data. The continuing extent of police misconduct needs to be hammered home. The Police Service trotted out its usual line to the Royal Commission.   The Police and Criminal Evidence Act 1984 has changed everything.   It 'strictly regulates their conduct.   They are, accordingly, 'more accountable, more open and, perhaps because of that, more vulnerable to criticism.'[3]   As a relative judgment, this may be factually correct. It is manifestly the case, however, that problems remain and that developments such as the Sheehy recommendation for performance-related pay may worsen them. PACE was, as one would have expected, no magic wand.

The research evidence is supported in a very practical way by a string of recent cases. A short survey of some that came to light in 1993 makes the point. Gary Binham was released after his conviction was quashed. He claimed that his confession had been concocted: his father alleged that his signature had been forged on a statement: eight relevant documents or files subsequently went missing from police custody. Stoke Newington police station in London has been revealed as a den of iniquity. For instance, James Blake and Francis Hart were released in February 1993.   The exhibits officer in their case was subsequently jailed for stealing the property of the man whom they were supposed to have murdered. He is now at the centre of a wider corruption enquiry, Operation Jackpot. The defendants always claimed that they had been 'framed'. Two weeks after

---

2   Maguire, M. and C. Norris (1993) *The Conduct and Supervision of Criminal Investigations*, Royal Commission on Criminal Justice, Research Study Number 5, London: HMSO, p. 115.

3   The Police Service of England and Wales (1991) 'Evidence to the Royal Commission on Criminal Justice', paras 1.1.1 and 1.1.5.

their release, the Court of Appeal quashed the convictions of Ida Oderinde, Dennis Tulloch, Everard Brown and Reggie Kingsley. All alleged in separate trials that evidence had been fabricated against them by Stoke Newington officers. Crown counsel acknowledged that 'there are police officers upon whom suspicion has fallen as to their reliability in any evidence they may give in court.' Police arrested the alibi witness of the Taylor sisters, who changed her testimony under threat of a charge of conspiracy to murder. And so the picture of sustained malpractice goes on.[4]

II THE RESPONSE

The Commission did not deny the magnitude of this type of problem. Its error lay in its theoretical approach. This was essentially management and systems orientated. The underlying message is that the criminal justice system can be made to work coherently if only its various component procedures contain sufficiently rigorous self-monitoring elements. If these can be made to work sufficiently well, there is no need for the intrusion of enforcement mechanisms of the kind that derive from notions of justice and which would require the abandonment of a prosecution or the overturning of a conviction where protective procedural provisions have been breached or qualms over such matters as 'the fruit of the forbidden tree', evidence obtained through inadmissible means. Thus, we get to the ultimately absurd position taken by the majority of the Commission in the light of the miscarriage of justice cases that led to its establishment: the powers of the Court of Appeal to quash a conviction should be restricted where procedural impropriety has been revealed. Professor Ericson's idea that the Commission is arguing for 'system rights', rather than defendants' rights, has force.

The Commission swallowed the line that criminal justice could be based on the tripartite co-operation of defence, prosecution and court, placing the onus on each to clean up their act. The naiveté of this was, no doubt, in part due to the extraordinary fact that the Home Secretary ensured that not one of its members had substantial recent experience of criminal defence work. Its co-operative principle allows the Commission to sit happily on the fence in relation to the traditional opposition of adversarial against inquisitorial models: 'we have not arrived at our proposals through a theoretical assessment of the relative merits of the two legal traditions. On the contrary, we have been guided throughout by practical considerations in

---

4 See LAG, *Preventing Miscarriages of Justice*, 1993, pp. 2–4.

proposing changes which will in our view, make our existing system more capable of serving the interests of both justice and efficiency.'[5]   The Commission rightly identified itself with neither an adversarial nor an inquisitorial model. It wants co-operation and, if correction is necessary, for this to be built into the system elsewhere, and earlier, than the court.

Only in the very last paragraph of Professor Michael Zander's third and last 'Note of Dissent' is there a statement of the ethical position which ought to underpin any viable approach to criminal justice: 'the process itself must have integrity .... The integrity of the criminal justice system is a higher objective than the conviction of any individual.'[6]

III MALPRACTICE

The position of the majority of the Commission, sometimes including the maverick Professor Zander, is consistent and should be made clear. They are not apologists for police malpractice: they do not deny that the criminal justice system faces a major problem. They accepted that 'confidence in the criminal justice system needs particularly to be restored among certain sections of the community'.[7]   They also stated, forcefully, that 'police officers must ... recognise that, whatever the motive, malpractice must not and will not be tolerated'.[8]

The problem is with the solution proposed: stringent protection by the court of defendants' rights is unnecessary; this can be done in other ways. The Commission assumes that the integrity of the participants in the system can be enforced by means other than the ultimate sanction, refusal to hear evidence directly or indirectly obtained and release of any defendant convicted on evidence subsequently tainted in this way. The Commission is not blind to the problems either of noble or ignoble cause corruption by the police. It wants to deal with them by way of better management and internal regulation. Its recommendations on police discipline are actually rather strong and pick up a number of proposals from the Police Complaints Authority's last triennial review.[9]   In particular, it calls for an end to the 'double jeopardy' rule by arguing that 'acquittal of a police officer in a criminal court should no longer be a bar to disciplinary proceedings on the same facts. Such proceedings should be capable of resulting in dismissal

---

5   Royal Commission on Criminal Justice (1993) *Report*, HMSO, Chapter 1, para. 12.
6   As above, *Note of Dissent* by Professor Michael Zander, para. 66.
7   As above, Chapter 1, para. 25.
8   As above, Chapter 1, para. 24.
9   Police Complaints Authority (1991) 'Triennial Review 1988 1991', London: HMSO, see appendix B.

where the officer's conduct shows that he or she is unsuitable to remain in the police force.'[10]

Pressure on the Government must continue for the implementation of recommendations such as these, for which pressure has been mounting. This does not mean that the Commission should not be criticised for shying away from the point made so eloquently by Professor Zander in relation to the Court of Appeal. The protection of the integrity of the criminal justice system demands that defendants must be released before, at or after trial simply because there was, ultimately, no evidence against them that had not been tampered with by the police or some other element of the prosecution. You stamp out fabrication of evidence by making the consequences so grave, in terms of acquittal of a defendant whom police officers consider is guilty and in terms of their own individual careers, that the game is not worth the candle.

IV RESOURCES

A similar response of 'yes but' should inform our approach to the Commission's proposals on resources. The Commission has tried a clumsy sleight of hand by explicitly suggesting that resources might be released by significantly increasing the number of cases in the magistrates' courts. This has attracted a barrage of adverse comment from civil libertarians rightly concerned to protect jury trial and barristers understandably influenced by the potentially diminishing worth of the restrictions on Crown Court advocacy. It was an absurd suggestion to make in the absence of any review of the quality of the magistrates' courts. The combination of material professional interest and philosophical objection will probably be enough to see it off. The Home Secretary, notably, could not wait to distance himself from this proposal immediately after the Report had been published.

The row over this suggestion should not, however, lead us to lose sight of the Commission's basic position on resources. It stated, loud and clear: 'we have, during our examination of the system, become aware that in many areas there is a lack of adequate resources.'[11] It cites, as examples, underfunding of forensic science, the Crown Prosecution Service, legal aid and judicial training.

To take one of these, legal aid, the Commission puts forward some strong suggestions. Legal aid for forensic tests should be available automatically:

---

[10] Royal Commission, Recommendation 76.

[11] As above, Chapter 1, para. 17.

'solicitors should be free to proceed ... in the knowledge that provided the costs do not exceed a stated figure, they will be paid.'[12]   The Criminal Cases Review Authority should be able to recommend the granting of legal aid.   The Commission expressed itself 'seriously concerned' if reform of criminal legal aid led to decreasing eligibility.[13]   Legal aid remuneration should be sufficiently high to attract suitably good practitioners.   Its most far-reaching proposal was that legal aid should become non-means tested on grant.   Contributions should be levied only after the case is concluded and collected along with any fines and contribution orders, implying that the acquitted should not pay a contribution.   Furthermore, it clearly did not favour contributions much at all: 'The initial contribution, if it had to be retained at all, could ... be levied at a flat rate which applied to everyone unless they were receiving unemployment benefit or income support.'[14]

These recommendations fly in the face of government policy.   The Lord Chancellor's Department stated in its three-year plan published in February 1993: 'in support of the Government's commitment to the control of public expenditure, the Department will give priority to controlling legal aid costs and containing expenditure on court services.'[15]   Pressure must, however, be maintained for a recognition of this aspect of the Commission's recommendations.   It is interesting to note that the neutering process can be seen beginning in the process of the production of the Report itself.   The relevant recommendation, number 172, dealing with the Commission's call for reworking contributions is worded in a way that conceals the force of the Commission's argument: 'The scheme recommended by the Lord Chancellor's Department's Legal Aid Efficiency Scrutiny in 1986 for the collection of the defendant's contribution to legal aid should be further explored.'

V TERRORISM

There are other parts of the Commission's Report which we should not overlook.   It is, for instance, quite remarkably outspoken on the Prevention of Terrorism (PTA) legislation.   This Commission contained the commandant of the Police Staff College, a former president of the Law Society, one peer, five knights, a former appeal judge and a practising recorder.   It gets as close as it could virtually to recommending abolition of

---

12 As above, Chapter 9, para. 54.

13 As above, Chapter 7, para. 70.

14 As above, Chapter 7, para. 71.

15 Lord Chancellor's and Law Officers Departments (1993) *The Government's Expenditure Plans 1993–94 to 1995–96* Cmnd 2209, London: HMSO, para. 8.

the PTA, saying: 'We agree that in principle the safeguards of PACE and its related codes should apply to all serious offences equally. Ideally, we would wish to dispense with the modifications to PACE that follow from the provisions of the [PTA].'[16] The only reason given for the Commission's failure so to recommend is the totally specious one that the PTA is voted upon annually by parliament. Its consideration should be given due weight when MPs debate this legislation in future.

VI CONCLUSION

The likely political deal offered by the Government on the Royal Commission Report will be the establishment of the Criminal Cases Review Authority at the expense of legislation a good deal more repressive than that suggested by the Commission. Standing in opposition to that deal will be not only those arguing against it but also, and this may be the real strength, the undeniable reality of experience. Miscarriages of justice are continuing to happen and they will continue to happen until the sanctions against malpractice are strong enough to discourage it adequately. In the end, after much suffering and hardship, innocence will generally out. The facts of cases like the Bridgewater 3 will, ultimately, defy all attempts to draw a line on miscarriages of justice as an issue of which politicians want to take note. These cases will not go away until the fundamental issues are addressed. In arguing this case, we need to be able to use the Commission's Report as well as to be able to abuse it.

---

[16] Royal Commission, Chapter 3, para 93–4.

27. For Action This Day

Russell Stockdale

English justice may be in crisis, not least because forensic science evidence has been exposed for what it always was and always will be – potentially fallible. Particular instances in which its fallibility have apparently come as a shock present foci for the wrath of the public at large and various partial groups with an axe or two to grind and, perhaps conveniently, for others who may wish to escape criticism themselves. A number have been sacrificed along the way and undoubtedly more may follow unless the courts and all concerned face up to the reality that forensic science evidence like any other cannot be accepted on the nod; it must be thoroughly probed and tested in order to expose weaknesses or room for reasonable doubt which can lie hidden from the lay observer behind an apparently unassailable façade of scientific accuracy and precision.

There is a popular and insidious misconception, perhaps fostered by the posturing of early practitioners whose feet were firmly planted in medicine, that forensic science holds the irrefutable answer to everything, that forensic science evidence is especially pure and objective and, in giving it, the forensic scientist is the harbinger of pristine truth. To my knowledge, most modern forensic scientists do not pretend any such attribute although there are still occasions when zealous counsel will seek to thrust it on them.

To us at Forensic Access, the precariousness of our positions, in our previous lives as Metropolitan Police and Home Office forensic scientists called by the prosecution, became all too apparent early in our careers. Increasingly we realised that, while eminently defensible in terms of pure science, the thrust of the evidence arising from our findings depended upon facts relating to context. While, as a matter of course, we would have settled everything in our minds in respect of a particular set of circumstances these often had radically altered by the time we got to court, and what had been carefully considered in one light was then being developed in quite another. If we were more than once startled by a particular line of questioning and the inferences drawn by our *extempore* responses, then so was the defence for, by and large, the so-called 'experts' on whom defence counsel relied, and often still relies for advice generally comprised a rough and ready band of quacks, charlatans and enthusiastic amateurs. They were unfamiliar with our sophisticated equipment and analytical capabilities and, in their often total ignorance of the application of science to crime investigation, they were as unfit to advise counsel as they were to give evidence themselves.

The prosecution held most of the cards while the defence had recourse to a pool of knowledge and expertise which was next to useless at best and positively dangerous at worst. It was in this climate that Forensic Access was established with the clear aim to help redress the balance and to provide the defence with high-quality forensic science advice and practical help both of which were hitherto the prerogative of the Crown.

Without wishing to suggest that just because forensic science evidence has been adduced by the prosecution, the defendant is automatically innocent, the importance of the sort of scrutiny of evidence and advice which we routinely provide is evident from the outcome of many of the cases we have investigated. At one end of the scale the prosecution may decide to drop the case altogether in the face of the challenge we have issued to the evidence. In a recent case a man was charged with possessing heroin with intent to supply, implying an amount of the drug in excess of 1 gram. The sample which the police had seized weighed 4.7 grams which apparently left a respectable margin. When we examined it we found that the sample also comprised carpet sweepings so that dirt, grit and other rubbish accounted for the larger part of its recorded weight. Having extracted the heroin from the debris, we calculated that there could not have been more than about a third of a gram there and, as a consequence, the charge was withdrawn.

There was nothing the matter with the original scientist's work; he had correctly identified the drug in response to the question, 'Does this contain heroin?'. Nobody had bothered to ask him whether the finding was suitable for extrapolation in support of an intent to supply charge. At court it is likely that his statement would have been read to the jury, in which case the scientist would not have been there to see what was happening and to intervene. Had we not become involved it seems clear to me that the defendant would have been found guilty on account of scientific evidence which was misapplied.

At the other end of the scale, we might say that the scientific evidence is so persuasive that anything which might be offered in rebuttal would have little or no impact – we do not pull our punches and lawyers have come to expect us to tell them how it is however unpalatable that might be to them and to their clients. In these sorts of cases the defendant often acknowledges that the prosecution's findings and interpretations have been authoritatively checked and verified and that it might be in his best interests to plead. One such case concerned a man who was supposed to have damaged a car by kicking in its side panels. There were marks on the damaged areas and these matched the soles of the man's boots. We found that the marks contained pattern and wear features which made them unique. It was inconceivable that any other pair of boots could have caused the marks – bad news for the client, but which he accepted.

However the majority of our cases come into a different category, one in which weaknesses and irrelevancies in the prosecution's scientific evidence are exposed for all to see and to explore. This sometimes leads to the evidence being withdrawn as the case proceeds, or sometimes to a successful submission of 'no case to answer' at half-time, but on every occasion the court is alerted and equipped to assess what weight should properly attach to it.

As an example, a man was linked to a serious offence through textile fibres found on his clothes and which the police scientist said could have come from a jumper sleeve fashioned into a mask and abandoned at the scene. He was right, they could have. But I found that, alternatively, they could equally well have come from either of two quite different jumpers belonging to the man himself – neither of which was like the sleeve mask. The police scientist agreed with me and informed the prosecution who did not seek to lead that part of the evidence. Incidentally, the remainder of the case seemed not to impress the jury over-much and the man was acquitted at the end of the day.

Again, there was nothing wrong with the original scientist's work which he had carried out over many weeks, meticulously and precisely. It was just that I decided to explore another avenue which, in the end, radically altered the context of his findings and turned the case on its head.

More recently, we investigated the scientific evidence in a rather unpleasant case of sexual assault. Without rehearsing any of the details, our reinterpretation of the scientist's findings, and expansion of the scope of the examination took support away from the prosecution's case and served to cast serious doubt over the complainant's account of events and the general circumstances surrounding the alleged offence. Although the case had been holed below the water line by our intervention it sailed on, albeit half-heartedly, until the defendant was formally acquitted just as soon as was judged to be decent after the complainant herself failed to turn up.

Perhaps from these few examples of our contribution to the justice system, which not only ensures that scientific evidence is fairly and squarely presented but, Lord Chancellor please note, can result in significant savings of court time and costs, the need every time for a fresh, independent look can be appreciated.

This is the key to an essential safeguard, but there are two major obstacles in the path of those who would use it. These concern the qualifications and experience of those purporting to practise forensic science, and the level of funding which the Government is prepared to commit to the forensic science needs of the defence.

I QUALIFICATIONS AND EXPERIENCE OF FORENSIC SCIENTISTS

The forensic science profession, like medicine, dentistry, accounting, law and so on, should be regulated to ensure that only those who are independently accredited as being appropriately and properly qualified, trained and experienced are permitted to practise in it.

With few exceptions the scientists working in the police and Home Office laboratories have been scrupulously honest, of a high calibre and rigorously trained. Lessons from the past have been well-learnt and, with the support of external accreditation and monitoring schemes instituted by NAMAS (the National Measurement Accreditation Service) and the British Standards Institute which are now being put into place there can be increasing confidence that the methodologies and operating procedures employed in the Metropolitan Police Forensic Science Laboratory (MPFSL) and in the laboratories of the Forensic Science Service (FSS) are as near flawless as it is in the power of the human animal to provide.

This does not absolve them from the requirement of personal, individual accreditation in specific areas of expertise. In the FSS at least and with the advent of agency status, forensic scientists are exposed to and deeply conscious of commercial pressures for the first time. Arguably, the far-reaching changes in the organisation and structure of the FSS have resulted in the loss from the laboratory bench of significant numbers of its most experienced scientists either to one or other of the new management functions which seem to abound, or to early retirement programmes designed to re-shape the age-structure of the Service into a convenient profile, more conducive to man-power modelling and forward-planning techniques. There is a consequent increasing reliance in case-work on relatively inexperienced staff and, at the same time, encouragement too for individuals to tackle broader and different ranges of evidence types when, in virtually every other field of scientific endeavour, scientists are becoming more specialised and less willing to stray into unrelated territories.

But it is outside the MPFSL–FSS network that concerns about honesty, quality and competence in forensic science are most acute.

Prior to the FSS becoming an agency and the changes in arrangements for funding whereby the police now pay for forensic science on a case-by-case basis, the police were effectively tied to the Service as their sole supplier. Because of the high standards demanded by the organisation itself, to all intents and purposes the rag-bag of quacks belonged to the defence. Although still largely the case, now that they can shop around in their search for 'value for money', whatever that is in a forensic science context, the police are increasingly likely to find themselves, along with the defence, with half a job poorly done.

It is not possible to overstate the seriousness of this development: we have already seen examples of private sector laboratories undertaking work for police seeking a cheap option and have been appalled at the incompetence and fundamental ignorance which would otherwise have lain unseen and unsuspected behind the emergent statements of seemingly impressive evidence.

In one notable case, an industrial laboratory – part of a huge organisation and whose charges significantly undercut the FSS – took on a complex case for the police which involved multiple transfers of textile fibres. Never mind the nuances of context and interpretation in this one: we found that because of the wholly unsatisfactory way they had gone about things, all the evidence could have been manufactured during the examination itself. None of it was safe, none of it could be relied on in any way. Fortunately our views were conveyed to the prosecution who wisely ditched the entire package before it reached the jury, thus avoiding the deep embarrassment our own evidence would have surely provoked.

Notwithstanding the generally very high standard of analytical work which routinely comes out of the MPFSL and the FSS, few of the scientists there would have the temerity to claim that they never made mistakes. It is always essential for the defence to have the opportunity to scrutinise the analytical procedures employed as to their appropriateness, and to check the results obtained to see how far they support what has been reported and what may be given in evidence.

It is also essential that the nature of the prosecution's scientific evidence and the interpretations which will be placed on the findings are crystal clear to the defence, and that there is sound advice to be had as to the significance of all of it in the context of the circumstances of the case at issue.

So-called defence 'experts' with little or no training in forensic science, or much of a grasp of the needs of the defence, often see their role in terms of either repeating the primary work of the police scientists or gratuitously rubbishing it, just for the hell of it. In most cases the former is impracticable or uninformative or both. This is because the relevant material might all have been used up, or it might have deteriorated to a point beyond which any results obtained would be reliable or meaningful or, owing to repeated handling and testing its integrity can no longer be assured. The latter is a ploy which is beyond contempt and it deserves no place in any respectable scientific forum.

Implicit in all of this is the heavy burden of responsibility which lies upon the prosecution's scientists who, by and large, will have the first and only opportunity to examine materials in their original state, and on whose detailed notes and records the defence scientist must rely.

Also implicit here is the need for the defence to appoint a properly trained and thoroughly experienced forensic scientist to advise them: one who understands and is completely familiar with all the techniques and procedures which will have been used.

As matters stand, there is no form of regulation of the profession whatsoever. Any Tom, Dick or Harry can set up in business as a forensic scientist – and they do, offering 'expert' services to the defence and now to the police as well. The practice is dishonest, misleading and an unjustifiable drain on the public purse. There is no doubt in my mind that the continued use of amateurs is building up a fresh store of potential miscarriages of justice.

II FUNDING THE FORENSIC SCIENCE NEEDS OF THE DEFENCE

Costs in criminal cases are met by the police at the investigation stage and by the Crown Prosecution Service (CPS) when the matter comes to trial. So far as the defence is concerned, most cases are funded by the legal aid scheme, a vote of money to the Lord Chancellor's Department (LCD), administered by local Legal Aid Boards and by the Lord Chancellor's men at the Crown Courts, all according to strict rules of entitlement – or perhaps that should be non-entitlement.

Fee scales for defence scientists are not generous and many genuine practitioners working in the private sector have been forced by commercial pressures to refuse legally aided cases in favour of more lucrative, privately funded work which is also free from the uncertainties of taxation – taxation is the novel device, arguably fraudulent, by which the LCD can agree an estimate of costs in advance and then renege on it once the work is done. The loss of these scientists from criminal practice is unfortunate because it reduces to a mere handful the number of properly qualified people who are able to assist the defence. It also encourages the cowboys who may be content to dabble in forensic science amongst all manner of other things.

In order to instruct a defence expert, a solicitor must apply to the Legal Aid Board for sufficient funds to cover the bill. Even in serious cases in which the defendant faces a custodial sentence if convicted, these funds may not be forthcoming at all, or are inadequate to cover the work which is required to be done.

Increasingly, Legal Aid Boards are denying defendants access to qualified and competent advice on cost grounds alone, while the police and CPS remain free to spend whatever they consider is an operational necessity in order successfully to investigate a crime and to secure a prosecution.

With alarming and increasing frequency solicitors tell us that this Legal Aid Board or that has said that in their lay view the scientific evidence against the client is overwhelming and there will be no money to have it independently checked. What we are seeing here is the insertion of a shadowy tier of summary justice orchestrated by administrators and clerks who are more concerned with balance sheets than with proper judicial process. Their pre-judgement of cases – out of sight of judge, jury and legal representative – are an unfair, unconstitutional, cynical and suspicious use of cash limits which serves only to ensure that the scales are tilted in favour of the prosecution. Such an attitude to his work by a Crown official, whether expressed or implied and whether or not encouraged by a Treasury-led policy of Government spending cuts, has no place in an English justice system. It puts me in mind of a police officer from some far-flung oppressive regime who told me that he saw no difficulty with fabricating forensic science evidence, just so long as he thought the man was guilty and got what was coming to him. That worries me.

Earlier in the year we were asked to investigate a case in the north of the country in which scientific evidence of a complex nature played a key role. The reply came back that a local firm, with about as much understanding of the issues involved as my cat, had quoted some 80 per cent less than we had and that the Legal Aid Board clerk was insisting the lower quote be accepted. Fortunately for the defendant, his defence counsel had a very firm grip of things and promised a Judicial Review if proper funds were not forthcoming to enable us to undertake the work. They were and we did, and the defendant was acquitted.

One wonders, had the Legal Aid Board got its way and things turned out differently, whether that case would have become a *cause célèbre* in the annals of miscarriages of justice and, in particular, whether the Lord Chancellor's man concerned would have been named and publicly pilloried in the Court of Appeal in place of the forensic scientist? I have my doubts. We have raised all these concerns in evidence before the House of Commons Home Affairs Committee in 1988 and, more recently, before Dainton and Runciman. So far as the latter is concerned, what provisions are there from the Royal Commission on Criminal Justice to ensure that the quality of forensic science is improved and maintained at a high level and the defence has proper access to competent advice?

Among the 352 recommendations contained in the Commission's Report potentially the most powerful one in terms of the future organisation of forensic science provides for the creation of a Forensic Science Advisory Council (FSAC) 'to report to the Home Secretary on the performance, achievements and efficiency of the forensic science laboratories'.

The vagueness of the recommendation, its failure to specify more precisely what roles and powers are envisaged for the new Council and, importantly, who should comprise it and under whose chairmanship, has provoked criticism in some quarters from those who sought a more detailed charting of the way forward. Nonetheless, we and others in the forensic science community broadly welcome it, provided that decisions about these and other issues are taken without delay save that necessary to ensure due and proper consultation to have taken place. It at least resisted the more radical and hysterical proposals for a complete structuring of forensic science services, presumably in recognition of Lord North's advice that, 'If it is not necessary to change, then it is necessary not to change'.

There is much for the new Council to do, particularly in the formulation, implementation and maintenance arrangements for the effective regulation of forensic science practitioners. Such regulation supported by external accreditation schemes and individual registration, and rigorously monitored as is the case in medicine for example, will ensure that the police, the prosecuting authority and the defence can be confident that they are instructing only scientists who are demonstrably up to the job.

As to funding the forensic science needs of the defence, sadly no direct recommendation was made save that, 'Clear rules should be laid down as to what scientific work defence solicitors can commission ...'. Here I would agree with its critics that the Commission has not gone nearly far enough. It should have seized the opportunity to ensure that scientific evidence is thoroughly scrutinised each and every time it is presented by insisting that the new rules must confer on defence solicitors the automatic right to commission their own scientists. Clearly, upper expenditure limits would need to be imposed initially, but these should not pose insurmountable problems provided that they were amenable to review as issues became clearer.

Another bone of contention on which the Commission did not focus at all concerns the perhaps little-known disparity between the very modest fees which can be claimed for preparatory work in a case – incidentally, less than the cost per hour of the humblest technician in the MPFSL or the FSS – and the quite different scales which apply to attendance at court. In the latter case, a defence scientist may spend whole days – conferring with counsel, listening to evidence in order to pick up on points arising and advising him as he proceeds with his cross-examination, as well as giving evidence himself – for significantly less than this. Such nonsense adds to the financial burden of practitioners in the private sector and helps to dissuade qualified scientists from entering it.

Perhaps more telling in a political arena, all of this means that whenever an FSS scientist is engaged by the defence, the police who remain the Service's prime customers are subsidising him through the higher charges which are levied on them! I wonder how many Chief Constables, if they knew, would be content with that?

The regulation of the practice of forensic science and funding the forensic science needs of the defence are two main areas of concern which should occupy places of high priority on the FSAC's agenda. Presumably it will fall to the Home Office to make the running and to set up the new Council. That being the case, I urge the Home Secretary to get weaving. Just as Sir Winston Churchill might well have written the minute to him, 'Pray, let me have your proposals', he would have certainly also marked the file, 'For Action This Day'.

28. It Couldn't Happen Today?

Andrew Hall

I WINDS OF CHANGE

The announcement of the Runciman Commission on Criminal Justice provoked, at least in some quarters, a distinctly sceptical response. Royal Commissions are rarely seen as appropriate vehicles for urgent and radical reform. On the contrary, they frequently provide an excuse for inactivity and prevarication. It is instructive to compare the alacrity with which the current administration has moved to legislate, and re-legislate, in relation to other issues in the criminal process, usually in response to the latest moral panic of the tabloid press. Abrupt U-turns in penal and sentencing policy, the creation of new offences to deal with perceived social threats, dramatic alterations to the funding of public legal services, and the introduction of market-testing ideologies to law enforcement and prison establishments, are all seen in rapid succession during recent months. The will to work and legislate against miscarriages of justice, however, is conspicuously absent from the political stage.

The wind of change which can be felt is a distinctly chilly and populist one. It brings a strong scent of Home Office policy, and more than a hint of Treasury corridors. We should accordingly not be surprised that the Runciman enquiry ultimately has lost its way, and that its proposals are timid and preoccupied with the efficient management of resources.

Indeed, it is perhaps less important to understand why the Commission has failed as to assess how the debate should be carried forward. At least part of the task is to understand the way in which public discussion of the concept of justice has been hijacked. Commonly-held misconceptions about the criminal justice system have coloured both the Report and its reception. It therefore seems an appropriate time to try to return to basics. To do that demands an understanding of what function the structure carries out, and what 'justice' is or may represent.

II INVESTIGATION AND TRIAL

To view the prosecution process as a simple mechanism for establishing 'truth' is an exercise in confusion. Investigative agencies can rarely be said to be impartial. Indeed, once criminal litigation has begun, they can rarely be expected to be. Police enquiries do not take place in a vacuum. They are informed by a variety of preconceptions and prejudices, and shaped by operational, political and public forces. Similarily, the organisation and presentation of evidence by the prosecution will inevitably be influenced by structural pressures, including that of achieving a conviction.

In much the same way, the function of the trial process must be understood. The court is not a laboratory in which technicians generate truth in a test tube. It is the arena in which the power of the State and the rights and liberties of the individual defendant are in opposition. The contest could barely be said to be an even one. Arrayed against the individual defendant is the power and unlimited resources of the State apparatus. Such trial concessions and privileges as s/he has, and such burdens as are placed on the Crown, are, in theory, designed to reflect and rectify that essential imbalance.

The verdict of a court or jury can only ever amount to informed but approximate accuracy. Its determination is not a statement of ultimate 'truth', but a conclusion reached on analysis of the available evidence and competing arguments, together with legal principles including the burden and standard of proof. In other words, the verdict is an attempt to make sense of disputed facts, constrained by the limitations of that very process and by the adversarial context in which it is reached. Most importantly, it represents a conclusion to be viewed in the light of the processes of law. 'Not guilty' is not intended to record the absence of factual responsibility but the failure of a forensic test of proof according to accepted process. That is as it should be. To view the determination in any other way is to assert scientific and not juridical accuracy. By this means it becomes possible to make the circular assertion that 'too many guilty people are getting away with it'.

A more helpful perspective is to recognise the many dimensions of a complex system of inquiry and adjudication, and the existence of competing interests and forces. The end product of the system – the determination – may, and we hope will, bear a close relationship to 'truth'. However, ultimately the trial is the final ritualised act in a process by which the State asserts culpability and seeks to apply sanctions to an individual. Whether 'justice' is achieved is determined as much by the integrity of the process as by its product.

To misunderstand the process invites considerable danger. By reifying a notion of objective 'truth', and by characterising the process as an inquiry rather than a contest, it is possible to undermine the protections which are available to suspects and defendants without criticism. Why should the right to silence survive if 'truth' is obscured? Should not a defendant make plain his defence before trial in the interests of the forensic search for 'truth'?

III A CONCEPT OF JUSTICE

The characteristics of a just system of criminal process are that it is effective, and that it commands widespread public confidence and support. The former demands the correct identification of 'wrongdoers', whilst protecting the rights and civil liberties of the individual. The latter requires impartiality, the elimination or miminisation of opportunities for corruption, and that the workings of the system should be public, subject to scrutiny and challenge, and under democratic control. The integrity of the whole is guaranteed by the certainty that the identification of the guilty shall be by means of due process and in accordance with law, and that the innocent should not risk punishment. Recognising the fallibility of all human endeavour, an effective appeals system should provide a guard against trial error.

IV A CRISIS OF CONFIDENCE

The current crisis in our criminal justice system arises precisely because the structure has been exposed as essentially unjust. It is neither seen as effective nor does it command general public confidence. The last ten years have chronicled a series of grave miscarriages of justice and led to widespread and genuine public concern as to old certainties. It is no accident that the majority of those cases disclose identical themes of corruption, incompetence and partiality. What has shocked many in the community is the apparent unwillingness or inability, over many years, properly to investigate and put right those cases of plain injustice. Whether the current Royal Commission has begun to address the question of injustice hinges on two simple tests. The first is whether its proposals positively decrease the future prospects of the innocent being convicted. Secondly, are they more or less likely to add to justifiable confidence in the integrity of the system?

It is the argument here that the Commission has manifestly failed to meet the concerns which have arisen over recent years and, indeed, led to its inception. Analysis of the miscarriage cases themselves has lacked rigour. As a result, a vital opportunity has been missed to learn lessons, paid for by an unfortunate few in years of unjustified imprisonment. In place of critical examination and radical change there has been a pre-occupation with 'efficiency' and economy in the court process. At the heart of this failure is an artificial separation between public and individual justice which echoes the reasoning of the earlier Commission on Criminal Procedure. In an attempt to create a 'balance' between 'individual rights' and 'justice' the indivisibility of the two is lost.

Moreover, there has been a parallel failure in public debate to clear the ground of those misconceptions described earlier. As a result we see an argument whose vocabulary defines the criminal justice process as a clinical search for truth. This is 'handicapped' to some extent by 'arcane rules' protecting the suspect or defendant from having to provide explanations for known facts. The participant investigators and prosecutors are seen as 'technicians' whose impartiality can be assured, at least with a few minor adjustments to curb professional over-enthusiasm. The criminal courtroom appears as a 'level playing field' upon which both sides share equal advantage. In so far as unfortunate cases of wrongful conviction have arisen, these are essentially isolated instances of mere 'historical interest'.

V UNDERSTANDING INJUSTICE

In more than one sense, miscarriages of justice are an inevitable product of any process of social control. The criminal law is a social and political construct and may reflect little more than the prevailing morality of the day. 'Injustice' may frequently be used to describe the relativity of that position and its impact upon those with competing views. I have used a more restricted notion but the same inevitability applies.

Where the State seeks to sanction an individual, the process is by its very nature coercive and unbalanced. Whether the imbalance is minimised, and coercion reduced to tolerable levels, provides a limited but useful working definition of 'justice'. From this viewpoint, 'miscarriages of justice' can be seen as failures of due process, producing determinations which are unfair by common standards, and likely not to reflect factual responsibility.

The extent to which injustice is perpetrated on a daily basis in our jurisdiction should not be underestimated. Every time a black youth in the inner city is unjustifiably stopped and searched unfairness arises. Each instance of police violence, malpractice or dishonesty, large or small, is an act of oppression. Those who praise the fairness and impartiality of our tribunals should spend a day observing the list in most Magistrates' courts. These are the venue for the vast majority of criminal adjudications and give a more accurate reflection of the inequalities and deficiencies of the system than is generally thought to exist. The everyday suit of injustice is mundane. I do not wish to undervalue the significance of this, or to suggest that the most important tasks lie elsewhere. However, the importance of the cases which have attracted massive publicity and concern is that they illustrate precisely the same injustices in a more extreme form. The analysis is identical.

The failure of the Commission adequately to analyse either is surprising. The common themes of recent miscarriage cases are there for all to see. It is, or should be, no surprise that many involve members of ethnic minorities. The majority arise in cases of serious violence, frequently in the context of political or quasi-political activity. Each crime and investigation has been the subject of widespread, and often lurid, media coverage which has in turn excited or exacerbated public emotions and fears. Enormous pressure has arisen for quick investigative results, with a consequent willingness on the part of the police to take investigative shortcuts in the light of tacit public and political approval. The results have been a series of grave charges supported solely by confessional evidence and, in some cases, dubious scientific material. Upon this the courts have impressed a seal of approval, proper evaluation of the evidence being hindered by prosecution failures to disclose relevant materials. Thereafter, notwithstanding widespread expressions of public concern, the appeal mechanisms have utterly failed to recognise the very serious forensic weaknesses which have resulted in convictions.

This is not to suggest that the Commission was entirely blind to the obvious. Rather that a degree of selective myopia has arisen which has enabled the accurate identification of a few trees, but not the wood of which they are a part.

Thus, we see proposals strengthening the right of access to informed legal advice during investigation, and preserving the right of silence at the investigatory stage. We do not see, however, a clear recognition of the fact that arrest and interrogation is an inherently hostile and coercive process. Questioning of the suspect is thus viewed as an opportunity for the detained person to deny and explain, rather than a process of obtaining material with which to convict. The police can be seen as technicians in search of truth. That admissions by an accused are often a very unreliable forensic tool is ignored. Arrest and detention is seen as the unquestioned process by which this is to be achieved.

Similarly, although there is acknowledgement that police malpractice exists, and long-awaited proposals are made in relation to the police disciplinary system, this goes only a short distance in addressing the ubiquity of misconduct. What it fails to recognise is the structural, or more properly 'functional' nature of malpractice. Oddly enough, this receives acknowledgement from the police themselves who are not unknown to justify rule breaking by arguing that otherwise their investigative functions would become impossible.

Well-documented research, available to the Commission, has made the existence of widespread misbehaviour well known. Moreover, what the miscarriage cases have documented is that in certain investigations the rules are not simply bent, but wholly disregarded. Under public and media pressure for results, and in dealing with political or ethnic minorities, the police feel justified in failing to apply the most basic civil liberty considerations. Disturbingly, but accurately, they have calculated that they will be forgiven for doing so by the courts and the public. Once again, fairness and legal process may, and are, sacrificed to expediency. That is only possible by virtue of a philosophy which can separate public justice ('efficiency') from individual justice ('due process').

That access to 'justice' and impartial treatment depends upon ethnic or political considerations is a very serious indictment. It is nevertheless a reality to which those on the 'wrong' side of industrial disputes in recent years would testify. However, the most glaring examples relate to those accused of offences of political violence and to whom wholly different rules and considerations apply. That the Commission should have excluded itself from consideration of this issue merely reinforces the point made earlier. Symptoms of some of the 'miscarriage' problems have been acknowledged, but the causes simply not addressed.

Similarly, the inherent imbalance between the State and the individual does not appear to be unduly problematic in the mind of the Commission. Recommendations relating to prosecution disclosure and improved access to scientific testing facilities are made. However, to take these two illustrations, at no stage does one have the sense that any fundamental imbalance of resources has been recognised by the Commission, or for that matter by the public. Indeed, the contrary appears to be assumed; once these adjustments are in place for the benefit of the defence it is thought perfectly safe to make equal and opposite adjustments in the form of defence disclosure.

It is the connection between structural imbalance, and key procedural and evidential precepts which is vital. Only the State has almost unfettered powers and unlimited investigatory resources. This will always remain the case. It follows that the burden of proof must always lie with the Crown and that the criminal standard of proof must be extremely high. It should not lie on the shoulders of the accused to prove anything, and for that reason s/he is entitled to remain silent. Nor should s/he have the tactical disadvantage of having to disclose the defence, or any evidential material, in advance.

Only in this way can one begin to address the initial imbalance, and recognise the process for what it is; an unequal contest in which fairness demands that the State should not be permitted to establish culpability and impose punishment except in accordance with accepted procedures and standards. Should this burden not be discharged, justice will always have been done irrespective of factual guilt.

To argue, as the Commission does, that some system of defence disclosure is desirable prior to trial is to risk undermining the fragile balance which currently engages public confidence. To do so on the basis that currently the defence has some unfair advantage over the prosecution is wholly misconceived. Dilution of those essential balancing mechanisms is a dangerous first step in a process of dismantling the whole. To fail to grasp the structural significance is to invite that process.

However, the most serious charge against the Commission relates to the issue at the heart of the majority of miscarriage cases, the uncorroborated confession. That it has manifestly failed to grasp this nettle is a cause of serious concern. Why it has failed to do so is perhaps made more clear in the light of the perspective I have suggested.

VI THE PRIMACY OF CONFESSION

By oversimplification of the complex process of criminal law enforcement and procedure it is possible to view the system other than as coercive and the arena of competition. Thus the obtaining of confessional evidence is both legitimate and desirable in the interests of efficiency. In addition it is unproblematically reliable. In crude form the argument is that the suspect is unlikely to concede liability if this is untrue since it is contrary to interest. The complicated psychological processes which lead to false confessions are acknowledged, but then paid little if any attention. Oppressive behaviour leading to admissions is recognised but can be remedied by relatively cosmetic rule changes.

In reality not only is confessional evidence frequently unreliable, but also the significance which it currently has in police practice is determined by the ease with which it is obtained and admitted in evidence. In other words, the confession is seen as the most direct and efficient route to conviction. For this reason it is often the case that more indirect but reliable investigative tools are discarded. In addition, once a confession has been obtained by police contrary indications of innocence are often undervalued, ignored or even deliberately hidden.

The din of alarm bells surrounding the subject of confessions has been sounding since the Fisher Report in the Confait case. It should have been deafening to both the Philips and Runciman Commissions. Once again, however, expediency triumphs. The risk of losing 'good' confessions is too great to outweigh the price of a few innocents being convicted, regrettable though this may be.

In truth it is in no-one's interests that false confessions, or admissions resulting from oppressive interrogation, should lead to convictions. Nevertheless, the obvious routes to dealing with this core problem have been ignored. It seems beyond argument that the police will continue to pursue the shortest route from their conviction of a suspect's guilt to his/her conviction by the court. This will be achieved using whatever technique is expedient limited only by the tolerance of the courts. Where rules of conduct exist they will be broken unless this is counterproductive to the desired end, that of a successful prosecution. Even where the rules are complied with, the danger of an untruthful or unreliable confession cannot be excluded.

A three-pronged attack might be thought both desirable and necessary for the reasons described. Independent or judicial supervision during the conduct of police investigations was the first route to be abandoned by the Commission. The second, an exclusionary rule of evidence applicable for breaches of the Codes of Practice, found few if any supporters. Finally, the necessity for corroboration of all confessions was thought to be both unworkable and unacceptable.

On reflection it is difficult to see what mechanism the Commission relies on in order to avoid future miscarriages based on false confessions, or those obtained through trickery, misconduct or plain oppression. Enormous faith appears to be placed on the current Codes of Practice, confidence in the professionalism of the police, and the safeguard of access to defence lawyers. It is those very 'safeguards' that recent cases, together with a vast body of academic research, have exposed as inadequate 'This couldn't happen today' is an argument which appears to have been adopted.

That this is a mere credo now seems to be beyond doubt. All of the Irish cases fall outside the 'normal' rules governing investigations. This fact is ignored. That the Tottenham 3 were arrested and questioned whilst the

Codes of Practice were in force appears irrelevant. That serious cases of non-disclosure, malpractice, and incompetence by both prosecution and defence lawyers continue unabated is noted but seems inconsequential. In place of radical change, the Commission's proposals allow confessions to continue as the bread and butter of investigation and prosecution.

That miscarriages have taken place could not, on the other hand, be ignored. In recognition of this is the proposed new Miscarriages Commission. This is a development to be welcomed, although perhaps not without reservation. The composition of the body is far from certain, and the fear is that limited powers of investigation and resources may result in it following in the unhappy footsteps of the Police Complaints Authority. Most significantly, however, what it represents is bolting the stable door after the horse has fled. It has often proved a bitter satisfaction to those wrongly imprisoned, and whose lives have been ruined, to be vindicated many years after the event. It may prove so again.

VII SUMMARY

The inevitable conclusion is that the Commission has failed to address the causes of miscarriages of justice and that its proposals are for the most part cosmetic. That fact, together with proposed abolition of 'live' committal proceedings and limitations on the right to jury trial, is a consequence of a fundamental failure to appreciate key theoretical and practical issues. This has resulted in a willingness to adopt spurious arguments against change. Our criminal justice system is likely to be shaped well into the next century by these flawed and timid proposals. Rather than fewer miscarriages of justice we are likely to see many more, and for many years to come.

References

Ackroyd, S., R. Harper, J. Hughes, D. Shapiro and K. Soothill (1992) *New Technology and Practical Police Work: The Social Context of Technical Innovation*, Buckingham: Open University Press.

ACPO/Home Office (1993) *A Guide to Interviewing/The Interviewer's Rule Book*, ACPO/Home Office, March.

Ashworth, A. (1985) *The English Criminal Process: A Review of Empirical Research*, Oxford: Centre for Criminological Research.

Ashworth, A. (1988) 'Criminal Justice and the Criminal Process', *BJ Crim*, 28:111.

Balbus, I. (1973) *The Dialectics of Legal Repression*, New York: Russell Sage.

Baldwin, J. (1985a) 'The police and tape recorders', *Criminal Law Review*, 695.

Baldwin, J. (1985b) *Pre-Trial Criminal Justice*, Oxford: Basil Blackwell.

Baldwin, J. (1992) *The Conduct of Police Investigations: Records of Interview, the Defence Lawyer's Role and Standards of Supervision*, RCCJ Research Study Nos. 2, 3 and 4, HMSO, London.

Baldwin, J. (1993a) 'Power and police interviews', *New Law Journal*, 143:1194.

Baldwin, J. (1993b) *The Role of Legal Representatives at the Police Station*, Research Study Number 3, Royal Commission on Criminal Justice, London: HMSO.

Baldwin, J. (1993c) 'Police Interview Techniques: Establishing Truth or Proof?', *The British Journal of Criminology*, 33 (3) Summer.

Baldwin, J. (1993d) *Preparing the Record of Taped Interviews*, Research Study Number 2, The Royal Commission on Criminal Justice, London: HMSO.

Baldwin, J. and M. McConville (1977) *Negotiated Justice*, Oxford: Martin Robertson.

Baldwin, J. and T. Moloney (1993) *Supervision of Police Investigations in Serious Criminal Cases*, Research Study Number 4, The Royal Commission on Criminal Justice, London: HMSO.

Bankowski, Z. and G. Mungham (1976) *Images of Law*, London: Routledge.

Beck, U. (1992a) *Risk Society: Towards a New Modernity*, London: Sage.

Beck, U. (1992b) 'Modern Society as a Risk Society', in N. Stehr and R. Ericson (eds), *The Culture and Power of Knowledge*, Berlin and New York: de Gruyter.

Bennett, R. (1993) 'Criminal Justice', *London Review of Books*, 15 (12), 24 June 3, 5–15.

Bentham, Jeremy (1827) *Rationale of Judicial Evidence specially applied to English Practice* (ed. J.S. Mill), Vol. 5, London: Hunt & Clarke.

Bevan, V. and K. Lidstone (eds) (1991) *The Investigation of Crime*, London: Butterworths.

Bittner, E. (1967) 'The police on skid-row: A study of peace-keeping', *American Sociological Review*, 32:5, 699–713.

Block, B., C. Corbett and J. Peay (1993) *Ordered and Directed Acquittals in the Crown Court*, Research Study Number 15, The Royal Commission on Criminal Justice, London: HMSO.

Bottomley, K., C. Coleman, D. Dixon, M. Gill and D. Wall (1991) *The Impact of PACE: Policing in a Northern Force*, Hull: The University of Hull.

Bottoms, A.E. and J.D. McClean (1976) *Defendants in the Criminal Process,* London: Routledge & Kegan Paul.

Box, Steven (1983) *Power, Crime and Mystification,* London: Tavistock.

Box, Steven (1987) *Recession, Crime and Punishment,* London: Macmillan.

Boyle, K., T. Hadden and P. Hillyard (1975) *Law and State: The Case of Northern Ireland,* London: Martin Robertson.

Braithwaite, John (1991) 'Shame and Modernity', *British Journal of Criminology,* 33:1.

Bridges, L. (1992) 'The professionalisation of criminal justice', *Legal Action,* August.

Bridges, L., B. Sufrin, J. Whetton and R. White (1975) *Legal Services in Birmingham,* University of Birmingham Institute of Judicial Administration.

Brogden, A. (1981) '"Sus" is dead: but what about "Sas"?', *New Community,* 9:44–52.

Brogden, M. (1984) 'From Henry III to Liverpool 8', *International Journal of the Sociology of Law,* Vol. 12.

Brogden, M.E. (1985) 'Stopping the People', in J. Baxter and L. Koffman (eds), *The Police and the Community,* London: Professional Books.

Brogden, M.E. (1991) *On the Mersey Beat,* Oxford: Oxford University Press.

Brown, D., T. Ellis and K. Larcombe (1992) *Changing the Code: Police Detention under the Revised PACE Codes of Practice,* Home Office Research Study 129, London: HMSO.

Bunyan, T. (1977) *The Political Police in Britain,* London: Quartet Books.

Burton, F. and P. Carlen (1979) *Official Discourse: On Discourse Analysis, Government Publications, Ideology and the State,* London: Routledge.

Cain, M. (1973) *Society and the Policeman's Role,* London: Routledge.

Calavita, K. et al. (1991) 'Dam Disasters and Durkheim: An Analysis of the Theme of Repressive and Restitutive Law', *Int. Jnl of Sociology Law,* 19:407.

Cape, Ed 'Defence Services: What Should Defence Lawyers do at Police Stations?', this volume.

Carlen, Pat and Anne Worrall (eds) (1987) *Gender, Crime and Justice,* Milton Keynes: Open University Press.

Carriere, K. and R. Ericson (1989) *Crime Stoppers: A Study in the Organization of Community Policing,* Toronto: Centre of Criminology, University of Toronto.

Carson, D. (1990) *Professionals and the Courts – A Handbook for Expert Witnesses.*

Cashmore, E. and E. McLaughlin (eds) (1991) *Out of Order?,* London: Junction Books.

Central Planning and Training Unit (1992) *A Guide to Interviewing,* London: CPTU.

Clare, I. and G. Gudjonsson (1993) *Devising and Piloting an Experimental Version of the 'Notice to Detained Persons',* Research Study Number 7, The Royal Commission on Criminal Justice, London: HMSO.

Cohen, L. Jonathan, 'Freedom of Proof' in William Twining, (ed.) (1983) *Facts in Law,* Wiesbaden: Franz Steiner Verlag GMBH.

Cohen, S. (1985), *Visions of Social Control,* Cambridge: Polity.

Colville, J.W. (1991) *Report on the Operation in 1990 of the Prevention of Terrorism (Temporary Provisions) Act 1989,* House of Commons Library.

Conlon, G. (1990) *Proved Innocent: The Story of Gerry Conlon of the Guildford Four,* London: Hamish Hamilton.

Cowell, D. et al. (1982) *Policing the Riots.*

Curtis, E. (1984) *Nothing but the Same Old Story: The Roots of Anti-Irish Racism,* London: Information on Ireland.

Dandeker, C. (1990) *Surveillance, Power and Modernity: Bureaucracy and Discipline from 1700 to the Present Day,* New York: St. Martin's.

Dennis, I. (1993) 'Miscarriages of justice and the law of confessions: evidentiary issues and solutions', *Public Law,* 291.

Departmental Committee on Legal Aid in Criminal Proceedings (1966) *Report*, Cmnd. 2934, London: HMSO.

Detention at the Police Station under PACE (1989) Home Office Research and Planning Study No. 104, London: HMSO.

Diplock Commission (1972) *Report of the Commission to consider legal procedures to deal with terrorist activities in Northern Ireland*, Cm. 5185 London: HMSO.

Dixon, D. (1991) 'Common sense, legal advice and the right of silence' *Public Law*, Summer.

Dixon, D., Bottomley, K., Coleman, C., Gill, M. and Wall, D. (1990) 'Safeguarding the rights of suspects in police custody', *Policing and Society*, 1:115.

Doherty, F. (1986) *The Stalker Affair*, Dublin: Mercier Press.

Douglas, M. (1992) *Risk and Blame*, London: Routledge.

Eggleston, (1983) *Evidence, Proof and Probability*, (2nd edn) London: Weidenfeld & Nicolson.

Enright, Sean (1993) 'Cost effective criminal justice' *New Law Journal* 1023–4.

Enright, S. and J. Morton, (1990) *Taking Liberties*, London: Butterworths.

Ericson, R. (1993) [1981], *Making Crime: A Study of Detective Work*, Toronto: University of Toronto Press.

Ericson, R. (1994) 'The Division of Expert Knowledge in Policing and Security', *British Journal of Sociology*, 45, March.

Ericson, R. and P. Baranek (1982) *The Ordering of Justice: A Study of Accused Persons as Dependents in the Criminal Process*, Toronto: University of Toronto Press.

Ericson, R., P. Baranek and J. Chan (1987) *Visualizing Deviance: A Study of News Organization*, Milton Keynes: Open University Press.

Ericson, R., P. Baranek and J. Chan (1989) *Negotiating Control: A Study of News Sources*, Milton Keynes: Open University Press.

Ericson, R. and K. Carriere (1994) 'The Fragmentation of Criminology', in D. Nelken, (ed.), *The Futures of Criminology*, London: Sage.

Ericson, R., K. Haggerty and K. Carriere (1993) 'Community Policing as Communications Policing', in Dölling, D. and T. Feltes (eds.) *Community Policing*, Holzkirchen: Felix-Verlag.

Ericson, R. and C. Shearing (1986) 'The Scientification of Police Work', in G. Böhme and N. Stehr (eds), *The Knowledge Society*, Dordrecht and Boston: Reidel.

Evans, R. (1993a) *The Conduct of Police Interviews with Juveniles*, Research Study Number 8, The Royal Commission on Criminal Justice, London: HMSO.

Evans, R. (1993b) 'Police interrogation and the Royal Commission on Criminal Justice', (forthcoming) *Policing and Society*.

Evans, R. and T. Ferguson (1991) *Comparing Different Juvenile Cautioning Systems in One Police Force*, London: Home Office.

Evett, I.W. (1992) 'DNA Statistics: Putting the Problems in Perspective', *Justice of the Peace*, 583–6.

Farrell, A. (1992) *Crime, Class and Corruption: The Politics of the Police*, Bookmarks.

Feldman, D. (1990) 'Regulating Treatment of Suspects in Police Stations: Judicial Interpretation of Detention Provisions in the Police and Criminal Evidence Act 1984', *Criminal Law Review*, 452.

Feuchtwang, Stephen (1992) 'Policing the streets', in S. Feuchtwang and A. Cambridge (eds), *Where you Belong: Government and Black Culture*, London: Avebury.

Findlay, M. and P. Duff, (1988) *The Jury Under Attack*, London: Butterworths.

Fine, B. and R. Millar (eds) (1985) *Policing the Miner's Strike*, London: Lawrence and Wishart.

Fisher, H. (1977) *Report of an inquiry into the Confait case*, London: HMSO.

Fitzgerald, M. (1993) *Ethnic Minorities and the Criminal Justice System*, London: HMSO.

Forensic Science Service (1993) *Annual Report and Accounts 1992–93* London: HMSO.

Foster, J. (1989) 'Two stations: an Ethnographic Study of Policing in the Inner-City', in D. Downes (ed.), *Crime and the City*, Basingstoke: Macmillan.

Foucault, M. (1977) *Discipline and Punish*, London: Allen Lane.

Frankel, M. (1975) 'The Search for Truth: An Umpireal View', *U. Penn. L.R.* 123:1031.

Galanter, M. (1992) 'Law Abounding: Legalisation around the North Atlantic' *Modern Law Review*, 55:1.

Garland, D. (1990) *Punishment and Modern Society*, Oxford: Clarendon Press.

Gee, D. (1987) 'The Expert Witness in the Criminal Trial', *Criminal Law Review*, 307.

Gelowitz, M.A. (1989) '"Yet he opened not his mouth": A Critique of Schedule 14 to the Criminal Justice Act 1988', *Criminal Law Review*, 198–206.

Giddens, A. (1985) *The Nation-State and Violence*, Cambridge: Polity.

Giddens, A. (1990) *The Consequences of Modernity*, Cambridge: Polity.

Giddens, A. (1991) *Modernity and Self-Identity: Self and Society in the Late Modern Age*, Cambridge: Polity.

Gilligan, O. (ed.) (1990) *The Birmingham Six: An Appalling Vista*, Literéire Publishers.

Gordon, G.H. (1981) *The Criminal Justice (Scotland) Act 1980*, Edinburgh: W Green & Son.

Gordon, G.H. (1982) 'Commentary on *McCuaig* v. *HM Advocate*', SCCR 128–9.

Gordon, P. (1983) *White Law*, London: Pluto Press.

Green, P. (1990) *Policing the Miners' Strike*, Milton Keynes: Open University Press.

Gudjonsson, G. (1992) *The Psychology of Interrogations, Confessions and Testimony*, Chichester: John Wiley & Sons.

Gudjonsson, G., I. Clare, S. Rutter and J. Pearse (1993) *Persons at Risk During Interviews in Police Custody: The Identification of Vulnerabilities*, Research Study Number 12, The Royal Commission on Criminal Justice, London: HMSO.

Hall, Stuart (1980) *Drifting into a Law and Order Society*, London: Cobden Trust.

Harman, H.J. and Griffith (1979) *Justice Denied*, London: National Council for Civil Liberties.

Harrison, Ross (1983) *Bentham*, London: Routledge & Kegan Paul.

Hart, H.L.A. (1968) *Punishment and Responsibility*, Oxford: Clarendon Press.

Hedderman, C. and D. Moxon (1992) *Magistrates' Court or Crown Court? Mode of Trial Decisions and Sentencing*, Home Office Research and Planning Unit Report 125, London: HMSO.

Helsinki Watch Report (1991) *Human Rights in Northern Ireland*, New York: Human Rights Watch.

Hill, P. and Bennett, R. (1990) *Stolen Years: Before and After Guildford*, London: Doubleday.

Hillyard, P. (1981) 'From Belfast to Britain: Some Critical Comments On the Royal Commission On Criminal Procedure', in D. Adlam et al. (eds.) *Politics and Power: Law, Politics and Justice*, London: Routledge & Kegan Paul.

Hillyard, P. (1987) 'The Normalisation of Special Powers', in P. Scraton (ed.), *Law, Order and the Authoritarian State*, Milton Keynes: Open University Press.

Hillyard, P. (1993a) *Secret Community*, London: Pluto Press.

Hillyard, P. (1993b) *Suspect Community: People's Experience of the Prevention of Terrorism Acts in Britain*, London: Pluto Press.

Hodgson, Jacqueline 'No Defence for the Royal Commission', this volume.

Holdaway, S. (1983) *Inside the British Police*, Oxford: Basil Blackwell.

Home Affairs Committee (1989) *The Forensic Science Service* (First Report for Session 1988–9; HC Paper 26–I), London: HMSO.

Home Office (1989) *Crime Statistics for the Metropolitan Police District, Analysed by Ethnic Group*, Statistical Bulletin 5/89.

Hood, R. (1992) *Race and Sentencing: A Study in the Crown Court*, Oxford: Clarendon Press.

House of Lords Select Committee on Science and Technology (1993) *Forensic Science*, HL Paper 24, London: HMSO.

Imwinkelried, (1990) 'The Evolution of the American Test for the Admissibility of Scientific Evidence', *Med.Sci.Law*, Vol. 30, No. 1, p. 60.

Inciardi, James A. (1980) *Radical Criminology: The Coming Crisis*, Beverly Hills: Sage Publications.

Inquiry into Police Responsibilities and Rewards (1993) *Report*, Cmnd 2280, London: HMSO.

IRR (1987) *Policing Against Black People*, London: Institute of Race Relations.

IRR (1991) *Deadly Silence: Black Deaths in Custody*, London: Institute of Race Relations.

Irving, B. and C. Dunningham (1993) *Human Factors in the Quality Control of CID Investigations*, Royal Commission on Criminal Justice, Research Study No. 21, London: HMSO.

Irving, B. and L. Hilgendorf (1980) *Police Interrogation: The Psychological Approach*, Royal Commission on Criminal Procedure, Research Paper No. 2, London: HMSO.

Irving, B. and I. McKenzie (1989) *Police Interrogation: The Effects of the Police and Criminal Evidence Act 1984*, London: The Police Foundation.

Jackson, J.D. (1990) 'Getting Criminal Justice out of Balance' in Livingstone, S. and Morison, J. (eds), *Law, Society and Change,* Aldershot: Dartmouth.

Jackson, J.D. (1993) 'Trial Procedures' in C. Walker and K. Starmer, (eds), *Justice in Error*, London: Blackstone.

Jackson, J.D. and S. Doran, (1990) *Judicial Fact-Finding in the Diplock Court in Northern Ireland*, Manchester: Manchester University Faculty of Law, Working Paper No. 2.

Jefferson, T., M. Walker and M. Seneviratne (1992) 'Ethnic Minorities, Crime and the Criminal Justice System', in D. Downes (ed.), *Unravelling Criminal Justice*, Aldershot: Gower.

Justice (1993) *Miscarriages of Justice: Defendants Eye View*, London: JUSTICE, June.

Kaye, T. (1991) *Unsafe and Unsatisfactory*, Report of the independent inquiry into the working practices of the West Midlands Police Serious Crime Squad, London: Civil Liberties Trust.

Kenny, A. (1983) 'The Expert in Court' *Law Quarterly Review*, 99:197, 200.

King, M. and C. May (1985) *Black Magistrates,* London: Cobden Trust.

Kirchheimer, O. (1961) *Political Justice: The Use of Legal Procedure for Political Ends*, Princeton, New Jersey: Princeton University Press.

Lacey, Nicola, Celia Wells and Dirk Meure (1990) *Reconstructing Criminal Law* London: Weidenfeld and Nicolson.

Lacey, N. (1994) 'Contingency and Criminalisation' in I. Loveland (ed.), *The Frontiers of Criminality*, London: Sweet and Maxwell.

LAG 1993 *Preventing Miscarriages of Justice*, London: Legal Action Group.

Lambert, J. (1970) *Crime, Police and Race Relations*, London: Institute of Race Relations.

Lander, E.S. (1989) 'Population Genetic Considerations in the Forensic Use of DNA Typing', in J. Ballantyne, G. Sensabaugh and J. Witwoski (eds), *Banbury Report 32:*

DNA Technology and Forensic Science, Cold Spring Harbor, New York: Cold Spring Harbor Laboratory Press, 143–54.

Law Society, The (1991) *Advising the Client at the Police Station*, London (3rd edn).

Law Society, The (1992) *Memorandum on the Future of Criminal Legal Aid: Evidence to Royal Commission on Criminal Justice*, London: Law Society.

Lee, J. (1981) 'Some structural aspects of police deviance in relations with minority groups', in C. Shearing (ed.), *Organisational Police De viance: Its Structure and Control*, Toronto: Butterworths.

Lee, T.R. (1981) 'The Public's Perception of Risk and the Question of Irrationality', in F. Warner (ed.), *The Assessment and Perception of Risk*, London: Royal Society, p. 5.

Leigh, L. and Zedner, L. (1992) *A Report on the Administration of Criminal Justice in the Pre-trial Phase in France and Germany*, London: HMSO.

Leng, R. (1993) *The Right to Silence in Police Interrogation: A Study of Some of the Issues Underlying the Debate*, Research Study Number 10, The Royal Commission on Criminal Justice, London: HMSO.

Levi, M. (1993) *The Investigation, Prosecution and Trial of Serious Fraud*, Research Study Number 14, The Royal Commission on Criminal Justice, London: HMSO.

Lewis, P. and J. Curtis (1971) *Apes and Angels: The Irishman in Victorian Caricature*, Newton Abbot: David and Charles.

Liberty, (1991) *Let Justice Be Done*, November.

Liberty, (1993) *Human Rights Convention Report 2: Criminal Justice and Civil and Political Liberties*, July.

Lord Chancellor's and Law Officers Departments (1993) *The Government's Expenditure Plans 1993–94 to 1995–96*, Cmnd 2209, London: HMSO.

Mackenzie, J. (1993) 'The Royal Commission on what?' *New Law Journal* 1035.

MacPhail, I.D. (1992) 'Safeguards in the Scottish Criminal Justice System', *Criminal Law Review*, 144–152.

Maguire, M. and C. Norris (1993) *The Conduct and Supervision of Criminal Investigations*, Research Study Number 5, The Royal Commission on Criminal Justice, London: HMSO.

Maher, G. (1983) 'Jury Verdicts and the Presumption of Innocence', *Legal Studies*, 3, 146–158.

Maher, G. (1984) 'Balancing Rights and Interests in the Criminal Process' in A. Duff and N. Simmonds (eds), *Philosophy and the Criminal Law*, Wiesbaden: Franz Steiner Verlag GmbH.

Malleson, Kate (1993) *Review of the Appeal Process*, Research Study No. 17, The Royal Commission on Criminal Justice, London: HMSO

Manning, P. (1977) *Police Work*, Cambridge, Mass.: MIT.

Manning, P. (1992a) 'Information Technologies and the Police', in M. Tonry, and N. Morris (eds), *Modern Policing*, Chicago: University of Chicago Press.

Manning, P. (1992b) *Organizational Communication*, New York: Aldine de Gruyter.

Marx, G. (1988) *Undercover: Police Surveillance in America*, Berkeley: University of California Press.

May, S.J. (1990) 'Return to an address of the Honourable the House of Commons dated 12 July 1990 for the inquiry into the circumstances surrounding the convictions arising out of the bomb attacks in Guildford and Woolwich in 1974', *Interim Report on the Maguire Case*, HC (1989/90) Cmnd 556, London: HMSO.

McBarnet, Doreen J. (1981) *Conviction: Law, the State and the Construction of Justice* London: Macmillan.

McCluskey, Lord (1992) *Criminal Appeals*, Edinburgh: Butterworths.

McConville, M. (1989) 'Michael McConville on Weaknesses in the British Judicial System', *Times Higher Education Supplement* (November 3), 5–6.

McConville, M. (1992) 'Videotaping interrogations: police behaviour on and off camera', *Criminal Law Review*, 532.

McConville, M. (1993a) 'An Error of Judgement', *Legal Action*, September.

McConville, M. (1993b) *Corroboration and Confessions: The Impact of a Rule Requiring that no Conviction can be Sustained on the Basis of Confession Evidence Alone*, Research Study Number 13, The Royal Commission on Criminal Justice, London: HMSO.

McConville, M. and J. Hodgson (1993) *Custodial Legal Advice and the Right to Silence*, Research Study Number 16, The Royal Commission on Criminal Justice, London: HMSO.

McConville, M. and C. Mirsky, (1990) 'Understanding defense of the poor in state courts', in A. Sarat and S.Silbey (eds), *Studies in Law, Politics and Society*, Vol. 10, JAI Press Inc., pp. 217–42.

McConville, M. and P. Morrell, (1983) 'Recording the interrogation: Have the police got it taped?', *Criminal Law Review*, 158.

McConville, M., A. Sanders and R. Leng, (1991) *The Case for the Prosecution*, London: Routledge.

McConville, M. and D. Shepherd (1992) *Watching Police Watching Communities*, London: Routledge.

McConville, M., L. Bridges, J. Hodgson and A. Pavlovic (1993) *Standing Accused: The Organisation and Practices of Criminal Defence Lawyers in Britain*, Oxford: Oxford University Press.

McEwan, J. (1992) *Evidence and the Adversarial Process*, Oxford: Blackwell.

McKenzie, I. et al. (1990) 'Helping the Police with their Inquiries', *Criminal Law Review*, 22.

McMahon, M. (1992) *The Persistent Prison?*, Toronto: University of Toronto Press.

Menzies, R. (1989) *Survival of the Sanest: Order and Disorder in a Pre-trial Forensic Clinic*, Toronto: University of Toronto Press.

Milton, K. (1991) 'Interpreting Environmental Policy: A Social Scientific Approach', *Journal of Law and Society*, 4: 5.

Miyazawa, S. (1992) *Policing in Japan: A Study on Making Crime*, Albany: State University of New York Press.

Moody, S.R. and J. Tombs (1982) *Prosecution in the Public Interest*, Edinburgh: Scottish Academic Press.

Morton, J. (1993) *Bent Coppers*, London: William Brown.

Moston, S. and G. Stephenson (1993) *The Questioning and Interviewing of Suspects Outside the Police Station*, Royal Commission on Criminal Justice Research Study No. 22, London: HMSO.

Moxon, D. and D. Crisp (1993) *Termination of Cases by the Crown Prosecution Service*, London: Home Office Research and Planning Unit.

Mullin, Chris (1990 edn) *Error of Judgement: The Truth about the Birmingham Bombings*, Guernsey: Poolbeg.

Munday, R. (1993) 'Jury Trial, Continental Style', *Legal Studies*, 13: 204.

Nelken, D. (1987) 'Criminal Law and Criminal Justice: Some Notes on their Interrelation', in T. Dennis (ed.), *Criminal Law and Criminal Justice*, London: Sweet & Maxwell.

Norris, C. (1992) 'Avoiding Trouble: the Patrol Officer's Perception of Encounters with the Public'in D. Downes (ed.), *Unravelling Criminal Justice*, Aldershot: Gower.

Norris et al. (1992) 'Black and Blue: An Analysis of the Influence of Race on Being Stopped by the Police', *BJ Soc*, 43:207.

O'Malley, P. (1991) 'Legal Networks and Domestic Security', *Studies in Law, Politics and Society*, Vol. 11. Greenwich, Conn: JAI Press.

Packer, H. (1968) *The Limits of the Criminal Sanction*, London: Oxford University Press.

Paley, Archdeacon W. (1809, 17th ed) *The Principles of Moral and Political Philosophy*, London: J. Faulder.

Palmer, S.H. (1988) *Police and Protest in England and Ireland 1780–1850*, New York: Cambridge University Press.

Parker, H., M. Casburn and D. Turnbull (1981) *Receiving Juvenile Justice*, Oxford: Basil Blackwell.

Pattenden, Rosemary (1982) *The Judge, Discretion and the Criminal Trial*, Oxford: Clarendon Press.

Pattenden, R. (1992) 'Evidence of previous malpractice by police witnesses and R v. Edwards', *Criminal Law Review*, 549.

Pearce, F. and S. Tombs (1990) 'Ideology, Hegemony and Empiricism: Compliance Theories of Regulation', *The British Journal of Criminology*, 30 (4), Autumn.

Peterson, Joseph (1986) 'Ethical Issues in the Collection, Examination and Use of Physical Evidence' in G. Davies (ed.), *Forensic Science* (2nd edn), Washington D.C.: American Chemical Society, pp. 35–48.

Plotnikoff, J. and R. Woolfson (1993) *Information and Advice for Prisoners about Grounds for Appeal and the Appeals Process*, Research Study Number 18, The Royal Commission on Criminal Justice, London: HMSO.

Police Reform (White Paper) (1993b) Cmnd 2281, London: HMSO.

PSI Report (1983) *Police and People in London*, Vols I–IV, London: Policy Studies Institute.

Punch, M. (ed.) (1983) *Control in the Police Organization*, Cambridge, Mass: MIT Press.

Punch, M. (1985) *Conduct Unbecoming: The Social Construction of Police Deviance and Control*, London: Tavistock.

Radzinowicz, Sir Leon and Hood, Roger (1986) 'A History of English Criminal Law and its Administration from 1750', Vol. 5: *The Emergence of Penal Policy*, London: Stevens & Sons.

Ramsay, M. (1988) *Effectiveness of Forensic Science Service*, Home Office Research and Planning Unit Study Number 92, London: HMSO.

Rawlings, P. (1985) '"Bobbies", "Aliens" and Subversives: The Relationship Between Community Policing and Coercive Policing', in J. Baxter and L. Koffman (eds), *Police: the Constitution and the Community*, Abingdon: Professional Books.

Reiner, R. (1985) *The Politics of the Police*, Brighton: Wheatsheaf.

Reiner, R. (1992) *The Politics of the Police* (2nd edn), Toronto: University of Toronto Press.

Roberts, P. and C. Willmore (1993) *The Role of Forensic Science Evidence in Criminal Proceedings*, Research Report Number 11, The Royal Commission on Criminal Justice, London: HMSO.

Robertson, G. (1993) *The Role of Police Surgeons*, Research Study Number 6, The Royal Commission on Criminal Justice, London: HMSO.

Rock, P. (1983) 'Law, Order and Power in Late Seventeenth- and Early Eighteenth-century England', in S. Cohen and A. Scull (eds), *Social Control and the State*, Oxford: Basil Blackwell.

Rock, P. (1993) *The Social World of an English Crown Court*, Oxford: Clarendon Press.

Romilly, Sir Samuel (1810) *Observations on the Criminal Law of England, as it Relates to Capital Punishments and on the Mode in Which it is Administered*, London: Mimeo.

Royal Commission on Criminal Justice (1991) Cmnd 2263, London: HMSO.

Royal Commission on Criminal Justice (1993) *Report*, Cmnd 2263, London: HMSO.

Royal Commission on Criminal Procedure (1980) *Report*, Cmnd 8092, London: HMSO.

Royal Commission on Criminal Procedure (1981) *Report*, London: HMSO.

Royal Commission on Criminal Procedure (1983) *Report*, London: HMSO.

Royal Commission on Criminal Procedure (1981) *The Investigation and Prosecution of Criminal Offences in England and Wales: the Law and Procedure, Report*, Cmnd 8092, London: HMSO.

Saltzburg, S. (1978) 'The Unnecessarily Expanding Role of the American Trial Judge', *Va. L.R.* 63:1.

Sanders, A. (1988) 'Personal violence and public order', *International Journal of the Sociology of Law*, 16:359.

Sanders, A., L. Bridges, A. Mulvaney and G. Crozier (1989) *Advice and Assistance at Police Stations and the 24-Hour Duty Solicitor Scheme*, London: Lord Chancellor's Department.

Scarman Report (1981) *The Brixton Disorder*, Cmnd 8427, London: HMSO.

Schlesinger, P., H. Tumber and G. Murdoch (1991) 'The Media Politics of Crime and Criminal Justice', *The British Journal of Sociology*, 42(3), September.

Scraton, P. (1985) *The State of the Police*, London: Pluto Press.

Scraton, P. (ed.) (1987) *Law, Order, and the Authoritarian State*, Milton Keynes: Open University Press.

Select Committee on Science and Technology (1993) *Forensic Science* (5th Report for Session 1992–3; HL Paper 24), London: HMSO.

Shearing, C.D. (1981) 'Subterranean Influences on Police Culture' in C.D. Shearing (ed.), *Organisational Police Deviance*, Toronto: Butterworths.

Shearing, C. and R. Ericson (1991) 'Culture as Figurative Action', *The British Journal of Sociology*, 42 (4) December.

Sheldon and MacLeod, (1991) 'From Normative to Positive Data: Expert Psychological Evidence Re-examined', *Criminal Law Review*, 811.

Simon, J. (1987) 'The Emergence of a Risk Society: Insurance, Law and the State', *Socialist Review*, 95.

Skogan, W. (1990) *The Police and Public in England and Wales: A British Crime Survey Report*, Home Office Research Study 117.

Smart, Carol (1976) *Women, Crime and Criminology*, London: Routledge & Kegan Paul.

Smart, J.J.C. 'An Outline of a System of Utilitarian Ethics' in J.J.C. Smart and Bernard Williams (eds) (1973) *Utilitarianism: For and Against*, Cambridge: Cambridge University Press.

Smith, D.J. (1984) 'A Survey of Police Officers', *Police and People in London*, Vol. 3 London: PSI.

Smith, R. (1993) 'The researcher's story', *Legal Action*, July.

Smith, R. (1991) 'Speaking out on Silence', *New Law Journal*, 141, p. 539.

Smith, 'Forensic Pathology, Scientific Expertise and the Criminal Law' in Smith and Wynne (eds) (1989) *Expert Evidence: Interpreting Science in the Law*, London: Routledge.

Smith, (1981) *Trial by Medicine: Insanity and Responsibility in Victorian Trials*, Edinburgh University Press,.

Smith and Wynne (eds) (1989) *Expert Evidence: Interpreting Science in the Law*, London: Routledge.

Southgate, P. (1982) *Police Probationer Training in Race Relations*, Home Office Research Unit, Paper 8.

Stehr, N. and R. Ericson (eds) (1992) *The Culture and Power of Knowledge: Inquiries into Contemporary Societies*, Berlin and New York: de Gruyter.

Steventon, B. (1993) *The Ability to Challenge DNA Evidence*, Research Report Number 9, The Royal Commission on Criminal Justice, London: HMSO.

Stockdale, Russell (1991) 'Running with the Hounds', *New Law Journal*, 141: 772–5.

Taylor, K. and K. Mumby (1990) *The Poisoned Tree*, London: Sidgwick & Jackson.

Taylor, P. (1987) *Stalker: The Search for the Truth*, London: Faber & Faber.

Taylor, I. (1983) *Crime, Capitalism and Community*, Toronto: Butterworths, p. 107.

Thomas, P.A. (1982) 'Royal Commissions', *Statute Law Review*, Spring, pp. 40–50.

Thornton, P., A. Mallalieu and A. Scrivener (1992) *Justice on Trial*, Report of the Independent Civil Liberty Panel on Criminal Justice, London: Civil Liberties Trust.

Tomlinson, M. (1980) 'Reforming Repression' in L. O'Dowd, B. Rolston and M. Tomlinson (eds), *Northern Ireland: Between Civil Rights and Civil War*, London: CSE Books.

Twining, William (1985) *Theories of Evidence: Bentham and Wigmore*, London: Weidenfeld & Nicolson.

Tyler, T. (1990) *Why People Obey the Law*, New Haven: Yale University Press.

Uglow, S. (1988) *Policing Liberal Society*, Oxford: Oxford University Press, p. 63.

Vagg, J. and J. Shapland (1988) *Policing by the Public*, London: Routledge.

Valverde, M. (1990) 'The Rhetoric of Reform: Tropes and the Moral Subject', *International Journal of the Sociology of Law*, 18(1), January.

Vennard, J. (1988) *Contested Trials in Magistrates' Courts*, London: HMSO.

Vogler, R. (1991) *Reading the Riot Act*, Milton Keynes: Open University Press.

Walker, M. (1992) 'Arrest Rates and Ethnic Minorities: A Study in a Provincial City', *Journal of the Royal Statistical Society*, Series A: Part II, 259–72.

Walkley, J. (1987) *Police Interrogation, A Handbook for Investigators*, London: Police Review Publishing Company.

Ward, J. (1993) *Ambushed*, London: Ebury Press.

Webster, M. (1992) 'DNA profiling evidence' (letter), *New Law Journal*, 1712.

Willis, C. (1983) *The Use, Effectiveness and Impact of Police Stop and Search Powers* Home Office Research and Planning Unit Paper No. 15.

Woffinden, B. (1988) *Miscarriages of Justice*, London: Coronet Books.

Woffinden, Bob (1991) 'How Justice is Blinded by Science' *The Independent*, 14 May 1991, 15.

Wolchover, D. and A. Heaton-Armstrong (1991) 'The Questioning Code Revamped', *Criminal Law Review*, 232.

Young, M. (1991) *An Inside Job*, Oxford: Oxford University Press.

Zander, M. (1993) 'Where the critics got it wrong', *New Law Journal*, 143:1338.

Zander, M. and P. Henderson (1993) *The Crown Court Study*, Research Study Number 19, The Royal Commission on Criminal Justice, London: HMSO.

Index